GLOBAL ROME

NEW ANTHROPOLOGIES OF EUROPE

Matti Bunzl and Michael Herzfeld, *editors*

Founding Editors
Daphne Berdahl
Matti Bunzl
Michael Herzfeld

GLOBAL ROME

Changing Faces of the Eternal City

Edited by Isabella Clough Marinaro and
Bjørn Thomassen

Indiana University Press

Bloomington & Indianapolis

This book is a publication of

Indiana University Press
Office of Scholarly Publishing
Herman B Wells Library 350
1320 East 10th Street
Bloomington, Indiana 47405 USA

iupress.indiana.edu

Telephone   800-842-6796
Fax   812-855-7931

Library of Congress Cataloging-in-Publication Data

Global rome : changing faces of the eternal city / edited
by Isabella Clough Marinaro and Bjørn Thomassen.
pages cm. — (New anthropologies of Europe)
Includes bibliographical references and index.
ISBN 978-0-253-01288-3 (cloth) — ISBN 978-0-253-01295-1
(paperback) — ISBN 978-0-253-01301-9 (ebook) 1. Rome (Italy)—
Social conditions—21st century. 2. Urbanization—Italy—Rome. 3.
Urban policy—Italy—Rome. 4. Community development—Italy—
Rome. I. Marinaro, Isabella Clough. II. Thomassen, Bjørn.
HN488.R6G56 2014
306.09456'32—dc23
2013044271

1 2 3 4 5   19 18 17 16 15 14

For Francesca, Paolo, Maria, Stella, and Chiara—
our Roman families. And for Terry Kirk, who
loved the city as passionately as we do.

Contents

Acknowledgments

THE EDITORS WOULD like to thank John Cabot University and the American University of Rome for funding the translations in this book.

GLOBAL ROME

Introduction

Into the City: The Changing Faces of Rome

Isabella Clough Marinaro and Bjørn Thomassen

Roma, Roma, at thy feet
I lay this barren gift of song!
For, ah! the way is steep and long
That leads unto thy sacred street.

> —Oscar Wilde (1881), "Rome Unvisited"

Chi non la conoscerà, questa superstite terra,
come ci potrà capire? Dire chi siamo stati?

[How will they understand us, those who will not know
this survived land? How will they say who we were?]

> —Pasolini, "A Bertolucci," *Bestemmia*, 544

PEOPLE RARELY THINK about what a miracle a city is. The city of Rome, the original *urbs,* is a living miracle, incorporating opposite extremes of almost everything human beings have ever produced. Its endless and timeless beauty persists side by side with urban degeneration, pollution, and crime proliferation in some of Europe's most desolate city areas, often built illegally. The warmth and openness of its inhabitants can turn into closure and xenophobia. With its chaotic traffic and the notorious loud talk of its inhabitants, with its manifold smells and noises, Rome can easily induce that "sensory overload" which Simmel described a century ago. Yet Rome is calm and relaxed in all its frenzy. The walking speed in its subway system is nowhere near that of Paris or London. Rome is a laboratory of intricate human relations and curious forms of sociability, of diffidence and civility, cynicism and humor, rudeness and kindness, a chaotic blend of distance and closeness, carelessness, apathy, and engagement which defines what everyone knows as "Roman-ness," an elusive term, but real enough in all its polysemy to be recognized by Romans and non-Romans alike: and if not for anything else, then for its language, *romanesco,* this swearing poetics growing out of the "Darwinian forests" of its slums, as Pasolini once said.

Rome is not one place; it is not one culture. It might better be captured as a way of life, to paraphrase Louis Wirth. Or perhaps, as ways of life. Rome is a vertical city, enshrined in its religious history, from the top of its hills decorated with crosses and churches, to the underground catacombs still being unearthed. Rome is a city cut in spatial and temporal layers of historical depth. The oldest monument of Roman engineering is the Great Sewer, the Cloaca Maxima, which dates from the sixth century BC and is still in use today. The main roads reaching out from the historic center, its water pipe lines, and aqueducts were all built more than two thousand years ago.

This Rome has been studied predominantly as a historical monument, focusing on the marvelous art and urban architecture that millions of tourists understandably come to visit every year. But what of contemporary Rome, its people, its politics and economy, its environment, the challenges of globalization? Both within and outside Rome's historic center, a variety of transformations are currently underway which make the city a privileged but as yet understudied site for reflecting upon the concomitant processes of globalization and urban change. Rome is both more and something other than what is conveyed by its global tourist image. Recent decades have seen the arrival of large numbers of immigrants, many of whom are becoming permanent residents and are changing the dynamics of the city. This new multicultural reality is affecting Rome's economy, its neighborhoods, its nightlife, and the arts. It has also become a highly contested issue in local politics. Mobility is not restricted to Rome's newcomers, and the city is undergoing gentrification, labor market transformations, geographic expansion. Conditions in its peripheries are now the subject of intense study, and urban planners are seeking new approaches to develop the city for a sustainable future. The issues of pollution, congestion, and calls for decentralization are more urgent than ever. Rome's identity as the national capital is also an issue for debate as moves for increased regional autonomy and questions concerning the role of the Italian nation-state itself develop. The fast-changing urban realities of Italy's biggest city and capital are the focus of this book, which is the first interdisciplinary social science approach to Rome in the English language.

The overall aim of the book is twofold. First, to fill the current gap in contemporary urban studies by examining a series of concrete urban realities beyond the historical city center. Second, to use the city of Rome as a springboard for reflecting on larger issues relating to theories of urban change within a context of globalization. The case studies presented in each of the chapters provide novel prisms to engage with central themes in contemporary urban studies: global city theory, urbanization as evidencing "multiple modernities," the relationship between capital cities and the nation, the informal city and urban change from below, and various models of sustainable urban growth that Rome exemplifies in its own paradoxical ways.

Part 1 of the book provides a panoramic view of the city and directly addresses the notion of the "global city" running through the whole volume, reflecting on what globalization actually means for Rome, and vice versa, how this city can contribute to sharpening our understanding of how globalization processes play out in different urban contexts. Although Rome is not considered a significant global city by scholars who focus predominantly on economic transformations, we argue that this perspective is too limited. Rome is indeed a global city in many ways. It is a hub for global diplomacy (not least because of the presence of several United Nations' agencies), immigration, religious pilgrimage and tourism, and it is one of the world's most known and "imagined cities," playing a central role in cinema and popular literature around the globe. Many of its current urban transformations are intertwined with global processes: deindustrialization, neoliberal policies, gentrification and housing segregation, emergence of new social movements, and a global idiom to bespeak cultural difference with what Herzfeld (2007) has called "benign racism." Part 2 provides case studies which further illustrate the complex relationships between the global and local levels, highlighting neighborhood transformations and their role in changing patterns of social interaction and identity politics in the city. With a view to spatial transformations and processes of inclusion/exclusion, several of the chapters discuss the role played by recent immigration.

A second core theme of the book concerns Rome's paradoxical status as the (often reluctant) capital of one of the world's economic powers and, simultaneously, its continuing expansion as an "informal" and "self-made city." Rome's ambivalent position and identity as both "core" and "periphery" within the Italian nation-state and Europe more broadly is an issue for debate within the contexts of increasing regional autonomy and European integration. Part 3 examines questions of identity linked to the city's history. Because Rome is so rich in historically rooted symbols and images, claims to the past often take on highly theatrical forms in the negotiation of boundaries of belonging. This is most visible in the articulation of Roman identity as daily fought out between fans of AS Roma and SS Lazio. Taking an anthropological approach to policy-making (Shore and Wright 1997), the section discusses the interplay between public sector projects and policies and the daily lives of citizens as well as the challenges and contradictions in the authorities' attempts to manage Rome's cultural heritage. It also addresses the impact of large-scale urban projects linked to global sports events. Part 4 examines how various neighborhoods and localities outside the city walls are developing as a bottom-up process and not as a result of urban planning. Rome is in many ways a collection of self-built neighborhoods, making its urban development comparable to numerous non-Western cities where the informal sector has driven change and expansion. This makes Rome a laboratory of interpersonal and informal networks, which sheds new light on urban dynamics in the "Western" city.

Situating Urban Studies Today:
Unfolding Ambivalences of Modernity and Globalization

Theorizing and understanding the city goes to the heart of disciplinary traditions in the social sciences. Sociology as it emerged in the late nineteenth century was in a very direct sense a study of how human beings could live together in cities, and how cities could be developed to accommodate the unfolding social forces of class, community, and diversity. The study of city life and social transformation was central to the founding figures of the social sciences, including Karl Marx, Max Weber, Ferdinand Tönnies, and Georg Simmel. It was their work that inspired American urban scholars, and in particular the Chicago school. The city represented both the problems and promises of modernity: How can the urban individual maintain the independence and individuality of his existence *against* the sovereign powers of society? A new individuality had grown out of the nineteenth-century experience, but would this individual survive the massification forces of the growing urban setting? Would the psychological foundation of this individuality be torn to pieces by the almost violent and ever-shifting stimuli that provided modern city life with its own particular emotional life? We tend to forget how dramatic an experience the city is, and how dramatic a change in style of life it was when cities started to grow rapidly in the late nineteenth and early twentieth centuries. What kind of community forms and interpersonal relations were possible in this new setting? Gabriel Tarde (1969) perceptively captured the emergence of the "public" in Europe's growing cities as a physical distribution of separated individuals "with a cohesion that is merely mental," largely anticipating Benedict Anderson's (1985) notion of "imagined communities."

Here was another paradox: As people were lumped together in city crowds, distance became a problem. Edgar Allan Poe noted, in "The Man in the Crowd" (1840), how isolated the persons seemed to be despite the "very denseness of the company around." In city life, an individual's horizon was enlarged; new possibilities were made available. The idea of an achievement-based society could never have fully developed in a village, because villages are too reliant upon determining hierarchies of wealth and status. But freedom came with a price. Marx called it alienation, Durkheim anomie, Simmel *Entfremdung,* and Weber analyzed the disenchantment that seemed to characterize modern, rational bourgeois life: a sense of loss and meaninglessness. Loneliness belongs to the city.

Parliamentary politics, public debate, and the very idea of a "public sphere" developed alongside urban growth. As Weber (1966) noted, and as etymology reminds us, the development of rights and duties and therefore of citizenship for people sharing the same space grew out of the long history of the occidental city. The working classes perhaps never united globally as Marx would have had it, but they did so in many cities, which is where they took to the streets. The division of labor that underpinned industrialization belonged to the city, as Engels understood so clearly. Capitalism spread from the city, but so did crime; whether celebrated by liberals or criticized by socialists, there was consensus about the priority of the city as the locus of modernity. The city holds the ambivalence of modernity within it.

The larger field of what we today know as *urban studies* started to reflourish from the 1980s; this time with the important contribution of the discipline of anthropology (Low 2005), which from the 1960s had increasingly started to focus on "complex society." Since the 1980s, urban anthropology has become established as one of anthropology's most important subdisciplines (Hannerz 1980). We certainly have to understand this general "return to the city" reflexively. Urban studies had not been a dominant field in the social sciences in the postwar period, and especially not in Europe. However, by the late twentieth century, a new series of challenges started to become evident, and just as a century earlier, they went to the heart of the modern project. The crisis of modernity, signaled by postmodernism, re-posed the question: What kind of community forms are meaningful in the postindustrial age? Identity became problematized from every angle of the social sciences. The nation-state was increasingly challenged as the monopolist of economic and political power and as a container for personal and collective identity. "Flows" of goods, money, ideas, people, and technologies were moving both below and beyond the nation-state in a general process of deterritorialization. Even our most cherished ideas of democratic forms have become challenged by legitimacy problems in a new type of "informational" mass society. This generalized sense of disorientation is currently deepened by ecological crisis and continuing population growth in "megacities." More than half the world population now live in cities, and the percentage as well as the total number is bound to go up, some say exponentially. As in the late nineteenth century, the ambivalences of (post)modernity are here for us to confront, and this is the context in which we live and think the city today.

Globalization debates from the 1990s forced new discussion about the city. The city became the locus for thinking differently about identity and belonging, and environmental concerns translated into various idioms of "urban sustainability." From the 1980s until today, urban studies have indeed been one of the most proliferating subcategories within academia and policy-making. As a field of study, it has brought together sociologists, anthropologists, architects, policy makers, political scientists, urban planners, literary scholars, companies, and street artists. What characterizes contemporary urban studies is the recognition of a shared space of discussion, not a convergence over methods or theories. The same must be said about this book. Still, the majority of our authors have a background in anthropology, cultural studies, or urban planning, and most chapters are based on ethnographic fieldwork in the city.

Normative positions likewise differ within contemporary urban studies debates. Some urban scholars tend to celebrate or at least look favorably toward new global cities as dynamic places for economic and political globalization and the emergence of a new cosmopolitanism "beyond" the outdated and limited national cultures (Friedman 1986; Brenner and Keil 2006). The new global cities are put on a pedestal as coordinators of information flows, knowledge economies, information exchange, and finance markets; of regional and transnational political integration and collaboration; as the motors behind decreasing barriers to trade, collaboration, and friendships tied across and beyond boundaries and continents. Yet the very same cities might be seen as representing everything negative about economically driven globalization: inequality, pollution, privatization of urban politics, fragmentation and polarization of communities, deepening class conflicts, exploitation of labor and immigrants, gentrification, the commercialization of urban culture, new mechanisms of exclusion alongside a frightening homogenization of spaces and identities. But even here lies an ambivalence, so evident also in Rome: the countercapitalist movements, often still relying on (neo-)Marxist critique, still hold the city as a promise: alternative movements, alternative economies, Occupy Wall Street, and the new global movements writ large emerge and institutionalize within cityscapes, creating forms of local identity-cum-alternative cosmopolitanism, antibourgeois and anticapitalist in nature, as can be seen in Rome's "social centers" (see Mudu, chapter 16).

The aim of this book is not to take sides in these debates. We work from the premise that cities are evidently both the motors and dustbins of globalization. Our concerns are more humble: What can we learn from the city of Rome that may inform these debates? How can an ethnography and anthropology of the city contribute toward a more finely tuned understanding of the interplay between local and global? Our aim is therefore also to entangle the too-often detached positions on globalization and its discontents to the reality of local settings. Any overall comparative discussion of urban/global change *needs* to return to the study of Rome. We are not arguing that Rome should replace Paris as "capital of modernity" (Harvey 2003) or New York as "capital of globalization"; we are arguing, however, that we urgently need to rethink the very notion of "model cities" and the spatially empowered metaphors of center and periphery that it relies and feeds upon.

Rome as Global City: Elements for Reflection

When global city theory developed in the 1990s, the models drawn upon were New York, Los Angeles, Tokyo, and London. How does Rome fit into existing theoretical frameworks in urban studies? The striking fact is that although Rome is one of the world's most known cities, it has practically never been a reference point for global city debates. More than mere neglect, this perhaps identifies a problem. Namely that contemporary global city theory somehow fails to accommodate anything that falls in between the dichotomy between "northern postindustrial hypercities" and "southern ever-growing megacities." Rome is neither. It is Western, even emblematically and foundationally so, and therefore not approachable within the frame of the "emerging southern capital." The European Union was born in Rome. Yet Rome is clearly peripheral to the global streams of capital, finance, and investment. Multinationals sell their products here, but none of them operate from here, whether in terms of production, investment, or marketing. Rome has no stock exchange, no finance center, no business hub. So can we place the city within any broader global city framework?

Our answers will be plural: Each chapter develops a specific aspect of the city and its urban life, and the perspectives developed cannot be contained within any single theoretical framework. We have no ambition to offer an alternative or competing paradigm for thinking of the global city. Rome defies easy generalization, but exactly here lies a merit. The study of Rome forces us to rethink what we mean by the *global* and how the local/global relations emerge in concrete settings. Here one has to avoid the temptation to dichotomize between the global as the dynamic flow of capital and information and the local as the traditional place of culture and community (Smith 2001). Urban development, also in the case of Rome, *is* indeed part of a multifaceted process of social, economic, and political change which provides the backdrop for the development of cultural forms that are locally specific just as they are globally entangled. Globalization is also an open-ended cultural process (Rotenberg and McDonogh 1993). And here Rome has a role to play, perhaps even a central one (see Thomassen and Vereni, chapter 1).

In contemporary globalization debates, and especially within the political sciences, globalization is often approached as a tension between state and market forces (Giddens 2002). Such a view would make little sense to most Romans. Here both *state* and *market* are most often considered external forces, impinging upon people's lives in ways that they cannot control. In fact, in the urban development of Rome, one can very frequently witness collusion between economic interest and political administration. In theory, the church offers an alternative to both. It has its own political administration and its own state within the city; its social philosophy, as argued very strongly by the current pope, Francis I, is critical of economic globalization and materialistic consumption. And yet, many Romans see the church as one more force "above them," part of that "palace city" which governs their life (and the housing market), but which Romans accept only very reluctantly. Globalization as seen from Rome is not market against state with religion as an alternative. It is about interacting forces and strategic games of power sifting through social body and physical landscape, in a continuous process of place-making where individuals and local communities try to cope with externalities through evasion, neglect, twisting the rules of the game, or suffering the consequences.

Thinking of urbanity and globality from the perspective of the city of Rome also represents a vantage point for addressing another central debate in contemporary urban global theory, namely the difference between American and European cities. As will be discussed in part 1 of this book, global city theory has been much criticized for being U.S.-centric in origin and nature. The idea that the city, much like a firm, should act as an entity that facilitates and provides infrastructure to economic growth is simply more plausible and feasible in America than it is in Europe. European cities are generally embedded with a welfare state system which exists to a lesser degree in America. Even after the neoliberal turn, European cities remain more firmly embedded in pre-existing political and cultural frameworks than do American cities which are "freer" to dynamically follow the streams of economic competition, but arguably they are also more fragmented and vulnerable to social inequality. This, however, does not mean that a city like Rome is not influenced by global capitalism, for it is indeed, and not least because of tourism and immigration.

Here *history* does play a role. European cities grew out of pre-existing towns, and the great majority of European cities are built on or around these historical town centers. In Rome, the *centro storico* has retained its spatial stretch for 2,400 years. Imperial Rome was built onto a pre-existing Etruscan village, tying together very ancient notions of centrality and sacrality. These histories have created genealogies of belonging and understanding of the *civic* (Herzfeld 2009) that differ in both nature and kind from the American urban experience. The overall point is that the effects of globalization are absorbed and reproduced very differently in European "historical" cities, which are more strongly ruled by local and national politics and cultural traditions and less autonomous than most American cities, for better or worse. To this point, one must add the very particular trajectories and concrete urban realities that have come to form each city. Let us therefore turn to the contours of contemporary Rome's urban setting: its histories, geographies, and peoples.

Framing the City: Layers of Place, History, and Memory

Rome can be described as a "reluctant capital" (see Herzfeld, chapter 2), a city which appears to resist fully taking on the functions of political center and representative of the nation. Italy's notoriously ambiguous sense of national identity and its history as a patchwork of regions, whose identities are still very marked today, play a large part in the unwillingness of Italians to see Rome as their core. Romans often appear equally disinclined to take center stage in the nation, as they made quite clear in their muted participation during the 2011 celebrations marking 150 years of national unity.[1] Rome is not new to the status of capital. It was capital city of the Roman Kingdom, the Roman Republic, and then the Roman Empire, without a doubt the most powerful city in the world for centuries. From the first century AD, it became the seat of the papacy and from the eighth to the tenth century the center of the Papal States. From 1871, it took on the role of capital of Italy and, in 1936, of the short-lived Italian Empire through which Mussolini tried to emulate the country's past greatness. Rome has always been a political city. It hosts an extremely large, centralized state administration, and it contains the world record number of embassies due to the presence of the Vatican as a separate state.

Romans frequently appear detached from their city's official status, often accused of provincialism and a resistance to change. In the last two decades, successive municipal governments have attempted to counter this image and instead launch the city as a global hub. Sports has been one of the most obvious means, with proposals to create a new Formula 1 race course, as well as the city's bid to host the 2020 Olympic Games (both of which have since been rejected), although the scandals concerning corruption and waste of public funds which followed the 2009 World Aquatics Championship did little to cleanse the city's reputation. Drives to give Rome more luster as a center of contemporary culture have led to it hosting an annual International Film Festival since 2006, and the unveiling of the MAXXI Museum of Twenty-First Century Art in 2010. That same year, the city officially took on the new name of "Roma Capitale," a status that gives it increased funding and local administrative autonomy to enable it to more effectively fulfill its functions as seat of government institutions and international diplomacy. Whether this new administrative structure is able to give the city the transformative impetus that is intended remains to be seen.

At the level of territorial and administrative units, Rome plays a central role within the rather complex web of Italian bureaucracy. Besides being the capital of Italy, Rome is also capital of the region of Lazio, which legislates on and manages an array of public resources including health, education, regional transport, and housing. The corruption scandal that exploded in late 2012 took place within the elected regional council and involved systematic pocketing of public funds by party groups and individuals. The region is divided into provinces, and the Provincia di Roma, with its more than four million inhabitants, is the most populated in Italy. It is often viewed as representing the larger metropolitan area of the city, which sprawls into rural areas and other towns. The provincia owns a part of the city's public property; manages elements of policing, urban planning, and public housing; and is led by an elected council, adding a further layer of bureaucracy. The Comune di Roma makes up a large proportion of the province and defines the boundaries of the city proper. The term refers not only to the geographic area but also to the municipal government, whose seat is on the Capitoline Hill (Campidoglio). This administrative body—run by an elected city council with the mayor at its head—is the core decision-making entity in the city, and most of the chapters in this book refer directly to its policies and practices. The Comune di Roma is in turn divided into 15 *municipi* (boroughs).[2] Created as an attempt at decentralization, the boroughs also have their own elected governments and manage local-level infrastructure and affairs. Finally, the historical center of the city is divided into 22 *rioni* (neighborhoods), which are very important in terms of identity, grassroots mobilization, and historical legacy, but which are not administrative units.

Rome's histories, ancient and modern, have been written about extensively and this book does not set out to duplicate or contribute to that field. Among others, Hibbert's (1985) by now classic biography of the city, Bosworth's (2011) more recent exploration of Rome's relationship with its many layers of history, and Caldwell and Caldwell's (2011) collection of essays on the city's representations and reconfigurations over time, are essential readings, as is John Agnew's (1995) geographic approach to the city's urban development. While this book is not about history, it must be noted that Rome *is* in many ways a "historical city." We propose to look at history as consisting of "archeological strata" (Foucault 1972), each of which constitutes a discursive formation and possible reference point for identity claims in the present. *Cultural memory* refers to the arsenal of symbolic forms, images, and myths that remain accessible across millennia that are reactivated and reinvented in concrete social settings by individuals and collectivities. As discussed in several chapters, in their identity claims, Romans, not surprisingly, make conscious use of the city's history, incorporating Rome's symbolic value into their cultural intimacy. These historical strata and layers of history remain visible and continue to shape the city's physical landscape—much in contrast to a similarly historical city such as Athens. As a consequence, Rome's urban development continues to evolve around its cultural heritage, sometimes a "blessing," sometimes a "curse" for attempts to redesign and "modernize" the city and its infrastructure (Higgins, chapter 12). Granted this importance of historical memory and symbolism, it is worth briefly noting the rapid transformations that the city has gone through in its short history as capital of Italy. Without just a hint of this background, few of the city's contemporary conflicts and idiosyncrasies make sense.

When Rome was taken by the Kingdom of Italy in 1870 and formally became its capital in 1871, "completing" Italian unification, it was an economic, cultural, and political backwater, suffering from introversion and stagnation caused largely by the papacy's defensive response to the political and social changes that had swept across the peninsula and Europe in the previous decades. Geographically, Rome was a tiny capital, made up of the Medieval, Renaissance, and Baroque core that Romans today refer to as the *centro storico,* a new development connecting Termini station to the center, and a very embryonic attempt to encourage indus-try by the river on the southern side. Its population was that of a small provincial town: about 229,000 residents (Babonaux 1983). Its new status as capital required massive physical development: the building of ministries, law courts, and other symbols of nation. With these institutions came an entirely new population that needed housing and other services, not just politicians and civil servants, but also the workers who would erect its buildings, lay its roads and other infrastructures, and serve its burgeoning bourgeoisie. While whole neighborhoods such as Prati and Esquilino were planned along the ordered lines of Piedmontese towns to house the city's official workers, the city was unprepared for the massive arrivals of unskilled laborers escaping the harsh conditions of the countryside and seek-ing any work they could find in the new capital. With them came the beginning of Rome's sprawl of slums, which remained a visible feature of the city's outskirts until the 1970s. This parallel development of Rome as self-made city, one largely untouched by formal planning but equally subject to intensive real-estate specu-lation, set the foundations for a trend that continues into the present (see chapters 4, 13, and 14 by Mudu, Cellamare, and Trabalzi). Within thirty years of becom-ing the capital, at the turn of the new century, Rome's population had almost doubled, reaching 442,000 (Babonaux 1983).

The late nineteenth century was a time of industrial development in Italy, mainly but not exclusively centered in its northern cities. Yet the capital's in-dustrial potential was not fully exploited then or at any time in the twentieth century out of a political choice to keep it untouched by the worker activism and protest that instead accompanied industrialization in the north. Some factories and power plants did develop, especially in the southern areas of Testaccio and Ostiense and, subsequently, in the eastern periphery. Nevertheless, these sectors never became a major force in the city's wealth and employment. What modern-ization and infrastructural growth did emerge in the early 1900s was brought to a standstill by the onset of World War I.

The fascist rise to power in 1922 instead heralded two decades of profound transformation of the city that it took as its main symbol of greatness, unity, and progress. The centralization and growth of the state apparatus under Fascism inevitably led to massive construction projects in the capital, again not only in terms of governmental and public buildings, but also residential complexes and neighborhoods to house the ever-increasing population. (By 1936, it had reached over a million inhabitants, four times its original size.) Public housing projects, especially for municipal and state employees, mushroomed and were, at least in the initial period, generally well integrated within the urban fabric. However, the colossal demolitions of parts of the historic center to create triumphal boule-vards and rationalize the city's roads were among the more traumatic assertions of fascist power in the capital. Not only did these *sventramenti* reduce to rubble entire sections of the old city—and in the case of Via dell'Impero, obliterate important archaeological remains—it made thousands of Romans homeless. These were forcibly rehoused, often in specially built *borgate:* new and isolated public housing projects located in the countryside beyond the city rim and often devoid of employment opportunities and more than minimal services. These were not organic working-class peripheries such as those that had developed in the more industrial towns. They were deposits in which to hide an impoverished and disgruntled population that did not fit the regime's self-image of progress and social unity.

Another world war again interrupted the directions in which the city was growing, most notably by halting the construction of Esposizione Universale di Roma (EUR), an entirely new area extending toward the sea which was intended to host the 1942 World's Fair and then to become the administrative heart of the city and the nation. The war was devastating for Rome. The Allied bombings of 1943 killed thousands of civilians and made many homeless, although its status as an "open city" largely protected its artistic and architectural treasures. Thousands of other Romans risked starvation and many escaped to the countryside to survive.

The postwar period of reconstruction and subsequent economic boom of the 1950s and 1960s brought with them the third and most radical period of the city's expansion. At this time, the population more than doubled again to reach almost 2.8 million in the 1970s, making it the country's biggest city in terms of both people and surface area. The decline of Italy's agricultural sector, especially in the south, coupled with booming job opportunities in the cities, led to urbanization of unprecedented proportions. Lacking industries to work in, the new Romans were mainly concentrated in construction, public administration, and services—the same sectors that continue to drive the city's economy today. The need to house these new arrivals quickly and to ward off the slums that continued to spread was partly met by the creation of public housing projects. Their numbers were most often inadequate and, with the collusion of the main political parties governing the city, the market was left open to rampant real-estate speculation and an urban sprawl of largely unplanned neighborhoods often devoid of the most basic services.

Home and Place-Making: Living the City

Many of the problems that Romans have to negotiate daily and that are immediately noticeable to its visitors have to do with its particular history of modernization. Despite the fact that most of the city center's tangled narrow streets are now closed to cars and there is a dramatic shortage of parking places in most areas, traffic congestion is endemic—with most of the ring road paralyzed at rush hours every day—and has not been significantly reduced by attempts to improve its public transport networks. Commuter trains are still overcrowded and often in abysmal condition. Rome has a very high number of cars for a European city: 695 per thousand inhabitants (ISTAT 2011). After Mumbai, Rome is the city in the world with the highest number of motorbikes per inhabitant. More shockingly still, 45 percent of Romans use public transport less than once a month or never (compared with 5 percent in Paris) (Eurobarometer 2009). Air pollution is consequently high: 89 percent of Romans view it as a major problem in the city and scientific studies confirm their view (Legambiente 2012). Rome has the highest density of green spaces of all the major Italian cities (131 m² per inhabitant) but not all of this space is easily accessible, and this has to do with another number: the mere 14 cm² of pedestrianized streets per person. Dirty roads, a lack of accessible and efficient services and, in recent years, fears of rising crime are among the most common concerns for residents. Compared to many other metropolises, Rome is not particularly dangerous or violent and its crime rates actually fell between 2006 and 2010 (Regione Lazio 2011). Nevertheless, a spate of murders in public places in 2011, 2012, and 2013, some clearly linked to expanding organized crime groups, has generated media-fueled alarm dubbing the city *Roma violenta, Roma criminale*. It is the city with the highest sense of insecurity among residents in the country, overtaking even those most commonly associated with high crime, such as Naples.

Rome does not score highly in any comparative study of livable cities. On Mercer's 2011 global ranking, it came fifty-second and it did similarly badly on the *Economist's* annual survey, far below most Western European capitals. It came twenty-third in similar national-level rankings, scoring particularly badly on feelings of safety and on employment opportunities (Sole 24 Ore 2011b). On the other hand, Romans came fifteenth in questions about happiness levels (Sole 24 Ore 2011a). Despite their ability to face many of the city's problems with their characteristically acidic humor, these challenges have pushed many Romans to flee the city and move to nearby towns in recent years. Its population shrank during the 1980s and 1990s and only began to rise noticeably in 2006, reaching a total of 2.76 million by 2012 thanks mainly to its growing numbers of immigrants which, at approximately 360,000 (circa 500,000 in the region of Lazio), now represent one in eight Romans. The city is now also home to a growing population of second-generation immigrants, which has given birth to new forms of cultural identity, hybridity, and resistance (Thomassen 2009).

The city's chronic shortage of affordable housing plays a large role in the decision of many families to leave: Housing prices are the highest in the country, both to buy and to rent. A 70 m² apartment costs on average around 1,000 euros a month (Sole 24 Ore 2011b) and it is no surprise that 89 percent of Romans declare it hard to find reasonably priced accommodations (Eurobarometer 2009).

Rome today is therefore colonizing its hinterland in new ways. While its outward sprawl has slowed down in recent decades, new residential, business, and mall complexes are continuing to spring up outside the ring road. As Cellamare argues (chapter 9), while these have been incentivized by local government as a way of decentralizing the city and generating urban renewal, services, and employment in the peripheries, those intentions have not been fulfilled. Meanwhile, the small towns around the province are increasingly becoming dormitories for Roman and immigrant workers.

Despite these changes and challenges, Rome's neighborhoods—both central and peripheral—still often have the feel of self-contained villages where locals stop to chat in shop doorways and children socialize in the sports facilities (the *oratorio)* of the local parish. This is by no means restricted to the twenty *rioni* which make up the historic center and the area near the Vatican. In fact, gentrification in many of those areas has forced countless families who had lived there for generations to move out, as Herzfeld's (2009) study of Monti chronicles. The tight-knit communities that some of us remember from our childhoods are therefore beginning to fragment, taken over by bijoux apartments for short-lets, boutiques, and restaurants which most Romans cannot hope to afford. The vast majority of the city's residents instead live in the residential neighborhoods built during the twentieth century that stretch from the edge of the old town to the ring road and beyond. These *quartieri* and the *borgate* and *borghetti* beyond them, while certainly less picturesque than the central *rioni,* are the contexts in which many of the city's battles and creative forms of negotiation and survival are occurring. Therefore, they are the backdrop to many of the chapters in this book. It is in the peripheral areas rarely explored by tourists that struggles for the right to a home and to the city occur (see Clough Marinaro and Daniele, Cellamare, Trabalzi, and Lombardi-Diop; chapters 7, 13, 14, and 15, respectively), as well as conflicts over access to schools (Vereni, chapter 6). These are the areas where many migrants are settling, creating new generations of hyphenated Italians, and changing local cultures and economies (see Cervelli, Broccolini, and Solimene; chapters 3, 5, and 8). These are also the locations in which attempts to bring agriculture back to the city are emerging (see Trabalzi, chapter 17).

These neighborhoods often feel far removed from Rome's more formal identities as Italy's political capital, the global center of Catholicism, and one of the world's major tourist destinations. The city receives between twenty and thirty million visitors a year, providing employment for its inhabitants, but also contributing to traffic and pollution, which add to the inhabitants' often conflicted relationship with the monuments and cultural heritage that are so crucial to the city's economy (Higgins, chapter 12). Is the splendor of its past the ruin of its present? Rome's status as capital, we have already seen, is an equally ambivalent one. While its ministries and institutions have in part driven the city's growth and wealth, they also fuel much of the residents' cynicism about political cor-ruption—or, at the very least, the perceived distance of the political class—and its effects on their daily lives, as the arguments by Martin and Mudu (chapters 10 and 16) explore in different ways.

Sacred and Secular, Fission and Fusion: Conflict Boundaries within the City

The "soul" of Rome is contested in many different ways. In Rome, *religion* and *secularity* are not abstract notions: They are spatial and semantic realities of ev-eryday life and have been so for two millennia. Public schools and hospitals are decorated with a crucifix. Some Romans jokingly call the pope an *extracomuni-tario* (the term refers to non–European Union citizens specifically but symboli-cally means someone not of "our community," a "foreigner"), with no right to interfere in their lives. The subtleties of such attitudes and the complex ways in which secular and sacred interweave in the everyday life of contemporary Ro-mans was one of the main themes of Herzfeld's ethnography (2009). It is not a coincidence that in Italy the tension between church and state took its modern formulation with the notion of the "Roman Question"—What role should the church play in the civic life of a modern nation-state?—a question that, in some form, is bound to endure. While Rome is a global icon for religiosity, from within the Italian experience, Rome has become a symbol of the *difficult* coexistence of state and church.

This book does not address the role of the church in any direct sense, yet its presence emerges in many of the chapters. This is because in the daily life of Romans the church has a down-to-earth importance. There are more than nine hundred operating churches in the city, another world record. Historically, the presence of some of Christianity's first and most holy churches and the establish-ment of the city as Christianity's administrative and spiritual center is what has brought people to Rome from around the world for centuries. Religious figures and holy shrines are still found on almost every street corner. Not that Romans should necessarily be regarded as particularly religious. The image of Rome as a "holy city" held by many visiting tourists (Christians or not) often contrasts with the disinterest in religious matters characterizing street debates and popular at-titudes among residents. The proportion of couples opting for a civil marriage (just above 50 percent) instead of a religious ceremony is surprisingly enough the highest in the country. For many, though, the church still fulfills a social func-tion. Parishes organize or provide the spaces for recreational life for young and old alike and religious institutions provide assistance to immigrants, making up for the empty slots left by the state. It is no surprise that the most accurate data on migration trends in Italy are provided by a church organization, Caritas, not the government. The church also owns a great part of the city's private property and is therefore a main player in the housing market as well as city politics. Of course, Rome is not only inhabited by Catholics. Due to recent immigration, Islam has become the city's second biggest religion, by far surpassing Judaism. The Jewish community has played its own non-negligible part of the city's history (Stow 2001; Coppa 2006). Interfaith dialog on the institutional level and religious diversity and coexistence in the city's neighborhoods are therefore ever-more defining features of a city whose identities are changing.

Rome's contested identities are also played out on the soccer field and, more acutely, among the fans of the city's two main teams, AS Roma and SS Lazio, which in many ways turns Rome into a moiety structure, where belonging to one or the other club is a categorical choice. As Dyal's discussion illustrates (chapter 11), the stadium is one of the main theaters where different interpretations of Roman-ness are performed, with repercussions for the larger city-space, where cars, motorbikes, personal belongings, and entire buildings are symbolically decorated with either the yellow and red (AS Roma) or white and blue (SS Lazio) colors. The symbolic struggle over ownership of the city is also ritually displayed via "graffiti wars" dominating public spaces. This illustrates one more Roman version of a segmentary system where mechanisms of fusion and fission take place from the smallest to the biggest units of social organization. As argued by Herzfeld (chapter 2), such localist factionalism must be seen as central to the political organization of everyday life. These Roman practices of segmentation fit well with the Catholic model of authority and administration and the principle of subsidiarity. This is one of the ways in which the sacred and secular forms of social life infiltrate and feed upon each other. It is also in this flexible system of fraction and coming together that Herzfeld identifies the Roman capacity for compromise and accommodation.

Rome, Open City

In sum, Rome represents a unique setting that has long been awaiting an in-depth social scientific study. Rome cannot be encapsulated in postcards or ready-made theoretical frameworks. Its hopeless beauty seems to abolish all standards of measurement and splinter any efforts at generalization. And yet it is the city's very peculiarity and its unique social texture that invites a study that throws light on local–global connections as these become tied together in concrete practices and lived experiences, and sometimes in unexpected ways. With this book, we wish to open up the city of Rome, dig into its intricate realties, and explore the city from within. Each city is its own cosmos. Or, as Goethe wrote in 1786, "Rome is a world, and it would take years to become citizens in it." However, Pasolini, in explaining his relationship to the city, once said that Rome acted "as an experience of a world, and thus, in a certain sense, of *the* world." Perhaps Rome, more than any other urban setting, is a globally significant spot from which to grasp the larger cosmos, this globality in which we all live, in one way or another.

Notes

1. There was, for example, a striking lack of national flags flying from windows and balconies compared to many towns in the north.

2. There used to be twenty, but one was eliminated in the 1970s, and four more were incorporated into neighboring *municipi* in 2013.

References

Agnew, John A. 1995. *Rome*. Chichester, U.K.: John Wiley and Sons.

Anderson, Benedict. 1985. *Imagined communities: Reflections on the Origin and Spread of Nationalism*. London: Verso Ed.

Babonaux, Anne-Marie Seronde. 1983. *Roma: Dalla città alla metropoli*. Rome: Editori Riuniti.

Bosworth, Richard J. B. 2011. *Whispering City: Modern Rome and Its Histories*. New Haven, Conn.: Yale University Press.

Brenner, Neil, and Roger Keil. 2006. *The Global Cities Reader*. London: Routledge.

Caldwell, Dorigen, and Leslie Caldwell. 2011. *Rome: Continuing Encounters between Past and Present*. Farnham, U.K.: Ashgate.

Coppa, Frank. 2006. *The Papacy, the Jews and the Holocaust*. Washington, D.C.: Catholic University of America Press.

Eurobarometer. 2009. "Perception Survey on Quality of Life in European Cities." ec.europa.eu/public_opinion/flash/fl_277_en.pdf. Accessed 9 November 2012.

Foucault, Michel. 1972. *The Archeology of Knowledge*. New York: Pantheon Books.

Friedman, John. 1986. "The World City Hypothesis." *Development and Change* 17: 69–83.

Giddens, Anthony. 2002. *Runaway World: How Globalization Is Shaping Our Lives*. London: Routledge.

Hannerz, Ulf. 1980. *Exploring the City: Inquiries toward an Urban Anthropology*. New York: Columbia University Press.

Harvey, David. 2003. *Paris as the Capital of Modernity*. New York: Routledge.

Herzfeld, Michael. 2007. "Small-Mindedness Writ Large: On the Migrations and Manners of Prejudice." *Journal of Ethnic and Migration Studies* 33 (2): 255–274.

———. 2009. *Evicted from Eternity: The Restructuring of Modern Rome*. Chicago: University of Chicago Press.

Hibbert, Christopher. 1985. *Rome, the Biography of a City*. New York: W. W. Norton.

ISTAT. 2011. "Italia in cifre." http://www.istat.it/it/files/2011/06/italiaincifre2011.pdf. Accessed 5 September 2013.

Legambiente. 2012. "Smog: Legambiente consegna il cigno nero al sindaco Alemanno." http://www.legambiente.it/contenuti/notizie-dal-territorio/smog-legambiente-consegna-il-cigno-nero-al-sindaco-alemanno. Accessed 5 September 2013.

Low, Setha, ed. 2005. *Theorizing the City: The New Urban Anthropology Reader*. New Brunswick, N.J.: Rutgers University Press.

Poe, Edgar Allen. 1840. "The Man in the Crowd." Reprinted Edgar Allen Poe. 1998. *Selected Tales*. Oxford: Oxford University Press.

Regione Lazio. 2011. "Rapporto sullo stato della sicurezza e sull'andamento della criminalità nel Lazio." http://www.regione.lazio.it/binary/rl_eell_sicurezza/tbl_contenuti/RAPPORTO_SICUREZZA.pdf. Accessed 5 September 2013.

Rotenberg, Robert, and Gary McDonogh, eds. 1993. *The Cultural Meaning of Urban Space*. Westport, Conn.: Bergin & Garvey.

Shore, Chris, and Susan Wright, eds. 1997. *Anthropology of Policy: Critical Perspectives on Governance and Power*. London: Routledge.

Smith, Michael Peter. 2001. *Transnational Urbanism, Locating Globalization*. New York: Blackwell.

Sole 24 Ore. 2011a. "Dove abita la felicità?" http://www.ilsole24ore.com/art/notizie/2011-12-02/felicita-segue-altre-170703.shtml?uuid=AaLP7hQE. Accessed 9 November 2012.

———. 2011b. "Qualità della Vita." http://www.ilsole24ore.com/speciali/qvita_2011/home.shtm. Accessed 9 November 2012.

Stow, Kenneth. 2001. *Theatre of Acculturation: The Roman Ghetto in the Sixteenth Century*. Seattle: University of Washington Press.

Tarde, Gabriel. 1969. *On Communication and Social Influence*. Edited by Terry N. Clark. Chicago: University of Chicago Press.

Thomassen, Bjørn. 2009. "'Second Generation Immigrants' or 'Italians with Immigrant Parents'? Italian and European Perspectives on Immigrants and their Children." *Bulletin of Italian Politics* 2 (1): 21–44.

Weber, Max. 1966. *The City*. London: The Free Press.

Part I
Rome: The Local and the Global City

1 Diversely Global Rome

Bjørn Thomassen and Piero Vereni

Urban Global Theory and the "Roman Question"

In Rome today, native-born Italians rub shoulders in daily life with immigrants from wildly different origins: Romanians and eastern Europeans who work in construction; Chinese men (and some women) running garment shops at the market of Piazza Vittorio; Bangladeshis working in restaurants and phone centers. In a new twist on the history of European colonialism, nuns from the Missionaries of Charity, the order founded in India by Mother Teresa, now come to the heart of Catholic Christendom, where they pray in English for the salvation of those living in the Roman peripheries.

An ethnographic approach to Rome forces us to develop a new understanding of globalization and the global city. Global city theory has relied too much on selected cities, such as London, Los Angeles, or New York, which have come to be seen as prototypical examples of the global. In the study of third-world cities, urban scholars have then tried to show how cities in the global "periphery" fit in—or not—with the prevailing models. It is time that we start to go deeper.

The emergence of theories linking the "new city" to an emerging economic global framework goes back to the early 1980s. The nation-state was increasingly challenged as the monopolist of economic and political power. The constructivist approach to the nation held by theorists such as Ernest Gellner (1983) and Benedict Anderson (1983) had produced among social scientists a widespread awareness of the recent dominion of the nation-state and made it possible to envision a future in which the state might not be central to political economy and cultural organization. The debates led to a serious, and much-needed, questioning of "methodological nationalism" (Chernilo 2006), that is, the tendency to posit the nation-state as the given unit of analysis. The emerging megalopolises around the world came to represent a new analytical tool and seemed to provide a sense of orientation for capturing the complexity of global flows. In John Friedmann and

Goetz Wolff's "world cities" (1992), the theoretical frame of Wallerstein's world-system theory was applied to urban post-Fordist society. New forms of capitalism, held up by a new international division of labor and the fast-developing financing of the global economy, were seen as shaping the very social, physical, and political contours of the city, and the city itself was the motor of this emerging system.

In the 1980s, urban studies returned to the forefront of the academic and political agenda, attempting to reposition the city as a main actor, to be studied in its own right. However, the excessive reliance on economic and functionalist frameworks easily ended up obliterating the city even as it was bespoken. This was perhaps most clearly the case in the work of Manuel Castells, considered one of the most important (neo-Marxist) theorists of globalization. Despite Castell's focus on network societies, his (early) works were representative of sociological traditions that, inspired by Durkheim and various strands of Marxism, consistently denied any specificity to the urban question, reducing the city to a passive scenery of struggles around capitalism (Castells 1977). Cities were considered as inert players in the game, passive subjects of external forces that they could resist as little as the similarly battered nation-states. This is arguably not the case with what we today recognize as "global city theory." Especially through Saskia Sassen's conceptualization (1991), during the 1990s, we became acquainted with the global city: novel spaces where new forms of economy integrate with streams of immigration in a global network of hierarchical nodes and layers.

There are different versions of this global city theory, but they do share a set of common features. The global city is considered a *new type of city* because:

1. It transcends the national city system, going beyond the state that geographically encompasses it.
2. It articulates its economy, demography, and society to a global form of capitalism. That is, it is an economy-driven city.
3. It is connected to other global cities in a network of nodes. And the nodes have their own hierarchy.

Global city theory was criticized during the 1990s, mostly in order to overcome its evident Western-based perspective. The original models drawn upon were New York, Los Angeles, and London, but the attempt to include non-Western cities made the theory itself somehow puzzling: What is the point of a theory that conflates New York and Cairo, Tokyo and Mumbai under the same label, *world cities*? And why would one rather than the other city be considered paradigmatic? Because it is more powerful? And if so, how should this be measured?

From the onset of the global city, debate analysts have tried to identify specific units and have systematically focused on economic and financial features. In one of the first references to global cities, Robert B. Cohen (1981) isolated a *multinational sale index,* measuring the relative strength of a city as a center of international business, and a *multinational banking index,* which measures the internationality of banking by comparing the share of foreign deposits to the share of domestic deposits held by each bank in each city. This approach gave way to more research on the role of transnational corporations as key indicators of a possible hierarchy of global cities (Friedmann and Wolff 1982). The subsequent attention on finance capitalism in the wake of Sassen's research brought about a new interest for the global location strategies of transnational firms (Taylor 2003). According to this approach, cities can be ranked on the number of offices owned by transnational firms, thus producing a hierarchical network. Measuring London's global reach, for instance, this method ranks Milan as an "important link" to London and Rome only as a "minor link" (Beaverstock et al. 2000). The fact that Milan seems more globalized than Rome does is on the one hand a truism (given the industrial history of Milan compared to Rome) and on the other a disappointing outcome of the analysis, since we are left with the annoying feeling that the whole analytical framework does nothing but confirm common sense, without a proper description of how globalization has affected minor links, which may be both theoretically and ethnographically more relevant in explaining globalization than prime, major, or important links.

Writers such as Friedmann, Sassen, Castells, and Taylor are right that some cities established themselves as dominant players within the global market economy, as power centers controlling the transnational service economy: what Sassen calls "nodes" of networks, capital flows, and human movement. But it is quite another step to posit these cities as "models."

This "hierarchical epistemology" dominating urban theory is in fact nothing new. All the merits of the Chicago school notwithstanding, members of the school such as Wirth, Park, or Burgess took certain characteristics of American city development as a blueprint for the city in general, generating universal models on the basis of a very limited number of cases. On the other hand, within the city proper, and falling into another kind of extreme, the Chicago school put an exaggerated, almost exclusive emphasis on certain marginal figures, or marginal forms of existence (crime, deviance), thus failing perhaps to address what really generates each city: its own "soul" and identities of belonging. There is something inherently deceptive about dominant trends in urban theory: They simply fail to capture the essence of lived, urban experience.

At the more comparative-theoretical level, contemporary global city theory equally fails to accommodate anything that falls in between the dichotomy between "northern postindustrial hypercities" and "southern ever-growing megacities." Rome is just such an in-between city: Western, even emblematically so, and therefore not approachable within the frame of the emerging southern capital. Yet Rome does not comply with almost any of the features of the northern global city. Rome is clearly peripheral to the streams of capital, finance, and investment that made a city like London truly global. Rome does not seem directly "connected" to other centers in a wider hierarchy of global cities making up today's worldwide economic architecture. Rome is not a base for transnational corporations and financial industries, nor is it a major headquarter for accountants, lawyers, and other professionals offering their skills to transnational corporations. In fact, Rome is one of Europe's few capitals without a stock exchange. So can we place the city within any broader framework of understanding at all?

Multiple Modernities: Rome as Alternatively Modern

Rome has gone through its own peculiar modernization process since it became capital in 1871. Rome is not "unmodern" or "late modern," rather its modernity has to be positioned against the city's history and the role the city came to play with respect to the formation of Italy as nation-state and, today, as a fast-developing global political/cultural economy. We argue that the globality of Rome can best be approached within a perspective of alternative or multiple modernities. From within this paradigm, modernity is considered an inherently ambivalent and open-ended process that implodes and develops differently within different cultural and geographical contexts (Eisenstadt 2000; Thomassen 2012). The development of the notion of multiple modernities was an important way for social theorists to move beyond Eurocentrism while still allowing for an analysis of modernity, now in the plural. Western modernity was/is but one particular trajectory of historical development; modernization and Westernization need to be disentangled as analytical categories and historical processes. This pluralizing must be continued within that Western context, as different cities, regions, and states modernized along wildly different routes even within Europe and its single states. Of huge relevance for positioning Rome, the multiple modernities paradigm, as developed by Eisenstadt in his elaboration of Weber, also put much more stress on modernity as a cultural force: Modernization processes, even within the economic and political spheres, are built upon values, worldviews, and types of life-conduct that cannot simply be deduced from an economic substructure.

While the theoretical framework tied to the idea of multiple modernities is by now well recognized and figures prominently in social theory (Thomassen 2010), it still has not informed urban theory to the extent one might have expected (but see de Frantz 2008). Yet there is hardly any area of research where the notion of multiple modernities becomes more directly applicable, and the city of Rome is but one case in point. Negotiations of urbanity in and across various contexts constitute urban politics as plural and open-ended (de Frantz 2008, 480).

Multiple modernities further translate into an understanding of "multiple globalizations," to multiple ways of dealing with globality (see also Smith 2001). The global city centers of the West may not necessarily be seen as the only producers of either modernity or globality. The decentering of Western modernity implied in the multiple modernities paradigm has several aspects to it, but one of them is certainly spatial and should invite us to think differently about position, territory, and power. Quite evidently, each major city in today's world is global, but from an anthropological point of view, this globality needs to be established from within, not by applying parameters of measurement that simply mimic those hierarchies of economic power that nobody should deny. The notion of multiple globalizations (Vereni 2012) does imply various layers of connectedness across the globe, but it also presupposes that various cities will find their own role and identity within wider, shifting national and global configurations. The diversity which unfolds, it must be noted, is also internal, as cities are composed of heterogeneous spaces and a multitude of actors, single and collective, who live the local and the global differently.

The ways in which a city like Rome becomes global is furthermore rooted in the particular historical trajectory of the city and is tied to the ways in which modernization has unfolded in contradictory and ambivalent ways. Without being rooted in the complexities of local reality, "global theory" comes to mean very little (McNeill 1999). Rome is shaped by economic, political, and cultural modernization, but in ways that defy any classificatory logic. Concretely, these historical complexities can be very briefly sketched as follows.

Rome in Recent History: Frictions of Modernity

Rome was not chosen as capital of Italy in 1871 because it was perceived as modern or avant-garde, quite the contrary. Already in the fourth century AD, Rome had seen street lighting; by 1870, there was none of the kind. By European but also North Italian standards, Rome was both an economically and politically "backward" area ruled by the papacy. The choice of Rome was based on symbolic more than political and economic reasons. Within Italy, Rome was the only potential capital that could boast a truly national reach. Italian nationalists from across the political spectrum agreed that without the twofold legacy of classical and papal Rome, the unification of Italy would remain incomplete. However, Rome was also useful for more mundane reasons: In order to win the souls of the emergent and still weak bourgeoisie in Italy, the political expansion of the Kingdom of Piedmont needed to permanently defeat localisms and parochialisms that had hindered the development of a united Italian political entity. A "neutral" point of balance had to be detected between the then most powerful and populated cities in Italy (Turin, Genoa, Milan, Florence, Venice, Naples); a steady pivot around which the whole unitarian project could be developed, minimizing the risks of jealousy and rivalry among the pre-existing local and regional powers. Rome perfectly suited this role, being neutral geographically, politically (devoid of a modern ruling class), and even economically (Caracciolo 1956, 17). Similar to Brussels and Strasbourg, which became the administrative and political centers of the European Union due to their marginality and lack of power in European politics, Rome became capital of the modern Italian state to compensate for this extraordinary political fragmentation, and mostly due to the city's weakness.

From the early *Risorgimento* in the nineteenth century, Republicans, Monarchists, and Unitarians all embraced Rome as the center of their political programs. Catholics close to papal power were among the few to resist the idea of Rome as the Italian capital. It was rejected exactly by those politicians and sectors of civil society which were actually living and operating in Rome. So, while "l'Italia ha bisogno di Roma" ("Italy needs Rome!") was a common slogan between 1861 and 1870 during the Unification of Italy, the inverse statement (e.g., that Rome needed Italy) was far less heard.

Rome's peculiar political history also relates to its economy. The fight against localism and regionalism was a necessity for the emerging Northern Italian bourgeoisie, striving to impose a fully fledged capitalistic mode of production. A national market had to be guaranteed beyond regional entrepreneurial and industrial traditions. Due to its economic weakness, only Rome could act as a neutral guarantor for the implementation of Italian capitalism. Capitalist farming and modern industries in Italy grew up predominantly in the northwest of the country, concentrated within the "industrial triangle" of Milan, Turin, and Genoa. As Rome became capital in 1870, this did not really change. The businesses that developed in the growing capital were all connected to transport, consumer sales, and administration.

In a very real sense, Rome was a "service sector" city long before terms like *information economy* and *postindustrialization* had been invented. Rome today is not "postindustrial," for it was never industrial in the first place. Indeed, after 1871, the new Italian political leadership purposefully avoided the development of industrial sectors in the Eternal City because they were afraid that a politicized proletariat in Rome would cause too much trouble (Caracciolo 1956, 61–62). Rome had to serve as a docile body of political centralization. Working-class neighborhoods, like those just barely visible today in Testaccio or Garbatella, grew up around trade and distribution of foodstuffs. Mussolini's plan for a self-sufficient national economy certainly did not make Rome independent in terms of consumer goods, except perhaps in the vegetables that were grown in the *agro romano* (the Roman countryside) and the various "garden cities" (see Trabalzi, chapter 17), especially as the economic crisis before and during World War II worsened. Italy's first "economic miracle," booming from 1957, radically altered Rome and its physical shape, with new *palazzine* (apartment buildings) mushrooming around and outside the historic center. But Italy's economic miracle still did not turn Rome into a center of production.

Here lies another feature of modern Rome discussed elsewhere in this volume: The built city was most often not the result of rational, centralized urban planning. Various periods of building booms massively expanded the city, in often chaotic and unplanned ways that still characterize it today. Italy's second economic miracle of the 1980s still had the Italian north as its center, this time gravitating toward the northeast. Rome kept growing in size, hand in hand with the burgeoning state administration, but could not attract companies such as Olivetti or Benetton, nor did small-scale family businesses in textiles, furniture, or the food industries start to flourish, as they did in regions such as Veneto or Friuli. There is a remarkable continuity here: Rome's economy still relies on bureaucracy, political administration, and religious tourism, a persistent feature for at least seven centuries. Modern Rome is certainly a "political city." Mussolini consciously played on the city's imperial past via fascist architecture and urban design (Kirk 2005); all the way back to 1871, Rome was developed by state planners as a symbolic and functional fixture of the centralizing and modernizing state.

Cultural identities and outlooks have been shaped together with these larger political and economic forces. Romans are often acutely aware of the city's history, even if their own families are mostly post-Unification immigrants. However, historical awareness and pride is in many contexts mixed with a sense of being peripheral and unimportant. Rome is Rome. The contrast to a capital city like Paris could hardly be more evident. Roman vernacular is considered, also by Romans themselves, a low-class dialect, whereas real and "cultural" Italian is spoken in Florence. Roman cooking is relatively simple and rustic, and Romans take pride in that very simplicity. In Piedmont and Tuscany, they excel in fine steaks and elaborate sauces, served with oak barreled wines. Roman dishes are cooked with tails, stomachs, and other offal, the cheap parts of the animal, and accompanied by uncomplicated table wines (white more than red). In most contexts, Romans do not feel they are living in any center, even if they evidently do so both geographically and politically. Michael Herzfeld (2009) has fittingly baptized Rome a "reluctant capital." All of these features of the city do not mean that Rome exists outside globality or modernity. Rome is different not because it has not been modernized. The city's fractured or alternative modernizations serve as an important background for understanding the ways in which Rome is globalized today. Nor is Rome simply a periphery in a larger international division of labor. Rome is both center and periphery, depending on perspective and subject matter. This can also be put differently: Urban development, in Rome as elsewhere, is tied to processes that are locally specific as well as globally entangled. This can perhaps be best exemplified with reference to how Rome is globally imagined.

Globally Imagined Rome

On the official 2010 Global Cities Index (each year elaborated by the Chicago Council on Global Affairs), Rome comes in at a decent position: number 28 worldwide. It is placed lower than cities such as Stockholm and Zürich, and evidently much lower than the "top" global cities, New York, London, and Tokyo.

According to another index, elaborated by the Globalization and World Cities Study Group and Network at Loughborough University, Rome is a beta+ city (while Milan is an alpha city, on a scale which is sorted into categories from alpha++, a label reserved for London and New York, to gamma–world cities). It is not our aim here to criticize the methodology behind such measurements. They make sense for certain purposes, and they certainly do indicate a degree of connectedness within the economic, political, and infrastructural realms, the global power flows in and out of cities. But there is at least one dimension or one variable that such indexes do not consider and which has a huge pertinence for a city like Rome: the degree to which a city is imagined and dreamed about by people around the globe.

Such imaginings can hardly be quantified, but they are certainly real enough and they create their own realities which are both cultural and economic. They become economic because the images of Rome are popularized via commercials and, especially, films, many of which are American produced and feed into tourism and various forms of consumption.

The global image of Rome is so pervasive in the social history of the West (and not only) that it has been equated to a template: "in its many historical incarnations, Rome more than any other single city has provided models and templates—architecturally, urbanistically, ideologically, and narratively—for the design and form of capital cities in the West" (Atkinson and Cosgrove 1998, 30). Rome was a global brand long before anybody was aware of globalization. Suffice to recall how many times an emerging political power named itself "the new Rome," from Constantinople, to Moscow, to Berlin under Nazism, not to mention the self-mimicry of Rome under Fascism. The worldwide presence of Roman political heritage is evident in common terminology such as *senate, parliament,* or *capitol (hill),* words that refer to political institutions and even localities of classical Rome.

Thanks to movements like the Beaux-Arts style, Rome has had a central role in a process of enduring aesthetic uniformity that started with the Renaissance. By imitating the late eighteenth-century neoclassicism, which mimicked the Renaissance, that in turn was copying classic Roman style, Beaux-Arts dominated most official construction from the second half of the nineteenth century to the first half of the twentieth, making Roman architecture visible and known throughout the Western (and Westernized) world (Atkinson and Cosgrove 1998).

With religious institutions as pilgrimage sites since early Christian times and their social and economic harnessing by political power since the fourteenth century through the invention of the Jubilee tradition, Rome (alongside other religious centers with a comparable artistic history) has been crucial to the development of modern tourism, which is now considered one of the main side effects of (economic) globalization.

The inherent internationalism of the papacy has been transformed into a veritable Roman mediascape (Appadurai 1990; Vereni 2012) that during the last two decades of the twentieth century further globalized the image of the Eternal City. The role of John Paul II in taking advantage of media to produce a truly global representation of the Chair of Saint Peter can hardly be overestimated. With Karol Wojtila, Rome took up the challenge imposed by the global media system and secured itself a prominent position on the world stage (Dayan and Katz 1992; Mazza 2006). A pontiff who—in order to travel and become a "citizen of the world"—leaves the isolated Vatican and its persistent aura of the past inevitably carries with him the icon of the city itself, contributing to its further popularization worldwide. The *Da Vinci Code* genre that now floods bookstores around the world (more than 2,200 titles labeled "religious thriller" at amazon.com) would not have been possible without the symbolic and imaginary support of a mysterious, ancient, and vibrant religious center such as Rome. You need New York if you want a president killed by international terrorism or economic lobbies, but you need Rome for an enigmatic murder that takes the reader to the mysteries of Templars or other sacred sects which still rule the world!

In brief, Rome is not only a system of economic interrelations or a knot in a hierarchy of world cities. In this symbolic and imaginary respect, Rome is first of all an icon, a brand, and a globally famous one. When Boston executive Thomas Di Benedetto purchased nearly 70 percent of Roma football club, he was quite aware of the symbolic relevance of the city to launch his business: "Rome is known for its culture, history and food and that brings a lot of people here," Di Benedetto said. "We want those people to also enjoy football. And we want them to become fans of our team, so that when they go back to their own countries they will be followers and supporters."[1]

Immigration: The Pulls and Flows of the City

One very concrete way in which Rome is globalizing from within is due to increasing immigration. During the last thirty years, Rome has undergone a profound and vast change. The former pilgrims have become resident immigrants, and now more than 10 percent of its approximately three million inhabitants are foreigners. In some neighborhoods, they make up more than 30 percent. This is a tremendous change in a very short time for the capital city of a nation-state that reached a positive migration balance only a few decades ago.

Yet the ties between this new immigration and the "big" economic processes worldwide are much more complex and entangled than is recognized in global city theories. While in London or New York the newcomers work for the transnational elite of the global corporations or as unskilled labor in the service sectors, in Rome there is not much of a global corporate elite for foreigners to work for. Many are still employed (like Italian immigrants in Rome during the first decades of the twentieth century) in the building industry. Others carry out domestic work as caretakers for children and elders, while others again run their small businesses in the food or garment industry, or are involved as nonskilled labor in the tourism services (restaurants and hotels). Indeed, one can count multiple factors pulling immigrants to Rome, and the strictly economic ones do not always seem to be the strongest.

At the beginning of Via Nazionale, there is the Church of St. Paul's Within-the-Walls, the Anglican Episcopalian church where one can see famous historical figures such as General Grant, Abraham Lincoln, and Giuseppe Garibaldi portrayed as saints. The first non-Catholic church within the city walls, inaugurated in 1876 as a durable example of freedom of worship granted by the new Italian state, the church now hosts in its crypt the Joel Nafuma Refugee Center, the only day center available to refugees and asylum seekers in Rome. From 10 AM to 2 PM some 150 men find some relief, a frugal breakfast, and outlets to recharge their mobile phones. They come mainly from Central Asia (Afghanistan) and the Horn of Africa. Like many other asylum seekers in Italy, while their applications for the status of refugee are being processed, they do not have a place to stay and must resort to squatting in empty buildings or seeking support from religious institutions (Caritas 2010). When asked why they chose Italy,[2] they give different answers that register the wide range of reasons that pull people, not only refugees, to the Eternal City:

"Rome is the city of the Pope. I trusted I could find help here from people of good will." Notwithstanding the fact that Rome (like Italy) does not have a coherent policy on asylum (let alone immigration), it can still boast an influential aura as a hospitable place due to its status as religious center. People from foreign countries with little or no connection to Italy find Rome "good to think" long before they are faced with the problems of living there. They are attracted by the enduring and now globalized image of a spiritual city that has always opened its arms to welcome pilgrims and the needy. Afghanis and Nigerians are national groups that often use this argument to explain the reasons for their coming to Rome.

"I am here just passing through, I will not stay. I want to go to Germany (Scandinavia/Great Britain/America) and Italy is an inevitable transit point, the gateway to Europe and to the West." Many foreigners in Rome who would be entitled to apply for the status of refugee have entered illegally simply because they do not want to stay so they do not fill out applications. They are aware that Italy offers fewer opportunities (in terms of jobs and rights) than other countries. Yet Italy is the first fully Western step for their final destinations and Rome, with her immense size, allows them to hide with ease, waiting for the opportunity to move elsewhere. Many Central African *sans papiers* come for this reason, as do people from Afghanistan and South Asia. All roads lead to Rome, but they also lead out of the city.

"I chose Rome because it is easy to find a little work here even though we do not have the right permit. Staying here as illegal immigrants is easier than in other major European cities, while we wait for the next amnesty that will allow us to stabilize our position." As Italy started to receive a slowly growing number of immigrants from the late 1980s, the Italian government faced the issue without a clear policy, preferring instead to address it as an "emergency," a classical theme of Italian politics. Since then, at least four different amnesties have regularized the position of 1,200,000 foreign workers who had entered without proper documentation. During the 1990s, many people came to Rome precisely because they knew that sooner or later their illegal position would be regularized. This is certainly one of the main reasons for the considerable size of the Bangladeshi community in Rome, now one of the largest in Europe. By word of mouth, the first Bangladeshis informed their relatives and compatriots that it was not impossible to find work in the gray market for a while, waiting for the next *sanatoria* (amnesty). Migrations organized by informal but highly structured agencies, such as the Bangladeshi and Chinese networks, took advantage of the loose-knit Italian law to settle with remarkable ease. In this case, the economic motivation was further caused by a political one.

"I wanted to come to Rome because it's the capital of a country I know and have many connections to." This argument is held by foreigners from different countries with different stories; from Somalis to Albanians who have past colonial ties to Italy; from Moroccans to Tunisians who have always had close contacts with the Italian geographic space. The arrival of many Romanians after the admission of their country to the European Union was also determined by motives that are "cultural": Romanians and Moldovans are the only Slavic people speaking a Romance language and the link with Rome and the at least imagined Italian culture persisted even during communism. From January 2007, Romanian citizens were entitled to travel freely across the European Union, but many of them chose to settle in Italy, and they are now the first foreign national group in Rome, 21.6 percent in December 2011 and constantly growing (+10.7 percent compared to 2010) (Caritas 2011). This perception of closeness might not be shared by Romans themselves.

If a mixture of cultural, symbolic, and economic factors has played a relevant part in determining the most recent flows of immigrants to the city, strictly political and historical causes have strengthened the foreign presence for much longer. Rome is the capital of Italy, and as such, it is home to embassies from around the world. At the same time, Rome hosts a formally autonomous state within the city limits, the Vatican. This independent and sovereign entity entertains diplomatic relations with many countries, with the result that Rome holds the world record for number of embassies. Moreover, since 1951, Rome hosts the United Nations' Food and Agriculture Organization with 191 member nations, each with its own delegation, offices, and personnel. Very few cities in the world count comparable numbers of international bureaucrats, and this takes Rome even further away from the stereotype of the global cities attracting foreigners primarily as an essential component of their post-Fordist economic system based on transnational corporations and finance capitalism.

Going further back in time, people have come to Rome from all over the world since antiquity (Sanfilippo 2011). Here the city's role as the heart of Catholic Christendom has guaranteed a steady presence of foreigners even when, after the seventeenth century, it was entirely marginal in international politics. Rome attracted the attention of the world even when it was little more than a provincial town. This international dimension has never been characterized to a decisive extent by the size or nature of its production system. There have always been more priests and nuns than executives in Rome, but this did not prevent Rome from becoming a city with a truly global reach.

Global–Local Rome

Rome is a globalized city. Its shape, its urban policies, and its everyday life are constantly affected by flows and streams of people and images making up its own peculiar global–local, or glocal, cityscape. Global Rome today exists at the margins of an international division of labor and the new finance economy. At the same time, the city keeps developing with its many layers of political administration. It also keeps developing as a part of lesser networks caused by demographic trends (which explain the presence of caretakers for the growing number of elderly people), historical trends (that made the city "the refuge of all nations" since the Middle Ages), and cultural trends such as its image as a center of religious heritage. Such images perhaps make Rome more similar to other religious centers which are undergoing their own peculiar form of globalization, such as Santiago de Compostela, Jerusalem, or Mecca. So we need a model for representing globalization within the city which takes into account culture and history in all its facets, from the outskirts of the still sprawling city to its historical center, and on the buses that connect its nodes, traffic permitting.

Rome is not a model city, nor can it be modeled after other cities. Rome today is undergoing urban transformations whose structure cannot be easily deciphered or apprehended through prevailing theoretical frames. Changes are brought about by interacting forces from below and above and by the cultural and political, as well as strictly economic dimensions, of globalization. At the theoretical level, such an opening is represented by a paradigm of multiple and alternative modernities and globalizations. The rest pertains to the study of concrete settings and concrete human beings; the rest pertains to ethnography.

Notes

1. As quoted by Associated Press 18 November 2011 at http://espn.go.com/sports/soccer/news/_/id/7250811/as-roma-new-us-owner-thomas-dibenedetto-reveals-ambitious-plans. Accessed 20 November 2011.

2. The quotes are taken from fieldwork notes based on informal conversation with visitors to the center.

References

Anderson, Benedict. 1983. *Imagined Communities.* London: Verso.

Appadurai, Arjun. 1990. "Disjuncture and Difference in the Global Cultural Economy." *Public Culture* 2 (2): 1–24.

Atkinson, David, and Denis Cosgrove. 1998. "Urban Rhetoric and Embodied Identities: City, Nation, and Empire at the Vittorio Emanuele II Monument in Rome, 1870–1945." *Annals of the Association of American Geographers* 88 (1): 28–49.

Beaverstock, Jonathan V., Richard G. Smith, and Peter J. Taylor. 2000. "World-City Network: A New Metageography?" *Annals of the Association of American Geographers* 90 (1): 123–134.

Caracciolo, Alberto. 1956. *Roma capitale: Dal Risorgimento alla crisi dello stato liberale.* Rome: Edizioni Rinascita.

Caritas di Roma. 2010. *Osservatorio romano sulle migrazioni: Settimo rapporto.* Rome: Centro studi e ricerche Idos.

———. 2011. *Osservatorio romano sulle migrazioni: Ottavo rapporto.* Rome: Centro studi e ricerche Idos.

Castells, Manuel. 1977. *The Urban Question.* Cambridge, Mass.: MIT Press.

Chernilo, Daniel. 2006. "Social Theory's Methodological Nationalism." *European Journal of Social Theory* 9 (1): 5–22.

Cohen, Robert B. 1981. "The New International Division of Labor, Multinational Corporations and Urban Hierarchy." In *Urbanization and Urban Planning in Capitalist Society,* edited by Michael Dear and Allen J. Scott, 287–315. New York: Methuen.

Dayan, Daniel, and Elihu Katz. 1992. *Media Events: The Live Broadcasting of History.* Cambridge, Mass.: Harvard University Press.

De Frantz, Monica. 2008. "Contemporary Political Theories of the European City: Questioning Institutions." *European Journal of Social Theory* 11 (4): 465–485.

Eisenstadt, Shmuel. 2000. "Multiple Modernities." *Daedalus* 129 (1): 1–29.

Friedmann, John, and Goetz Wolff. 1982. "World City Formation: An Agenda for Research and Action." *International Journal of Urban and Regional Research* 6 (3): 309–344.

Gellner, Ernest. 1983. *Nations and Nationalism.* Ithaca, N.Y.: Cornell University Press.

Herzfeld, Michael. 2009. *Evicted from Eternity: The Restructuring of Modern Rome.* Chicago: University of Chicago Press.

Kirk, Terry. 2005. *The Architecture of Modern Italy.* Vols. 1 and 2. New York: Princeton Architectural Press.

Mazza, Giuseppe, ed. 2006. *Karol Wojtyła, un pontefice in diretta: Sfida e incanto nel rapporto tra Giovanni Paolo II e la TV.* Rome: Rai-Eri.

McNeill, Donald. 1999. "Globalization and the European City." *Cities* 16 (3): 143–147.

Sanfilippo, Matteo. 2011. "L'immigrazione in Roma antica." In Caritas, *Osservatorio romano sulle migrazioni: Ottavo rapporto,* 165–171.

Sassen, Saskia. 1991. *The Global City.* Princeton, N.J.: Princeton University Press.

Smith, Michael P. 2001. *Transnational Urbanism.* New York: Blackwell.

Taylor, Peter J. 2003. *Global City Network.* New York: Routledge.

Thomassen, Bjørn. 2010. "Anthropology, Multiple Modernities and the Axial Age Debate." *Anthropological Theory* 10 (4): 321–342.

———. 2012. "Anthropology and Its Many Modernities: When Concepts Matter." *Journal of the Royal Anthropological Institute* 18: 160–178.

Vereni, Piero. 2012. "Le modernità di tutti. Il contributo di Arjun Appadurai al dibattito sulla globalizzazione." In Arjun Appadurai, *Modernità in polvere: Dimensioni culturali della globalizzazione,* vii–lxi. Milan: Cortina.

2 The Liberal, the Neoliberal, and the Illiberal

Dynamics of Diversity and Politics of Identity in Contemporary Rome

Michael Herzfeld

THE ASCENT TO power of Pope Pius IX anticipates in many ways the paradoxical status of the Eternal City. Hailed as a liberator (and, more to the point, as a liberal), he soon demonstrated his repressively conservative and antirevolutionary colors and is now principally remembered as a cruel tyrant who authorized a virtual orgy of executions in the desperate and ultimately unsuccessful attempt to perpetuate Vatican control of Rome. His motives were not those of the Greek patriarch of Constantinople, whose opposition to his compatriots' national revolution was inspired more by justifiable fear of Ottoman reprisals—they eventually executed him despite his stance—than by any principled disagreement with the revolution's ideals. Pius IX, by contrast, did not fear the existing authority; he represented it in his own person. What he did fear and resist was the Vatican's political collapse that, over a period stretching from the nationalist insurgents' capture of Rome in 1871 to the Lateran Concordat signed with Mussolini in 1929, he and his successors were ultimately forced to accept.

Echoes of the Illiberal

Today Italians face a new paradox of liberalism, and it is one that to a striking degree reproduces its first iteration. The shocking intolerance that characterizes the political Right, in Italy as elsewhere, bears the name *liberal* in another sense: the neoliberal doctrine that sends the socially and economically weak to the wall of despair, evicts long-standing populations from the *centro storico* and other segments of Rome, and monumentalizes the past in way that further alienates the dispossessed from their erstwhile haunts even as they return on weekends from the often unpleasant and relatively inaccessible suburban districts to which they have been exiled in a sad, vain attempt to reconstitute as a living social reality the now-vanished nexus of artisans, workers, and small merchants.

In the central square (locally known as the "little piazza," or *piazzetta*) of the Monti district *(rione),* for example, such weekend returnees from exile alternate between disconsolate longing and upbeat camaraderie. Both emotions often merge with intense dislike of the East European migrants who also throng the square. Ironically, the self-described exiles frequently subscribe to the right-wing, economically harsh ideology of which they are the victims, instead blaming the left-wing governments and even the clergy for multiculturalist policies that, they claim, have displaced them from their rightful homes. Their absorption of a hegemonic ideology that has treated them so harshly reproduces the political alchemy of Mussolini's fascism of seven or eight decades earlier.[1] This rhetoric and these practices go right to the gut—indeed, sometimes literally so, as when rightist Mayor Gianni Alemanno (elected in 2008) replaced the gastronomic diversity of ethnic foods in Rome's school, which was the result of an intentional educational move of a previous, left-leaning city administration—with the view that Italian (and especially distinctively Roman) pasta dishes should be especially favored. (His move paralleled a ban on opening more "ethnic" restaurants in the historic center of Lucca promulgated around the same time by that city's rightist mayor.)[2] While food may seem a trivial arena for serious political confrontation, its very ordinariness makes it an appropriate context in which to explore the impact of ideology on everyday actions and perceptions.

Such windows on the soul of a city are vitally important to understanding the dynamics of current political change. This is all the more true inasmuch as the official rhetoric of tolerance and political correctness has generated a deceptive jargon that requires constant decipherment. Alemanno's occasional expressions of horror at the violence committed against immigrants and gays appear to express more irritation with the necessity of making such pronouncements than genuine solidarity with the groups thus targeted.[3] More generally, the rhetoric of political correctness and especially of tolerance on the one hand and victimhood on the other serves ideological and political ends that are the very opposite of what this rhetoric was originally devised to promote. This apparent contradiction between rhetoric and practice informs much of the way in which Rome today confronts the challenges and possibilities of cultural diversity.

The people of Rome generally pride themselves on both their distinctive local culture and, as part of it, their acceptance of difference. While some would point to the city's ancient history as the source of Romans' acceptance of cultural difference,[4] such historical and cultural determinism is less useful as an analytic tool than it is as the expression of an ideological reading of past and present that informs current attitudes; the claim to have always been generous hosts smacks of the same conditional stance as today's equally common claim that Romans are by definition not racists. Both are claims that call for critical analysis. In their framing, two key words—*tolleranza* and *accommodazione*—recur with great frequency. But they do not mean one and the same thing.

Indeed, the distinction between them reveals a dynamic that in some respects is quite specific to the heirs to the repression of papal Rome. *Tolleranza* is about "putting up with" people who are different; when they become too different, they hit the nadir known as "zero tolerance" (*tolleranza zero*). Far from representing an unqualified embrace of difference, tolerance in this sense has instead the ring of the contradiction that the French anthropologist Louis Dumont (1982, 238–239) identified in the American segregationists' slogan "separate but equal"—an oxymoron that breaks down in practice, because separation breeds mutual distrust rather than an equitable sharing of goods and resources. Dumont saw in the land that so fascinated De Tocqueville, the paradoxical desire to maintain privilege while adhering to democratic values. His observation, however, fits a much wider range of cultural contexts. Ideological generosity—as we see in Bruce Kapferer's (1988) fine comparative study of Australian egalitarian "mateship" and the pacific ideology of Sri Lankan Buddhism—can easily morph into racism, sexism, and violence. It is the logic and process of such transformations that concern us here.

Self-Deceptions of the Liberal

Tolerance, I suggest, is no less prone than mateship is to this kind of inversion.[5] Indeed, recent scholarship on attitudes to migrants in some southern European societies, with their strong emphasis on the obligations of reciprocity, illustrates his point particularly well. Thus, Efthymios Papataxiarchis (2009) has persuasively argued that only a short distance separates the generous initial reception of immigrants and refugees from highly specific accusations of ingratitude—accusations that are grounded in the social practices and self-stereotypes associated with hospitality. Long before southern Europe attracted massive migration, such attitudes already informed local responses to tourism (Herzfeld 1987, 81–86); the rhetoric of tourism was similarly couched in the idiom of hospitality and of its centrality to local tradition. While that rhetoric may serve to lure customers,[6] it also effectively disguises the implicit right to resentment and anger that it confers on hosts who feel that their "guests"—a concept also embedded in the notion of immigrant "guest workers" (German *Gastarbeiter*)—have abused the hospitality offered to them.

"Explanations" of Roman adaptability that merely invoke the complex culture of the ancient empire, which was after all based on conquest and slavery, thus explain very little in reality. Roman Jews—one of Europe's most ancient Jewish communities, dating at least as far back as the Sack of the Second Temple in 70 A D—are seen as preservers of the ancient traditions of the Roman table. But this emblematic role never protected them from the opprobrium of the popes (see Kertzer 2001) or from petty harassment at the local level, although it provides a template ("we were never anti-Semitic, unlike the Germans") for today's globalized expressions of politically correct tolerance.[7] While it is not uncommon for modern rightists to praise the Jewish community as the last of the true Romans, we should not forget that under Mussolini, too, an initial willingness to tolerate the Jewish presence (and a concomitant support for Mussolini on the part of mercantile segments of Italian Jewry in particular) gave way to active persecution, whether primarily because of Nazi pressure or because the new circumstances that pressure created enabled (and for some also alibied) the emergence of a hitherto latent racism in its most overt and vicious form. Here, indeed, we see exemplified in especially dramatic form the actual processes through which an apparently welcoming social ideology always contains within itself the capacity to become, instead, the expression and instrument of repression and even genocide.

It is certainly not the case today that Romans have suddenly become racists and bigots. Even among those who embrace explicitly fascist attitudes, open expressions of intolerance create embarrassment. Many Romans, especially those of more determinedly progressive views, are actively engaged in fighting against racism, often supporting the immigrants' desire to achieve acceptance at a distinctively local level. This way of framing their position has deep historical roots and is connected to the powerful forms of localism for which Italy is famous. Most dramatically, perhaps, a well-known monument in the Roman Ghetto inclusively describes the local Jewish Holocaust victims as "Roman citizens" (rather than as Italians). Within an expanded notion of racism that for Italians includes *all* forms of intolerance and prejudice, and thus homophobia as much as racism based on skin color, many heterosexual Romans joined in the World Gay Pride demonstrations of the 2000 Jubilee and thus braved the hostile glare of the Vatican and of the Rutelli municipal administration now strangely, given its leader's initial and perhaps equally opportunistic (or accommodating?) displays of anticlericalism, fawning on the church and its prelates. And many see close parallels between the circumstances of the immigrant poor and those of their own compatriots who, in earlier ages, ventured abroad in search of a decent living they could not find in the poverty-stricken cities and towns of Italy.

Nonetheless, the discourse of tolerance that a now-globalized liberalism has promulgated provides cover for acts and attitudes that are unquestionably intolerant. Romans are experts at using courtesy as menace, and the new political correctness—itself a form of "civilized politeness" (*civiltà*, the practice of being *civili*[8])—affords ample play to such inversions. Semi-underworld operators, for example, are known to make unctuous offers of help with moving out of apartments in a gentrifying area—offers that conveyed, in a more sinister way than mere threats would achieve, that refusal would have unspecified but unpleasant consequences (Herzfeld 2009, 256–258). In this matrix, tolerance talk paved the way for the banning of ethnic foods, the persecution of street vendors whether Jewish (during the Jubilee of 2000[9]) or West African, the attempts to reduce the use of Chinese and other foreign writing systems in signage displayed in public spaces, the hounding of Roma, and the determination of police officials to "protect" white citizens from immigrants.

Indeed, when I wanted to film a very peaceful antidiscrimination protest on Via dei Fori Imperiali, I was stopped by a police officer who told me, "It's for your own safety" (*È per la Sua incolumità*). The officer's disingenuous explanation invoked menace at multiple levels. Not only did he use an expression of polite concern to hint that disobedience on my part would not be tolerated, but, consciously or (more probably) otherwise, his security-based rhetoric implicitly invoked older discourses about "dangerous populations" worthy of Mussolini's surveillance of the left-wing working classes.

Such an affectation of concern reproduces, I suggest, the same ambiguous logic that we find in the practice of tolerance and its underlying model, hospitality: a rhetoric of generosity that always carries within itself implications of potential contempt and even violence, whether (in this case) against the immigrants and demonstrators or against a pesky individual with a camera. In the Roman context, this particular version of encompassment turns on the logic of what anthropologists call political segmentation, a point that requires some further elaboration.

Despite its status as the national capital, Rome exhibits precisely those features of extreme localism that more generally characterize the Italian nation-state. Where else in the world does a country's historically most stable government include members of a party—the Northern League—that periodically swears to dismember the nation-state and declare the independence of its most prosperous regions? In the much-despised capital of this self-dismembering polity, solidarities are inevitably fragile and transient, and social interaction has long reflected that fragility. This is "accommodation" in social practice: Rhetorical flexibility is always preferable to direct attacks and belligerent language. All social relations in Rome are friable; they are classically "segmentary"—that is, relative to each social actor's relationship to the parties to each dispute. While segmentation exists everywhere, it gains particular prominence in a city where districts affect to despise each other, but split internally—sometimes on clearly spatial lines—to contest more restricted sets of material and affective interests. Allies today are foes tomorrow and allies again the day after; the weakness of human nature is taken as a given, so that enmity should not be permanent (who, after all, is perfect?), but should reflect only a provisional and situational separation of interests in the totally understandable flux of social life.[10] Such adaptability is the stuff of which that self-ascribed Roman characteristic of *accommodazione* is made. Romans explain their adaptability by reference to the long centuries of Vatican repression and the necessity of coming to terms with such absolute power. There is probably more than a smidgeon of truth to such claims. But they also smack of the cultural determinism that I opened this essay by rejecting—and there are good reasons to reject it, at least as a totalizing explanation of a complex social idiom. Other European societies have labored under repressive regimes without exhibiting obviously segmentary tendencies—tendencies, moreover, that were far from quashed by the emergence of the equally fractious Italian nation-state.

Countenancing the Neoliberal

How is this feature of Roman society connected to questions of tolerance and racism? In a segmentary structure of sociopolitical relations, encompassment becomes an active principle, since the objects of one's condescending acceptance at one moment easily become the targets of competition, jealousy, and ire at another. Given a context of rampant neoliberalism, especially one in which the state has been demonstrably unable to protect itself from specific leaders scheming to protect their sectional interests, the one circumstance that could seem to "justify" racism in cosmopolitan Rome was competition over resources. The current situation of economic uncertainty, the condition of *precarietà* that particularly afflicts the young, is a highly combustible breeding ground for resentment. It also exposes the fault lines of a segmentary social order.

In so doing, it illuminates the micropolitics of Roman social life. Romans, for example, see no contradiction on excoriating the speculators who evict old Roman families while also exhibiting hostility toward newly arrived immigrant families that replace the evicted. Both the wealthy speculators and the indigent migrants are, to local right-wingers, dangerous and alien forces—and, to make matters worse, they have by definition rejected any hint of *accommodazione*. What is more, both are identified with the left-leaning political parties, the largest of which, the Democratici di Sinistra, "liberalized" the real-estate market in legislation enacted in 1994. This action allowed proprietors to evict tenants more easily than before and to raise rents at dizzying speeds, and it thereby created the very situation that is now generating such tension. The Italian parliamentary leftists, exemplifying in perhaps extreme form a betrayal of principle that was becoming disturbingly common among European left-wing socialists in the 1990s, thereby exposed their own involvement in economic practices that were radically at odds with their Marxist ideological pretensions and gave the very term *liberalization* an odious name. Since the Left more generally is seen as the political space of intellectuals, and since intellectuals and artists are among those seen to have "invaded" the "traditional" spaces of life in Rome's historic core, it was perhaps inevitable that many disaffected working-class Romans would utterly reject the presence of the wealthy, of intellectuals, and of immigrants, all in one conflated and detested package, and would all too easily be lured by right-wing populism.

I am acutely aware that to argue that Romans are nevertheless not racist is to court obvious parallels with the politically correct pronouncement, "I'm not a racist, but . . ." (*non sono razzista, però* . . .).[11] This conventional (and internationally widespread) disclaimer is a clear statement of Dumontian encompassment. It shows that people can be ideologically nonracist at the same time as they display racist sentiments in practice. Indeed, the politically correct language of antiracism thereby sustains a substantively racist attitude. Those who are more unabashed about their racism can openly frame it in terms of the *romanità* celebrated by Mussolini and the Ultrà troublemakers at today's football matches (see Dyal forthcoming)—a defensive localism that, like Roman identity in the national context more generally, wallows in a sense of rejection and marginality.[12] For these social actors, then, being Roman has come to stand in opposition *both* to the nation-state *and* to the new waves of immigrants. A segmentary polity is, ipso facto, a diverse one. Romans pride themselves on their internal *social* diversity, pointing to their famous ability to achieve the cohabitation of different social classes in a single area while also distinguishing among different districts on the grounds of class differentiation. This structural attitude, however, favors a rejection of *cultural* diversity; hostility—of the Monticiani toward the Trasteverini, for example—is expressed by rejecting the other side's speech habits, forms of social life, and other cultural features. From this stance, it is only a short step to rejecting the more modern idioms of mutual respect that come under the label of *multiculturalism*. At the same time, the state is increasingly rigidifying the appearance of the city, creating a more ordered and homogeneous and bureaucratic whole in place of the former riotous array of local differences; and this, too, reinforces a growing tendency to essentialize Roman identity in opposition to that of immigrants and other groups. Thus, the neoliberal management of the city's spaces works against the allegedly traditional forms of Roman social life, offering in its place a vision of Roman "identity" that, by a further twist, resembles nothing so much as the cultural separatism of the Northern League.

On the one hand, it seems that ideally the state would like to break the back of the virtual separatism of the capital. On the other, however, it is precisely these culturally dissident forces that furnish the right-wing parties with the majority of their converts, proletarian and artisanal sectors bereft of their once clearly left-wing identity through what they see as cynical betrayal. In this way, short-term opportunism trumps the desire to create a unified state—a rather distant prospect in any case, given that the right-wing coalition is so dependent on the Northern League, which, in addition to its frequent forays into separatism, also openly expresses anti-immigrant and racist sentiment.

Rome, moreover, encapsulates a local version of this dynamic. The affluent residents of places like the bourgeois and once military-dominated suburb of Parioli may affect to believe that the dispossessed—known as *coatti* (literally "forced"—that is, to live in the outer suburbs)—are the dregs of society, their lilting but disrespectful Roman speech the defining mark of their abjection. But the latter are pragmatically the backbone of the Right's support among young people, and their aggressive localism is strongly associated with the new media, especially the Internet, which has become a vehicle for the rapid reincarnation of the Roman dialect as a language of dissidence and hostility to foreigners as well as of the robust, salty humor for which Romans have long been justly famous. So right-wing politics finds itself a perhaps too-willing hostage to forces to which it must formally deny legitimacy.

Italy's current paradox is indeed a national politics that depends on localist politicians. It is not mere coincidence that some of the strongest advocates of Italian unity in recent years have been leftist politicians (see especially Thomassen 2011). The rightward drift reinforces precisely the tendencies that these politicians most fear: Roman "accommodation," while often producing an outward display of tolerance matched in some cases by a real commitment to cultural, religious, and social diversity, can, by tripping the wires of Romans' open opportunism, morph—at the extreme end of Roman right-wing politics—into a morose and self-absorbed localism that thinks nothing of expressing open hatred for otherness, turning to "counter-Enlightenment" thinkers such as Evola and Nietzsche in order to justify its muscular insularity.[13] It should be apparent by now that simply describing even a segment of Roman society as either racist or tolerant does not advance our understanding of the current situation. Both terms figure in a rhetorical matrix that is a component of the present dynamic. Such ambiguities are not new to Rome. Whatever one thinks of the ongoing debates over how far Italians' fascism resisted the Nazis' racist campaign of extermination, for example, even today there are black-shirted nostalgics who yearn for Mussolini's rule and yet who also insist on the Jewish contribution to modern Roman culture and who love to relate tales of how their families sheltered Jews from the Nazis.

This does not imply wholesale acceptance, nor is it only a reflection of the important symbolic role the Jewish community plays in Rome today. Rather, the model had already been set by the Vatican, which appointed itself the protector of the Jews while at the same time putting enormous pressure on the Roman Jews to convert to Christianity. The Vatican needed the Jews to keep its finances running profitably, especially as, for many centuries, the clergy could not openly practice usury. Concentrating the Jews in a single space also meant assuming responsibility for them in some sense. But it did not mean treating them with kindness, or even with the lofty tolerance of present-day political correctness. Properly examined, it exposes the cynical underpinnings of the ostensibly benign practice of "protection"—an attitude that, in this regard, seems not unlike the "friendship" professed by mafiosi toward their victims or the "protection" (*pizzo*) offered to car owners wishing to park in crowded spaces. Politeness, service, protection, hospitality, and, yes, tolerance: all "encompass" sanctions against those who do not materially recognize the material obligations that they impose.

In short, the idea that a benign rhetoric could mask enormous and sometimes brutal power has always been part of the Roman experience. Romans understand the performance of unctuous politeness, whether from mafiosi or politicians or even the clergy, without any literal-minded illusions. The performance of politeness *as* a threat is a reality, and a dangerous one at that. Romans know this and comment on it frequently and with a mixture of concern and amusement. Such manifestations of encompassment are not uniquely Roman. Rather, what perhaps makes Rome unusual is the explicitness with which the potential terror behind the jocular smile is repeatedly acknowledged.

I am attempting here to place the relationship between social structure and historical experience in a broader theoretical context. Social structures are always historical products, but again the Roman case is made notable by the explicit recognition of this diachronic depth, particularly the frequent invocation of how Romans had to adapt to the harshness of Vatican rule over two millennia. The cultural determinism that we should reject as an analytical tool is, rather, an ethnographically interesting and important phenomenon; it is an integral part of the nexus of attitudes I am seeking to decipher here. This determinism has social significance; it may, for example, be somewhat defensive, since Roman accommodation is often viewed by outsiders as pusillanimous hypocrisy.

It certainly does not conform to the larger regional pattern. Accommodation in this sense contrasts sharply with the usual agonistic image of southern European society, as does the pride Romans take in the aggressive behavior of their women and the public way in which these women allegedly used to shame their husbands by staging elaborate and very public screaming matches. Rome both belies the classic stereotype of "Mediterranean society" (in which women were expected to be demure) and, at the same time, ironically offers an explanation that reproduces a key feature of that stereotype: strategic denial of collective blame, here in the form of seeing the lingering effects of harsh ecclesiastical rule in the alleged tendency to seek accommodation at almost any cost.

It is not, I suggest, too far-fetched to view "accommodation" as a variant of the stereotypically Italian penchant for *l'arte dell'arrangiarsi* (the art of getting things fixed up). But it is a variant that pays particularly close attention to performance. As such, it is a proactive and rhetorical defense of immediate familial interests, and in this sense perhaps also approaches the familistic values attributed—with variable degrees of sophistication and credibility—to other Mediterranean societies. But its rhetoric and practice are distinctive. Romans neither endorse nor, apparently, enjoy the swaggering and confrontational stance that supposedly typifies Mediterranean society, and that certainly characterizes many of the local societies of the region. Continual and opportunistic adaptation, not fierce moral grandstanding, has—perhaps in consequence of this history—emerged over long centuries as the preferred social idiom.

Such a stance, as I have pointed out elsewhere, makes possible another important feature of Roman and indeed of Italian life.[14] This is the *condono edilizio*—the legal practice of allowing citizens absolution from past fines by allowing them to pay a small percentage of what they owe in exchange for a document guaranteeing them immunity from further prosecution for the same offenses. Largely on the basis of local practitioners' observations, I have compared such documents to the indulgences offered by the church in exoneration of minor sins. It is not a coincidence that the *condono* is especially favored by the right-wing parties, which, perhaps even more than their hardly less corrupt left-wing opponents, play up an idiom of calculation of what it takes to avoid punishment and moral responsibility for infractions already committed; trumpet the value and significance of a national heritage they are nevertheless willing to outsource and ransack for its financial advantages; and thus once again lay out a model of how to endorse "tradition" while in practice seeking the proactive means of being able to continue to offend against its supposed norms.

Taking Liberties: Rome Today and Tomorrow

In this way, contemporary Rome maintains practices that have been kept in place by the continuing power and influence of the church. Such templates of collective self-justification translate easily into the secular sphere. As a right-wing architect remarks in my film *Monti Moments* (Herzfeld 2007a), abuse of the law is "practically a tradition here in Rome!" The dominant aesthetic of Roman architectural restorations leaves stucco façades weather-stained and crumbling in a display of the mortality of all things human in which we might wish to see the architectural equivalent of corruption in the political sense. The same attitude arguably also informs the local authorities' remarkable tolerance of graffiti. If we consider that a high proportion of the graffiti are daubed by right-wingers and are not infrequently couched in the Roman dialect rather than in standard Italian, they provide a pointed contrast to the formal rejection of foreign language signage and new "ethnic" restaurants. They also, however, remind us that an increasingly right-wing proletariat will not necessarily be welcomed to the spatial realms carefully cleansed of the riff raff in expensive designs by the famous architects and planners collectively known as Maxi-Stars. Municipal leaders, right- and left-wing alike, have been thinking big, and little people find themselves increasingly excluded from the official aesthetic of the city as a grandiose artwork.

Rome has long been the theater of a peculiar tension between the ethically permissive and the bureaucratically repressive. This tension has produced in the population a reciprocal ambiguity, in which apparent acquiescence in the demands of the powerful—"accommodation"—vies with collusion against the structures the powerful claim to represent. The resulting micropolitics produces shifting social fractures at multiple levels. While this may make the population of Rome relatively ungovernable in a formal sense, it also allows for a more robust pursuit of self-interest than is possible in more directly regulated and politically compact populations. It also, however, makes resistance to official power extremely difficult to sustain over long periods of time: protectors too easily decline into opponents; neighborhood associations collapse in furious rivalry; promises evaporate; and imagination about an ideal urban future far outstrips willingness to turn plans into places.

In such a context, ideologies are as evanescent as the alliances through which they are given material existence. Declarations of cultural tolerance morph, with dizzying unpredictability, into the rejection and violence that they potentially always encompass. From a liberal pope who became one of history's notorious oppressors to a left-wing regime that "liberalized" home ownerships and thereby launched the current orgy of gentrification and its attendant *emergenza casa,* and from a culturally diverse *imperium* celebrated as the glorious past of a despised capital that practices a localism worthy of its disaffected northern and southern provinces, Rome's urban and political ecology has always defied simple categorization. The planners and bureaucrats who are charged with the future of Rome are trying to reverse this pattern, which—as they apparently fail to realize—is at least as ancient and entrenched as any of the virtues they attribute to the Eternal City. They want to turn productive forms of conflict and confrontation into passive acquiescence in a grandiose vision of undying glory in which urban harmony emblematizes national unity.[15] They resist the perception that it is precisely the aspects of Roman life they most fear and despise—in a nutshell, its segmentary fractiousness—that have the deepest historical roots, the best fit with the experienced proclivities of the national political order, and thus the most convincing lien on, if not eternity, at least a promising future. Their chances of reversing that reality are as vanishingly slim as those of keeping the graffiti artists away from the architectural inventions of the Maxi-Stars.

Notes

I would like to thank the co-editors of this volume as well as two anonymous reviewers, both for their helpful comments and for their encouragingly enthusiastic reception of the contents of this essay.

1. For a full account of Monti and of my field research there, see Herzfeld (2009), as well as Herzfeld (2007a, 2007b, 2011).

2. See, e.g., Tiziana Guerrisi, "Alemanno e il menu etnico: 'Da mal di pancia ai bimbi,'" *La Repubblica,* Rome section, 19 July 2008, p. 1; http://www.o6blog.it/post/3339/via-il-menu-etnico-dalle-scuole-si-torna-alla-carbonara; the petition against Alemanno's policy at http://

www.petizionionline.it/petizione/no-allabolizione-del-menu-etnico-dalle-mense-scolastiche-comunali-di-roma/2755. (Both URLs accessed 17 September 2011.) On the restrictions in Lucca, see "Lucca, stop ai ristoranti etnici—'Salvaguardare la tradizione,'" *La Repubblica*, "Cronaca," 26 January 2009.

3. This, at least, is the view of gay activists, and it appears to be borne out by his willingness to have local police harass gays for public kissing. See Jeff Israely, "Gay-Rights Clash over Rome Coliseum Kiss," *Time*, 24 September 2008, http://www.time.com/time/world/article/0,8599,1844012,00.html (accessed 17 September 2011).

4. E.g., Eamonn Canniffe, review of Herzfeld (2009), in *GUTTAE: Above and Below Architecture*, http://guttae.blogspot.com/2011/06/review-michael-herzfeld-evicted-from.html (accessed 22 August 2011).

5. Dumont's (1970) notion of "encompassment" anticipates the present analysis, although it is arguably Kapferer's (1988) reading of Dumont that has clarified its relevance for a critical understanding of the sometimes violently destructive transformations of modernist liberalism.

6. Nonetheless, the late-capitalist term *hospitality industry* does rather give the game away!

7. On the history of the Roman Jews, see also Caffiero (2004); Sarfatti (1999); Todeschini (1989).

8. See Silverman (1975): 1–8. On the distinction between the civic and the civil and its relationship to extortion, see Herzfeld (2009): 181–217.

9. See Emanuele Coen, "La rivolta degli ambulanti ebrei," *La Repubblica*, Rome section, 28 December 1999, p. 4.

10. For discussion and further references, see Herzfeld (2009): 89–101.

11. See Herzfeld (2007b) for an extended analysis of this expression and its implications.

12. Liah Greenfeld's (1992) notion of *ressentiment* may be even more applicable to such dynamics than it is to the state-oriented nationalisms that she discusses.

13. For a detailed account of these sources, see Ferraresi (1996); Dyal (forthcoming) explores their translation into political practice in the violence propagated by football fans in Rome.

14. On the *condono edilizio*, see especially Herzfeld (2009): 131–136.

15. On conflict, see Scandurra (2005): 10; on widely varying perspectives on the forms, justifications, and modalities of social and political confrontation in Rome, see Cellamare (2008); Dyal chapter 11, this volume; Goñi Mazzitelli (2010); Herzfeld (2009): 77–79.

References

Cellamare, Carlo. 2008. *Fare città: Pratiche urbane e storie di luoghi*. Milano: Elèuthera.

Caffiero, Marina. 2004. *Battesimi Forzati: Storie di ebrei, cristiani e convertiti nella Roma dei papi*. Rome: Viella.

Dumont, Louis. 1970. *Homo Hierarchicus: The Caste System and Its Implications*. London: Weidenfeld and Nicolson.

———. 1982. *On Value*. London: Oxford University Press.

Dyal, Mark. forthcoming. *Ultras Contra Modernity*. London: Arktos Media.

Ferraresi, Franco. 1996. *Threats to Democracy: The Radical Right in Italy after the War*. Princeton: Princeton University Press.

Goñi Mazzitelli, Adriana. 2010. *Se ci sei battiti: Nuevas Políticas Urbanas basadas en procesos y prácticas culturales locales, con el aporte de la antropología contemporánea a la planificación participada.* PhD thesis, Università di Roma Tre.

Greenfeld, Liah. 1992. *Nationalism: Five Roads to Modernity.* Cambridge, Mass.: Harvard University Press.

Herzfeld, Michael. 1987. "'As in Your Own House': Hospitality, Ethnography, and the Stereotype of Mediterranean Society." In *Honor and shame and the unity of the Mediterranean,* edited by D. D. Gilmore, 75–89. Special Publication no. 22. Washington, D.C.: American Anthropological Association.

———. 2007a. *Monti Moments: Men's Memories in the Heart of Rome.* Video, filmed and produced by Michael Herzfeld. Berkeley, Calif.: Berkeley Media LLC.

———. 2007b. "Small-Mindedness Writ Large: On the Migrations and Manners of Prejudice." *Journal of Ethnic and Migration Studies* 33: 255–274.

———. 2009. *Evicted from Eternity: The Restructuring of Modern Rome.* Chicago: University of Chicago Press.

———. 2011. *Roman Restaurant Rhythms.* Video, filmed and produced by Michael Herzfeld. Berkeley, Calif.: Berkeley Media LLC.

Kapferer, Bruce. 1988. *Legends of People, Myths of State: Violence, Intolerance, and Political Culture in Sri Lanka and Australia.* Washington, D.C.: Smithsonian Institution Press.

Kertzer, David I. 2001. *The Popes against the Jews: The Vatican's Role in the Rise of Modern Anti-Semitism.* New York: Alfred A. Knopf.

Papataxiarchis, Efthymios. 2009. "Stin akri tou vlemmatos: I krisi tis 'filoksenias' tin epokhi ton dhiaperaton sinoron" ["At the edge of the gaze: The 'crisis' of hospitality in the age of porous borders"]. *Sinkhrona Themata* 107: 67–74.

Sarfatti, Michele. 1999. "Il razzismo fascista nella sua concretezza: La definizione di 'Ebreo' e la Collocazione di Questi nella Costruenda Gerarchia Razziale." In *Nel Nome della Razza: Il razzismo nella storia d'Italia 1870–1945,* edited by Alberto Burgio, 321–332. Bologna, Italy: Il Mulino.

Scandurra. Giuseppe. 2005. "Che cos'è conflitto? Conflitti metropolitani." In *Mappa e conflitti nel territorio metropolitano di Roma. La riva sinistra del Tevere,* edited by M. Berlinguer, 54–57. Rome: Transform.

Silverman, Sydel. 1975. *Three Bells of Civilization: The Life of an Italian Hill Town.* New York: Columbia University Press.

Thomassen, Bjørn, and Rosario Forlenza. 2011. Renarrating Italy, Reinventing the Nation: Assessing the Presidency of Ciampi. *Journal of Modern Italian Studies* 16: 705–725.

Todeschini, Giacomo. 1989. *La Richezza degli Ebrei:Merci e denaro nella riflessione ebraica e nella definizione cristiana dell'usura alla fine delMedioevo.* Spoleto, Italy: Centro Italiano di Studi sull'Alto Medievo.

3 Rome as a Global City

Mapping New Cultural and Political Boundaries

Pierluigi Cervelli
(translated by Isabella Clough Marinaro)

Spatial Practices and Urban Transformation

The analysis presented in this chapter is the result of a research project concerning the use of space in Rome by men and women belonging to various immigrant groups: Chinese, Bangladeshi, Romanian, Albanian, and Roma. Their "spatial practices"[1] appear to be based on an ability to innovatively and strategically interpret the relationships between areas which developed out of the sociopolitical model of urban space defined by Fascism—a model which outlived the regime and endured well into the postwar period (in my view until the 1980s). Studying the spatial practices of these immigrant groups allows us to make out the incipient transformations, the new political conflicts, and the emerging religious and linguistic cultural stratifications that make contemporary Rome a global city, profoundly different from the city it was a few decades ago. In order to verify this hypothesis on a macro level, I compare the urban model which developed through Rome's transformations between 1871 and 1940 with the spatial practices of these groups, investigated through an examination of their sociodemographic data.

I situate the appearance of this model during Fascism, between 1925 and 1940, because this was the period in which the enormous transformations in the city's monumental, urban planning, and demographic organization occurred (Insolera 1970; Racheli 1979; Sanfilippo 1994). It was in this phase that the relationship between city and countryside was radically altered, entire medieval and renaissance sections of the historic center were demolished, and the system of roads was overhauled. In this process, urban space took on a political dimension and an ideological organization through two main maneuvers. First, Fascism manipulated the "cultural memory" (Lotman 1985) expressed by urban space. By making theatrical use of space, the ancient monuments were inscribed into a network of walking routes and panoramic view points in order to express a historical-political narration in which the fascist state model was presented as the "natural" and coherent outcome of Italian history, directly tied to the imperial past and the events of the Risorgimento (the creation of the Kingdom of Italy and the unitary state), but also fused with the country's religious identity (Cervelli 2008). Some urban scholars (e.g., Birindelli 1978) argue that this process culminated in the creation of a single center in the city—something which had not previously existed in Rome—with Piazza Venezia as its fulcrum; a choice which was not coincidental, since the office of the fascist leader, and consequently the heart of political power, was located there. In my opinion, this is linked to another maneuver: that of the even more radical "territorialization" of the urban population, the most obvious result of which was the forced relocation of the city's poor inhabitants (lower middle class and working class) from within the historic center to the urban fringes. This was achieved first through the liberalization of rental prices and then directly through the destruction of their homes (5,500 dwelling units were demolished just in the building of Via dell'Impero, now Via dei Fori Imperiali) and their progressive deportation to the *borgate*, undifferentiated agglomerates of cheap housing separated from the rest of the city by a "no-man's land": a belt of uncultivated terrain that extended for many miles (Insolera 1970).

The building of the *borgate* was fundamental because their position outside the urban space allowed the city to then be imagined as a single, spatially and socially sealed whole. They made it possible to delineate the city limits and expel beyond them the social "others" that Fascism wanted to exclude, facilitating their control and surveillance. Through these transformations, the fascist regime projected a political template onto the surface of the city; a spatial model composed of concentric belts, closed by a visible boundary, in which distance from the political center expressed the *borgate* residents' position on the lowest rung of the social hierarchy. Thus simplified and codified, the urban territory became a "readable" space and took on the function of a diagram, capable of transmitting "the exact communication of power relations" (Foucault 2005, 26). Rome became so important for Fascism (Gentile 2007) because its urban structure laid out the cartography of class and power relations and a selective view of Italian history that served to legitimize the regime's existence. This spatial system, which we can call "disciplinary," to borrow Foucault's terminology, was only partially accomplished from an urban planning point of view; nevertheless, it guided the control of the city's population.[2] Examples of this are the city council ordinances that required the demolition of slums, starting first with those located within three kilometers of the Aurelian Walls and gradually extending outward (Insolera 1970). This disciplinary organization of space was aimed at the biopolitical control of the poor population, which potentially threatened the regime. Indeed, the process was carried out by continually mapping spatial practices and urban life though the collection of highly detailed statistical data (concerning, for example, demographics and population movements, dietary trends, places of death and medical conditions of children), which focused on the relationship between population and space and were published in the magazine *Capitolium*.[3] The urban model this governmentality initiated, based on a fundamental binary opposition between interior and exterior, and which we could describe as "radio-centrically disciplinary," appears to have influenced the geographical location of the population and the city's development for a long period thereafter. The position of the unauthorized settlements, which were partly built by Italian migrants who arrived in the 1950s and 1960s and were partly developed by real-estate speculators in the same period on state-owned land (see Mudu, chapter 4), appears to have been based on a recognition of the city boundary traced by the no-man's land, which in fascist times separated the city from the *borgate*, and beyond which these new agglomerations were set up.

The location of the new and squalid peripheries, which were developed in the 1980s, represent a continuation of that model. These are high-density neighborhoods of public housing built at a great distance from the city center, surrounded by urban voids, lacking in public spaces, and with few transport connections. It is important, however, to note one change which did occur in the interim period: The boundary of the city shifted from being fixed and uncrossable to a "mobile border" (which was also functional to real-estate speculation), forming a belt into which the city progressively expanded, incorporating the forms of marginality which were once on the outside.[4] The spatial practices of the immigrant groups discussed in this chapter seem to be dismantling this spatial radio-centric disciplinary model, taking advantage of the opportunities offered by its deterioration and thus accentuating its decay. At the same time, they make the contemporary confines of global Rome visible. These are boundaries that are political, linked to strategies for controlling the population as in the case of Romani men and women; socioresidential, connected to the large size of the current metropolitan area underlined by the location of Romanian, Albanian, and, to a lesser extent, Polish, groups; and cultural, related to the appearance of specifically global neighborhoods which cannot be reduced to a single nationality and within which local forms of cultural cohabitation emerge that are typical of international borders but which do not simply reflect existing frontiers between states. This is the case in urban areas where, for the first time, groups who had no relations prior to their immigration (such as Chinese and Bangladeshi communities) live side by side. This radically new situation is forming a new set of internal boundaries which are both local and transnational and which make Rome a truly global city, a frontier city which reproduces within itself the borders that once only delimited states. The data presented in the next section provide a mapping of these new boundaries.[5]

Theoretical Debate and Methodology: Cultural Boundaries and Technologies of Power

The specificity of my approach lies in its aim of returning to and updating the analytical themes concerning urban space identified by Michel Foucault and Michel de Certeau, on the one hand distinguishing the strategies of power and governmentality within urban space, and on the other hand mapping spatial practices and their relationship with those strategies. The work intersects with the study of urban planning (see Cervelli 2009 for a critique of the definition of "periphery" presented in the latest urban master plan for Rome), with geography (in terms of "rethinking peripherality," Davis 2006), anthropology (Piasere 1999), and sociology (Sassen 2008).

The methodology is semiotic, based mainly on the theories of Lotman (1994) and de Certeau (1980), in dialogue with Foucault's research. The data were collected through direct anthropological observation as well as the analysis of urban configurations, demographic statistics, political discourses and historical sources. In Lotman's (1985, 1994) theory of culture as "semiosphere," a culture's identity is built through two processes: the production of "self-definitions," which involve varyingly complex sets of models of identity (from the most basic binary ones to more multiform webs of broader categories), and the demarcation of "semiotic boundaries," understood as all the points of contact between the cultural system and what lies outside it (other cultures). These boundaries are not barriers but filters, places in which elements of one cultural system are translated and pass into another. The specificity of one cultural system is thus constructed through the "invention" of differences with other cultures (or through radically simplifying other cultures) while simultaneously inserting external elements within one's own system. Without this latter process, no culture could mutate and survive. In this way, culture is conceived as a dynamic system which is not sealed but rather is in constant osmosis with other cultures, incorporating elements which are filtered through its own models of identity, thus achieving stability as well as transformation. These processes of stabilization (the production of models of identity) and transformation (translation) are carried out through all the "languages" the culture has at its disposal. According to Lotman, though, the most important communicative devices are language and space. Through these processes, boundaries are constructed that are both external to the culture and internal (i.e., that reproduce the mechanism of relationships with the other within itself). These boundaries are pictured as a hierarchy, at the center of which are the areas of stability (or "semiotic centers") that are more codified and thus simpler—where contact with what is considered "other" is forbidden—and more dynamic areas, which are more permeable to hybridization, are defined as *peripheries* and made up of all the "borders" where various cultures come into contact.

In this chapter, I explore how Rome was used to define Italian identity and how, through the management of urban space, an image of cultural center and margin was created in the process. I also examine how that relationship changed with time. I am not only concerned with the "ideological" use of space but also how it functions as a "technology of power" (Foucault 2004), an issue that Lotman does not address. In order to analyze the possible forms of resistance (or simply avoidance), I consider the relationship between political use of urban space and spatial practices in terms of the distinction made by de Certeau between strategies and tactics. For de Certeau, *strategies* are systems for organizing time and spatial relationships in order to make a place immobile and unchangeable, in which the subjects that are incorporated have no choice but to occupy the positions that the dominant (technocratic or political) power establishes for them. The *tactics* are instead the myriad ways in which those who are "dominated" evade those strategies without openly overcoming them but by exploiting the aporias they present. The way spatial practices function as tactics essentially consists of "subjectifying" places, thereby transforming them from a collection of immobile elements to "practiced" spaces. The relationships between places are redefined by the people who cross them with varying speeds and in various directions. I argue from this point of view that the spatial practices of immigrant groups restructure the relationship between urban areas in a way that is equivalent to de Certeau's tactics, exploiting the contradictions and underlining the enervations of the model of disciplinary political space and, in the case of the Roma, the emergence of new practices of political control of urban space. It should be emphasized that at times de Certeau's approach appears to consider the relationship between dominators and the dominated in a rather static way. I argue that it is instead necessary to examine how those who on one level of analysis appear to be homogeneously dominated can instead be divided by inequalities of power and forms of exploitation. Equally, I think that considering those groups' spatial practices only as forms of resistance would be to idealize them. What I consider instead most interesting is the way in which they can help us understand how—with varying means and motivations—the model of political space is being surpassed and how the city is being transformed.

Spatial Practices among Rome's Immigrant Communities

My argument takes its inspiration from a number of direct observations: starting from the visibility of various immigrant groups in certain areas of Rome, I began to explore their residential practices across the whole city. I examined the official data concerning residence status as of 31 December 2006, originally collected by the national statistical agency (ISTAT) and reworked by the Caritas Observatory on Migration (*Osservatorio romano sulle migrazioni* 2007, 2008, 2010, 2011). I then chose to focus on the groups whose spatial practices seemed to reinterpret the radio-centric model discussed earlier.[6] This choice enables us to consider some of the ten largest migrant groups in the city and Province of Rome.[7] It should be noted that the scale of analysis necessary for considering the whole of the urban area means that gender dynamics are not highlighted, producing a certain "homogenization" of the immigrant groups which thus appear as monolithic wholes, whereas in reality there are internal divisions and inequalities of power within them (see, for example, Daniele 2011, concerning Roma). When discussing the residential modalities of Roma groups,[8] I focus on their uses of space that seem to constitute a tactic in response to strategies of political control (see chapter 7 for a discussion of the recent "security emergency" and living situations of Roma in Rome).

Bangladeshi and Chinese groups are not the largest groups in the city, but they are certainly the most concentrated and thus most visible.[9] These groups live mainly in two boroughs (the first and the sixth *municipi*) in central areas that are strategically important in terms of mobility and rising real-estate value. Until about fifteen years ago, these neighborhoods were considered unsafe and subject to urban decay and were consequently not attractive to Italian residents. Today, both are affected by gentrification in which their potential for development has been widely recognized. This potential already existed at the turn of the millennium but it has accelerated thanks to a process of rediscovery and repopulation in which immigrants have participated actively (including through a large range of entrepreneurial activities—see Mudu 2006) and in which some groups of Italians have also begun to be involved.

The issue of spatial concentration is particularly noticeable: In 2007, 39.72 percent of Bangladeshis and 34.84 percent of the city's Chinese population were resident in the two boroughs (out of Rome's nineteen *municipi*). Their residential patterns are very distinctive; their concentration is highly localized in certain neighborhoods and translates into their almost complete absence in many other boroughs.[10] We thus have two immigrant collectivities who presumably had no interactions before their migration to the city and who present the same levels of concentration and settlement patterns. This concentration is most visible in the Torpignattara neighborhood in the sixth *municipio* where approximately 10 percent of the Bangladeshi and Chinese populations live (see also Broccolini's ethnographic study of the Bangladeshi community in that neighborhood in chapter 5). A similar phenomenon exists in the Esquilino area (zone 1E of the first *municipio*) where more than 12 percent of the city's Chinese and approximately 7 percent of the Bangladeshis reside. This is presumably a stable population since it is made up of equal proportions of men and women.[11] The data we have for 2008 seem to confirm these tendencies; although there was a slight fall (1.34 percent) in the number of Bangladeshis compared to the previous year, the Chinese population showed an increase of about 2 percent. If we examine these data in light of the oldest statistics available (2003), we see that their spatial concentration has risen. At the time, Chinese groups resident in the two boroughs represented about 32 percent of the total Chinese population, while 39 percent of Bangladeshis lived there. The diachronic dynamic of patterns of residence shows that there has been a progressive move of Bangladeshis from the tenth and the eleventh *municipi* to the first and sixth and of Chinese from other areas in the sixth and ninth boroughs—where they tended to be concentrated during the 1990s (Campani et al. 1992)—toward the Esquilino. The most recent data available (31 December 2010) seem to confirm this trend: 39.23 percent of Bangladeshis and 47.47 percent of Chinese were resident in the two *municipi*.[12] The dynamic we have identified was therefore stable for the Bangladeshi population and intensifying for the Chinese. It is highly significant that this occurred in parallel with a notable rise (of about 60 percent) in the absolute size of both groups between 2006 and 2010 (from 8,927 to 14,466 Bangladeshis and from 7,064 to 12,013 Chinese).

This point seems particularly important because it demonstrates how this progressive concentration has involved both collectivities and how, just as the massive rise in house prices was beginning to occur in Italy and especially in Rome (an increase of approximately 90 percent between 1991 and 2010 [Nomisma 2010]), both were able to identify and position themselves strategically in the areas where a rise in real-estate value would be most likely. Their settlement choices indicate an ability to read the spatial organization of the city on two levels, the global and the local, based on an understanding of the hierarchies of spaces and the gaps that these have created. These groups have in fact positioned themselves with an *interstitial logic of compact settlement* within the "internal peripheries" in the center of the city, enhancing the value of neighborhoods that Italians considered marginal. Indeed, the Esquilino neighborhood was intended be one of the "centers" of post-Unification Rome in the late 1800s, accommodating the class of civil servants who moved to the capital from northern Italy. However, the area was left on the fringes of the political center as it was delineated by the fascist spatial model (it was one of the hubs of the project of spatial reorganization closely tied to the presence of the Italian royal house of Savoy, which clashed with Mussolini's subsequent plans for the city). Due also to the low quality and large scale of the buildings, the population had started to diminish in the 1950s and plummeted further in the 1980s because of its proximity to Termini railway station, which meant that it was frequented by many drug users. Torpignattara's blight was instead due to problems of housing and high levels of crime. Despite being very close to the city, it was socially separated from it: Located in what was once an industrial district, its population was predominantly working class (to this day it is in the part of the city that has the lowest proportion of university graduates). The area included Pigneto, which today is its most gentrified neighborhood (and the nearest to the city center) but which originated as a partly illegally built *borgata,* separated from nearby urban areas by uncultivated land.

The settlement patterns of Romanian and Albanian groups point to a different but equally distinctive dynamic:[13] They tend to be located near the city's administrative boundaries and especially beyond them, in various municipalities within Rome's province (particularly Fontenuova and Ladispoli, but also Tivoli, Guidonia, Fiumicino, Pomezia, Monterondo, Mentana). Their concentration in the Province of Rome, rather than the city, becomes clearer still when we compare it not only to the Bangladeshi and Chinese groups, but also to the population more generally: 68.47 percent of the inhabitants of Rome's province live within the capital's confines, with only 31.53 percent dispersed outside the city. Romanian and Albanian citizens are highly concentrated in the province, with 49.43 percent and 57.83 percent, respectively, living in a municipality outside Rome, whereas only 4.34 percent of Banglandeshis and 9.58 percent of Chinese reside there. If we compare these data with their presence in the towns where they are most numerous, we note that this "dispersal" is actually a *marginalized concentration.* They are distributed along the boundaries of the capital's metropolitan area, which is much larger than the administrative limits of the Comune di Roma. This settlement pattern is connected to the idea of centralized space which has now, however, extended to a belt of land that is no longer circular but has taken on a regional dimension and which is expanding progressively, absorbing other towns as if they were new neighborhoods and adding them onto the existing city.[14] It is important to underline, though, that the scale of this research, which covers the entire urban area, makes it impossible to explore the diversity of personal motivations underlying migrants' choices of where to live, and therefore only considers the relationship between a group's geographic concentration and the city's structure.

Finally, the spatial practices of Roma who live in unauthorized settlements made up of tents and shacks appears to have a political dimension. Their use of space is the means through which they resist the forced nomadism caused by the bulldozing of their encampments and whose ultimate aim is to expel them from the city altogether. An analysis of their settlement patterns is crucial to this study because it entirely belies the spatial relations that underpin the radiocentric model, but perhaps it enables us to make out the forms of urban territorial control that are currently underway. Before presenting the data, I reiterate that, as with the other groups studied here, unfortunately we cannot delve here into the individual choices and patterns of settlement and mobility of different families involved. The Roma's migratory patterns alter significantly and often very quickly; they are also often circular and thus potentially reversible. Moreover, the type of accommodation can frequently change—moving from a house to an unauthorized camp, a prefabricated container to a shack—without this being a linear process that can be conceptualized as a trend toward greater or lesser stability. Chapters 7 and 8 explore these processes in greater depth.

According to the available data—which is very fragmented and constantly changing due to the Roma's frequent evictions and relocations—at the end of August 2008, there were 133 unauthorized shanties, inhabited by 4,179 people (some of whom were not Roma), and about 50 percent of which were children.[15] The camps are spread throughout almost the whole city, in eighteen of its nineteen boroughs, with the exception of the third *municipi* The encampments usually lack running water, electricity, and plumbing, and their contact with welfare services is scarce or nonexistent. They are very small, often home to between five and thirty inhabitants belonging to one or two families. Only 8 of the 133 camps were home to one hundred people and only 1 contained more than three hundred. Thus, 2,818 people were living in 125 camps. This has not always been the case in Rome, though; the number of unauthorized encampments tripled from less than 70 to approximately 220 between 2006 and 2011 as the policy of forced evictions and camp demolitions intensified (see Clough Marinaro 2009),[16] producing ever smaller and more hidden microshanties generally inhabited by a few families, most of which are Eastern European and of recent migration to Italy (Motta 2011). This rise in the number of camps did not happen because of a growth in the population but rather because the size of the encampments shrank radically. In 1995, a census found that there were 5,467 Roma distributed in 51 unauthorized camps (Motta and Geraci 2007). In 2002, the municipal authorities provided minimal services to some of the settlements, such as chemical toilets, electricity, and a few public drinking fountains. There were thirty-two such official camps, located in sixteen of the boroughs, in addition to just under sixty unauthorized ones where about six thousand Romanian Roma lived (Motta et al. 2006).[17] By August 2008, twenty-six of the original fifty-one camps were still inhabited and had been transformed into legal camps, but the roughly sixty unauthorized camps of 2006 had doubled in number, even though the population counted in the studies diminished from 6,000 to 4,179 (probably in part due to the option of "voluntary repatriation"—for which they received a small amount of money—following the forced evictions, although many of them then returned).

The fact that the number of unauthorized camps more than doubled without there having been a growth in the population is extremely important.[18] These camps seem to be structured like "dust particles," as one of Italy's most eminent scholars in the field, Leonardo Piasere (1999), eloquently defined this phenomenon when discussing his ethnographic experience and his view that Roma make themselves invisible at times when repression against them is at its most intense, to then reappear when the situation calms down again. The rise in unauthorized microcamps is thus tied to a tactic for creating invisibility, which is only possible with small agglomerations that can be hidden and moved quickly. It is no coincidence that these settlements are often located "under" or "inside" the city: in abandoned underpasses, along riverbanks, next to isolated bicycle tracks, under bridges, and along bypasses, in empty buildings or in the least accessible areas of public parks. It should be stressed that this residential mobility is certainly not a form of nomadism; rather, it makes it easier to return quickly to the places from which they have been evicted.[19] We can hypothesize that this use of space in reality aims to avoid the forced nomadism that the current strategies for politically controlling Roma in Rome produce, both through the destruction of unauthorized camps and through the Roma's relocation in so-called solidarity villages made up of prefabricated containers (about 28 m² each, housing between eight and ten people) introduced in 2005 and whose regulations are all based on the notion that the Roma's presence is transitory (some of them are converted former tourist campsites). The regulations limit the Roma's right to live there to six years, divided into three two-year periods at the end of each of which the authorities evaluate whether to permit them to stay on (see Cervelli and Pota 2011).[20] It is important to add that long-term residence in these "villages," in addition to being against the rules, is strongly discouraged by living conditions within them; they are all located far from the city center and are overcrowded, lacking in spaces for recreation, and precarious in terms of services and hygiene (for example, in one of the camps the author tasted the drinking water; it was salty). How do the new forms of control of urban territory that are thus being tested on Roma function? This is a strange form of power which instead of expelling the subjects it is trying to control, or immobilizing them as occurs in the radio-centric disciplinary model, seems to continuously chase them, moving the boundary that excludes them into every place in which they stop: a *marginalizing power* which controls people by keeping them on the move rather than obstructing their circulation.

Changing Faces, Changing Places

This study of the spatial practices of different immigrant groups allows us to identify three distinct ways in which they reinterpret the radio-centric disciplinary model of urban space as it was defined during the fascist period. The first of these, underlying the settlement patterns of Chinese and Bangladeshi groups, considers the urban area as a whole in which the value of its neighborhoods decreases as one moves away from the center (as in the fascist model) but which offers some gaps into which the two collectivities have inserted themselves in a very compact way. The second approach, used by Romanians and Albanians, reproduces some features of the patterns of Italian migrants in the 1950s and 1960s, treating Rome as a whole made up of a set of boundaries along whose margins they position themselves, thereby pushing those boundaries substantially outward. They thus identify the current area of influence of the metropolitan region whose radio-centric model is no longer fixed but is now inserted in an expanding belt of territory of varying widths. The third model is instead inferable from the organization of small unauthorized Roma encampments. This territorial model is centerless and stratified; it does not recognize any hierarchy of space (that is, there is no inequality of value between center and periphery) or any of the boundaries defined by *gağé* (non-Roma). What counts instead are issues of accessibility/inaccessibility and the ways in which the Roma can escape control and encirclement by making themselves invisible and continuously mobile. In this field of strategic maneuvers and tactics, the spatial practices of immigrant groups reveal—in dialogue with the history of transformation in the Eternal City—the new possibilities and tragic pathologies of contemporary Rome.

Notes

1. De Certeau (1980) also defines these as "arts" that constitute "walking rhetorics."
2. The building of the Esposizione Universale di Roma (EUR) district, which was intended as the new center of Rome, positioned between the historic city and the sea, is a dramatic exception to this model and demonstrates the change in the regime's approach and scale of action following the conquest of Ethiopia and the proclamation of the empire in 1936 (Gentile 2007). I would argue that it can be interpreted as the kernel of a future project of imperial centrality whose area of reference was to be the entire Mediterranean Sea.
3. *Capitolium* was the monthly report, founded in 1925, of the activities of Rome's governorate. See in particular the issues published between 1925 and 1930. I have thus far examined about 1000 pages of statistical data and 3,300 pages of articles which constitute the foundations of a larger research project.
4. These marginalities were not socially included, however, but simply surrounded spatially. The old fascist *borgate* continue to be recognizable as places "apart" and their residents socially stigmatized, although less so since the 1990s as immigration from abroad became a consolidated phenomenon. In colloquial Roman speech, *borgataro* (resident of the *borgate*) is synonymous with being uncouth and ill-bred.
5. A part of these data is also presented in Cervelli (2009).
6. I have excluded Filipino groups from the analysis because although they are one of the most geographically concentrated collectivities in the city (over 90 percent live in the first borough (Municipio 1), this is strongly influenced by the fact that many of them are domestic workers who live with their employers.
7. Residence data concerning the province are from 2007.
8. I use the term *Roma* here only as shorthand, since they speak different variants of the Romani language and do not consider themselves to be a single entity.
9. Data are for 31 December 2007. The unpublished raw data were obtained from the statistics office of the Comune di Roma and reelaborated by the author.
10. Nine of the nineteen boroughs have extremely low levels of concentration (less than 2 percent of the Bangladeshi population in each). This is also the case with Chinese groups in six boroughs.
11. The ratio is exactly even among Chinese, whereas there is a larger proportion of young men among the Bangladeshis in both neighborhoods, which seems to reflect the current characteristics of Bangladeshi immigration patterns. One apparently anomalous phenomenon should be noted, though: About 11 percent of Bangladeshis officially reside in Trastevere (zone 1B, first *municipi*), a historical and very expensive neighborhood which attracts many tourists and where gentrification occurred about three decades ago. It is now home to a large number

of foreigners from Western Europe and the United States. This phenomenon can be explained by the fact that two organizations which provide assistance and support to immigrants are based there; the Comunità di S. Egidio and the Bangladesh Cultural Institute of Italy. Many immigrants declare the organizations as their official residence, a choice which is presumably motivated by their lack of a stable place of residence in the city. Based in part on direct contact with these groups, I hypothesize that these people, who are mainly young men (only 18 of the 1,269 individuals resident there are women), in reality live in the neighborhoods where their communities are particularly concentrated and in which there are frequent situations of cohabitation and overcrowding in apartments. A walk through those neighborhoods is in any case enough to note a large presence of Bangladeshis, not least due to their businesses and the numerous notices and publications in Bengali.

12. Data provided by Caritas (2008, 2010), based on statistics collated by the Comune di Roma.

13. And Polish groups to a lesser extent (35.64 percent residing in the province).

14. On the basis of employment data, we can assume that these people work predominantly in Rome (Caritas 2008).

15. Data on unauthorized settlements in 2008 were provided by Arci-Karin. I use data collected from diverse sources since—significantly—accurate official statistics on the Roma population in Rome do not exist. This means that the data can only provide us with a partial impression of the situation, which at most gives a very general sense of trends, rather than a precise temporal and geographical mapping.

16. Declaration made by Rome's mayor, Gianni Alemanno to *Il Messaggero* (23 April 2011)

17. These were counted during a health campaign to vaccinate Roma children. It was the second edition of a project titled "Health without Exclusion: Campaign for Access to Health and Education Services for Roma and Sinti in Rome" (*Salute senza Esclusione: Campagna per l'accessibilità dei servizi socio-sanitari e l'educazione della salute in favore dei Rom e Sinti presenti a Roma*).

18. If we add these 4,179 residents to the approximately 7,900 which, according to data from Caritas (2006, 2008), lived in "serviced or semi-serviced" camps recognized by the city authorities in 2006, the total population amounted to 12,079 people, far fewer than the approximately 20,000 Roma who the right-wing candidate for mayor, Gianni Alemanno, suggested should be expelled from the city (Vitale 2007).

19. An emblematic example is a camp in Milan inhabited by about fifty Italian Roma which in 2009 was evicted fifty-two times in eight months (once every three days), only to be recreated fifty-two times in the same place (Senesi 2009). Despite the content of the *Corriere della Sera* article that reported it, the box next to it referred to the Roma only as "the nomads."

20. These regulations were recently declared illegitimate by Italy's highest court for public administration, the Council of State.

References

Birindelli, Massimo. 1978. *Roma italiana: Come fare una capitale e disfare una città*. Rome: Savelli.

Campani, Giovanna, Francesco Carchedi, and Alberto Tassinari, eds. 1992. *L'immigrazione silenziosa. Le comunità cinesi in Italia*. Turin: Fondazione Giovanni Agnelli.

Caritas di Roma. 2007. *Osservatorio romano sulle migrazioni, III rapporto*. Rome: Edizioni Idos.

———. 2008. *Osservatorio romano sulle migrazioni, IV rapporto*. Rome: Edizioni Idos.

———. 2010. *Osservatorio romano sulle migrazioni, VI rapporto*. Rome: Edizioni Idos.

———. 2011. *Osservatorio romano sulle migrazioni, VIII rapporto*. Rome: Edizioni Idos.

Caritas/Migrantes. 2006. *Dossier statistico Immigrazione, XVI rapporto*. Rome: Edizioni Idos.

Cervelli, Pierluigi. 2008. *La città fragile*. Rome: Lithos.

———. 2009. "Vuoti, stratificazioni, migrazioni. Programmazioni urbanistiche e forme dell'abitare a Roma." *Lexia* 1 (2): 95–111.

Cervelli, Pierluigi, and Matteo Pota. 2011. "Doppia marginalità e provvisorietà permanente: I nuovi campi rom nel Comune di Roma." In *Dossier statistico immigrazione, VIII Rapporto*, edited by Caritas di Roma, 197–202. Rome: Edizioni Idos.

Clough Marinaro, Isabella. 2009. "Between Surveillance and Exile: Biopolitics and the Roma in Italy." *Bulletin of Italian Politics* 1 (2): 265–287.

Daniele, Ulderico. 2011. *Sono del campo e vengo dall'India. Etnografia di una colletività rom ridislocata*. Rome: Meti edizioni.

Davis, Mike. 2006. *Planet of Slums*. New York: Verso.

de Certeau, Michel. 1990. *L'invention du quotidien*. Paris: Gallimard.

Foucault, Michel. 1975. *Surveiller et punir*. Paris: Gallimard.

———. 2004. *Sécurité, territoire, population. Cours au Collège de France (1977–1978)*. Paris: Seuil/Gallimard. Translated to Italian, 2005, Sicurezza, territorio, popolazione, Milano: Feltrinelli.

Gentile, Emilio. 2007. *Fascismo di pietra*. Bari-Rome: Editori Laterza.

Insolera, Italo. 1970. *Roma moderna*. Torino: Einaudi.

Lotman, Jurij Michajlovič. 1985. *La semiosfera. L'asimmetria e il dialogo nelle strutture pensanti*. Venice: Marsilio.

Motta, Fulvia. 2011. "I rom a Roma: Emergenza o integrazione?" in *Dossier statistico immigrazione, VIII Rapporto*, edited by Caritas di Roma, 172–180, Rome: Edizioni Idos.

Motta, Fulvia, and Salvatore Geraci. 2007. "Rom e Sinti a Roma, un'emergenza sempre rinnovata." In *Osservatorio romano sulle migrazioni, III rapporto*, edited by Caritas di Roma, 296–298. Rome: Edizioni Idos.

Motta, Fulvia, Salvatore Geraci, and Massimo Converso. 2006. "Rom, Sinti e Camminanti in Italia." In *Dossier statistico Immigrazione, XVI rapporto*, edited by Caritas di Roma, 145–154. Rome: Edizioni Idos.

Mudu, Pierpaolo. 2006. "L'immigrazione straniera a Roma: Tra divisioni del lavoro e produzione degli spazi sociali." In *Roma e gli immigrati*, edited by E. Sonnino, 115–164. Milan: Francoangeli.

Nomisma. 2010. *La condizione abitativa in Italia: I trend e le prospettive alla luce delle più recenti novità fiscali*. Rome: Nomisma.

Piasere, Leonardo. 1999. *Un mondo di mondi*. Naples: L'ancora.

Racheli, Alberto Maria. 1979. *Sintesi delle vicende urbanistiche di Roma dal 1870 al 1911*. Rome: Facoltà di architettura di Roma, Istituto di progettazione.

Sanfilippo, Mario. 1994. *La costruzione di una capitale: Roma 1945–1991*. Cinisello Balsamo, Italy: Silvana.

Sassen, Saskia. 2008. *Una sociologia della globalizzazione*. Turin: Einaudi.

Senesi, Andrea. 2009. "Il campo nomadi sgomberato 52 volte." *Corriere della sera*, August 1.

Vitale, Giovanna. 2007. "Rom, romeni e criminalità è scontro sulla sicurezza." *La Repubblica,* on-line edition, December 24. http://ricerca.repubblica.it/repubblica/archivio/repubblica/2007/12/04/rom-romeni-criminalita-scontro-sulla-sicurezza.html?ref=search. Accessed 10 October 2012.

4 Housing and Homelessness in Contemporary Rome

Pierpaolo Mudu

THE HISTORY OF contemporary Rome is one of urban development led predominantly by private interests which have caused an enormous burden of social conflict (Insolera 1993; Berdini 2008). In order to understand this development it is necessary to be familiar with a range of recurrent terms such as *borgate, borghetti, palazzinari, abusivismo,* and *condono* that describe important features in the evolution of the city's housing market. Since 1870, Rome's demographic growth has gone through four main phases. The first period followed Rome's appointment as capital in 1870, when there were approximately 200,000 inhabitants. In the second period, in the 1930s, during Fascism, its inhabitants passed the one million mark (Rossi 1959). The third period was between World War II and the end of the 1960s. The fourth period concerns the last forty years, in which there has been a population decrease in the city of Rome and a growth in the rest of the province, generating sprawl and the creation of an extended environmentally unsustainable metropolitan area.

Rome as capital has always been a city of immigrants, formed initially by a century of migration flows from other Italian regions (mostly southern and central) and then, in the last three decades, from abroad (Mudu 2007). Housing thousands of new inhabitants has historically constituted a device of power that has kept large strata of the population outside the "free market." Rome is Italy's capital of evictions, *sfratti* (6,626 eviction orders issued in 2011), and the number of people homeless or in precarious housing conditions is estimated on the order of 5,000–15,000 individuals (Mastrandrea 2004; Cortellesi et al. 2007). In this chapter, I investigate under what conditions and with what effects the right to housing is exercised, focusing particularly on poverty and homelessness, housing policies in the three main periods of urban growth, and the formation of the *periferia,* as well as forms of resistance practiced against the structural housing conditions and speculation-driven policies.

Poverty and Homelessness

> Urban marginality can be defined as the inability of the market economy, or of state policies, to provide adequate shelter and urban services to an increasing proportion of city dwellers, including the majority of the regularly employed salaried workers, as well as practically all people making their earnings in the so-called "informal" sector of the economy (Castells 1983, 185).

The array of terms through which poverty can be discussed is reminiscent of the high variety of words available to stigmatize homosexuality. Similar to the sphere of sexuality, poverty is an important issue in power-related discourses and practices. Poverty does not exist in itself; rather it represents a large range of deprivation processes that include lack of housing and food as the most visible indicators and other factors such as an individual's accentuated marginality in social networks. In recent decades, the debate on poverty has shifted toward focusing on "social exclusion," mainly in Europe, on an "underclass" in the United States, and on *marginalidad* (marginality) in Latin America (Fassin 1996). This shift is justified by the need to rely on multidimensional and relational conceptualizations rather than limiting the analysis to a "simple" lack of resources.[1] These concepts assume three different symbolic topologies of poverty: inside/outside, high/low, center/periphery (Fassin 1996). However, there is little consensus about these concepts, and it has been argued that debates about exclusion and underclass lack a theoretical basis (Fassin 1996; Martinelli 1999). Furthermore, the three concepts suggest a binary social vision that does not take into account social transformations; instead, they contribute to stigmatizing victims of poverty (Fassin 1996). Another relevant definition has been proposed by Wacquant (2008), who identifies "advanced marginality" as the novel regime of sociospatial relegation and exclusionary closure that result from the uneven development of the capitalist economies and the recoiling of welfare states. Poverty cannot be separated from the social processes that produce sociospatial segregation. Thus, in addition to statistics concerning people who sleep in the streets, in parks, or emergency shelters, it is equally important to examine data on the dynamics that transform independent individuals into homeless and vice versa (Tosi 2009). For example, contemporary studies include divorced people earning 2,000 euro a month but who are expected to devote 70 percent of their money to child support and a mortgage. In Rome, there are an estimated 90,000 potential newly poor individuals (Caritas di Roma 2011).

Poverty is a constitutive dimension of homelessness (Rauty 1995); however, homelessness can affect large sections of the population, not only the poor. Rome city government statistics show that of 5,182 homeless assisted by municipal social services in 2002, 64.9 percent were foreigners and 79.2 percent were male. In 2009, 17.0 percent of families claimed they had great difficulty making ends meet, whereas in 2007, they were 15.4 percent (Corriere della Sera 2010). In 1999, social pensions (that is, pensions of about 600 euros per month that the Italian National Social Security Institute pays to individuals over 65 years of age with no income), were requested by 37,212 individuals, 7.5 percent of the population over 65 in Rome (Caritas di Roma 1999), whereas in 2004, these had risen to 61,076 (73.3 percent of them women) and in 2008 to 68,569 (70.8 percent women), respectively, 11.9 percent and 11.4 percent of the population over 65. The number of unemployed in Rome increased in proportion to the national average (between 8 and 10 percent), but youth unemployment (between 15 and 34 years) is particularly high among individuals with high levels of education (71.6 percent compared to the Italian average of 57.4 percent) (Villani 2010).

It has to be recognized that we need to shift our perspective from the "inability of the market economy, or of state policies, to provide adequate shelter" to the "ability" to actively neglect these. Ability should be conceptualized as the will and capacity to conceive and produce particular devices for social control. In Rome, this ability not to provide adequate housing is a historical process that is worth deconstructing.

Home and Housing after 1870 and the Heritage of Fascism

"Free" market and neoliberal policies largely oriented the development of the city after 1870, with the exception of three brief periods under the Pianciani (1872–1874 and 1881–1882), Nathan (1907–1913), and Argan-Petroselli (1976–1981) administrations. At the end of the nineteenth century, popular housing was becoming an important social issue (the construction of the Testaccio neighborhood started in 1883 and San Lorenzo in 1884). In 1903, the institute for popular housing (Istituto Autonomo per le Case Popolari [IACP]) was set up, suggesting that the market-led situation was going to change. Unfortunately, though, due to the opposition of landlords and real-estate companies, the IACP was never able to take a leading role in the popular housing market, except with the building of San Saba in 1920 and a few other examples. The fascist dictatorship (1924–1944) openly favored the upper and middle classes in their housing needs and used any means to ghettoize, remove, and evict the working-class population from the center of the city. *Borgate* were planned and built between 1923 and 1937 to host people that had been evicted from the center as well as the poor. The term *borgate* was used for the first time in 1924 when Acilia was built, 15 km from Rome in a malarial area for the inhabitants evicted from housing near the Roman Forum (Insolera 1993). Insolera clarifies the meaning of *borgata* thus:

> This is a derogatory term that derives from the word *borgo* [village]: it is either a piece of city whose organization is not complete enough to be called a "neighbourhood" or a rural agglomeration which is still blocked by a feudal economic system that hampers its development as a complete organism. *Bor-*

gata is a subspecies of the "borgo": a piece of city in the countryside, which, really, is neither one nor the other (Insolera 1993, 135. My translation).

Aldo Tozzetti (1989) describes the mechanism of surveillance and control set up by the regime for the *borgate*, where the fascists were constantly present, and which were also regularly patrolled by the police. For example, the fascists visited *borgata* Gordiani several times a day, first in the morning to distribute milk, second in the afternoon to offer snacks to the children, and third in the evening for political propaganda. Under the regime, the use of housing as a mechanism of power to control the lower classes was explicit.

The Reconstruction of Rome after World War II and the *Palazzinari*

The situation did not progress much after the Second World War when Rome hosted 35 legal *borgate* (planned by the fascists) and 87 *borghetti*: illegal *borgate* (Tozzetti 1989). The dynamics that led to the emergence of *borghetti* were similar to the ones for the *borgate*. Areas far from the city center were illegally occupied, and shacks or small houses were built on them (Clementi and Perego 1983). From 1947, for almost thirty years, the Christian Democrat Party (Democrazia Cristiana) controlled the municipal government, allied with the same landlords and real-estate speculators active during the dictatorship (Scalera, Talenti, Tudini, Vaselli, Torlonia, Gerini, Chigi, Lancellotti), and additionally supported a new generation of *palazzinari* (Armellini, Bonifaci, Caltagirone, Francisci, Mezzaroma, Toti). A *palazzinaro* in Roman slang is the builder of *palazzine*, a derogatory term for an edifice that does not reach the status of a *palazzo*. In Rome, the term *palazzinaro* refers broadly to housing developers and to owners of several buildings, property speculators that exploit rentals from tenants. The *palazzinari* have always been male figures who emerged in the postwar period as prominent actors in Rome's "development." Their capacity to control city councilors and clerks in municipal technical offices became so strong that they were able to violate the city's master plan or adapt it to their needs. Their widespread failure to respect building regulations resulted in the creation of poor quality houses with few services. A famous example is the Magliana neighborhood built at the end of the 1960s, below the level of the Tiber River, with a high density of houses and no urban infrastructure or public services at all.

After World War II, poverty and poor housing conditions could be "justified" and "accepted" as part of the "reconstruction" rhetoric, but this was no longer plausible at the end of the 1950s when the Italian economy was booming and it became clear that the Christian Democrat Party was not interested in providing decent housing for immigrants, squatters, and poor people. Still, in 1968, the grassroots association Centro cittadino delle Consulte Popolari (Civic Center for Popular Consultations) reported the existence of approximately fifty-seven concentrations of shacks and *borghetti* "hosting" 16,506 families, or 62,351 individuals (Insolera 1993). These shacks formed an arc-shaped constellation between the northeast and the southeast of the city (Mudu 2006a). One study defined Rome city government's management of housing as "against humans" (D'Apice and Mazzetti 1970).

Popular and Illegal Housing and the Making of the *Periferia*

In 1949, Parliament passed two bills aimed at creating thousands of publicly funded apartments (Law No. 43/1949, the Piano INA-Casa, and Law No. 408/1949, the Tupini Law). The *borgate* and *borghetti* did not disappear, though; they increased. Often, after people were moved to new decent housing, shacks were not demolished but were left abandoned and then squatted by new inhabitants. In 1962, the new Urban Master Plan for Rome was approved. Its main goal was to stimulate further real-estate speculation with the intention of developing the city to accommodate up to five million inhabitants (the population at the time was 2,278,882).

At the end of the 1960s, the construction of neighborhoods known as "167" (named after housing Law No. 167 of 1962) began without an organic project. Housing for about 165,000 people was planned and built on the eastern and southeastern side of Rome, the first of which was Spinaceto. The political marginalization linked to *borghetti, borgate,* and slums was reproduced in the large housing blocks built in Tuscolano and Monteverde, Corviale, Laurentino 38, and Torbellamonaca.[2] In each case, these projects were built as single "episodes," not as integrated parts of the city. This is the common trait of all the recently planned and built *periferie*.

In 1977, "the historical" suburban *periferia* of Rome was surveyed and official boundaries established (fifty-five illegal areas covering more than 3,000 ha). Water, sewage, gas, and electricity facilities were provided. In practice, a large portion of the *periferia* was integrated with the rest of the city (Leone 1981). In 1980 alone, four thousand "improper houses" were demolished. The municipality engaged in a massive effort to control the eviction of thousands of people ensuring "from house to house" (*da casa a casa*) mobility, meaning that nobody was evicted if a new place to stay was unavailable (Perego 1981). Following the work carried out by the left-wing administrations between 1976 and 1983, the conditions of marginality of the Roman *periferia* weakened (Martinelli 1995). Suburbs increasingly became places of residence, work, and consumption as well as sites of production of alternative cultures, such as social centers (see Mudu, chapter 16).

Despite the fact that the Plan for Popular Housing Construction started in the 1960s and another followed in the second half of the 1980s, most real housing policy interventions were linked to *abusivismo* (illegal housing construction) that in the 1950s and 1960s became hegemonic. Illegal housing construction means building without legal authorization and a license from local authorities who ensure its conformity to the urban master plan (Brazzoduro 1989). The word *abusivismo* refers to the unusual use of a resource (land), its overexploitation, and a practice benefitting private individuals to the detriment of the whole city (Clementi and Perego 1983). In practice, *abusivismo* generates entire portions of the *periferia,* when production, exchange, and consumption of houses are not guaranteed by public institutions. In the 1960s, *abusivismo* became the ordinary means of house construction, responding—in an illegal way—to the need for accommodation of lower social strata excluded from the market. Retrospective building amnesties (*condoni edilizi*) then ensured the transition of a building's status from illegal to legal. Three such amnesties have been introduced in recent decades: in 1985, 1994, and 2003. Speculation increased the need for housing and generated a completely distorted market where people moved from rent to purchase, and a real "reserve army" of rentable dwellings was kept out of the market. In 1951, 20 percent of Rome's population lived in an apartment they owned; in 2001, the percentage was 65 percent.

In 1951, there were approximately ten thousand vacant dwellings, accounting for 3 percent of all households. After 20 years, their number tripled, and by 1981, vacant dwellings represented 11 percent of the available stock (corresponding to 113,000 apartments). This percentage has since remained stable.

The *Periferia Clandestina* of Immigrants in Rome

In 1953, seventy areas close to Rome's consular roads were slums that hosted immigrants from the center and south of Italy. According to the 1951 census, more than 100,000 people (8.7 percent of the whole population) in Rome were living in "improper housing," such as shacks, caves, basements, warehouses, and garrets. This number decreased in the following years, and in 1961, approximately seventy thousand were considered to be living in improper housing; by 1971, this number had fallen to 20,000. In 1981, the census category of "improper housing" was replaced by "other types of accommodation," and the official statistics thus produced underestimated figures of the most critical housing situations (545 in 1981; 184 in 1991; 1,471 in 2001). Processes of segregation, similar to urbanization patterns in Latin America, Asia, or Africa, are emerging in contemporary Rome (Mudu 2006a, 2006b). The problem of improper housing has not disappeared, as the ghettoization, expulsion, and deportation that the Roma population has suffered demonstrates (Clough Marinaro 2003; see also chapters 3 and 7). Housing settlements defined as improper can be divided into five subcategories: (1) improper accommodation within a house; (2) shantytowns; (3) night shelters; (4) squatting; and (5) homelessness. In addition to these categories, there are the two extreme spaces: prisons and Centers for Identification and Expulsion of illegal immigrants. Fifty years on, albeit with many differences and varying proportions, shantytowns are still being reproduced to house some immigrants. However, unlike in the 1950s, the question of housing for immigrants is entirely absent from the political agenda. Class and ethnic hierarchies as well as social networks produce diverse housing outcomes for migrants. For example, Chinese immigrants never live in shacks, but they are found in overcrowded housing, whereas immigrants from Romania who work in the construction sector are more likely to be homeless or living in a shack.

Intense housing segregation is often linked to a lack of legal residence documents. Approximately eight thousand to fifteen thousand immigrants survive in improper housing or are homeless (Mudu 2006a). Tracking and identifying the most extreme forms of poverty suffered by these groups provides a useful starting point for understanding how segregation processes have spatially and socially expanded, while other patterns have become cyclical. Unlike the 1950s, marginal housing conditions are now scattered across the whole metropolitan area and Rome has record numbers of homeless (Mastrandrea 2004).

The Housing Market in Contemporary Rome

In the last twenty years, neoliberal policies in Rome have been implemented in ways similar to many other cities: (1) the administration of the city is increasingly and openly class-oriented, and upper classes dominate decisions and flows of public money; (2) distribution and circulation of resources (housing is the best example) are not priorities for policies that are aimed at private profit and land valorization; (3) security policies are instrumentally used not to contrast illegal activities but to enforce social control. There are a number of additional features that are instead different from most other cities: the presence of a religious apparatus that is largely allied to neoliberal forces and, as we will examine later, the existence of widespread disjointed forms of resistance that challenge the social order.

The dominance of neoliberal policies has relied on conflicts of interest and corruption as important factors in giving away public housing stock, the heritage of decades of collective investments. In fact, some politicians and their supporters have obtained apartments in the center of the city for the price of a car (Lillo 2007). The last twenty years of local government have seen massive withdrawal of the public sector from the housing market. In 1981, popular housing for rent directly managed by the city authorities and the IACP represented around 17 percent of total housing (Abate and Picciotto 1983). After a decade, the stock of housing owned by the IACP and other public institutions was below 10 percent (Cresme 1995). In the 1990s, public intervention for housing was drastically reduced, so that the percentage of homes owned by the IACP and other public institutions was about 8.2 percent in 2001. The city of Rome, led by center-left coalitions from 1993 to 2008, sold apartments and shops in the city center to buy housing in the suburbs and in other municipalities of the province of Rome, for example, in Lunghezzina, Cinquina, Cerveteri, Anzio, and Pomezia (Mudu

2007). The city government unequivocally refused to pursue a policy of conservation and protection of popular housing, shifting toward supporting financial investments and real-estate speculation. The local policy is set within a similar national context; in fact, real-estate speculation was boosted during the five years of center-right national government between 2001 and 2006 that sold thousands of apartments by creating a company for property sale called *Scip*. The law did not allow local governments to buy housing; it was an exclusively private business (Pilla 2001). According to the Court of Audit (Corte dei Conti), from 1994 to 2003, 71,000 apartments were sold with very poor results (Del Vecchio and Pitrelli 2007); the housing market fell entirely into the hands of speculators. This means that it is impossible to guarantee public housing in most cities, while the market generates social segregation. With very few exceptions (e.g., Pilla 2001; Carlini 2005), newspapers and political parties commented positively on the blanket sale of publicly owned housing (see, for example, Liguori 2007). An expected outcome of this political choice was the possibility of evicting thirty thousand low-income families in ten years, particularly in the metropolitan areas of Rome and Milan (Pilla 2001). The eviction of the old city center inhabitants began under Fascism and continued without interruption after the Second World War (Sonnino 1976). Currently fewer than 100,000 inhabitants live in the center; that is less than one quarter of its residents in 1951 (436,000 inhabitants).

The minimum average prices for selling apartments in different toponymical subdivisions between 2001 and 2011 help to clarify some trends.[3] The range of the lowest values for sale has been reduced and prices have leveled upward. Similarly, the range of maximum prices has been reduced too. This means a more limited supply in terms of prices now than in the past. This leveling has happened mainly in the suburban areas. The houses built in the periphery in the 1950s became semicentral in the 1990s and the increased land value was privatized by selling the apartments to the tenants (whether these were legitimate or not) at very low prices and then resold by the new owners at market prices (Abate and Picciotto 1983; Del Vecchio and Pitrelli 2007). Low-cost housing is mainly concentrated in the eastern part of the city, whereas few people can afford to buy an apartment in most of the city center and in large sections of Municipi (boroughs) 2, 3, and 17. Just over 5 percent of all apartments are in the historical center (Municipio 1) but they are worth approximately 34 billion euro: 23.8 percent of the whole of Rome's real-estate value (Santarpia 2007). Comparatively high prices are also charged in the immediate vicinity of Municipio 20 and the Esposizione Universale di Roma, or EUR, section of Municipio 12. Due to these trends in prices, which partly arose due to buyers' preferences and partly as a consequence of demographic processes, these areas are now mainly inhabited by the upper middle classes.

In Italy, between the mid-1970s and mid-1980s, rent absorbed on average less than 15 percent of workers' salaries. The proportion of expenditure on rent rose slightly in the second half of the 1980s and reached around 18 percent in the first half of the 1990s. Since the mid-1990s, rents have been growing rapidly and constantly, absorbing about 30 percent of employees' salaries at the beginning of the new century. The cost of an apartment remained relatively stable during the 1970s and the 1980s, requiring an average investment of approximately seven years of an individual's income. During the 1990s, the cost of an apartment increased to 14 years' income (Poggio 2009). Since 2001, rent and sale prices have more than doubled, and Rome is the city which has exhibited the highest increase in house prices and the largest gap between the most wealthy and poorest areas (Liquori and Manzella 2003; Giordano 2006). Rome is estimated to be the worst city in Italy in terms of renting possibilities for immigrants: 69.3 percent of their income is spent on rent (CNEL 2010). Renting an apartment in the central or semicentral areas of Rome, and in many peripheral parts, is impossible also for the middle-class population (Ares2000 2002). Families with an annual income of less than 20,000 euros cannot rent an apartment in Rome, where rent now absorbs 44 percent of a family's income, according to estimates by Nomisma (Santori and Ammendola 2005). After 1979, the rent market was regulated by the Equo Canone law (Law No. 392/1978) that capped rents at affordable prices for low- to medium-income tenants. In 1992, a new law in favor of the owners was passed, and in 1998, the rent market was completely liberalized.

In the last five years, 15 percent of public housing residents in Italy have not paid the rent, and in 2004, around forty thousand homes were illegally occupied, constituting 6.73 percent of all housing in the Lazio region (Del Vecchio and Pitrelli 2007). In 2010, in Rome, around forty thousand people applied for public housing (Righetti 2010) and the house stock of Azienda Territoriale per l'Edilizia Residenziale (Ater, formerly IACP) is de facto predominantly supporting middle-class families and not poor people (Del Vecchio and Pitrelli, 2007). In 2008, only 1.5 percent of apartments in Rome (737 of 47,804) owned by Ater were assigned to foreign immigrants (Righetti 2010), and the Province of Rome holds Italy's worst record for evictions: 1 of every 220 families. The largest number of evictions were executed, first, against tenants in arrears (60 percent of cases) and, second, because the rental contract had expired. An average of 2,851 evictions per year were carried out between 1983 and 2011 and the number has since remained stable, while there are more serious oscillations in the number of requests for evictions ordered by the bailiff, which tend to rise when there is an increase in social problems.

Resistance to Housing Policies

Three phases of struggles over housing have emerged in the postwar period. The first went from 1950 to 1960, the second from the late 1960s to 1980, and the third has developed during the last twenty years, with a new dynamic in the last decade. The first phase was principally led by the Partito Comunista Italiano (Italian Communist Party), whereas the second saw the emergence of the extraparliamentary left organizations, especially in the 1970s. Since the end of the 1980s, radical left organizations have surfaced that are not directly linked to any party and have adopted new forms of protest.

After the Second World War, the PCI organized the movement of Consulte Popolari per la Casa (Popular Associations for Consultation on Housing) to obtain services such as electricity, sewage, transport, and schools for thousands of people (Tozzetti 1989). Several neighborhoods were built in the middle of nowhere, 10 km away from the city center, in order to increase the value of the land between them and the city.[4] The main objective of the Consulte Popolari (Groups for Popular Consultation) and Comitati per la casa (Housing Committees) was the recovery of the *borgate* and the integration of all neglected peripheral neighborhoods. The PCI had a twofold attitude, demanding that planning and house building be carried out legally and, at the same time, that the illegal houses built during the weekends by poor southern immigrants be legalized (Tozzetti 1989). In 1961, after a long battle, the fascist Law No. 1092/1939 was revoked. This law had aimed to curb migration to urban centers and denied thousands of Italian migrants, illegally resident in Rome and elsewhere, the possibility of being listed in the population registers. This meant that they could not vote or receive health and welfare assistance (Berlinguer and Della Seta 1976). Between 1963 and 1966, unassigned public housing was squatted in Trullo, San Basilio, and Tufello, representing the end of a long cycle of protest (Tozzetti 1989).

The second phase of the struggle for housing was very intense and produced some of Europe's greatest squatting campaigns ever. For two years until 1971, extensive squatting of empty houses took place, reaching its peak on October 29. For two days, 3,300 apartments were occupied, mobilizing thirteen thousand to fourteen thousand families. Another big wave of squatting occurred in 1974 when hundreds of families camped out in front of city hall for 68 days demanding a house (Comitati autonomi operai di Roma 1976). The struggles of working-class people from the *borgate* converged with broader national protest movements that started in 1968 and lasted throughout the 1970s. While the national association of public housing tenants (Unione Nazionale Inquilini Assegnatari) only promoted squatting of public housing as a means to negotiate with the institutions, extraparliamentary organizations (for example, Autonomia Operaia—Autonomist Workers' Group) targeted also private housing, demanding a rent equal to 10 percent of one's salary. A famous slogan graffitied around the city in the 1970s was "*La casa si occupa, l'occupazione si difende*" ("occupy houses, defend occupation"). These intense struggles cannot be isolated from the climate of social and police violence which prevailed in Italy at the time. The most dramatic episode occurred in the San Basilio suburb of Rome in September 1974, when a radical left-wing activist was killed during a clash between police and squatters. In the mid-1970s, there were four thousand squatted apartments in Rome (Comitati autonomi operai di Roma 1976). The political counterparts recognized as responsible for the lack of housing were identified as: the builders' association (Acer), real-estate firms linked to Fiat, the Banca Nazionale del Lavoro, and insurance firms (Comitati autonomi operai di Roma 1976).

The situation changed in the 1980s, after the integration of the old *borgate* within the city, when the need for housing led many people to squat permanently, not as a means to negotiate with authorities. Coordinamento cittadino lotta per la casa (Citizens' Committee for the Fight for Housing) was created in 1988, and 350 apartments were squatted in San Basilio. In the 1990s, the locus of squatting, particularly for the Movimento di lotta per la casa, was in abandoned public buildings such as schools (fifty schools were squatted by the movement). But, in September 1993—during Rutelli's center-left administration—the Coordinamento cittadino lotta per la casa C occupied the FederImmobiliare complex in Ostia, three large apartment blocks generated by speculation and abandoned for over ten years. This was the first occupation which involved many foreign immigrants (approximately 40 percent of the 220 squatters represented nineteen different nationalities) after the occupation of the Pantanella former pasta factory at Porta Maggiore in 1990. This marks the development of an intercultural social movement in a context where the right to housing for migrants is not recognized in Italy. The most recent case is the Metropoliz squat organized by the Blocco Precario Metropolitano (Precarious Metropolitan Block) in Via Prenestina, since March 2009.

In 1999, the association Diritto alla casa (Right to Housing) was created (and became Action in 2002), denouncing real-estate speculation and the complicity of the city administration in not providing housing for a large share of the population. To complete the picture, it is worth bearing in mind that other associations also operate in Rome: Comitato inquilini del centro storico (Historic Center Tenants' Committee), Comitato popolare di lotta per la casa (Popular Committee for the Housing Struggle), Comitato obiettivo casa (Committee for Housing Objective), Unione inquilini (Tenants' Union). Many associations have networked in recent years to advance joint requests and protests.

Some positive results have been achieved. For example, in September 1999, a "protocol on emergency housing" (*Protocollo sull'emergenza abitativa*) was ratified in Rome, providing 170 billion lire (approximately 85 million euros) to purchase new housing and more funding for six projects and other self-recovery initiatives in various suburbs. Approval and implementation is time-consuming, however, and the housing crisis was intensifying. In 2005, the municipality ratified Resolution 110 on Rome's housing emergency (*Deliberazione Programmatica sulle politiche abitative e sull'emergenza abitativa nell'area comunale romana*),

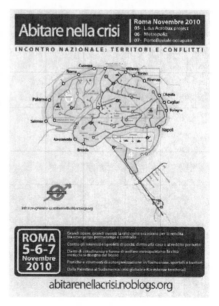

Recent public meetings about housing. *Photographs by the Pierpaolo Mudu.*

which would eventually unlock funds and resources to plan public housing. The new resolution requires each borough to: create a "home for evictees" (*casa dello sfrattato*), providing temporary accommodation; build entire lots of new social housing in the 167 areas; buy houses owned by public bodies that have not yet been sold; provide contributions for rent. Despite some tensions caused by Action's activities, the city government recognized their importance and the center-left mayor Veltroni (2001–2008) requested that Action collaborate with the municipality. In 2005, the Coordinamento cittadino lotta per la casa was even received by a U.N. delegation reporting on housing rights. On the other hand, the housing rights resistance movement was treated with hostility by the center-right parties and the *palazzinari*. In fact, political action by the *palazzinari* intensified (Desario 2009), and in 1996, the daily local newspaper *Il Messaggero* was bought by Caltagirone, while *Il Tempo* was purchased by Bonifaci, both real-estate magnates.

In terms of the population involved in squatting, we can distinguish three typologies. Until the 1970s, squatting was carried out by people living in shanty-towns *(baraccati)* or homeless, whereas during the 1980s, evicted tenants started squatting big public housing units (Transform! 2004). The end of the century marked a further change in the composition of the squatters; these are now not only evicted tenants, but also a variegated set of precarious unemployed, students, and migrants. In fact, in the 1950s and 1960s, the saving model of middle-class families was to rent an apartment, setting aside savings which after a few years were enough to put down a deposit with a constructor. The new apartment could then be let and passed on to the next generation (Giustiniani 1981). This administration model for family budgets went into crisis during the 1970s and was replaced by a model whereby people's savings were invested in thirty-year mortgages to buy the apartment they were living in. This model, which dominated during the following thirty years, could not survive the neoliberalization of the city.

Housing means the creation of a relationship between a society and a particular space, and it is one of the most powerful devices in designing a city. The current ability to generate improper housing has been a long historical process of oppressing lower classes and controlling middle classes. This mechanism of power shifted from being explicit in post-Unitary Rome, during Fascism, and with the Christian Democrats, to an indirect bureaucratic system, nourished by debt (both for mortgages and rent), directed by financial and real-estate speculators. Contemporary Rome is far removed from the modern model of poverty that featured a clear spatial pattern of concentration in *borgate* and *borghetti* created by the authorities or Italy's internal migrants. That poor population, which was supported by political parties and in turn influenced the institutions in the three decades after World War II, has since been abandoned. Foreign immigrants who now constitute a large proportion of the urban poor, have not been supported by political parties. There has been a process of extension and heterogeneitization of poverty and Rome's poor are now a mix of the weakest international migrants and the most vulnerable groups of Italian citizens (those with problems of mental health, alcohol, or income). The numbers are astonishing: forty thousand people applying for public housing (Righetti 2010), five thousand to ten thousand homeless, fifteen thousand evicted or awaiting eviction, four thousand individuals squatting (Mastrandrea 2004). Poverty has a "home" in myriad precarious spaces, disconnected from political institutions and connected through forced mobility of thousands of individuals. There is not a center-periphery dichotomy for the poor, there is just a spiral peripheric condition that can move and locate people at any scale (Mudu 2006a; see also Cervelli, chapter 3). The scale of homelessness includes streets, rooms in basements, riverbanks, roadway bushes; while the scale of popular housing includes large housing blocks dispersed in the metropolitan area of Rome. There is thus no direct relationship between the number of people living in the city and the number and utilization of houses and, moreover, there is a total mismatch between the increase in homelessness and institutional public intervention. The ability to deny housing rights and the progressive spreading of situations of poverty from specific parts of the city to an area that covers the whole province has been met by the refusal of the political class to take on any responsibility, instead transferring the problem to the private market and religious organizations.

The solution to the housing problems of the most deprived individuals that migrated from the south and center of Italy to Rome for a hundred years between 1870 and 1970 is linked to a vast history of struggles led by the Communist Party and by the extraparliamentary left. Currently, foreign immigrants whose interests are not supported by institutional parties have found, at least for housing, the support of grassroots associations such as Coordinamento cittadino lotta per la casa or Action. The struggles of the housing rights movement have intentionally and effectively protected a right recognized by international treaties but violated by governments. Unfortunately, this protection cannot be extended to all those entitled to it. Economic crises are periods that often wipe out social achievements in terms of more equal distribution of resources. In the short term, the housing conditions of the city can only worsen as the most important goal of urban policy has become to mobilize city resources for market-oriented economic growth.

Notes

1. In fact, poverty in official statistics and many discourses is measured and presented in terms of "relative" or "absolute" poverty. In Italy, the relative poverty threshold for a two-member family was calculated by the national statistical institute (Istat) as an average monthly

expenditure per person of 983 euros in 2009. Absolute poverty is calculated as the minimum monthly expenditure necessary for a family to purchase a basket of goods and services considered essential for an acceptable standard of living.

2. Corviale is a building that is almost 1 km long; a "linear city" planned to host 6,500 inhabitants. It was started in 1974 and finished in 1982–1983. The Vigne Nuove neighborhood, built between 1972 and 1979, was planned for 3,400 inhabitants. Laurentino 38 was planned for thirty thousand inhabitants, its construction started in 1975 and finished in 1980. Tor Bellamonaca was a joint public-private venture for twenty-eight thousand inhabitants.

3. These are prices by single square meter and are related to an approximately 100 m² standard apartment on an intermediate storey (Borsa Immobiliare 2011).

4. The neighborhood built by INA-Casa in Valco San Paolo in 1949 favored development along via Marconi, the INA-Casa neighborhood in via Tuscolana generated urbanization between Tuscolana and Cinecittà, other INA-Casa projects were located at Torre Spaccata (the twelfth kilometer of the via Casilina) and Casale Bernocchi (completely isolated and connected by private coaches to Acilia).

References

Abate, Matelda, and Massimo Picciotto. 1983. *La casa a Roma.* Rome: Dedalo.

Ares2000. 2002. *Rapporto sul mercato delle locazioni a più di tre anni dalla riforma (legge n. 431 del 1998).* Rome: Ares. Berdini, Paolo. 2008. *La città in vendita.* Rome: Donzelli.

Berlinguer, Giovanni, and Piero Della Seta. 1976. *Borgate di Roma.* Rome: Editori Riuniti.

Borsa Immobiliare di Roma. 2011. *Listino Ufficiale. Valori correnti di mercato di Roma e Provincia.* Rome: Camera di Commercio Industria Artigianato ed Agricoltura di Roma.

Brazzoduro, Marco. 1989. "L'abusivismo come processo di espansione spontanea della città." In *Abitare a Roma,* edited by Aureli Cutillo Enrica and Mignella Calvosa Fiammetta, 215–248. Milan: Franco Angeli.

Caritas di Roma. 1999. *Disagio e povertà a Roma.* Rome: Anterem.

———. 2011. *Le cifre dell'accoglienza.* Rome: Caritas.

Carlini, Roberta. 2005. "La Roma che conta e quella che costa." *Il Manifesto,* 29 October.

Castells, Manuel. 1983. *The City and the Grassroots.* Berkeley: University of California Press.

Clementi, Alberto, and Francesco Perego. 1983. *La metropoli "spontanea." Il caso di Roma.* Bari, Italy: Dedalo.

Clough Marinaro, Isabella. 2003. "Integration or Marginalization? The Failures of Social Policy for the Roma in Rome." *Modern Italy* 8 (2): 203–218.

CNEL (Consiglio Nazionale Economia e Lavoro). 2010. *Indici di integrazione degli immigrati in Italia.* VII Rapporto. Rome: Consiglio Nazionale Economia e Lavoro.

Comitati autonomi operai di Roma, ed. 1976. *Autonomia Operaia.* Milan: Savelli.

Corriere della Sera. 2010. "Cinque mila senzatetto a Roma, ma la vera povertà dilaga in provincia." *Corriere della Sera,* 4 May.

Cortellesi, Giulia, Paolo Venezia, and Silvia Carelli. 2007. *Casa: Un diritto di tutti.* Rome: Lunaria.

Cresme. 1995. *Radiografia di una metropoli.* Rome: Cresme. D'Apice, Carmela and Giovanni Mazzetti. 1970. *Roma: La città contro l'uomo: Le baracche e gli altri problemi urbani nella loro dimensione storica ed attuale.* Rome: Schirru.

Del Vecchio, Gianni, and Stefano Pitrelli. 2007. "Quel mattone è molto impopolare." *L'Espresso,* 6 December.

Desario, Davide. 2009. "Occupazioni, 80 situazioni sotto stretta sorveglianza." *Il Messaggero,* 2 September.

Fassin, Didier. 1996. "Exclusion, underclass, marginalidad." *Revue française de sociologie* (1): 37–75.

Giordano, Attilio. 2006. "Cercando casa. A tutti i costi." *Il Venerdì di Repubblica,* 24 February.

Giustiniani, Corrado. 1981. *La casa promessa.* Turin: Einaudi.

Insolera, Italo. 1993. *Roma moderna.* Turin: Einaudi.

Leone, Anna Maria, ed. 1981. "Il recupero degli insediamenti abusivi." USPR Documenti n. 1. Rome: Comune di Roma. Liguori, Anna Maria. 2007. "Da Garbatella a viale Togliatti il Comune vende 13 mila case." *La Repubblica,* 23 November.

Lillo, Marco. 2007. "Casa Nostra." *L'Espresso,* 30 August.

Liquori, Alessio, and Gianpaolo Manzella. 2003. "Economia e società a Roma nell'ultimo decennio: I numeri del cambiamento." In *Dieci anni di una capitale,* 155–192. Rome: Donzelli.

Martinelli, Franco. 1995. *Poveri senza ambiente.* Naples: Liguori editore.

Mastrandrea, Angelo. 2004. "La capitale dei senza casa." *Il Manifesto,* 17 November.

Mudu, Pierpaolo. 2006a. "La circonferenza apparente: La periferia romana tra luoghi comuni e non comuni." *Parolechiave* 14 (2): 115–140.

———. 2006b. "Patterns of Segregation in Contemporary Rome." *Urban Geography* 27 (5): 422–440.

———. 2007. "L'immigrazione straniera a Roma: Tra divisioni del lavoro e produzione degli spazi sociali." In *Roma e gli immigrati: La formazione di una popolazione multietnica,* edited by Eugenio Sonnino, 101–149. Milan: Franco Angeli.

Perego, Francesco. 1981. *L'Urbanistica della sinistra in Campidoglio.* Roma: Edizioni delle autonomie.

Pilla, Francesca. 2001. "Mattone pubblico affare privato." *Il Manifesto,* 24 October.

Poggio, Teresio. 2009. "Le principali dimensioni della disuguaglianza abitativa in Italia." In *dimensioni della disuguaglianza in Italia: Povertà, abitazione, salute,* edited by Andrea Brandolini, Chiara Saraceno, and Antonio Schizzerotto, 273–292. Bologna: Il Mulino.

Rauty, Raffaele. 1995. *Homeless.* Genoa, Italy: Costa and Nolan.

Righetti, Chiara. 2010. "La casa popolare resta un sogno." *La Repubblica,* 25 February.

Rossi, Dario. 1959. *Aspetti dello sviluppo demografico ed edilizio di Roma.* Rome: Istituto di demografia.

Santarpia, Valentina. 2007. "Centro storico, roba da ricchi. Un patrimonio da 34 miliardi." *City,* 23 May.

Santori, Aldo and Teresa Ammendola. 2005. *La provincia capitale: rapporto annuale sull'area romana 2004.* Rome: Provincia di Roma.

Sonnino, Eugenio. 1976. "Il movimento della popolazione e lo spopolamento del centro storico di Roma negli ultimi venti anni." *Notiziario ai soci* [newsletter]. Rome: Italia Nostra Sezione di Roma.

Tosi, Antonio. 2009. "Senza dimora, senza casa: note di ricerca." In *Dimensioni della disuguaglianza in Italia: Povertà, salute, abitazione,* edited by Andrea Brandolini, Chiara Saraceno, and Antonio Schizzerotto, 355–367. Bologna, Italy: Il Mulino.

Tozzetti, Aldo. 1989. *La casa e non solo: Lotte popolari a Roma e in Italia dal dopoguerra a oggi.* Rome: Editori Riuniti.

Transform! 2004. *La riva sinistra del Tevere. Mappe e conflitti nel territorio metropolitano di Roma.* Rome: Carta.

Villani, Clementina, ed. 2010. *Mercato del lavoro a Roma 2009–2010.* Rome: Comune di Roma.

Wacquant, Loïc. 2008. *Urban Outcasts.* Cambridge, U.K.: Polity Press.

Part II
Changing Faces, Changing Places

5 Torpignattara/Banglatown

Processes of Reurbanization and Rhetorics of Locality in a Suburb of Rome

Alessandra Broccolini
(translated by Jennifer Radice)

ONE WINTER MORNING in 2010, I was strolling along a street in the Torpignattara neighborhood on the outskirts of Rome, where I have been engaged for some years in an ethnographic study of the Bangladeshi community in the area, when I saw a piece of plastic that had been taken from the rebuilding of a phone center and fixed to a wall. Someone unknown, who obviously wanted to annoy the Bangladeshi community, had written on the piece of plastic the name of a nonexistent street: Via della Banglanella. This very visible sign, opposite the sign with the street's real name—Via della Marranella—was a mocking allusion to the massive colonization of that district by the Bangladeshi diaspora. For the whole morning, this improvised street sign, probably written by an Italian, remained on the street in full view of passersby until someone threw it into a nearby litter bin, where it nevertheless remained very visible for the rest of the day.

It seems to me that this anecdote, relating as it does to old and new names for urban spaces, serves as a good introduction to an essay that considers the new forms of urban settlement initiated by the Bangladeshi diaspora.

Torpignattara, a Roman neighborhood

Torpignattara, a historic district in Rome's eastern periphery, has been the destination during the past fifteen years for large numbers of immigrants, especially from Bangladesh, who have brought about major changes in social life (see also Cervelli, chapter 3). This area, historically working-class and of ill repute, was a place of internal migration from central and southern Italy at the beginning of the twentieth century. In the 1980s, it suffered a progressive fall in its population, owing among other things to a high crime rate. Today the original inhabitants, themselves migrants of an earlier generation, do not recognize the district's new face; they idealize the poverty and insecurity of the past and regard the changes as a "deterioration" brought about by the immigrant presence.

The Bangladeshi community, by contrast, are settling into the area and creating forms of social, economic, and community life that they perceive as positive improvements to the area. It is a form of migration that moves within global and transnational frameworks; yet it is recreating a "locality" between the lines of a diaspora's policy that makes use of mainly Western values—such as "urban regeneration"—as a defense of their own national values.

This process is being defined in particular by leaders of the Bangladeshi community who are trying to refound an urban space (with the assignation of names such as "Banglatown") and to define rhetorically the course to be taken by the diaspora's political mission: to upgrade a rundown area and integrate with Italian social life, bringing to it "traditional" (national and religious) values of "morality" and "dignity."

From the town-planning and social perspective, we can perhaps regard the settlement of Bangladeshi immigrants in Torpignattara as a form of "reurbanization," which bypasses the concept of "gentrification," understood as an upgrading of central areas of a city by the affluent middle classes.[1] Even though we are not considering a central area or the involvement of the upwardly mobile middle classes, the presence of Bangladeshi migrants who are active entrepreneurs and strong supporters of community life represents a form of regeneration which throws light on local sociocultural processes of change within the urban fabric, linked to larger global flows of people, ideas, and values.

Torpignattara is an area where the future in present-day Italy of policies that acknowledge differences and "Italian-style" multiculturalism is at stake (see Grillo and Pratt 2002). Here, perhaps more than elsewhere, processes of regeneration, rhetoric about urban upgrading, the policies of the diasporas, and use of spaces all play a part in mediation and negotiation between the various parties who make this social space into a frontier zone in Italian society.

The Bangladeshi Community in Torpignattara: Depopulation and Repopulation

The influx of Bangladeshis into Torpignattara started in the mid-1990s,[2] in a district that showed strong evidence of an exodus by the original inhabitants. Indeed after the progressive arrival in Torpignattara of migrants from central and southern Italy up to the 1960s and 1970s, its population started to fall in the 1980s owing to its bad reputation, petty crime, and the rundown condition of the housing stock. In 1983, the big fascist-era Cinema Impero (Empire Cinema) closed its

Torpignattara 2011—*Il Cinema Impero. Photo by Alessandra Broccolini.*

doors and today lies idle like a crumbling "monument," waiting to be converted into a shopping center or flats. From 1971 to 2005, the area that now makes up the sixth borough lost around 57,000 inhabitants.[3] At the beginning of 2000, the number of migrants in the area seemed to be constantly increasing, while the number of original inhabitants continued to fall.[4] According to data collected by the Osservatorio Romano on migration into Torpignattara (Caritas Roma 2009, 408ff), 49,117 people lived there in 2005, but by the end of 2009, the number had fallen to 47,500 inhabitants.[5] According to recent, informed estimates from within the Bangladeshi community, there are now about five thousand Bangladeshis in the neighborhood (more than 10 percent of all residents).

This repopulation of a rundown district has had considerable repercussions not only on social behavior, between people of different origins, but has also given the district a "multicultural image"; this has opened a range of scenarios of acceptance, narrow-mindedness, social anxiety, and forms of peaceful coexistence.

Most of the employed in the Bangladeshi community are male, with a gradual increase in recent years of nuclear families. This is a community that for the most part engages in trade, as street sellers or in services such as bartenders, chefs, and pastry-cooks.[6] The majority—mostly males—consists of the "invisibles," young new arrivals who do not speak Italian and who work illegally as street sellers. Then there are a lot of workers and regular employees who work in restaurant kitchens, bars, and workshops. Finally there is self-employment, signifying the achievement of a life objective.

Living in the Banglatown of the *Borghetti:* Torpignattara on a Local and Global Scale

One of the most apt expressions coined by urban sociology to define certain "hybrid" urban spaces was introduced by Giovanni Laino, who, when speaking in the 1980s about the historic center of Naples, defined it from the social perspective as an area that was "as spotted as a leopard" (Laino 1984, 50).

The phrase "as spotted as a leopard" conjures up a picture of spaces that are very mixed not only from the social but also the architectural, urban planning, and above all cultural perspectives, owing to the presence of migrants who try to insert themselves into pre-existing social groups.[7] At a first glance, the urban space characterizing the neighborhood is highly stratified; many "instant" buildings stand next to 1970s conversions into enormous blocks of flats, with uneven pavements and fragments here and there of the urban villages that were inhabited in the postwar years by the lower working classes.[8] In the district, there are four *borghetti* or urban villages, areas with spontaneous and unauthorized buildings (small single-story houses with a patch of garden) that sprang up between the wars.[9] Around these areas, like the leopard's spots, is a scattering of early twentieth-century working-class housing consisting of small but smarter apart-

Torpignattara 2010—What is left of the Marranella *borghetto*.
Photo by Alessandra Broccolini.

ment blocks that are between two and four stories, some of them today in a very poor state, and the ubiquitous 1960s and 1970s "mega-blocks" with eight to ten floors. Scattered around, one can also find semirural buildings, today cottages, that are linked to small plots of land, and some abandoned farmhouses typical of the "agro Romano" (the Roman countryside). Finally, the district counts some important archaeological remains scattered about the Casilino territory: the mausoleum of Saint Helena, the Alessandrino aqueduct, and the catacombs of Saint Marcellinus and Saint Peter.[10]

The Bangladeshis have moved into the network of streets starting from Via della Marranella and continuing along Via Eratostene, Via Pavoni, and Via Maggiolo. The leopard's spots give a good idea of the social and cultural configuration that this area is experiencing.

A young woman working for the government, originally from Calabria, had lived in Torpignattara for about ten years and was trying to move house; she did not like this area with "all those black people" and identified a clear frontier between one street and another; beyond a certain "zone" there were "the blacks," she told me, where she would never go and live. Another woman, also in

The murals at Largo Pettazzoni. *Photo by Alessandra Broccolini.*

the public service, was by contrast very active in the neighborhood committee, created about fifteen years earlier, and had no intention of moving from an area that she loved and considered to be an "important" place from the viewpoint of culture, archaeology, and intercultural dialogue. The closer you move toward Via Prenestina, the smaller the immigrant presence, and, according to the received wisdom, this raises the social status of people living in the seclusion of the apartment blocks. Beyond the frontier, in the "Bangladeshi zone" of Torpignattara, the original inhabitants consist mainly of elderly people, pensioners (former brick-layers or manual laborers of various types, small shopkeepers) and their offspring who have a sentimental attachment to the place. A recently arrived group of new residents is represented by students and single people, attracted by being near Pigneto and by the "multicultural" air of the zone;[11] they live side by side with low-income families from various backgrounds, who in general are less attracted to ideas of cultural "otherness."

The network of streets with a high proportion of Bangladeshis (known to the older inhabitants as the Marranella) has for some years been renamed Ban-glatown by the Bangladeshis themselves: a renaming that indicates, as we shall shortly see, a process of creating a locality that follows the routes of migration with a strong transnational character.

Torpignattara 2010—Provocative graffiti: The spaces' new names and a football fan's irony.
Photo by Alessandra Broccolini.

The commercial activities engaged in by Bangladeshis include groceries, greengroceries, minimarkets, phone centers, service agencies, restaurants, and bars. They show that the diaspora has become well-established in the district,[12] strengthened by the presence of their nuclear families, with children who go to the Carlo Pisacane primary school.[13]

Throughout the streets, the leopard's spots clearly mark out the urban landscape from the cultural perspective. Next to the "historic" "Wines and Oil" shop and the bar that boasts of having been there since 1946, one finds a swarm of people around the money transfer office, phone centers, Indian clothing shops, and Bangladeshi supermarkets that often decorate the streets with posters written in Bengali. These, incomprehensible to the other residents, conjure up a picture of a social life full of concerts of Bengali music, meetings with community leaders, purchase and sale of goods, and trade advertisements.

During the day, the number of people in the streets may fluctuate and activities range from trading, going to school, and using community services; but in the evening, especially in summer, Banglatown is transformed into a place for socializing. Many young Bangladeshi men, when they come back from work, spend the evening on the pavements outside the phone center, drinking beer, chatting

Torpignattara 2010—Streets in *Banglatown*. *Photo by Alessandra Broccolini.*

to each other, and eating *gal muori* or spiced fluffy rice, sold on the streets by their compatriots.

Not far away, the old trattoria Da Francesco, with its austere look, reassures the old residents that change has not yet swept away all their memories and sends out a message of authenticity to the new Italian residents who seek out "the old Rome." They are supplemented by the Roman trattoria Betto e Mary, a temple of "Roman-ness" in the Villa Certosa area, and the Signorini pastry shop, which, because of its sign "founded in 1931," evokes a historical authenticity that needs no comment. But the nearby Punjabi Bar and the Indian-Italian restaurant offer a glimpse of hybridity that makes the original residents feel disorientated and conjures up a very multicultural scenario for the others.

There remain a few somewhat seedy bars, meeting points for elderly men of outmoded appearance, and a few gambling clubs, evidence of what was an unlawful activity in the past. Everywhere the mobile telephone shops, international forwarding agencies, and Internet centers connect the busy lives of others, while on the roofs of the houses (even the most fragile edifices) a forest of satellite dishes make one think, as Appadurai (1996) has written, of the forces that drive "the work of the imagination" toward many people elsewhere, toward other "centers," sought out and reproduced in domestic scenes far away from an old district in the outskirts of Rome.

Torpignattara has a lively social life: there are numerous Bangladeshi associations that print magazines in Bengali, while the local neighborhood committee promotes cultural initiatives and projects for improving quality of life.[14] There are also a local newspaper, two parishes, and the headquarters of various parties.

During the years preceding Bangladeshi immigration, the media used to refer to Torpignattara in disparaging terms, owing to local crime in Rome that was linked to the "Marranella gang."[15] But it was after the arrival of the Bangladeshis from the mid-2000s that the media began to portray the district in terms of conflict and intolerance. In April 2007, for example, Torpignattara was shaken by news reports on the difficult relationship between the original inhabitants and the Bangladeshis. The murder of a Bangladeshi man by a Sardinian, arising out of a quarrel in a condominium in the Alessandrino *borghetto*, provoked discussion and demonstrations on the dangers of racism.[16] More recently, the media have reported a number of incidents of violence against Bangladeshis, carried out in Torpignattara by "original" inhabitants.[17] All these episodes were reported by the media in terms of racial aggression, thus suggesting a bleak urban scenario, brought about by problems of coexistence, which were presented as typical of the entire area.

Torpignattara was back in the news again in 2010 with an article in *La Repubblica* that raised the specter of a suburb in danger. According to the article, the influx of Bangladeshis into Torpignattara was putting a strain on the community and thus increasing the risk of clashes. The large presence of migrants in a suburban neighborhood caused the media to talk up the existence of a conflict, in terms of both racism and "retaliation" and to decry problems of "blight" and "infestation" without examining the dynamics and context of the situation.

> From 1997 to 2007 the number of immigrants in this district has risen by 81%. In some streets you see almost only Bengalis with their food shops and internet centers. . . . There is a very tense atmosphere. "We are no longer in our own home," say the Italians, who accuse the Bengalis in particular of making the town dirty, making a noise far into the night outside their shops, infesting the condominiums with their smells of garlic and other spices. . . . There have been assaults in the foreigners' shops. Up till now the Bengalis, most of them born in Italy, have not reacted, but there is the danger that one spark may trigger an explosion. Our research indicates that this district is one of the most at risk. This is a dangerous suburb.[18]

Urban Upgrading and the Bangladeshis: Leadership and Rhetoric in the Locality

In contrast to portrayals by the media evoking the image of the suburbs and in contrast also to the original inhabitants' nostalgia for an "authentic" district that no longer exists, what the Bangladeshi community have to say about their neighborhood clearly identifies the positive and beneficial role that they have played in an area seen in the past as impoverished, beset by petty crime, and barely active in commercial life. What emerges is a concept of urban, social, economic, and moral regeneration, upheld by the moral and cultural values of their nation.

Those who call themselves the leaders of the community by virtue of a political and economic authority built up over time represent their own migratory history within the concept of a community that is growing on Italian territory. An ethos of "hard-working people" and the moral values attributed to their "national" culture and to Islam are displayed as signs of economic, moral, and cultural advancement: this makes the diaspora an engine, reestablishing the space where they arrived within a concept of national belonging. In this sense, the Bangladeshi leadership is trying to reestablish an urban space (with place-names like Banglatown) and to define the parameters of a genuine political mission for the diaspora: positive "colonization" of a rundown area and assimilation into Italian social life, bringing the "traditional" (national and religious) values of morality and dignity.

The figure of Asraf, a Bangladeshi leader who lives in Torpignattara, is a good example. Asraf is a man of about 50 years, strong, smartly dressed, and always smiling. He lives in Torpignattara with his wife, who has a shop in the same district selling traditional Bangladeshi and Indian clothes. He sees himself as a leader, runs an association, engages in import/export business, organizes events, and supplies various services to members of the community. He defines himself as right-wing, a member of the Bangladesh Nationalist Party.

The romantic and nationalist language used by Asraf, who is aware of his political and cultural role, is symptomatic of the diaspora's mission within a lively political dynamic that links these migrants to their country of origin in more than one way. As leader of a new diasporic generation, Asraf moves within a global framework through different worlds and different centers. His language, inspired by a nationalist mission that is infused with the moral values of dignity and honor, uses romantic concepts that are strongly essentialist:

> In Torpignattara there is a large Bangladeshi community. That means that we need true professionals who can help us to fight for our rights. I devote myself to the Bangladeshi community; the community needs management, it needs professionals who will one day be capable of acting. . . . This community of ours is big. They need guidelines and leadership. And since we are not Italians, we must represent our country here. We must have an honorable identity. If a Bengali commits a robbery or is a criminal, people tar us with the delinquency brush and say that Bengalis are a bad lot. We in Rome can say proudly that the Bangladeshi community is the only one that co-exists very harmoniously and acts as one body (28 April 2010).

As for the Torpignattara district, Asraf outlines the positive contribution made by the Bangladeshi presence and clearly depicts the role of "control" of the territory operated by various different "leaders":

> We are well known as a community and have a good relationship with everyone, because thanks to our social engagement the Bangladeshi community does not commit much crime. This part of the community in this neighborhood is fairly peaceful and lives respectably. This zone is inhabited by our community; we who live in this district feel as if we were more in Bangladesh than in Italy. Do you know that we in this district named the area Banglatown three years ago? The name existed before then, but only among ourselves. Now our kids, our own kids, have got a football team together in this district, called Banglatown Friends. Since we feel that we are living in Bangladesh, we want to promote our own culture, the culture of our society. We have women, families, children. I want my daughter and my wife to go about the district in peace without being hassled. . . . In this area we do not have full control of society. We have had to work to obtain it. In the past this area seemed to be out of control. I represent an association. We settled here in 2007. Torpignattara at that time seemed to have no guardian, nobody who was committed to watch and to intervene, things were very different then. But in the recent years of our presence we have managed to overcome obstacles of this kind. In recent years I have seen that the district has been pacified.

This interesting process of creating the leadership of the Bangladeshi diaspora takes place within the dynamics of Bangladeshi national politics, in that the leaders are linked to the two main political parties of Bangladesh and to the country's political and administrative organization. The chairmen of local government in rural areas in Bangladesh (known as unions and Upazila councils) have the same title of "leader." In the Italian (and Roman) diaspora, the Bangladeshis reproduce the system of leaders that exists in their national division of territory, but they do it through cultural associations, each one ruled by a leader (chairman) who governs a territory. The close attachment to associations that informs the social, cultural, and economic life of the Bangladeshi diaspora echoes Bangladesh's two main political parties: the Bangladesh Nationalist Party (a center-right nationalist party, anticommunist, liberalist, and Islamist) and the Bangladesh Awami League (a social democratic party of the center-left).

The Bangladeshi settlement in Torpignattara is ruled by leaders who are heads of various "associations" that have a base in the district with shops, service agencies, and so on. With the increase in the number of Bangladeshi migrants in Rome, the first association, created in 1994 and which represented all Bangladeshis in Italy, broke up. From this breakup, there emerged various associations (today around fifty, sometimes in disagreement among themselves concerning the leadership) which, up until now, have not acquired a hierarchical structure but are horizontal and territorial creations. Thus the leaders of the diaspora are scattered in all the Italian towns where there are Bangladeshi communities. The Bangladeshi leaders speak also of a "management" of the community, made up of an ensemble of leadership in Italy, each one equal to the others; these leaders form a network in the name of defending Bangladeshi national values, helping their compatriots but also controlling the "morals" of "our boys," the safety of the community's members and its relationships with Italian society. This management boasts that it has succeeded in keeping "the community" away from the degraded fabric of Italian society that pervades the territory.

Many Bangladeshi traders in Torpignattara are aware that they have been a beneficial presence in the district, bringing about the reopening of shops and the return of a wholesome social life. Khan, a Bangladeshi trader about 30 years old, is a very industrious young man. He said to me explicitly:

> When we arrived here there was nothing but crime and closed shops. We have rebuilt the life of the district and have caused local property prices to rise again. Yesterday the Italians let properties to us that nobody wanted to rent; today their offspring feel regret and quarrel with their parents because accommodation costs more (18 March 2010).[19] Mukhtar, who is a chef and lives in Torpignattara with his wife and two children, is of the same opinion, and, in his conversation, introduces the image of light and dark to define, in visual fashion, his opinion concerning the beneficial effect of the arrival of the Bangladeshis in the district:
>> Beforehand there was no light here, when I arrived there was no light, it was completely dark. Now there is light, one can walk about, we feel safer. When I arrived here ten years ago it was practically dark in this area, I re-

member it well, there was just one bar, we always went there, but the street was always dark, not like now when it is well-lit and there are always people about. Then lots of foreigners arrived. Now there are nearly 5,000 just from my own country (22 May 2010).

The image of light and dark, referring to the presence of commercial activities in the district, becomes a metaphor of social life and of a positive view of the arrival of "peasants" in urban space. Babu is 47 years old and has a travel and services agency with its headquarters in Torpignattara. He too has similar things to say about the district:

> I got to know Torpignattara in 1990. I came here to visit a friend and when I went to his house it was completely dark, there was nobody about and none of my countrymen. Now when I came this month I found, as it were, a town called Little Bangladesh, like those who live here and call this district Banglatown. It used to be completely dark because at first there were no street lamps, not so many inhabitants, not so many immigrants, that's what the darkness meant. Now if I go out of my shop I meet three or four of my countrymen. Today most of my countrymen want to live in this area, they want to work here. (15 April 2010)

Rony is 40 years old and has a degree in political science from a Bangladesh university. In Italy, he organizes Bangladeshi cultural events. Editor of a newspaper and founder of the Italian Institute of Bengali Culture, which has its office in Torpignattara, Rony promotes and organizes Bangladeshi culture in the diaspora in essentialist and nationalistic forms. He too emphasizes that the Bangladeshi presence has brought security and well-being to the district:

> The Bangladeshi community started coming to Rome between 1987 and 1990. After 1990–1992 some of them acquired houses in Torpignattara. Why did we go there? At first it was too dark, there were no people about, it was such a shit district, armed gangs, prostitution, drugs, drug dealers, the lot. Most people there were criminals, if you got off the 105 bus you wouldn't keep your wallet for more than three seconds. Ordinary people like working women or students never went there, neither during the day nor in the evening. But the Bangladeshi community, since many of them were arriving with their families, needed somewhere nearby to live. And they all went to Torpignattara because they saw that accommodation was very cheap; this was because here there were no conventions, no municipal regulations for building blocks of flats, everything was unauthorized. So the district became famous for us because it was cheaper. That's how Torpignattara has now become the unique district, the most famous one in Rome, we community leaders say. And that's how it has gradually become a big community. (15 May 2009)

According to Rony, this process of urban regeneration is linked to the Bangladeshis' economic needs, but also to their moral values that are presented as national virtues. A Bengali, says Rony, citing a general example, would never request help from an organization outside his community; he would rely on the community to support him:

> Let's take an Italian boy of 20 with his mother and father here; he's 20 years old, doesn't work and doesn't care a bit. Because he's got a home, he's got food, he has no expenses, Mum and Dad give him everything. But a Bengali who arrives here can't relax, he has to pay the rent every month, then he owes money for his journey here, he has to eat, he needs a minimum of 500 euro to support himself. He even has to remit money to his family, he has to work like a high-speed train, not a slow one. Now this 18-year-old Bengali will have 10,000 euro in his pocket by the time he is 30. No Bengali would seek help from Caritas, he would turn to his own community, he wouldn't go to Caritas because he would feel uneasy at the prospect. But an Italian graduate of 30 is still looking for work. (15 May 2009)

Counterhegemonic Regeneration, Essentialism, and Cultural Hybridization

Men such as Asraf, Rony, Babu, Mukhtar, and many others are pioneers who are perhaps unaware of a counterhegemonic process of cultural settlement, but they are also representatives who are conscious of a diasporic community that, in activating settlement politics in a national and local territory, redefines itself in essentialist and nationalist forms. The positions of those who act as spokesmen prompt a series of questions that relate to what we may call, from urban planning and social perspectives, a form of "regeneration" of Rome's suburbs: a process that as well as generating change, bypasses dominant and hegemonic values such as urban regeneration, usually attributed to the middle and upper segments of the original inhabitants.

Even though the percentage of Bangladeshis in Torpignattara is no higher than that of "original" inhabitants or other migrants, the area is in fact well known as Banglatown. Some of the media have noticed this, and television dramas have already been shot in the "Via della Banglanella"; it is predictable that other media products, documentaries, and reportages about this area will soon be produced, reinforcing the district's multicultural image. The consequence of this will probably be that groups of young people will be attracted to the area, to the annoyance of the original low-income families and the elderly working class who at present are not happy to live side by side with economically successful migrant groups.

It is perhaps not the task of the anthropologist to establish whether or not a settlement process falls into a category borrowed from town planning (upgrading, regeneration, renewal, etc.), nor to identify objective parameters that do or do not relate to the improvement of quality of life. Our purpose as anthropologists is rather to analyze these dynamics in the context of cultural identity-building and to elaborate on the reflections that this provokes within the theme of identity politics.

Nevertheless, this "regeneration" process has the effect of overturning those Western values that portray migrant communities as occupying a marginal position, with a precarious social status and little money. If the idea of urban regeneration is associated with the presence of the middle and upper classes, who upgrade the area by bringing in new facilities and a token amount of new capital (and pushing out lower classes and immigrants), then the economic and "moral" rise of the Bangladeshi community in the district, even if it functions by virtue of the "identity" rhetoric of leaders who are well placed in relation to the diaspora, puts a strain on that Western "global hierarchy of values" (Herzfeld 2004) which expects migrants from developing countries to be globally marginalized, passive, and alienated from the main power centers. Such a process goes well beyond Torpignattara and extends to the whole urban space in the era of global migration. If the concept of gentrification is associated by urban planners with selective improvement that is created by middle- and upper-class Westerners, how can we interpret a process of regeneration that is acknowledged to be on the rise but has been created by a diaspora from one of the poorest countries in the world?

As well as creating a short circuit in terms of dominant values, the process underway in Torpignattara opens up new dynamics in relations with the original population, offering the prospect of scenarios that move from the implementation of hybrid practices to forms of cultural essentialization, but also include conflict and resistance from both parties. All this also generates marked changes in the original population: in some cases, they manage to defend their power and authority, dictating the economic (e.g., renting of properties) and cultural conditions of the district, whereas in other cases, they have to defend themselves against the new owners of their houses and new practices.

In an earlier essay on Torpignattara (Broccolini 2009), I told the story of an old greengrocery in Banglatown, a historic shop run by a Roman and patronized by a great many of the original inhabitants; when the shop was taken over by a Bangladeshi, it became visibly deserted. For some time, I have noticed that the shop has returned to the Roman's ownership; in order to indicate to the original inhabitants that the shop has been "repatriated" to Italian ownership, the shopkeeper has put a large notice outside the shop that says "under former management." This is an interesting reversal of values in commercial communication (generally such notices say "under *new* management"), which presumes a code of shared values (we Romans are back) and which we can take as the metaphor of a form of wearied resistance on the part of the original residents, who fail to hide their feelings about a new emerging form of marginality.

It is difficult to foresee how in the future the so-called second generation of Bangladeshi immigrants (at present still of school age) will understand the district: Will they reinforce the diaspora's frontiers in more rigid and politically organized forms? Or will the practices of hybridization reduce the ethnic element in their social life? I have always found it remarkable and very allegoric, almost a "historical nemesis," that the Banglatown settlement should establish itself right around that abandoned monument called Cinema Impero, a large fascist-style building that with its still legible insignia dominates the streetscape like a ruin from the colonial past. Still more remarkable is the fact that this settlement is being presented as having benefited and improved an area with such a bad reputation: The "Empire" decays but its "impure" fruits are being born and are growing up around it, reclaiming the surrounding territory. As Clifford (1993, 29) once put it, "the victims of progress and of the empire are weak, but rarely passive."

Notes

1. On gentrification from the social and town planning perspective, see Piccolomini (1993), Semi (2004), and Annunziata (2007, 2008, 2011)

2. Officially, the number of Bangladeshis in Italy is 65,556, 11,500 of them in Lazio, mostly concentrated in Rome. In the migration chain, the Bangladeshis (usually young men) start off as street traders in the black market; next, they go to work in restaurant kitchens as dishwashers, sales assistants in markets, barmen, or workmen, and then as cooks; then, if they are successful, they become entrepreneurs or self-employed small shopkeepers. These migrants dream of reuniting their families, being self-employed in a business, and returning to Bangladesh toward the end of their lives for their old age.

3. Statistics Office of Rome city council; see *ViaVai*, February 2007, p. 2.

4. In 2006, the sixth municipality lost 5,000 more inhabitants (falling from 129,000 to 124,000), but the number of migrants rose from 9,600 in 2002 to 12,000 in 2006. In 2008, the area lost a further 1,000 "old" inhabitants (falling to 123,000), but the number of migrants rose to 14,000.

5. Statistics Office of Rome city council—written in the register on 31 December 2009.

6. There are no specific writings later than the mid-1990s about Bangladeshi migration to Rome. This was when the geographer Melanie Knight, at the time of the first Bangladeshi arrivals, studied their economic activities in Rome. She identified in the particular structure of the migratory chain one of the factors (people-trafficking organized by various regional dealers) that drove immigrants toward Rome. However, Knight focused on the economic aspect of the "network economy"; she did not take into account the political dynamics of the diaspora and its repercussions on the construction of a "locality" in a specific territory (Knight 1997). A book about Bangladeshi migration to Rome, specifically in the area of the sixth municipality, has been published very recently (Pompeo 2011); see also Riccio (2007) on Bologna.

7. Various areas of Rome's outer suburbs, also "as spotted as a leopard," contain conglomerations that are characterized by marked social stratification and rapid change. You can wander from one street to the next, from one block of flats to the next, and sense a marked change in horizons, inhabitants, and landscapes.

8. Concerning Torpignattara, there are some studies from oral sources that relate to the World War II period (Ficacci 2007) and some authentically local writings (Sirleto, 2002; Dionisi and Della Pietra 1994). See the classic study by Ferrarotti (1970) for more information about suburbs and urban villages in postwar Rome.

9. Alessandrino *borghetto,* next to the Alessandrino aqueduct; the Angeli *borghetto,* joined to the *Villa Certosa;* and the *borghetto* of Marranella.

10. By "Casilino territory," I mean the area along the Via Casilina that in ancient times was called "Ad Duas Lauros," once a property of the Emperor Constantine, which today is part of the old Roman Campagna measuring about 140 ha; here, in addition to the archaeological remains that I have mentioned, is a 12-ha public park called Villa de Sanctis, the Centocelle park, and many private plots with abandoned farmhouses.

11. Il Pigneto is a historic Roman suburb next to Torpignattara, well known in the latter area because in the past 10 years it has undergone a considerable amount of gentrification, already studied by sociologists, town planners, and anthropologists; see Annunziata (2008, 2011) and Scandurra (2007).

12. I have written elsewhere about the commercial activities of Bangladeshis in Torpignattara and the relationship between old and new residents (Broccolini 2009). According to a mapping of commercial activities that I carried out in 2007, about 25 percent of the shops in the Banglatown area are run by Bangladeshis.

13. This school has for years been at the center of controversy and political debate because of its high percentage of immigrants' children. For further details, see Vereni, chapter 6.

14. A spontaneous and nonpolitical association of original residents, formed in 1996.

15. This was a criminal group that was generally supposed to have risen from the ashes of the more famous "Magliana gang," who went in for robbery, loans at extortionate rates, and drug-dealing.

16. E. Ranalletta, "Dopo l'omicidio di Via Niutta, imponente corteo contro il razzismo," *ViaVai,* May 2007."

17. In April 2009, a Bengali boy was robbed and beaten up in Torpignattara by Italians ("Raid razzista contro un bengalese a Tor Pignattara" [Racist attack on a Bengali at Tor Pignattara] 1 April 2009, www.abitareaRome.it [accessed 20 January 2011]). In March 2010, some Bangladeshi boys were attacked in the same area by about 20 young Italians ("Aggressione razzista a Torpignattara" [Racial attack in Torpignattara], 29 March 2010, www.abitareaRome .net [accessed 20 January 2011]).

18. The article reports data from research carried out by the sociologist Stefania Della Cueva of the Catholic University of Milan. J. Meletti, "Gang, palazzi ghetto e poco lavoro. La mappa delle banlieue d'Italia," *La Repubblica,* 12 May 2010.

19. In some cases, I have used a pseudonym for my Bangladeshi interlocutors.

References

Annunziata, Sandra. 2007. "Se tutto fosse gentrification: Possibilità e limiti di una categoria descrittiva." In *Territori della città in trasformazione: Tattiche e percorsi di ricerca,* edited by Alessandro Balducci and Valeria Fedeli, 165–187. Milan: F. Angeli.

———. 2008. "Urbanità e desiderio." In *Tracce di quartieri: Il legame sociale nella città che cambia,* edited by Marco Cremaschi, 66–82. Milan: F. Angeli.

———. 2011. "The desire of ethnically diverse neighbourhood in Rome. The case of Pigneto: an example of integrated planning approach." In *The Ethnically Diverse City,* edited by Frank and John Eade, pp. 601–623. Berlin: Berliner Wissenschafts-Verlag.

Appadurai, Arjun. 1996. *Modernity at Large: Cultural Dimensions of Globalization.* Minneapolis: University of Minnesota Press.

Broccolini, Alessandra. 2009. "Lavorare a Banglatown: Attività commerciali e relazioni interculturali nella periferia Romana di Torpignattara." In *Identità mediterranea ed Europa: Mobilità, migrazioni, relazioni interculturali,* edited by Maria Rosaria Carli, Gioia Di Cristoforo Longo, and Idamaria Fusco, 243–298. Naples: Consiglio Nazionale delle Ricerche Istituto di Studi sulle Società Mediterraneo.

Caritas Italiana. 2009. *Immigrazione: Dossier Statistico 2009.* 19° rapporto sull'immigrazione. Rome: Edizioni Idos.

Caritas Roma. 2009. *Osservatorio Romano sulle Migrazioni: Quinto Rapporto.* Rome: Caritas.

Clifford, James. 1993. *I frutti puri impazziscono. Etnografia, letteratura e arte nel secolo XX.* Turin: Boringhieri.

Dionisi, Davide., and Gennaro. Della Pietra. 1994. *Torpignattara I luoghi della memoria.* Rome: Circolo Culturale Ricreativo SS. Marcellino e Pietro.

Ferrarotti, Franco. 1970. *Roma da capitale a periferia.* Bari-Rome: Editori Laterza.

Ficacci, Stefania. 2007. *Torpignattara: Fascismo e Resistenza in un quartiere Romano.* Milan: F. Angeli.

Grillo, Ralph, and Jeff Pratt, eds. 2002. *The Politics of Recognizing Difference: Multiculturalism Italian-Style.* Ashgate: Aldershot. Italian edition. 2006. *Le politiche del riconoscimento delle differenze: Multiculturalismo all'italiana.* Rimini, Italy: Guaraldi.

Herzfeld, Michael. 2004. *The Body Impolitic. Artisan and Artifice in the Global Hierarchy of Value.* London: The University of Chicago Press.

Knight, Melanie. 1997. "Migrants as Networkers: The Economics of Bangladeshi Migration in Rome." In *Southern Europe and the New Migration,* edited by R. King and R. Black, 113–137. Brighton, U.K.: Sussex Academy Press.

Laino, Giovanni. 1984. *Il Cavallo di Naples: I Quartieri Spagnoli.* Milan: F. Angeli.

Piccolomini, Michele. 1993. "The Gentrification: Processi e fenomenologie dell'urbanizzazione avanzata." *Sociologia e Ricerca Sociale* (40): 49–75.

Pompeo, Francesco, ed. 2011. *Pigneto-Banglatown: Migrazioni e conflitti di cittadinanza in una periferia storica Romana.* Rome: Meti Edizioni.

Riccio, Bruno. 2007. "Processi di trasformazione urbana e costruzione di confini: Migranti dal Bangladesh e dal Pakistan nel centro di Bologna." In *Mappe urbane: Per un'etnografia della città,* edited by Matilde Callari Galli, 105–123. Rimini, Italy: Guaraldi.

Scandurra, Giuseppe. 2007. *Il Pigneto: Un'etnografia fuori le mura di Rome. Le storie, le voci e le rappresentazioni.* Padua, Italy: Cleup.

Semi, Giovanni. 2004. "Il quartiere che (si) distingue: Un caso di gentrification a Torino." *Studi culturali* 1 (1): 83–107.

Sirleto, Francesco. 2002. *La Storia e le memorie: Il Municipio VI del comune di Roma. Un territorio, la sua storia, le memorie dei suoi protagonisti sconosciuti.* Rome: ViaVai.

6 Foreign Pupils, Bad Citizens

The Public Construction of Difference in a Roman School

Piero Vereni
(translated by Jennifer Radice)

A PRECISE QUANTIFICATION OF the presence of foreigners seems to be one of the main worries of Italian political institutions. "How many are they?" is a common question even in public schools. The Ministry of Education considers it extremely important to set apart Italian pupils from those "of non-Italian citizenship" independently of their actual linguistic competence and their level of socioeconomic integration (Miur-Ismu 2011a, 2011b). This quantitative attitude certainly derives from the "blood" principle of Italian citizenship, according to which one is Italian or foreign based on the nationality of one's parents, notwithstanding one's place of birth (i.e., the *ius sanguinis* principle). Yet the deeper reason for this fixation on numbers also relates to a more widespread social anxiety toward otherness felt by ordinary Italians, caused by a very rapid demographic change still underway. After a century of emigration, Italy became a receiving country during the 1970s (Colombo 2004) without being socially and politically ready for this unexpected turn. The number of incoming migrants has only accelerated since the turn of the millennium. Facing an unanticipated growing foreign presence, Italian institutions set in motion a numbering strategy which is readily understandable, since the objective annotation of sheer numbers constitutes a "minority" as a politically controllable entity and reinforces the status of the "majority" that is in charge of counting (Appadurai 2006).

This defensive attitude has been mirrored by Italian legislation, which has tied immigration with securitization by positing an almost necessarily positive correlation between the *numbers* of foreigners and the idea of social *danger*. Local incidents and contextual situations have been reconfigured (Herzfeld 1997, 2003) to the institutional and national level through their numerical dimension. Starting from the assumption that foreigners are indeed a social problem, quantification has been presented not only as a possible analytical tool, but sometimes as the real solution: *Count* them, and you will be able to *limit* them.

But how does this occur in practice? In the case presented here, it will be shown that the negative social connotation associated with a primary school on the outskirts of Rome was first "ethnicized" in numerical terms and then transformed into a question of national identity, via the efforts of various interested parties and institutions: the "local moms," worried about their children's schooling; the school's various management teams; the regional directors of education; the local councilor for public education; a member of the Italian parliament; and, finally, the minister for public education. The thread connecting these individuals was formed first by the borough itself (with which all of them had a personal connection, except for the minister) and second by a series of personal links of acquaintanceship and friendship that constituted a channel of communication. Once this channel between the local and institutional level was established, it was very difficult for alternative versions to reach any public space; they were relegated to the margins and regarded as utopian or indeed mendacious portrayals.

An Ill-Starred School

The number of pupils without Italian citizenship in Italian schools has increased steadily in the last decade and recently reached the level of 7.9 percent of the total number of pupils (Miur-Ismu 2011a, 5), although clearly these statistics synthesize completely different situations: Some schools have almost no foreign pupils while others have a very visible multiethnic presence. In the Torpignattara district, in Rome's eastern periphery, the Carlo Pisacane school is famous for the fact that more than 80 percent of pupils are technically foreigners, as they do not have an Italian passport, even though the great majority were born in Italy or arrived there before they were of school age and thus speak Italian just as well as children of the same age who are native speakers. In short, we are talking about a school attended for the most part by bilingual children whose parents are immigrants, and where the number of Italian pupils is much lower than the national average and than the presence of Italians in the district. The Carlo Pisacane school currently has 140 pupils, of whom 115 are foreigners and only 25 Italians, divided among nine classes, two in each year except for year 2, which is unique for reasons that we shall see shortly.

How can it be that *no* other primary school in the district has ever had more than 30 percent of pupils per class with a foreign passport, while at the Carlo Pisacane school, the same figure in the last decade has never fallen below 80 percent? To answer this question, we need to start with an observation that few people have made in facing up to the "peculiarity" of the Pisacane school, namely the words of Maria Grazia Cascio, a teacher at the school:

I personally think that what should arouse our concern at Pisacane school is not the presence of foreign children: that is absolutely predictable, they live round here, all of them are our neighbors so naturally they come to this school. What should arouse our concern, but does not . . . , is the fact that the Italian families have gone away; indeed the Italians are saying, send our children to that school? We'd rather take them to another school by car in the morning.[1]

The reasons for the lack of Italian pupils are complex: some may be linked to Italy's legal system, others derive more from the local context. Before we set the Pisacane story in the social context of the district, let us take a brief look at the legal framework for teaching the second generation of immigrants.

Immigrant pupils in Europe have an overall lower school performance than do native pupils. Immigrant pupils drop out or have to repeat a year more frequently and, in secondary school, are concentrated in lower-level institutions (Ricucci 2008). This distance between newcomers and natives lessens in the second generation—pupils born of foreign parents who received their entire "secondary socialization" (primary school attendance and formation of a group of peers) in the receiving country—who score in between the two previous groups in their educational achievement (Di Bartolomeo 2011).

This also holds true for Italy, with the addition of some special features relating to the Italian legal system. Although the rights of foreign minors are formally safeguarded by Italian legislation (which requires compulsory schooling for all minors notwithstanding their residency status, the possibility to enroll at any time of the year, and the right of pupils not to be in a class with an excessively high number of children), these principles often do not lay down clear instructions for their implementation (Liddicoat and Díaz 2008). As a consequence, schools know quite well *what* they are supposed to offer in terms of rights for their pupils, yet they do not know *how* to fulfill those legal expectations (Ricucci 2008, 453) and "teachers, especially head teachers, are increasingly worried about the practical applicability of the legislative provisions" (Gilardoni 2011, 452). In this context of uncertainty concerning the application of regulations in practice, the minor case of the Pisacane school has risen from the working-class suburbs of Rome to the national level.

Up until the 1950s, most inhabitants of Torpignattara were laborers, clerical workers, and shopkeepers. Rapid urbanization in the postwar period led to a worsening of social conditions in the whole of Rome, with consequences that were most evident in the suburbs. From the 1960s onward, an image of local crime, linked to prostitution and an increase in drug-dealing, began to be associated with Torpignattara; the general perception was that most criminal activity took place around Via della Marranella (see also Broccolini, chapter 5), where the Pisacane school is situated.

Before 1969, Pisacane, built in 1928, was the only school in the district, but the very rapid growth in the number of children enrolled (these were the years of the Italian baby boom as well as rapid urbanization) led to the construction of a second primary school, the Grazia Deledda, on the south side of the Via Casilina. This is one of the radial roads that cross the city and the neighborhood developed along it.

The Pisacane school, simply by virtue of its geographical location, began to have a more and more negative image among residents as the "school for the local crooks." For reasons of social distinction, anyone who could manage to, sent their children to Grazia Deledda, thus triggering a downward spiral in which Pisacane gradually became known as the school for "those Marranella types."

From the 1980s, the population of the neighborhood began to fall, owing to the demographic crisis that affected many areas across Rome. The low demand for housing and the Marranella district's bad reputation kept property prices very low, whereas they began to rise in other parts of the district, such as Pigneto (Pompeo 2011). Immigrants arriving from the late 1980s onward found that the Marranella area was just what they wanted. Prices were low and young foreign workers found that the trains going along Via Casilina were a good (if spartan) way of getting to the historic city center, where they often worked in bars and restaurants (Pompeo 2011). Following the five successive amnesties enacted under Italian law between 1990 and 2009,[2] many of them obtained a residence permit that allowed family members to join them. Over the years, the Torpignattara district witnessed an increase in the number of foreigners, in particular Bangladeshis, Egyptians, and, a few years later, Chinese. Even though many groups of single male immigrants continued to live in the decrepit apartments of Marranella (Priori 2011), the number of reunited families grew rapidly. They began to use the municipal services available in the district, including the schools; and Pisacane was there, very large and effectively underused as regards numbers of pupils, given that many parents (as we have seen) preferred to send their children to Grazia Deledda and to leave Pisacane for "those Marranella types."

In the second half of the 1990s, when the immigrant presence in the district was becoming evident, a further factor contributed to the ongoing exodus of Italians to other schools. The headmistress at that time is remembered as someone who was reluctant to engage in dialogue and was often in conflict with the teaching staff. Thus a vicious circle was created in which the school, already burdened in the 1970s and 1980s by ill repute for those who attended it, saw its reputation worsen in the 1990s with regard to the education that it offered, given the excessive turnover of the teachers who went elsewhere as soon as they could.

It was only at this point (when the number of Italian pupils was falling in any case) that the presence of the foreign parents became substantial. Most of them had settled in the Marranella district, yet they were inevitably uninformed about the bad reputation of the local school, given their restricted social contact with Italians in the neighborhood. They turned to Pisacane as the "natural" school when the time came to enroll their children in infant and then primary school.

Pisacane's notoriety was interpreted by many Italian families as the consequence of the incipient "ethnic diversity," provoking Italians to distance themselves further. Having started as a school for (Italian) problem families, Pisacane ended up by being "the immigrants' school" without losing its negative image—indeed seeing it reinforced.

But while the number of Italian children was steadily falling, the immigrants in the district continued to send their children to Pisacane, and it was this unbalanced ratio between Italians and foreigners that at the end of 2007 prompted a group of parents to form a committee that was self-styled—without any irony—as Moms for Integration. The entrenched inadequacy of Pisacane was interpreted by the committee as a direct consequence of the presence of immigrants. At the political level, this was argued as having been caused by the excessively left-wing policies of the school's management and some of the teachers. After years in which the gossiping and negative judgments had been expressed in chitchat between individuals, Pisacane was now being attacked publicly.

This politicized interpretation soon aroused institutional interest. The first person to make himself publicly heard was Fabio Rampelli, a member of Parliament belonging to the PDL (Il Popolo della Libertà, Italy's main center-right party). He had a long history of right-wing political activism in Rome and was a leading light from the 1980s in the Fronte della Gioventù (the youth section of the then "Movimento Sociale Italiano") in Colle Oppio. There Rampelli had come to know the Marsilio family, two boys and a girl, who lived a few steps from Marranella. The four of them formed a friendship that was to lead Laura Marsilio to be elected several times from 1993 onward as a local councilor in the sixth borough (the Torpignattara *municipio*), a position that enabled her to get to know the district and its residents very well (meanwhile her brother Marco would be elected to the first *municipio,* in the center). After being elected regional councilor in Lazio, Rampelli entered Parliament with Marco Marsilio in 2006, and he was elected again in 2008, this time forming part of the majority coalition, thanks to the Italian right's victory under the leadership of Silvio Berlusconi, who appointed the young lawyer Mariastella Gelmini (PDL) as minister for Public Education. But Fabio Rampelli's new parliamentary role by no means led him to forget his old companions and their many political battles. When after many years, the left lost control of Rome in the municipal elections of May 2008, the new mayor Gianni Alemanno (who had a political background similar to that of Rampelli) invited Laura Marsilio to join his team and made her the city councilor for education and schools.

The very strong political ties between Member of Parliament Rampelli and the Marsilio family, on the one hand, and between Laura Marsilio and the sixth *municipio* (where the Pisacane school is located), on the other, thus constituted the individual connections that caused the Pisacane question to "take on new life" and to become a national cause célèbre: The local "problem" turned into a matter to be dealt with through appropriate legislation of the Italian state facing the issue of integrating foreigners into its social fabric. Let us examine the main stages of this process and its ramifications.

From Neighborhood School to Political Drama

The matter flared up before Christmas 2007, when some of the mothers opposed the preparation of a cardboard Nativity scene conceived as a "global village," an initiative that required the children's parents to make a contribution in accordance with their own cultural traditions so as to celebrate an occasion that would exclude nobody, certainly not the non-Christians. On 22 December, Rampelli issued a press release in which he expressed regret at not having been allowed to visit the school in person to check how many people the term "some of the mothers" referred to. He then added, somewhat contradictorily:

> During my inspection I established that at least 76 percent of the school roll consists of foreign pupils of the Muslim faith, that in one class there are 18 foreign children and only one Italian, that many Italian families have been forced to leave after suffering discrimination against our identity and against the Catholic faith, to the point where there have been instances of linguistic regression. . . . The parents are in despair because their children are frightened by the completely veiled women who bring the Bangladeshi children to school (Rampelli 2007).

But the attack on Pisacane started for real only about a year later, when Laura Marsilio was city councilor for education and Fabio Rampelli was in Parliament as a majority member of the Culture Committee, together with the Minister for Education Gelmini, who belonged to the same party (PDL). While awaiting the enrollments for the 2009/2010 school year, the parents of thirteen Italian children in the final year of the infant school at Pisacane unanimously decided for the first time, with a clear "political" intention, not to enroll their children in the primary school in the same complex, and the thirteen children were instead enrolled in other schools. Their motives were that there were too many foreign children at Pisacane; the consequence was that the prophecy fulfilled itself, and in 2009/2010 the school, instead of having two entry classes—each of which would have had about ten foreign and six or seven Italian pupils—had just one with eighteen pupils, all of them foreign.

By now, the problem had been brought into focus: there were not too few Italian children at Pisacane but too many foreign ones. Thus instead of finding a way of making the school more attractive to Italian parents, tempting them to enroll their children at Pisacane, and thus increasing the number of pupils with an Italian passport, the opposite solution was proposed: put a cap of 30 percent on the number of foreign children in each individual class.

This objective was pursued at the same time by Rampelli—who declared on 5 February 2009 that "it is necessary to establish a reference point, a maximum percentage of foreign children in each class" (Rampelli 2009a)—and by the councilor Marsilio, who on the same day summoned the representatives of the sixth borough, Department XI (the regional education office for Lazio), and the primary schools of the sixth *municipio* with the intention of jointly signing a "network agreement" that would put a definite and quantified limit on the presence of foreign children in school classes. But the agreement, thanks to the joint efforts of school principals and local left-wing politicians, once signed, actually steered toward the opposite solution, with a recommendation that Italian parents in particular should be incentivized to enroll their children in neighborhood schools, given that (as noted by Giammarco Palmieri, chairman of the sixth *municipio*):

> The municipality has received a request to fulfill the requirement for a more balanced composition of Italian and non-Italian pupils in our schools. Precisely because of the great importance of the contents of the agreement *the Sixth* Municipio, *supported by the great majority of head teachers of scholastic institutions, has rejected the insertion into the agreement of an upper limit on the presence of non-Italian children*... (Abitare a Roma 2009, emphasis added)

Some weeks later on 17 March, Rampelli harshly criticized the network agreement: "The maximum quota was not approved, owing to its boycotting in the sixth *municipio* and by certain head teachers." According to his reading of the facts, the ever-smaller number of Italian children enrolled in the primary school was attributable not to previous causes or the provocatively anti-immigrant attitude of the Moms for Integration committee, but to the management of the school: "It is the failure of a presumed utopian and stupid model arbitrarily imposed on citizens by a presumptuous and ideologized school board.... There are two possible explanations if only 21 children are enrolled at Pisacane with only 2 Italian children: incompetence or malice" (Rampelli 2009e).

But by now it was clear that a local solution was no longer possible. The Pisacane issue would have to be resolved by bringing in the most weighty institutional hierarchies, and the task of galvanizing the minister became more urgent. During that same month of March, the news that some mothers had asked permission to move their "Italian" children from Pisacane to other schools had "forced Minister Gelmini to announce a cap on the number of foreign children in schools, fixed at 30 percent" (*Roma Today* 2009).

Indeed, the next move was the involvement of the government with a decision taken in the Committee for Culture, Science, and Education on 1 April 2009. Rampelli was the first signatory of this resolution, which obliged the government to introduce "a maximum quota of 30 percent for foreign pupils" as soon as possible. One sentence in the resolution makes its final aim very clear, where it declares that the government undertakes, inter alia,

> not to introduce in the first years any differential treatment between recently-immigrated foreign children and second-generation foreign children, so as to allow the latter to perfect their cultural and social integration, this having up until now been insufficient owing to the lack of adequate measures of support.

However obscure this may sound (what does "in the first years" mean and what is understood by "treatment"?), the general sense of this obligation is clear: foreign children (*whatever* their practical level of integration and linguistic competence) must be treated on an equal basis and thus the cap on their presence in class is due simply to the fact of their being foreign. Thus a child of immigrants born in Rome, who speaks Italian as his or her first language with a strong Roman accent and is happy to speak Roman dialect with classmates, must be treated and included like a foreign child who arrives in Italy at the age of 8 or 9 years, knows no Italian, and has been educated in a different educational, linguistic, and cultural system. Or rather, the resolution insists that this equal treatment will serve to encourage cultural integration of the second generation, which is presupposed (we do not know on what empirical data) to be "less capable of achievement owing to the lack of adequate support." Scientific reports do indeed confirm that the educational achievement of second-generation immigrants falls between that of native Italians and those who have arrived when already of school age (Di Bartolomeo 2011). Those reports also indicate that foreign children who have done all their secondary socialization in the host country have specific needs that differentiate them from both native Italians and immigrants who arrive in Italy after having had some sort of formal education in their country of origin (Ricucci 2008). It may be difficult to think of second-generation immigrants as the same as Italians in all respects, but it seems just as misguided to think that they are at the same level as other foreign citizens. One should make further distinctions, given that vast categories such as "second generations" or "young immigrants" bring together people who differ enormously in terms of their desires; expectations; life projects; religious, political, and cultural affiliations (Thomassen 2010; Bello 2011). The types of identity are particularly stratified in second-generation immigrants, and to reduce them to a general cultural adhesion to the civic principles of the state where they have grown up does not allow us to grasp how much the institutional, participative, and affective dimensions interact in unforeseeable ways in bringing about integration (Colombo et al. 2011). And yet, Rampelli, when asked for an adequate interpretation of the governmental obligation advocated by him, confirmed that:

> Integration is a cultural fact, not only a linguistic one, and therefore cannot be proven by the fact that a child was born in Italy. . . . We need gradually to reach

the stage of considering the new generation of immigrants to be integrated from the cultural, not merely the linguistic, point of view and therefore we should not regard birthplace as a conclusive factor (Rampelli 2011).

By making such a rigid distinction between linguistic integration (that is, competence at native level) and cultural integration, Rampelli seems to dismiss any possibility of identifying a specific group of second-generation students, not "completely" Italian nor even superior to the new arrivals. Or rather, the lumping together of all foreigners on the basis of their passports, without any regard for their linguistic competence, reveals a political ideology that is scarcely aimed at facilitating integration. It is not surprising to find that this legalistic position was confirmed by the Ministry of Education which, in a research project commissioned by the Iniziative e Studi sulla Multietnicità foundation (Miur-Ismu 2011a), classified the "pupils with non-Italian citizenship" in schools by calculating their attendance record and scholastic achievement without making any distinction between the performance of the second generation and that of the new arrivals, as is normally done in research projects of this kind (Ricucci 2008; Di Bartolomeo 2011).

Pressure on the minister continued not only at institutional level, but also from below; on 7 September 2009, Flora Arcangeli, the spokeswoman for the Moms for Integration committee expressed her disappointment to the press: "Minister Gelmini promised to put a cap on the number of foreign children in school classes, but nothing whatever has come of it" (*Il Tempo* 2009). On that occasion, Ms. Arcangeli also made an embarrassing statement that gave away the depth of her prejudice against the foreign pupils and their families:

> Given the prevalence of Influenza A, we have a further concern: until last year, no health certificates were requested from foreign children who came back to school after travelling to their country of birth. We hope that attention will now be paid to this at least (*Il Tempo* 2009).

The next day, 8 September, Rampelli made another reference to the Pisacane school and to the "Utopian fantasies" of the school's management and asked the minister to impose a cap of 30 percent: "I hope at this juncture that Minister Gelmini will issue as soon as possible a ministerial circular on the introduction of a 30 percent cap on foreign children" (Rampelli 2009c). This request was reasserted a few days later on September 14: "The first day of term at Carlo Pisacane school in Rome has served to sanction the objective of our proposals on the introduction of a cap of 30 percent on foreign children" (Rampelli 2009d).

Once again, the only solution put forward foresaw a cut in the number of foreign children, not a move to increase enrollments of Italian children. All this pressure yielded results and finally on 8 January 2010, Minister Gelmini issued Ministerial Circular No. 2, "Indications and recommendations for the integration of non-Italian pupils." As was to be expected, the new text bore no formal trace of its entirely fortuitous genesis, but City Councilor Laura Marsilio frankly admitted that she had played a central part in its making: "Look, I know it by heart because it was I who wrote virtually all of the circular, side by side with the minister" (Marsilio 2011).

Once the objective of imposing an obligatory cap on foreign children had been achieved, one of Councilor Laura Marsilio's last public acts was the inauguration of the 2010/2011 school year. On 10 September, she arrived at the Pisacane school and publicly reasserted her conviction that "the children of immigrants born in Italy are not Italians" and therefore it was right for them to be regarded as foreigners (Corriere Roma 2010). Even though the declaration aroused much controversy, it was in complete accordance with the government's commitment of 1 April 2009 not to make any distinction between "foreigners," who were all considered to be equally "inadequate." Rampelli made another public statement on 17 September, starting once again with the Pisacane but ending up by speaking of citizenship and *ius soli,* defining the latter as "a true presumption of superiority and thus a racist attitude. To oblige someone who was born in Italy to disown the roots of his own family and to foist on him a definition of 'Italian' was a clear example of racism" (Rampelli 2009b).

With this statement, the reconfiguring of the Pisacane affair was complete: a school abandoned by dozens of people from the lower middle class in Rome's periphery and attended lately by immigrants' children becomes a symbol of how to belong to the Italian nation, or to a nation in general. According to the picture that emerges from this affair, one does not "belong" because one shares *learnt* values, principles, and cultural attitudes; one must belong where these values, principles, and attitudes are *inherited,* transmitted by the blood line. A primary school has become the basis for formulating a very general principle of belonging for ethnic reasons, as opposed to any civic citizenship. Constrained between *obliging* someone to belong and *forbidding* someone to belong, this principle neglects one of the basic dimensions of Western liberal identity: the possibility of *choosing* where one wants to belong.

Another Pisacane?

The old stereotype of the district that portrayed the "Marranella school" as a source of potential peril for respectable people has acquired a new lease of life from the presence of foreign pupils: the other (now the ethnic other) is lying in ambush and wants to replace us, to take our place. In consequence, the ministerial circular of 8 January 2010, although it did not sanction the breaking-up of the classes at Pisacane—given that most of the foreign children speak Italian as their mother tongue—certainly legitimizes (from the cultural perspective) some practices that are now established in the institutional "filter" that prevents the enrollment of foreign children in certain schools. Even if the circular did not apply in the case of Pisacane, it certainly helped to give legitimacy to the negative views concerning the school.

Once entrenched at the institutional level, the prejudice against Pisacane can spread elsewhere, reinforced and legitimized in its public expression through petty day-to-day bureaucracy. This, more than any circular, directive, or formal act creates Pisacane's segregation and the fact that it is a "case." For example, a mother tells the story of a significant episode in another local school in the same neighborhood. A little girl born in Italy, the daughter of an Italian mother and an Arabic-speaking father and thus with a recognizably foreign surname, was informally refused admission to that school on the grounds that there were no longer any places; she had to resort to Pisacane. On the same day, an Italian girl who lived in the same building and had an Italian first name and surname was accepted in the very same school.

But there are many anecdotes along these lines. An Italian mother had offered to help a foreign mother who had just arrived in Rome and wanted to enroll her daughter in the infant school. The Italian mother thought that Pisacane would be a good choice:

> First I went to speak to the teachers, because my request was outside the normal time of year. The teachers told me: We have no problem with this, but you must go to the borough's office. So I went to the office and the woman there said to me: "But why do you want to enroll your friend's daughter at Pisacane school? Don't you know that it's the school for foreigners? Why not enroll her in another infant school?" She took it for granted that I, an Italian, did not have a Lebanese friend and obviously thought that the child to be enrolled was Italian.[3] A further incident told to me by the people involved further underlines how stereotypes are produced. Someone who works in the education office spoke to a teacher at Pisacane, emphasizing the fact that "well-off parents and intelligent migrants who paid their taxes sent their children to the Deledda school, whereas no Italians went to Pisacane because the immigrants enrolled there came from disorderly families who were in trouble with the law."[4] It will be noted that the old conception of the school for "the riffraff" is superimposed with almost exact precision on the newer one of the school "for foreigners."

The "Pisacane affair" has evolved from this discrimination expressed by small gestures, words that are barely weighted, and shared "common sense." It is on the basis of common sense that the wind of political debate has been able to blow strongly, legitimizing an interpretation of the school to the point of making it predominant. The general sense that emerges from all this is clear: For many of the residents in the district, especially those who need to demonstrate their respectability in contrast to the disreputable Torpignattara district, there are dangerous types prowling around Pisacane who could endanger collective well-being and who, it is feared, will displace the present inhabitants. Foreigners are perceived as an *alternative to us,* a close-knit group that confronts us with an "either-or" situation.

And yet, seen from the perspective of the teachers and the small number of Italian parents who still send their children to Pisacane, that school could offer an opportunity of enrichment for all. These people instead regard the Italian-foreign couple as a "both-and" situation. That is to say, they see in the multiethnic group-ings in Pisacane a wealth of opportunity, the chance to expand the horizon of our concept of humanity, the other as an *alternative for us.*[5] In this binary opposition, the school may be seen as either a *ghetto* or an *oasis* (Benadusi 2009). The teach-ers in particular seem to be aware that teaching at Pisacane is an opportunity for growth also for them. The original text voted for in the "network agreement" of 5 February 2009 went in that direction of addressing Italians so that they would recognize the value of multiculturalism—only then to be symbolically defeated by Ministerial Circular No. 2.

Thus the teachers' vision of Pisacane school as a space for dialogue, mutual enrichment, and collective civic growth for Italians and foreigners, a vision that is put into practice daily, remains suppressed and invisible. This vision finds no space of its own to evolve; it remains confined to the local context of those who share it because there are still no official channels to encourage it and give it pub-licity. And yet, it is a concept that could have its own appeal not only for Rome but for the whole of Italy, a country that has not yet found a way to come to terms at the symbolic level with its recent role as a country of immigration, after having been a country of emigrants for over a century.

In the light of these final considerations, I would like to end this chapter with an amusing episode. I will tell it without further comment, as it seems to me to summarize perfectly the cultural space that could be opened up in a school of this kind, a space that the Italian children of the neighborhood unfortunately do not yet have the opportunity to experience to the full.

In the fourth year class of a primary school, the teacher proposes an exercise of reciprocal description. One at a time, the children come to the teacher's desk and their classmates try to recite their main features. The purpose of the exercise, as intended by the teacher, is for them to discuss openly the difference between one classmate and another, inviting them to think about it and to express their doubts.

It is the turn of S., a very Roman son of Filipino parents.

"What is S. like?" asks the teacher.

"He has very sleek black hair."

"He has olive skin."

"He is thin and has very white teeth."

G. (an Italian girl) adds: "He has almond eyes!"

The teacher takes advantage of the fact that G. has identified an "ethnic" feature to try to speak about the relationship between physical and cultural diversity and to explain it: "Why does S. have almond eyes? See if you can tell me, G.!"

Her answer seems odd to those Italian adults who have grown up in a uniform cultural environment, but it expresses poetically a new way of seeing that could be created only in a context such as that of Pisacane school:

"Because he's always laughing!"

Notes

1. These statements by the mothers and teaching staff at Pisacane school were made in various informal conversations and collected in the course of two discussions recorded on 4 April and 24 May 2011 in places near the school.

2. The Martelli Law in 1990, the Dini Government's Decree Law in 1995, the Turco-Napolitano Law in 1998, the Bossi-Fini Law in 2002, and the "amnesty for caretakers" in 2009 gave a complete amnesty to over 1,600,000 immigrants without official residence permits (IDOS 2012).

3. Given the sensitive nature of this episode, I was asked to maintain the anonymity of the persons concerned.

4. Again, in reporting these judgments I am maintaining the anonymity of my interlocutors.

5. I have stolen this juxtaposition of *alternative to us* and *alternative for us* from Clifford Geertz (1986).

References

Abitare a Roma. 2009. "Una più equa distribuzione degli alunni stranieri nelle scuole del VI." *Abitare a Roma.* 6 February. http://www.abitarearoma.net/index.php?doc=articolo&id_articolo=11627. Accessed 11 September 2013.

Appadurai, Arjun. 2006. *Fear of Small Numbers.* Durham, N.C.: Duke University Press.

Bello, Barbara Giovanna. 2011. "Empowerment of Young Migrants in Italy through Non-Formal Education: Putting Equality into Practice." *Journal of Modern Italian Studies* 16 (3): 348–359.

Benadusi, Mara. 2009. "La scuola già e non ancora interculturale. Memorie e narrazioni dal campo." *Lares* 75 (3): 469–504.

Colombo, Asher. 2004. "Italian Immigration: The Origins, Nature and Evolutionof Italy's Migratory Systems."*Journal of Modern Italian Studies* 9 (1): 49–70.

Colombo, Enzo, Lorenzo Domaneschi, and Chiara Marchetti. 2011. "Citizenship and Multiple Belonging: Representations of Inclusion, Identification and Participation among Children of Immigrants in Italy." *Journal of Modern Italian Studies* 16 (3): 334–347.

Corriere Roma. 2010. "Marsilio: 'I figli di immigrati nati in Italia non sono italiani.'" *Corriere Roma,* 16 September. http://roma.corriere.it/roma/notizie/cronaca/10_settembre_16/marsilio-figli-immigrati-non-italiani-1703772473524.shtml. Accessed 11 September 2013.

Di Bartolomeo, Anna. 2011. "Explaining the Gap in Educational Achievement between Second-Generation Immigrants and Natives: The Italian Case." *Journal of Modern Italian Studies* 16 (4): 437–449.

Geertz, Clifford. 1986. "The Uses of Diversity." *Michigan Quarterly Review* 25 (1): 105–123.

Gilardoni, Guia. 2011. "Segmented Assimilation in Italy? The Case of Latinos." *Journal of Modern Italian Studies* 16 (4): 450–464.

Herzfeld, Michael. 1997. *Cultural Intimacy: Social Poetics in the Nation-State.* New York: Routledge.

———. 2003. "Localism and the Logic of Nationalistic Folklore: Cretan Reflections." *Comparative Studies in Society and History* 45: 281–310.

IDOS (Immigrazione Dossier Statistico). 2012. *1951–2011: Le migrazioni in Italia tra passato e futuro.* Rome: Edizioni Idos.

Il Tempo. 2009. "Scuola Pisacane, gli iscritti sono al 97% stranieri." 8 September. http://www.iltempo.it/2009/09/08/1067412-scuola_pisacane_iscritti.shtml. Accessed 11 September 2013.

Liddicoat, Anthony J., and Adriana Díaz. 2008. "Engaging with Diversity: The Construction of Policy for Intercultural Education in Italy." *Intercultural Education* 19 (2): 137–150.

Marsilio, Laura. 2011. Interview recorded at the Italian Senate on 22 November 2011.

Miur-Ismu. 2011a. *Alunni con cittadinanza non italiana: Scuole statali e non statali. Anno scolastico 2010/2011. Anticipazione dei dati Ottobre 2011.* Ministero dell'Istruzione, dell'Università e della Ricerca. Typescript.

———. 2011b. *Comunicato stampa Miur-Fondazione Ismu: Rapporto nazionale sugli alunni con cittadinanza non italiana Anno scolastico 2010/2011. Anticipazione dei dati 24 Ottobre 2011.* Ministero dell'Istruzione, dell'Università e della Ricerca. Typescript.

Pompeo, Francesco, ed. 2011. *Pigneto-Banglatow. Migrazioni e conflitti di cittadinanza in una periferia storica romana.* Rome: Meti.

Priori, Andrea. 2011. "'Per la casa chiedo a amici, parenti, per il lavoro chiedo a Dio!': Condizione alloggiativa, inserimento lavorativo e riterritorializzazione nella Banglatown romana." In *Pigneto-Banglatow. Migrazioni e conflitti di cittadinanza in una periferia storica romana,* edited by Francesco Pompeo, 57–90. Rome: Meti.

Rampelli, Fabio. 2007. "Scuola: alla Pisacane,presepe con moschea e donne in chador al posto dei pastor[i]" http://www.rampelli.it/articolo730.html. Accessed 11 September 2013.

———. 2009a. "Immigrazione, subito quote massime bambini stranieri nelle scuole." *http://www.rampelli.it/articolo1147.html. Accessed* 11 September 2013.

———. 2009b. "Marsilio, commenti della sinistra farneticanti." http://www.rampelli.it/articolo1456.html. Accessed 11 September 2013.

———. 2009c. "Pisacane, fallita integrazione progressista." http://www.rampelli.it/articolo1265.html. Accessed 11 September 2013.

———. 2009d. "Pisacane, tetto 30% per evitare scuole ghetto." *http://www.rampelli.it/articolo1268.html. Accessed* 11 September 2013.

———. 2009e. "Scuola Pisacane, risultati fallimentari della dirigenza scolastica." http://www.rampelli.it/articolo1164.html. Accessed 11 September 2013.

———. 2011. Telephone interview recorded on 21 October 2011.

Ricucci, Roberta. 2008. "Educating Immigrant Children in a 'Newcomer' Immigration Country: A Case Study." *Intercultural Education* 19 (5): 449–460.

Roma Today. 2009. "Scuola Pisacane a Torpignattara: Le mamme italiane ritirano i propri bimbi." March 20. http://pigneto.romatoday.it/torpignattara/mamme-scuola-pisacane-ritirano-i-propri-figli.html. Accessed 11 September 2013.

Thomassen, Bjørn. 2010. "'Second Generation Immigrants' or 'Italians with Immigrants Parents'? Italian and European Perspectives on Immigrants and their Children." *Bulletin of Italian Politics* 2 (1): 21–44.

7 Evicting Rome's Undesirables

Two Short Tales

Isabella Clough Marinaro and
Ulderico Daniele

GLOBAL ROME'S IDENTITY today is not only fashioned by the flows of people who use it and move through it, but also by the migrants who have made it their home. Tourists, diplomats, and religious personnel, as well as refugees and economic migrants, contribute to the divides between extreme wealth and power and extreme poverty which are part of the specific global identity of the Eternal City. From a broader temporal perspective, Rome's recent history as capital has been marked by a series of migratory waves which have been accompanied by a continuous dynamic of inclusion and exclusion of peripheral areas and communities. The locus of this dynamic, which has involved especially migrants, both Italian and foreign, has often been the city's *borghetti:* shantytowns inhabited until their forced demolition in the 1970s and replaced by an urban sprawl of low-income housing, which absorbed into itself the small villages and towns of the Roman countryside (Ferrarotti 1970). Most new Romans' practices of settlement in the city have had to face a form of urban development deeply intertwined with real-estate speculation that has resulted in an economically inflated private housing market compounded by gravely inadequate public housing policies (see Mudu, chapter 4). The arrival of large numbers of foreign migrants since the 1990s further reinforced speculation and exploitation in the housing market and simultaneously amplified the conflicts over access to public spaces. Rome's piazzas, parks, and peripheral neighborhoods thus became the new arena of those contemporary struggles that, according to Bauman (1998), are typical of global cities.[1] Roma migrants to the city—first Italians until the 1960s and then ever-rising numbers of foreigners since the 1970s—have been a part of those dynamics and struggles. However, unlike most other migrant communities, which have not tended to be the explicit targets of local government intervention and policies,[2] Roma groups have, since the 1980s, been the objects of a clear strategy of management of urban spaces which has selectively dictated which parts of the city are accessible to them and which are off-limits. This exclusive attention to Roma has been motivated by notions of "otherness" and danger—their alleged propensity to bring crime and urban degradation—that have been historically associated with those labeled *zingari* and *nomadi* (gypsies and nomads). Of all the capital's communities, the Roma are the group most frequently "evicted from eternity" (Herzfeld 2009) or, more precisely, they are those most commonly subjected to policies of displacement (see also Cervelli, chapter 3).[3] The last decade has seen a dramatic intensification in the municipal authorities' rhetoric concerning a perceived need to achieve order and security in the city. Much of this securitizing discourse, and the practices it has spawned, have focused on managing the Roma population.[4] The Roma have long been targeted by drives to distance them from Rome and other Italian cities; however, we argue that today's exclusionary practices are occurring within a new urban order which is redesigning the city's spatial and social geographies. The many recent projects to transform and rehabilitate parts of the city have often had as their corollary the removal of Roma from residence and commercial activity in its neighborhoods and public spaces. This is effecting a clear erosion in their right to the city; a right which not only concerns the possibility of living within its boundaries but also the right to stable social relations, to visibility, and to a recognition of their needs and expectations.

Most scholarship on Roma in Italy's cities takes a top-down approach, analyzing laws, institutional policies and practices, and the effects that these have on Roma communities. In this chapter, we instead focus on the microlevel, taking two small episodes which have involved the city's Roma and which concern their living spaces, possibilities of income generation, and political participation. Rather than viewing Roma as passive victims of state power, we aim to highlight some of the dynamics of interaction between local authorities and Roma's strategies for reentry and reappropriation of parts of the city, stressing, though, that the relationship is a highly asymmetrical one which produces a cycle of expulsion, reentry and, ultimately, further expulsion. This microapproach enables us to grasp some of the very human consequences of much larger processes of globalization, gentrification, and the regimentation of urban space, underlining how the modernity that seeks to monitor and manage its subjects and spaces intersects with individuals' informal strategies of presence, creation, and reappropriation.

From Center to Periphery and Back Again

Until 2005, one of the largest Roma settlements in the city was located on vicolo Savini, a narrow street in the Ostiense neighborhood, just a few minutes' walk from the tourist hubs of Trastevere, the Basilica of Saint Paul Outside the Walls, and the Porta Portese flea market.[5] The camp was surrounded by abandoned industrial buildings and empty lots whose long-term purpose had remained undecided for decades. Despite its proximity to the city center, the camp was hidden from the view of local residents. Due largely to this invisibility, in the 1960s and 1970s, the street had hosted wooden or stone shacks built by a few dozen migrants from southern and central Italy. In the 1970s, a small number of Roma families originally from Bosnia also moved into the neighborhood,[6] setting up homes along the banks of the Tiber and under Ponte Marconi. The imminent threat of the river breaking its banks in the winter of 1985 forced the Christian Democrat (Democrazia Cristiana) city government to intervene and, despite vociferous protests from neighborhood residents, forty-four Roma families were given permission to make their homes—some of them caravans provided by the *protezione civile*—along vicolo Savini. The area was delineated with a fence, marking the beginning of an institutionalized separation between the Roma and the rest of the neighborhood. The creation of this "nomad camp" reflected a broader trend that was emerging throughout Italian cities in the 1980s, whereby the only policy envisaged for Roma was to accommodate them in camps, areas that were segregated from the rest of the city and equipped with emergency facilities such as chemical toilets and prefabricated huts.

In the following years, other Roma families who had settled in this area of the city were evicted from their illegal encampments and moved to vicolo Savini by the authorities, causing a significant increase in the camp's population. At the same time, the internal organization of the camp began to change: Many of the caravans were enlarged and reinforced and, in some cases, replaced with camper vans or much more solid wooden structures which could accommodate the ever-expanding families. Other caravans instead started to fall apart and were patched up with scrap materials such as plastic sheets and wooden planks. It was not until 1995, ten years after its inauguration, that the city government did some maintenance work, laying a new pavement and installing some showers and toilet facilities. This new attention on the part of Rome's recently elected left-wing administration also generated various social projects aimed at the camp's residents: initiatives to encourage school attendance, employment integration, health education, and disease prevention. However, various programs were carried out exclusively within the camp and thereby reinforced the Roma's isolation from local society by discouraging them from accessing public spaces and services in the vicinity (see also Clough Marinaro 2003 and Clough Marinaro and Daniele 2011). Nevertheless, some of the camp's inhabitants, particularly young Roma who had been born or grew up within its confines, began to frequent the neighborhood on a daily basis. The nearby bar, sports facilities along the riverbank, and shops and stalls along Viale Marconi all become places in which to interact and build friendships with the Italian and growing foreign population in the area.

At the end of the 1990s, the camp again became the focus of political and media attention since its population had swollen to close to a thousand residents, a large proportion of which were young children. The maintenance work carried out by the municipal authorities had done little to improve conditions in the camp: The toilet facilities were often broken and many areas of the compound were constantly flooded. This situation generated various internal tensions between young people and elders who had grown up in very different contexts, among neighbors who were now sharing even more restricted spaces, in relations with the institutions and nongovernmental organizations (NGOs) whose resources were never sufficient to meet the inhabitants' desire for long-term improvements. Moreover, shortly before 2000, the administration, faculty, and students of the nearby Roma Tre University began protesting about the camp's presence, claiming that the Roma were carrying out petty thefts in the car parks and entering the university's premises to use the toilets. The proximity and contact with the camp led to high-ranking members of the academic community demanding a much stronger division between the two areas, declaring that the Roma's cultural identity was "difficult to reconcile with our own" and that the camp was producing "a closeness that is impossible to manage" (Gubbini 2000). The tangible outcome of the demonstrations was the construction of a wall blocking access to the university from the camp; however, the protests also marked a turning point in perceptions of the camp as a problem not only for the people living in it but also for its incompatibility with the projects for postindustrial renewal of the whole neighborhood that the municipality and the university were beginning to develop.

Five years of demonstrations and meetings between Roma, local authorities, and NGOs followed until, in September 2005, a definitive solution was found; the city government moved approximately eight hundred people from vicolo Savini to a site near the town of Pomezia, 25 km outside the ring road which serves as Rome's symbolic boundary. The new camp, known as Castel Romano, was defined by the left-wing mayor at the time, Walter Veltroni, and by his right-wing successor, as a "solidarity village," a model solution for the problematic presence of Roma in the city. The camp is bordered on three sides by the Malafede nature reserve, while the fourth side lies directly on the Via Pontina, a high-speed road which is also the camp's only point of entry. Beyond the fast traffic and the dense vegetation of the nature reserve, the only nearby buildings are a high-end shopping mall and industrial complexes, while the nearest residential neighborhood is more than 5 km away and accessible only by car.

Initially, Roma were housed on the site in large tents where they spent the winter, but these were replaced after various months by "containers," prefabricated huts made of plastic and metal that were designed for temporary residence. Electricity was installed immediately, whereas it took a number of years of vocal protests before drinkable water was provided (see Iowa State University Rome Architecture Studio 2008). Social projects as complex and costly as those provided in vicolo Savini were activated in the new camp, but these were further hampered by the large distance between the site and the Ostiense neighborhood to which children had to be shuttled in order to maintain continuity in their schooling. The equally severe isolation from health services became a critical barrier in the possibility of many people, particularly the elderly and women, accessing health care. This distance from the city and the lack of public transport led many Roma, especially children and adolescents, to lose all the opportunities for interaction and social contact which they had developed in their old neighborhood, restricting their possibilities for employment or leisure activities to the very few resources available within the camp. Despite these problems, city governments have since continuously increased the camp's population by transferring to it Roma evicted from other encampments around Rome. By 2011, over one thousand people in Castel Romano were experiencing the city's new model for managing and "integrating" Roma: a policy which focuses on concentrating them in increasingly invisible spaces detached from the rest of the city.

Meanwhile, vicolo Savini has been entirely transformed. The road once lined with caravans and wooden shacks is now paved with a perfect strip of asphalt which ends at the entrance to a state-of-the-art sports complex containing Olympic-sized swimming pools, lodgings, and a large car park. Its glass walls and wavy roof gardens are the most noticeable and paradoxical signs of the latest of Rome's monumental public works projects, an initiative which originally aimed to utilize the 2009 World Aquatics Championship as a catalyst for urban renewal of the entire surrounding area. The complex was never completed, though, as construction was blocked by judicial investigations concerning corruption in the public sector (see Martin, chapter 10). Nevertheless, every Saturday and Sunday morning, the inhabitants of Castel Romano as well as many other Roma from former Yugoslavia and Romania return to the street to set up the last remaining trace of their history in this fragment of Rome, the *pijats romanò*, a market for secondhand and recycled goods run by Roma who used to live on vicolo Savini. It attracts many of the neighborhood's residents, both Italian and foreign, who seek bargains among the salvaged and recycled objects, and is also a space for the Roma to socialize, as men and children catch up with friends and family while the women manage the stalls.

The creation of this *pijats* followed the same pattern as others which have sprung up in Rome in recent years and which were triggered by a common cause: the forced exclusion of Roma from another of the city's social and commercial hubs. At least since 2003, most Roma families had sold their goods in a marginal section of Rome's largest and most famous flea market, Porta Portese. Not only was their presence in the market extensive but, as De Angelis (2007) emphasizes, they had become well-established over the years, developing close and mutually beneficial commercial relations with their Italian clients (collectors, antiquarians, etc.), which allowed them to earn a legal and adequate income. Moreover, it gave many women an unprecedented central role both in family finances and in relations with non-Roma clients, since they were the ones primarily responsible for collecting and selling the goods. As the anthropological literature documents (Leiris 1951; Bestor 2001; Aime 2002), Porta Portese and many other smaller neighborhood markets had become a space of interaction and exchange, enabling Roma to develop strategies of inclusion through commercial activities. Their presence in Porta Portese was brought to a halt by constant municipal police checks due to allegations of illegal activities there.

In response to this exclusion, Italian NGOs and Roma groups sought alternative locations in which to resume commercial activities and created various *pijats*, often merging with smaller markets which had formed to display Roma craftsmanship. These exclusively Romani spaces gradually mutated into new contexts for interaction with the rest of society. There are currently at least four such *pijats* on the southern side of the city and although the vicolo Savini one was established by a family that had lived on that street for over twenty years, sellers include Roma from both legal and unauthorized camps in the vicinity. Like the other Roma markets, this one has always had a very precarious status. Its organizers have so far been unable to obtain official permits for the stalls despite repeated appeals to the authorities underlining that such permits would help them regularize their legal and tax status in the country. Instead, this lack of institutional recognition of the *pijats* keeps them in a state of constant instability since, as has already happened various times, the authorities can disrupt business at any moment, confiscating material and checking people's immigration status. The precariousness of the *pijats* thus becomes an extension of the condition of insecurity and fear of police controls which haunts the daily life of many Roma in the city. This regime of instability is evident in the management of formal "nomad camps" such as Castel Romano, but is even more critical for those who live in unauthorized encampments and for whom the collection and sale of recycled goods is often the only source of income.

From Shantytowns to Global Media and Back Again

Since the winter of 2007, the presence of unauthorized settlements has been one of the most pressing issues of political debate in the city; they are generally defined as a major source of insecurity and degradation, requiring decisive and direct intervention on the part of the institutions. These settlements are mostly, though not exclusively, the result of recent migration flows from Romania, which were already becoming substantial in 2001 and increased further with the country's accession to the European Union in 2007. The encampments vary in size;

some are inhabited by a few dozen people, while others accommodate over a hundred residents. They have developed in many of the spaces that have historically sheltered Rome's precarious populations: the banks of the Tiber and the Aniene Rivers, scraps of wasteland close to the center, unused and abandoned structures in its built-up areas. From the Roma's point of view, the main criterion in choosing a location is that it must guarantee a high level of invisibility from non-Roma neighbors and police forces so that residents can live there undisturbed for as long as possible. Another fundamental factor, especially in terms of providing a marginally improved quality of life, is proximity to sources of water and parishes or NGO headquarters where the Roma can have access to bathrooms and some minimal form of aid. The stability of the encampments largely determines the kind of homes within them. The most basic form of shelter is a tent, known among Romanians as *kortine,* often bought in the shopping malls dotted around the urban periphery. Shacks built from recycled wood planks and plastic sheeting, which can be heated with wood stoves and divided into separate areas or rooms, constitute a more stable type of housing. Many Roma families instead live in the same van that they use to collect scrap metal and often move from one parking area to another every night. In all of these settlements, the hygienic conditions are dire and hazardous: the lack of water, toilets, and spaces for garbage collection; the proximity of the river; and distance from services cause a wide range of health problems in all the encampments. Some of them have also seen tragic deaths such as those of five children between 2010 and 2011.

For many of these individuals seeking to settle in the city, the greatest hope is to be given a home in one of the municipality's authorized camps, which they see as a haven of permanence and safety. Indeed, the migratory experiences of most Roma are marked by the constant fear of the authorities destroying what little stability they manage to build for themselves, since municipal policy establishes that all unauthorized camps must be evacuated and the homes within them bulldozed, forcing Roma onto the streets without any shelter and with all the material goods that they were able to save from destruction held in suitcases and plastic bags. This precariousness has been a central element in the condition of most Roma in the capital since 2007, when a policy of forced evictions began, aimed at pushing them to repatriate and discouraging the creation of new settlements. Mayors of both the left and right wings have persevered with this zero-tolerance approach to unauthorized settlements—galvanized both by residents' protests and the deaths in camps—flaunting statistics about evictions and repatriations as evidence of their success but without opening any discussion about the effectiveness of the evictions and potential alternative strategies. Despite the continuation of these demolitions, which consume many of the funds formally earmarked for integration policies, the phenomenon of unauthorized camps has continued unabated and their residents have generally not fled the city. These families are continuously evicted, pushed by the authorities into a condition of forced nomadism, and obliged, after each police raid, to rebuild a minimal level of security and quality of life in the same spots or in ever more isolated and dangerous spaces. By 2011, nothing had changed in this dynamic except that the right-wing municipal authorities were pushing the national government to develop new policies to facilitate the expulsion of European Union citizens, while NGOs continued to denounce the failures of the municipality's repressive approach. During Easter week of that year, though, events appeared to reach a breaking point. Within the space of a few days, the authorities had evicted four of the largest unauthorized encampments. As with previous such raids, the municipality's Emergency Social Service (Sala Operativa Sociale del Comune di Roma) offered Roma women and their youngest children shelter for a limited period in the large Red Cross center for asylum seekers almost 40 km outside Rome at Castelnuovo di Porto. The vast majority of Roma refused the offer which would otherwise have forced their families apart; thus, over a thousand people found themselves on the street.

In the case of one of the evictions, which targeted a camp near Via Tiburtina on Easter Friday of 2011, many of the families that had been driven away from their homes refused to disperse to seek yet more hidden locations in which to settle and instead headed for the Basilica of Saint Paul Outside the Walls, accompanied by volunteers and members of local NGOs. Preparations were underway in the basilica, one of Rome's key tourist attractions, for the imminent Easter celebrations as various dozen Roma entered the building and were later joined by other evicted families. Their arrival was met by astonishment on the part of the basilica's security personnel and Vatican authorities who were unsure how to react to the presence of men, women, and children sitting in silent, orderly rows along the church pews. The city's lay authorities were equally unprepared for such a demonstration in a space where they had no jurisdiction. The Roma immediately wrote an open letter declaring that theirs was not a violent action against the church but rather a request for sanctuary and shelter so that their families would not have to be separated. It was a very simple request which the Catholic Church could not ignore but which would soon prove to have a highly disruptive effect on the city authorities.

On Easter Friday afternoon, while the Roma continued to sit quietly without obstructing services and tourist visits, the cloister began to fill with journalists and news crews, local politicians, and members of the city's antiracist organizations. Various members of the municipal government appeared and made public statements, among them the administration's head of social policies, the head of security, and two spokesmen for the prefect and the state police. Each one put pressure on the Roma to back down, but they refused to leave the church and accept accommodation which would divide their families. The standoff only came to an end when, after sunset, the basilica's management reassured the Roma that they could stay in one of the halls of the complex until the situation was re-solved, and the use of force by the police was thus avoided. However, the greatest achievement of this unprecedented protest was the fact that these shantytown residents had managed to briefly move into the limelight and dominate political and media debate, becoming the focus of interest and mediation on the part of the Vatican and Catholic welfare organizations, especially Caritas and the Co-munità di Sant'Egidio, as well as various Italian government ministries. During the following two days of tension and negotiation, the Roma were housed within the basilica; after the first hours of elation, though, their resentment grew as they found themselves cut off from any contact with the outside, unable to dialogue with the NGOs that had supported their protest, and, especially, isolated from family and friends. The initial sense of protection that the church afforded the Roma soon faded, especially as the need to clear the building for the Easter ser-vices intensified and even members of some Catholic organizations began to put pressure on them to accept the city government's proposal and leave.

From the morning of Easter Saturday, television crews from around the world converged on the gardens as the protests gained coverage beyond Italy, at-tracting attention especially in other Catholic countries and in Eastern Europe. The outside of the church also became a place of anxiety and hope for those Roma who had left the basilica to buy milk, sandwiches, and cigarettes and were now shut out from events developing inside which concerned them directly. As the interviews, attempts to gain up-to-date news, and improvised football match-es continued outside, the issue of the Roma's separation from the rest of their families became ever more tense and, by evening, various police vehicles began to circle the area, causing many to leave in fear. NGOs became more vocal in their lobbying of the basilica's administrators, also drawing into their protests many faithful attending Saturday evening services. The police eventually raided the gardens, destroying the tents that Roma and *gağé* (non-Roma) had put up symbolically.

On the political level, an opaque process of negotiation—from which the Roma themselves were excluded—was underway. The pope publicly expressed his solidarity with the Roma inside the basilica and his declaration was soon followed by criticisms of the city government by high-ranking members of the Vatican. Representatives of the national government, including the Interior Min-istry, also became involved. Despite the attention of the highest levels of church and state institutions, nothing changed in practice and much of Easter Sunday passed without any decision being reached. At last, an unexpected solution was announced in the late afternoon: The Roma would be given accommodation in a hostel run by the Catholic organization, Caritas, in the city's eastern periphery. This would ensure that the families could stay together and would allow those that had been divided in recent days to be reunited. Initial declarations to the media suggested that Caritas had offered this solution autonomously and, given the city government's unyielding position, would deal with the needs of the Roma alone and without any outside funding. Nevertheless, in the following weeks, rumors circulated that the municipal authorities had participated in finding this solution, although the exact nature of its involvement behind the scenes remains unclear. These events were highly significant for the city and especially for the Roma who had orchestrated one of the biggest and most forceful protests of the capital's marginalized population, bringing onto center stage the needs of people who are by definition invisible in their illegal shanties and usually only the objects of political decisions and police raids. Their achievement in physically and symbolically occupying the city center and the tenacity which eventually resulted in their objectives being met was a watershed in asserting their organizational abilities, influencing relations with the institutions, and forcing their interlocutors to dwell on the principles and values involved in the practical management of social exclusion. The confrontation between the municipality and the Catholic Church did not, however, lead to any alteration in Rome city government's policies. Indeed, just a few weeks later, it resumed its forced evictions of unauthorized encampments and continued to offer the same inadequate accommodation solutions, while also adding another level of threat by making some mothers sign a form declaring their understanding that if they did not accept municipal accommodation, their children could be taken away from them (see Pompeo and Daniele 2011). It thus confirmed its refusal to develop a policy in conjunction with Roma to make the city accessible and livable for all. Furthermore, the long-term outcome for the Roma who had protested proved to be far from ideal: although Caritas originally intended to help them find integrated housing, work, and access to schools, the need to clear its overcrowded hostel took priority and the Roma were moved to a complex on the Via Salaria where hundreds of Romanian Roma were already living in conditions of extreme overcrowding and squalor (Associazione 21 Luglio 2011).

These two stories are symptomatic of how Roma are drawn into dynamics currently playing out in the city and redefining its social geographies. The outward relocation of "nomad camps" that were originally positioned in semicentral areas of the city, planned and carried out by both left- and right-wing city governments, should be read, we argue, as closely connected to the processes of gentrification affecting many of the neighborhoods near the historic center. These have often been facilitated by clearing and freeing up areas with potentially high commercial value, such as vicolo Savini or the former slaughterhouse in Testaccio, and developing urban regeneration initiatives that merge public projects with private interests, in a form of state-complicit market-led gentrification. When Roma have found themselves in the way of these developments, they have been forcibly moved into areas which, conversely, have little value or potential in terms of quality of living. The new generation of "solidarity villages" for Roma, such as Castel Romano, are entirely detached from the urban fabric and from any long-term urban planning. The Roma's Sunday flea markets,which have survived within the city's symbolic boundaries, are the only small weekly window within which the Roma's visible presence is still allowed or, at least, tolerated. Thus, we see, on the one hand, public drives to separate Roma more and more from the rest of the urban population, similarly to the other "excess" groups which the city claims it cannot accommodate, such as undocumented migrants and asylum seekers held in increasingly isolated compounds (Rahola 2011). On the other hand, despite these segregationist forces, Roma are participating in informal practices to regain public spaces and reestablish social relations in the city. These attempts are no longer occurring within accessible and amenable urban contexts such as neighborhoods, though, but are instead restricted to the few remaining marginal and ethnicized niches of the city that are still available to them. Thus, the Roma's eviction from Porta Portese and consequent creation of a distinct "ethnic" market reflects a political trend within which migrants' identities and diversities are made publicly recognizable, at the cost, though, of reducing them to stereotypes and underlining their distinctiveness. Through these urban policies, the city thus loses the mission of integrating differences that modernity assigned it and, rather than facilitating interaction and negotiation, appears to be reinforcing social distances and divides between migrants and natives, concretizing in urban space processes of ethnicization and essentialization of difference.

The Roma's difficulties in accessing shared public spaces are thus connected to the persistence of stereotypes and prejudices surrounding "gypsies" and "nomads" in Italy and are matched by the obstacles to their visibility in the political arena. The few forms of institutionalized representation which Roma have acquired in recent years—such as the nomination of a Romani consultant to the mayor and recognition of official spokespersons for the authorized camps—are entirely ethnicized and subaltern roles (Clough Marinaro and Daniele 2011). The local government's strategy of separating Roma issues not only from those of the native population but also from other immigrants and their demands has resulted in Roma's political mobilization adopting an equally ghettoized approach. In this context, Roma only obtain brief visibility when tragic deaths occur in the unauthorized camps or when national institutions and other high-profile actors such as the Vatican take on the Roma's requests and needs. However, these moments of public visibility, generally accompanied by emotional expressions of solidarity and calls for urgent and permanent solutions, serve only to reinforce the municipal government's approach. At these times, especially, Roma issues are managed according to the model that Foucault (2009) defined as "pastoral care" in which local institutions treat them as needy of specialized protection and services, sometimes to protect their lives, while simultaneously constructing them as a threat to order and security in the city, to be distanced and controlled through surveillance and regimentation in order to protect our lives and property.

The two cases we analyze here clearly show the complementary relationship between the two faces of Rome government's policy for managing Roma through a perpetual state of emergency (Agamben 1998, 2005). The global profile of the Eternal City is today being created through a continued dynamic of exclusion and inclusion of Roma and many other marginal groups. Moreover, Roma's attempts at participation, through informal practices within the city's hidden spaces and economies, are being carried out primarily in response to local government's actions explicitly aimed at isolating them. Reading global Rome through the experiences of the Roma reveals a city in which public apparatuses continue to exert fundamental power over spaces and people; a power, which through its forced evictions and transfers, directly determines the Roma's right to the city. In contemporary Rome, Roma are the ultimate "redundant population" (Bauman 2004), relegated to specialized dumping grounds by the politics and economics of modernity.

Notes

1. The neighborhood of Esquilino, and its famous Piazza Vittorio in particular, was the first public setting for encounter and conflict (both physical and symbolic) with the autochthonous population. Similarly high concentrations of immigrants' homes and businesses subsequently became visible in other parts of the city such as Anagnina, Torpignattara, and Via Magliana, generating transformations which were often perceived by Romans as "invasions" in those areas too. A sensitive picture of these dynamics is provided by Lakhous in his novel *Clash of Civilizations over an Elevator at Piazza Vittorio.*

2. Notable exceptions have been the forced evictions of immigrants from Pantanella in 1990 (a former industrial building subsequently converted into high-value apartments) and Residence Roma in 2007 (see Lombardi-Diop, chapter 15).

3. We use the Roma as a shorthand term to refer to a very complex reality of different Roma and Sinti groups in Italy who often do not see themselves as a single or even related ethnic group. Although there are some similarities in their languages and cultures, the issue that most connects them is a history of stigmatization, widespread poverty, and their frequent residence in camps rather than in standard housing (see Clough Marinaro and Sigona 2011 for a brief overview). Rome is the city with the largest Roma population (approximately 12,000), the vast majority of which live in camps. These are divided into state-built "villages" (see our discussion of Castel Romano) where about a quarter of the Roma population reside; legally ambiguous encampments made of shacks and caravans, where a further 2,500–3,000 live; and illegal shanties which are home to more than half of the city's Roma. The last two types of camps are vulnerable to frequent forced evictions. A small minority of Roma were given public housing in 1981 following the first major camp eviction, and a few hundred live in private houses. Although nationwide about half of Roma and Sinti are Italian citizens, the majority of camp residents in Rome are foreigners, mainly from the former Yugoslavia and Romania.

4. The securitization of migration has spread globally in recent decades, especially in developed countries (Bourbeau 2011; Huysmans 2006; Watson 2009), and Italy is no exception. The media and politicians from left to right have widely contributed to explicitly constructing migrants as a threat to local and national security (see, for example, Palidda 2011). On the criminalization of Roma in the capital, see Sigona (2008) and Clough Marinaro (2009).

5. This section summarizes and develops part of the findings published in Daniele (2011).

6. These arrivals were part of the beginning of what Piasere (2004) has termed the third wave of Roma migrations from Eastern to Western Europe. Matras (2000) provides an overview of recent Roma migrations, while Lockwood (1986) focused on those from former Yugoslavia.

7. According to a survey of Roma residing in the capital in 1985 published by Karpati et al. (1986), several dozen Roma were living in this area and other small settlements were scattered throughout the Ostiense neighborhood.

8. See Daniele (2011, 95–122) and Solimene (2010) for a chronology and analysis of anti-Roma protests in the 1980s and in the last decade.

9. Italy's civil protection agency which provides immediate logistical intervention and emergency relief in the case of natural and other disasters.

10. Between 2008 and 2011, the city government under Mayor Alemanno closed two authorized camps (Casilino 900 and La Marmora), relocating over a thousand Roma in existing camps. The Tor De Cenci camp was demolished in 2012, and, at the time of writing, its approximately 400 residents were expected to be moved to the La Barbuta camp, which had just been built, and to Castel Romano. The eviction and demolition of unauthorized camps is frequent and ongoing, continuing the policy which began under left-wing Mayor Veltroni. There are startling similarities in the way the two mayors have underlined the number of Roma repatriated as evidence of their policy's success.

11. In 2007, the left-wing administration signed a "Security Pact for Rome" which explicitly defined camps as sources of urban insecurity that required intensive policing. In the same year and shortly before the municipal elections, a Romanian Rom murdered Giovanna Reggiani, a middle-class Roman woman, triggering intense anti-Roma discourses by both left- and right-wing candidates. See Clough Marinaro and Daniele (2011) for an analysis of how the victorious right-wing proceeded to manage the presence of Roma in the capital.

12. Fires in unauthorized camps in Rome killed a small child in August 2010 and four other children in February 2011. See: http://tg24.sky.it/tg24/cronaca/2010/08/27/incendio_campo_rom_muore_bambino_roma.html and http://www.corriere.it/cronache/11_febbraio_06 /roma-incendio-baracca_5c213c98-3230-11e0-a054-00144f486ba6.shtml (accessed 12 October 2012).

13. Although residence in these camps is also temporary and conditional, as Cervelli underlines in chapter 3.

14. For an additional account of these events, see Chiodo 2011. The English version can be viewed at: http://www.cronachediordinariorazzismo.org/wp-content/uploads/Chronicles-of-ordinary-racism-2011_versionedefinitiva2.pdf (accessed 12 October 2012).

15. In delegating the management of this problem to Caritas, the municipal government acted in line with its broader system of social services aimed at the Roma, which provides initiatives targeted exclusively at them and is run by a limited number of NGOs. This case provides a clear example of the state's increasing outsourcing of social services to the voluntary sector, coupling retrenchment of welfare with new forms of control and regulation (see Muehlebach 2011 for an excellent analysis of this phenomenon in Italy).

16. Mayor Alemanno has accorded various business and entertainment personalities the status of representatives of some of the immigrant communities in the city, giving them a formal public role in negotiations with the city government.

References

Agamben, Giorgio. 1998. *Homo Sacer: Sovereign Power and Bare Life.* Stanford, Calif.: Stanford University Press.

———. 2005. *State of Exception.* Chicago: University of Chicago Press.

Aime, Marco. 2002. *La casa di nessuno: I mercati in Africa Occidentale.* Turin: Bollati Boringhieri.

Associazione 21 Luglio. 2011. "La Casa di Carta." http://www.21iuglio.com/index.php?option=com_content& view=article&id=38:esclusi-e-ammassati-2&catid=21:report&Itemid=170. Accessed 3 October 2012.

Bauman, Zygmunt. 1998. *Globalization: The Human Consequences.* New York: Columbia University Press.

———. 2004. *Wasted Lives: Modernity and Its Outcasts.* Cambridge, Mass.: Polity.

Bestor, Theodore C. 2001. "Markets, Anthropological Aspects." In *International Encyclopedia of the Social and Behavioral Sciences,* edited by Neil J. Smelser and Paul B. Baltes, 9227–9231. Oxford: Pergamon.

Bourbeau, Philippe. 2011. *The Securization of Migration: A Study of Movement and Order.* Abingdon, U.K.: Routledge.

Chiodo, Serena. 2011. "Roma caccia i rom. L'accoglienza mancata." In *Cronache di ordinario razzismo. Secondo libro bianco sul razzismo in Italia,* edited by Lunaria, 158–162. Rome: Edizioni dell'Asino.

Clough Marinaro, Isabella. 2003. "Integration or Marginalization? The Failure of Social Policy for the Roma in Rome." *Modern Italy* 8 (2): 203–218.

———. 2009. "Between Surveillance and Exile: Biopolitics and the Roma in Italy." *Bulletin of Italian Politics* 1 (2): 265–287.

Clough Marinaro, Isabella, and Ulderico Daniele. 2011. "Roma and Humanitarianism in the Eternal City." *Journal of Modern Italian Studies* 16 (5): 621–636.

Clough Marinaro, Isabella, and Nando Sigona. 2011. "Anti-Gypsyism and the Politics of Exclusion: Roma and Sinti in contemporary Italy." *Journal of Modern Italian Studies* 16 (5): 583–589.

Daniele, Ulderico. 2011. *Sono del campo e vengo dall'India.* Rome: Meti Edizioni.

De Angelis, Roberto. 2007. "Uomini e pulci." In *Architetture dello shopping,* edited by Alessandra Criconia, 153–168. Rome: Meltemi.

Ferrarotti, Franco. 1970. *Roma da capitale a periferia.* Bari-Rome: Editori Laterza.

Foucault, Michel. 2009. *Security, Territory, Population: Lectures at the ColleÂge de France.* Basingstoke, U.K.: Palgrave Macmillan.

Gubbini, Cinzia. 2000. "Il rettore: 'così non si può'." *Il Manifesto,* 19 May.

Herzfeld, Michael. 2009. *Evicted from Eternity: The Restructuring of Modern Rome.* Chicago: University of Chicago Press.

Iowa State University Rome Architecture Studio. 2008. "Castel Romano. A Report on the Conditions of Habitation." http://www.public.iastate.edu/~kbermann /castelromano/index.php?pageToBeDisplayed=Home. Accessed 3 October 2012.

Huysmans, Jef. 2006. *The Politics of Insecurity: Fear, Migration and Asylum in the EU.* Abingdon, U.K.: Routledge.

Karpati, Mirella, Francesca Porcari, and Giorgio Viaggio. 1986. "Rom a Roma." *Lacio Drom* 5: 5–36.

Lakhous, Amara. 2008. *Clash of Civilizations over an Elevator in Piazza Vittorio.* New York: Europa Editions.

Leiris, Michel. 1951. *Race et civilisation.* Paris: Unesco.

Lockwood, William. 1986. "East European Gypsies in Western Europe: The Social and Cultural Adaptation of Xoraxanè." *Nomadic People* 21-22: 63-72.

Matras, Yaron. 2000. "Romani Migrations in the Post-Communist Era: Their Historical and Political Significance." *Cambridge Review of International Affairs* 13 (2): 32-50.

Muehlebach, Andrea. 2011. "On Affective Labor in Post-Fordist Italy." *Cultural Anthropology* 26 (1): 59-82.

Palidda, Salvatore. 2011. "The Italian Crime Deal." In *Racial Criminalizations of Migrants in the 21st Century,* edited by Salvatore Palidda, 213-236. Farnham, U.K.: Ashgate.

Piasere, Leonardo. 2004. *I rom d'Europa.* Bari-Rome: Editori Laterza.

Pompeo, Francesco, and Ulderico Daniele. 2011. "Protezione dei minori e 'cultura zingara.' Ambiguità e contraddizioni nelle pratiche della ragione umanitari." In *Osservatorio romano sulle migrazioni, VIII Rapporto,* 147-159. Rome: Eidos.

Rahola, Federico. 2011. "The Detention Machine' in Palidda." In *Racial Criminalization of Migrants in the 21st Century,* edited by Salvatore Palidda, 95-106. Farnham, U.K.: Ashgate.

Sigona, Nando, ed. 2008. *The Latest Public Enemy: The Case of Romanian Roma in Italy.* Commissioned by Organization for Security and Cooperation in Europe/Office for Democratic Institutions and Human Rights. www.osservazione.org. Accessed 23 October 2012.

Solimene, Marco. 2010. "1987, 2007: Roma and Rome between Change and Continuity." Paper presented at: Conference on Contemporary Rome: Changing Faces of the Eternal City, the American University of Rome, 26-27 November.

Watson, Scott. 2009. *The Securitization of Humanitarian Migration.* Abingdon, U.K.: Routledge.

8 The Rootedness of a Community of Xoraxané Roma in Rome

Marco Solimene
(translated by Jennifer Radice)

ROMA GROUPS WHO originally came from Yugoslavia have been present in the Rome area for decades.[1] Some settlements (for example, the Casilino 900 or Via Candoni camps)[2] represent historically constituent elements of the outskirts of Rome, but a considerable number of Roma are to be found in small and transient settlements, dispersed among the interstices of the urban area and in spaces left empty by the people and institutions of Rome (see also Cervelli, chapter 3). The Roma, with their settlements under bridges and on the banks of the Tiber and the Aniene Rivers, their camper vans and caravans parked in wasteland, cross the city and live their lives among Romans. The Romans, for their part, have often viewed (and still view) this "otherness"—brazenly close and unpleasantly recognizable as "the gypsies"—as an alarming invasion.

The model adopted in most of the discourse on "nomads" in Italy is one that "degypsifies" society, both practically and symbolically. On the one hand, it is asserted as a matter of ideology that the Roma are separate from the history and the social fabric of the territory that offers them "hospitality"; on the other hand, policies concerning the Roma seem to be inspired primarily by a model of "inclusion by means of exclusion." A glaring example of this are the nomad camps that, like all types of camp, mark the separation between those who live in them, human rubbish that cannot be recycled, and mainstream society.[3] Yet Italy is anything but degypsified: The Roma are not only "part of the landscape," but also a continuing source of interactions that are more or less wanted, sporadic, personal, or confrontational. The Roma's relational networks, far from being closeted within a form of collective isolation, extend into networks of Italians and, in some instances, are kept up for many years. Thus, there seems to be a close and durable relationship between specific groups and specific territories. To speak of the Roma in terms of their being alienated from Rome and the Romans means ignoring one of the important dimensions of the Roma presence in a territory: their stability.

One could think of stability in the emotional sense, as attachment to a territory that symbolizes one's "own place"; but thinking it through to the end, one could be emotionally, yet not socially, established in a physical territory, in an exaggerated version of that condition described by Hannerz ([1980] 1992) as "encapsulation": in other words, being among other people but nevertheless strangers to them. To make this vague concept of stability easier to grasp, this chapter will speak in relational terms: that is, about stability as the consequence of ongoing relationships, the fruit of coexistence—maybe contentious but nevertheless enduring—between the people of Rome and the Roma; in other words, something that belongs to the daily experience of lives that are interwoven in sharing the same territory, whether out of choice or necessity.

Stability

My main concern in this study is to provide some examples of the territorial stability of Roma who have arrived from the former Yugoslavia, and of the combination between this stability and some forms of mobility.[4] I shall focus on a group of Bosnian Xoraxané Roma, the Bijeljincuri (or Bijeljinakuri) and the Vlasenicakuri (they hail, respectively, from the towns of Bijeljina and Vlasenica).[5] The stability of these Roma is the outcome of a long process of settlement; this started in the 1960s, continued in subsequent decades, and intensified during the conflict in Yugoslavia in the early 1990s.

The main settlement area for the Vlasenicakuri and the Bijeljincuri is the district to the southwest of Rome, surrounding the Magliana quarter and extending south to the neighborhoods of Ostiense, Marconi, Garbatella, San Paolo, Villa Bonelli, Trullo, Corviale, Eur, Tor di Valle, and Muratella. Some Vlasenicakuri families, insofar as I have been able to reconstruct the information from my interlocutors, were already present and settled in the territory from the 1970s. But the first arrivals of the Bijeljincuri, linked to the Vlasenicakuri by kinship and a shared past in Vlasenica,[6] began in the late 1980s. Between 1991 and 2003, the Roma from Vlasenica and Bijeljina lived mainly in the camps of Via Candoni and Muratella. After the forced eviction of the latter in August 2003, the Roma were dispersed: Some of them went to live in other cities or abroad, but most of them stayed in Rome. Of these, various Vlasenicakuri families moved to other districts (mainly Bastoggi, around the official camp on Via della Cesarina—near the Via Nomentana—and the Roman coast), although some of them have continued to frequent the Magliana area. The Bijeljincuri, after two years of moving between Rome (invariably the southwest quarter) and the Adriatic coast, found accommodation for the most part in the official camp in Via Candoni; other

Vlasenicakuri families continued to live in and around Magliana, in car parks, on riverbanks, in areas little used by Italians, sometimes sharing the space with other Roma groups.

For the Vlasenicakuri and the Bijeljincuri, Magliana is not merely the district that hosts (or used to host) their camp: It is where they have lived out their lives for years, where their young people have grown up and attended school. In short, there seems to be a relationship of shared choice and belonging between these Roma and the Magliana district. To give a precise explanation as to why it should be this district rather than any other would be to hazard a guess without knowing the facts. It must be said, however, that in the past Magliana was a shantytown, scarred by unlawful building, a frontier, in short, between city and countryside where institutions have always struggled to assert themselves. Magliana is still today a territory full of areas which are not exploited by Romans and which in part are out of the range of influence and control of formal institutions (this is demonstrated by the marked amount of unauthorized land use—vegetable gardens, buildings, plots of land—practiced primarily by nongypsies and not yet eradicated). Furthermore, Magliana hosts quite a few scrap metal dealers, known in Rome as *sfasci*,[7] thus attracting people who collect scrap iron. For all these reasons, the territory of Magliana has a strong Roma presence, mainly Bosnians and Romanians, who live for the most part in illegal settlements (the only authorized "nomad camp" is the one in Via Candoni, which currently accommodates two separate communities of Bosnians and Romanians).

In my experience, the Roma settlements symbolize, for non-Roma society and especially for the neighborhoods where they are to be found, an ambivalent reality. On the one hand, they arouse revulsion and discontent; on the other hand, they exercise a significant force of attraction for a range of different social actors. In addition to representatives of institutions (social workers, the police, and volunteer organizations), the camps are regularly visited by Slavs selling products imported from Bosnia (foodstuffs, music, clothes) and who prepare Slavic cuisine (such as *ćevapćići, burék,* or *dolma*)[8] and even supply prostheses and gold teeth. I have seen street sellers (the so-called *bibitari*)[9] stationed at the entrance in order to sell sandwiches, sausages, and drinks. Italians and foreigners go there on business, for example, to buy spare parts for a car from someone who is a metal dealer or to take on laborers for building sites (paid under the table, of course). Some people go for the purpose of fly tipping, using the camps as rubbish dumps—often without the permission of the residents. There are others who come to enjoy themselves, who feel at ease in the company of certain families or friends, for religious reasons, or as a lifestyle choice.

The Vlasenicakuri and the Bijeljincuri seek to maintain good relations with the people who live in the immediate neighborhood of the settlements. During the period of my field research, for example, the local car dealer often scowled at the Roma living with their camper vans on the site of the abandoned factory in Via dell'Imbrecciato (adjoining the Via della Magliana). But all the Roma got on well with Mario, the old man who collected scrap iron with his Piaggio three-wheel truck, leaving it on the unauthorized site under the flyover near where the Roma pitched their camper vans and tents. Still in Magliana, the Roma from the settlement on the banks of the Tiber had good relations with the Italians who, just as unlawfully, occupied the high-water bed of the river with their shacks and vegetable plots.

Furthermore, although it may be true that the Roma are less worried about neighbors' sensibilities when the settlement is a long way from houses and inhabited buildings, when they live in areas that are not physically separated from the Italians (for example, in the case of some car parks), the Roma try not to attract too much attention or to cause inconvenience to people who live in the neighborhood. That is to say, they avoid lighting fires, keep their music at a low volume, make sure that their children are not too noisy, and try to keep the site clean.

Good neighborliness assumes wider forms in the maintenance of a harmonious relationship with the residential district that they visit every day. Magliana, for the Roma who still live there, is where they do their shopping, have a coffee, play video poker, buy clothes, post a letter, or surf the Internet to watch a video of their favorite singers. The Roma need bars, tobacconists, Internet points, and food, and since the non-Roma supply these things, relations with them must be peaceful. As long ago as 1989, Asséo wrote that relations between Roma and non-Roma had historically taken the form of an individual integration accompanied by a collective rejection. The Vlasenicakuri and the Bijeljincuri appear to have grasped this fact clearly. Indeed, they tend to disperse in their habitual visits to the district, so as to reduce the perception—on the part of the non-Roma—that the Roma are a burden on the area. At group level in recent years, the Vlaseni-cakuri prefer the Magliana–Villa Bonelli district and the Bijeljincuri, the Trullo neighborhood. Furthermore, each family "in residence" (by this I mean a group made up of various married couples and their children, as a rule closely related and living in the same place) habitually goes to a limited number of bars, stores, and food shops, avoiding those frequented by other Roma. It is in fact important not to be perceived, in one's "own" bars (or supermarkets or shops) as "yet another gypsy" who will annoy customers and frighten them away. Thus, it is precisely the collective rejection of the gypsies that obliges the Roma, in their relationship with the non-Roma whom they meet daily, to free themselves from what Hannerz ([1980] 1992) calls "role discrimination," in this instance connected to their own ethnic category. So they have to introduce themselves as Max or Maria; gypsies, indeed, but different from the other gypsies and above all specific individuals.[10] Thus, every Roma in the district has "their own *gaĝé*" whom they have known for years.[11] These relationships are key to the Roma's rootedness in a given territory, and they tend to fulfill multiple purposes at the same time. One Roma may be friends with Francesco the mechanic, whom he often asks to lend him some tools and to give him some advice about repairing his car; another knows the ice-cream seller, for whom he worked for a few months and who helped him to obtain a residence permit; another knows the waiter in a restaurant because they were at school together; still another knows the bartender or shopkeeper who gives him credit, to whom every now and then he sells a spare part for the car, and with whom he has gone dancing at the Palacavicchi;[12] then there is the one who is a friend of the warrant officer (*maresciallo*) of the local *carabinieri*, who sold him a car some time ago and had a son in the same class as other Roma children in the former camp at Muratella; and there is the friend of Ahmed, the kebab seller who often gives him credit and once in a while visits the camp for a chat "because he is a Muslim like us"; and the one who when she has a problem (a sick child, an eviction, or needs a contact name and address for the purchase of a mobile phone SIM card) can depend on a family of Italian friends; finally, the one (especially among teenagers) who has a girlfriend or boyfriend in the area.

The Roma also put down roots in districts where they do not reside, but where they carry out their economic activities. For example, scrap metal workers (most of the Bijeljincuri and some Vlasenicakuri families) frequent the Roman coast. Besides being relatively near to where they live, the coast is also an area where it is easy to find metals because construction there, whether by individual families or businesses, is booming.

The Roma regularly work the same districts, according to a system of rotation. Every day they follow a sort of outline itinerary and each district in this itinerary is meticulously sifted, street by street; they often use a megaphone to broadcast a prerecorded message that announces the arrival of "your scrap metal dealer," while hunting for metal left in the street or near the refuse containers. But the main part of the scrap metal collection business depends heavily on the individual's interpersonal abilities. It is in fact by getting to know the residents of the district being worked that a network of regular customers can be built up and maintained: These are the ones who do not turn to the "competition" to get rid of their metal; who call the mobile phone number if there is any work to be done; who will tip off the dealer about anyone who is clearing out their basement; or who gives some acquaintance who wants to get rid of a gate or a water heater without hassle a tip about their own "reliable scrap metal dealer."

In the course of their itinerary, the Roma habitually stop in certain bars to have a *cornetto* and a coffee, buy cigarettes for their Romanian "employees" (usually Roma) and perhaps to see if there is any news about scrap metal that needs collecting. Also important are good relations with the police, which ensure that one can go about one's business in peace and not be suspected in the event of thefts from building sites and because these same police send work in their direction.[13] Their regular working of the districts allows the Roma to have a "feel" for the territory, since over the years they have begun to know the formerly anonymous human beings who live behind the gates and inside the houses and to become known to them in turn.

Perhaps the best example of the establishment of the Roma in areas of work is Trastevere. This is a strategic area for those who live in the southwestern sector of Rome and a point of contact between the southwestern outskirts and the city center; it is furthermore one of the crucial junctions for the flow of tourists arriving at and departing from Fiumicino airport. Trastevere has for many years been the focal point for the crossings of the Vlasenicakuri and the Bijeljincuri (by "crossings," I mean a way of being present in a place, rather than a simple walk across a space), and not only the adults, since many youngsters begin to explore the non-Roma world on their own by wandering around the very streets of Trastevere and the nearby zone of Campo de' Fiori.

For many of the Bijeljincuri and Vlasenicakuri who live in Magliana, Trastevere station is the starting point for working activities and a place to meet up after work. In the area around Piazza S. Maria in Trastevere, instead, many women beg, sharing out the territory without too much animosity (in accordance with the unwritten rule that the post "belongs" to whoever got there first until they leave it) among each other or with the residents.[14] By contrast, there have been some confrontational episodes with the police and with the tramps who also go begging around the square. Many of these women come almost every day; some, who live far away, come every now and then (especially on Sundays, to stroll around the flea market in Porta Portese before going to beg).

Begging takes place by the entrance to churches, at traffic lights, and in the street; sometimes the beggars display a notice with a written message or photograph that describes the beggar's own circumstances; sometimes they hold out a small basket with holy pictures. They often recite the same phrase mechanically repeatedly, without any visible listener (a sort of "spoken message board"). Some women keep their heads down and cover them with the traditional headscarf (*červa*), to the point of being difficult to recognize. In other words, they are acting out—and this does not necessarily mean that they are lying—a stereotype: that of the good-natured smiling gypsy, the gypsy mother with many children driven to despair, the refugee from the war in Bosnia, and so on. They turn into a stereotype and make it a tool to interact with people.[15] We are dealing here with relationships embedded in the tight circle of a transitory and impersonal interaction, aimed at receiving money. Each individual woman has also developed within the district an independent network of special relationships that she maintains for years. This is because a substantial part of the income deriving from begging, as in scrap metal dealing, depends on the ability to build and maintain special relationships with the non-Roma in the district, particularly residents, traders, and regular customers. These are more personal and longer-lasting relationships, resources which are not only financial but also social, political, and cultural.[16] Because of special relationships of this type, Trastevere is a familiar place for women who beg, where they are known not only as one of the numerous gypsy beggars but also as Maria, Brenda's mother, or as Vesna, who lives at the Caritas hostel.

A group of Vlasenicakuri, some of them closely related to each other, have found that the railway station is a good place to spend time. It is the nerve center for the men's business affairs and meetings and the starting point for the women's "collecting" expeditions when heading to the city center; for some women and youngsters, it is sometimes a place to beg: at the traffic lights, on the pavement, and by the bus stop. At Trastevere station, as well as being well-known (if not always welcome) in the bars, newsstands, market stalls, and snack bars, the Roma have a sort of post office in a bar. Since the Roma have no fixed address (or none that is officially recognized), the bar is their fixed point for receiving letters, which the landlord hands over to the addressee.

Trastevere continues to be visited often by those who have not lived in Magliana for years: because they know which streets are frequented by hordes of tourists; because they have acquaintances and know where to obtain a cappuccino and a *cornetto* for their children, or where they can ask the stationer for a pen and a notebook, or some small change and clothes from the "nice lady" who always comes along Vicolo del Cinque before her lunch; because they also know the policemen, among whom (despite rumors that they are "really nasty") there are some who are less intransigent and who may admit, even when the woman is begging with a baby in her arms, that "a woman who asks for alms is not, after all, Italy's biggest problem; but if she just left the baby at home it would be better. . . ."

It is by focusing on these relationships that one can better understand why activities like scrap metal collecting or begging are carried out well away from the Roma's place of residence. Italians are not always happy to have under their windows a gypsy dealer who collects scrap iron and uses a megaphone, or a gypsy beggar-woman surrounded by "a clutch of dirty and ragged children." So to avoid the risk of damaging their relationships with the other residents in the quarter where they live, the Roma tend to keep their residential and work networks separate from each other.

It would seem that the Roma tend to be more "multifaceted" in their work territories than in the place where they live. In the latter, they seek a more personal rapport with the neighborhood, whereas elsewhere things are done in a more ambivalent way. Indeed, outside the residential territory, the Roma mingle with the "background noise" of the city, a terrain of anonymity and thus of stereotypes (among which the gypsies figure prominently); yet they reclaim the "localness" of places, even those that are commonly defined as nonplaces (Augé [1992] 1993), by building up and maintaining relationships with those who live that space as their own place; that is to say, relationships where the stereotype makes way for a person with a name, a history, and an identity.[17] Furthermore, we should not underestimate the fact that some self-representations linked to the field of procurement (Hannerz [1980] 1992) could lead to a "relational short-circuit," since they would be difficult to reconcile with the self-representations that the Roma perform in their relations with neighbors (relations that aim mainly toward the acknowledgment of personal individuality and respectability).

We have seen how in the daily crossings of the Roma women in Trastevere there is an interplay between acting out a stereotype and claiming an individuality beyond "role discrimination," between creating a state of need and flaunting one's own respectability, between pursuing one's own activities regardless of possible repercussions on relationships with a territory and wishing at least to be tolerated and to maintain some special relationships. It is worth noticing, nevertheless, that ambivalence of roles, in the sense posited by Hannerz ([1980] 1992) of "targeted situational involvements," is to be found also in residential territories, if only to a lesser degree. In Magliana, indeed, the women (sometimes, and discreetly) have a look at the refuse containers like the Romanian Roma, whom they criticize for rummaging "like tramps" right in the neighborhood where they live, or beg in the district, though only from their own special contacts.[18] As well, in their settlements, the Roma pursue the noisy and dirty business of separating and selecting metals. Their vans pass through Magliana every day, laden with scrap iron, on their way to the large metal dealers in the area (where the owner will pay a better price, be less likely to cheat when he weighs the metal, and where one is unlikely to run into any Roma with whom there is "bad blood"). Even the "rule" of maintaining good relations with neighbors is sometimes disregarded, as when the Roma drive through the district with their radios blaring at top volume, revving the engine defiantly, and talking very loudly in the neighborhood streets when returning to the camp late in the evening.

Mobility and Rootedness

Having highlighted the dimension of stability, we now go on to consider what in common parlance seems to be the antithesis of stability: mobility. The Roma move for a number of reasons: harassment by the police, deteriorating relations with the quarter's residents, a conflict with other Roma who live in the same area, some more tempting opportunity in another place, or simply to visit a relative who lives a long way away. My purpose in these final pages is to demonstrate the link between the various forms of mobility and stability that mark the presence of the Vlasenicakuri and Bijeljincuri in Rome.

A predominant form of mobility, currently characteristic in particular of certain Vlasenicakuri families, concerns patterns of movement within the urban territory. In the short-term, movements are generally local. The Roma, even when they are constantly moving, tend to gravitate around the same quarter, or around the same encampment lived in by Roma that belong to their own network; routes to places of work radiate from these areas, which serve as magnets and centers of everyday life. During the period of my field research, all the families of Vlaseni-cakuri living in illegal settlements moved several times between car parks, Roma encampments, riverbanks, and beds of reeds, but always within a territory that extended between the zones of Viale Marconi and Muratella, along an imagi-nary axis formed by Via della Magliana. The families moved independently of each other, dispersing on their own, but maintaining their "base" in the area and their daily frequentation of Trastevere. In this case, mobility itself can have its roots, in that it is limited to a restricted territory; thus the daily practices in both place of residence and place of work are not impaired. It would seem that precisely the possibility of moving between various spaces within one territory allows the Roma to stay in a specific zone of the city, since their presence is di-luted and individual places are thus relieved of the gypsy "pressure." In other words, discontinuity becomes the other face of continuity.[19] Habits of mobility relating to periods of time lasting several years, instead, often take on an urban rather than local neighborhood dimension; thus, it is the place of residence that changes, while the workplace remains unchanged. The places chosen for resi-dence are preferably ones with good connections to the work area (which basi-cally does not vary); in general, they are zones already known to the Roma and/or inhabited by other Roma belonging to their own relational network. During the past five years, there have been three main places that attract the Vlasenicakuri and Bijeljincuri: the Bastoggi quarter (Via di Boccea, near the ring road); the Via della Cesarina camp (Via Nomentana, just after the ring road); and the Magliana quarter.[20] Sometimes various nuclei belonging to the same extended family dis-perse to different territories. This is what happened to Tony's family, whose sons with their respective families spread all over Rome at various times: Some were living in Trastevere (where a few Vlasenicakuri found accommodation near the station), some in Bastoggi with relatives, some in various car parks along the Via Nomentana (together with other relatives who had part of the family living in the Cesarina camp), and some in Magliana. The fact that different family nuclei, related to each other, gravitated around different focal points and relied on the specific Roma communities based there intensified the link between the various centers of attraction and made a range of city territories easily accessible at any time to all the nuclei belonging to Tony's family.

Here we touch on a point of fundamental importance for understanding the logic of the Roma presence: it is the existence of a sort of "base" for the Roma that makes it possible for someone who no longer lives there or has never lived there before to cross or move into a given territory. For example, Fred, having moved into a house on the coast to the north of Rome, continued to frequent Magliana and relied on the camps, both authorized and not, in that area. In general, he made use of the settlements that were far from built-up areas to sort out the metals that he had collected on the coast and sell them on to his trusted metal dealer in Magliana. He would seize the opportunity to "sit together" with the Roma of the locality (some of them related to him) and perhaps pursue some sort of business, making good use of the possibilities opened up by his rootedness in two places.[21] Frequent visits paid to relatives who live far away similarly offer an opportunity to transact various business deals.[22] The same thing occurs when there are other types of mobility that make it more difficult for individual nuclear families to maintain continuity with a territory: for example, when they move to another Italian city or abroad for an extended period of time, maybe even for years. With this system in place, someone who returns to Rome after living elsewhere easily resumes his place in the territory, as if the territory were still familiar.

For individual family nuclei, their own relational networks (both those between Roma and the ramifications of such networks in the local population) are the key to familiarity and maintenance of contact with a territory. In particular, continuity within an area seems to be achieved by means of a wide Roma network held together mainly (but not solely) by ties of kinship and friendship and bringing together a range of families originating from various towns in the former Yugoslavia. This network changes constantly, its composition alters as much as its configuration, but it is precisely this flexibility that confers its characteristic persistence, going beyond the vicissitudes of individuals or single families. In short, the "baton" is preserved within the Roma world: It may be passed from one person to another, but it is not lost.

The Roma system of having a "base" also permits new arrivals to put down roots rapidly in a territory that is unknown to them, as is demonstrated by previous migration experiences. Migration from Bosnia provides a good example: the fact that in Italy there were Roma families, especially in cities like Rome, Milan, Naples, and Florence, to whom the Vlasenicakuri and the Bijeljincuri were in some way connected meant that those newly arriving from Bosnia settled in quickly and easily. Many Roma—according to what they have told me—were helped to settle in by those who were already living in Rome. These people taught them important sentences in Italian and a basic socioanthropological knowledge, enabling them to survive and make money; they also put their relational networks at the disposal of the new arrivals. At the same time, those who started out from Bosnia left a network in place there guaranteeing that contacts would be kept up, good use would be made of the opportunities opened up by the rootedness in both old and new establishments, and a possible return to Bosnia would prove less traumatic.

The vast number of Roma networks between Bosnia and Italy has allowed individual families to keep a foot in both places. The same mechanism seems to continue today more or less unchanged. The Roma relocate for shorter or longer periods, almost always knowing where they are going, since there will be someone there to mediate between them and their new territory and someone else to "keep warm" the post they have left. In short, the Roma network guarantees continuity and mobility in equal measure. This emphasizes how stability and mobility complement, rather than oppose, each other. Some forms of this stability, for example the "post office" at Trastevere station, could not exist without other forms of corresponding rootlessness. In other words, this stability is the exact consequence of types of mobility. In fact, impermanence seems to be one of the best ways of persuading non-Roma society to accept the very existence of the Roma, an existence that is therefore rendered fluid and changing; thus, it is precisely this definitive character of transitoriness that makes the presence of the Vlasenicakuri and the Bijeljincuri continuous.

Tony belongs to a family of *čergarja,* as they call themselves and as other Roma (who do not consider themselves to be in that category) call them: They are "those who keep moving on and live in tents" (*čerga* in *Romanès* means "tent"). He arrived in Italy with his family in the 1960s. First, they traveled around northern Italy, then they moved south as far as Rome. For a long time, they oscillated between Bosnia and Italy and also gave Paris a try in the 1970s, along with others from the same village, but they soon retraced their steps. As the years passed and ever more family members arrived in Italy, the family's center of gravity began to shift. Tony has nephews who have not returned to Bosnia for 40 years; his own center of gravity shifted definitively to Rome in 1984. This choice had the type of finality that the Roma assign to such a concept: a very firm intention, but no planning. He went with some of his sisters at the beginning of the 1990s to Milan, where two of his children (from his two wives) were born, but he soon came back, because he did not like Milan and by then "we had got used to Rome." In Rome, or more precisely in Magliana, his children grew up and went to school; in 2000, Tony left for Germany with his family, living in Berlin and Cologne, but after two years he came back to the Muratella settlement in Magliana. After the camp was demolished, he moved all over Rome, and his family dispersed throughout the city only to join up, disperse again, and join up again.

In short, Tony moved about through Rome, through Italy, and through Europe; in the past five years, he has changed his place of abode more than ten times; he has lived in a house, in official camps, in unauthorized ones, in car parks, in a prefabricated hut, in a shack, in a camper van, and in a tent. Therefore, he is emblematic of how mobility and stability are not irreconcilable terms, since throughout this period, Magliana has remained a reference point for him and his family; Piazza S. Maria in Trastevere remains the place where his wife and daughters-in-law go to beg; and Trastevere station is the place where he continues to spend time, more or less regularly. At any rate, for the time being.

Notes

1. The original version of this chapter, "Il radicamento di una comunitá di xoraxané romá a Roma," appeared in 2009 in a monographic section of *DIPAV-Quadrimestrale di psicologia e antropologia culturale* (24: 67–84), published by Franco Angeli. I thank both Franco Angeli and the University of Verona for authorizing the publication of this English version.

2. At the time that the original article was written, the authorities had not yet demolished the Casilino 900 camp.

3. See Agamben (2003), Rahola (2003), Piasere (2006), Bauman ([2004] 2007).

4. The data presented in this study are taken from field research carried out between April 2007 and May 2008.

5. Concerning the transcription of these names, bear in mind the following notes about spelling: č is pronounced like the *ch* in *church;* c as in *ts;* ǧ like the *j* in *jam;* k as in English; š like *sh* in *shut;* and *x* like *ch* in the Scots word *loch.*

6. The Bijeljincuri in Rome belong to an extended family grouping that moved from Vlasenica to Bijeljina after a blood feud.

7. These dealers acquire metal that is collected from "wrecks," a trade practiced in the past by Rome's "underclass," today mainly by the Roma. Note that the link between the Roma and Rome also has repercussions at the linguistic level, in that the *Romanés* spoken by these Roma has appropriated some terms from Italian and the Roman dialect in the form of neologisms, or as a substitute for older terms. *Sfascio* is thus one of many examples of Roman dialect terms that have been fully absorbed in the *Romanés* (as well as the Italian) of the Roma.

8. Respectively, small spicy sausages, puff pastries filled with meat, and meat roulade.

9. This is the name in Rome for the street sellers of food and drink who generally have a van or three-wheeler truck where they store and if need be prepare the food.

10. The names used here, whether Romani or Italian, are fictitious. On one occasion we went into a Magliana bar with Zahid, who lived in Ladispoli but often strolled around the district. Zahid began to joke with the landlord, whom he knew well, and to flirt with the girl behind the bar, promising to come and abduct her because she was so beautiful. When Zahid went to the bathroom, the landlord confided to me that "Tony" (that was how Zahid was known to the Italians) was a great guy, one of the few decent ones of "that lot."

11. In the *Romanés* of these Xoraxané Roma, gaǧó (plural gaǧé) is the term used to refer to non-Roma.

12. A multiplex nightclub in Ciampino (a small town southwest of Rome, a little beyond the ring road), frequented by Italians but also by many foreigners.

13. I have not been able to witness these happenings in person. Nevertheless, the Roma relate that sometimes a *carabiniere*, or a police officer, perhaps in the course of a check, takes a Roma's telephone number and later asks him to dismantle an old kitchen or clean out a basement. I have also been told about an occasion when some Roma loaded whole lorries with old metal taken from a *carabinieri* station, at the request of the officers.

14. As far as engaging in *manghél* (literally "asking," that is to say begging) is concerned, we can say that although Bijeljincuri women used to do this in the past, today it is an activity carried out primarily by Vlasenicakuri women. Piasere (1995) had already noted that the same

"rule" about "ownership" of a begging spot had been adopted by a group of Xoraxané Roma from Kosovo who lived in the Verona area in the late 1970s.

15. It is interesting to note how a certain way of presenting oneself can be found in various forms both in begging and in scrap metal dealing: that is to say, by constantly repeating impersonal stock phrases that play on the impersonation of an "ethnic" stereotype, rather than displaying the specific characteristics of the individual.

16. This is what Piasere (1985) called "*Gaǧikanó* capital."

17. After all, this ambivalence reflects the ambivalence of urban relations generally and that pertaining to the area itself: Trastevere is at the same time a place for some people and a nonplace for others.

18. Pamela, for example, often stops to talk to some of the ladies she knows to ask them for "some spare change" and perhaps a toy or clothes for her children; in the evening (but only every now and then, so as not to spoil their good relationship), she goes and asks Ahmed the kebab seller for a bit of the food left over unsold at the end of the day.

19. Something of this kind also happens in seasonal nomadism, when regular Roma presence in a territory permits reciprocal familiarity but discontinuity becomes the key to the presence of gypsies being accepted.

20. A new concentration of Roma along the coast south of Rome has recently emerged.

21. As Saletti-Salza (2003, 102) has illustrated, this "sitting together" is an "important social occasion" among the Xoraxané Roma, which can assume various nuances according to who invites whom to sit, and where (in general, it will be a space that is very well-known as belonging to the person who does the inviting). In every case, it involves sitting down to pass the time together without counting the minutes as they pass, drinking coffee, smoking, talking, and eating. It is thus a gesture that reasserts social vicinity, confidence, and reciprocal respect, or at least a willingness to establish or reestablish a relationship in accordance with such criteria. Fred's "sitting together" means paying a visit to his own relatives, being their guest for a coffee, a bit of chat, a few cigarettes.

22. For example, Golub often goes to Holland to visit his daughter; Dino goes every now and then to Madrid and Barcelona (where he also lived for two years) to visit some relatives; Valter goes to Milan, where he has relatives; and in the same way, Velo lives in Marseilles but is often seen in Rome visiting his family.

References

Agamben, Giorgio. 2003. *Stato di eccezione.* Turin: Boringhieri.

Asseo, Henriette. 1989. "Pour une histoire des peuples-résistance." In *Tsiganes: Identité, Evolution,* edited by P. Williams, 121–127. Paris: Syros.

Augé, Marc. [1992] 1993. *I non-luoghi.* Milan: Elèuthera.

Bauman, Zygmunt. [2004] 2007. *Vite di scarto.* Rome: Editori Laterza.

Hannerz, Ulf. [1980] 1992. *Esplorare la città.* Bologna, Italy: Il Mulino.

Piasere, Leonardo. 1985. *Māre Roma: catégories humaines et structure sociale: Une contribution à l'ethnologie tsigane.* Paris: Études et Documents Balkaniques et Méditerranéens.

———. 1995. "L'organizzazione produttiva di un gruppo di xoraxané Roma." In *Comunità girovaghe, comunità zingare,* edited by L. Piasere, 345–365. Naples: Liguori.

———. 2006. "Che cos'è un campo nomadi?" *Achab* 8: 8–16.

Rahola, Federico. 2003. *Zone definitivamente temporanee: I luoghi dell'umanità in eccesso.* Verona, Italy: Ombre Corte.

Saletti-Salza, Carlotta. 2003. *Bambini del campo nomadi: Roma bosniaci a Torino.* Rome: Cisu.

9 Ways of Living in the Market City

*Bufalotta and the Porta di Roma
Shopping Center*

Carlo Cellamare
(translated by Jennifer Radice)

An IMPORTANT AND entirely new feature of recent urban development in Rome is the creation of several large conglomerations, mostly placed along the GRA (the Grande Raccordo Anulare or ring road) or near the main roads and motorways. These conglomerations have come into being primarily with the creation of large shopping complexes, often connected to extensive residential areas. There are now more than twenty-eight large malls *(centri commerciali)*, some of them the largest in Europe, which have had a marked impact on the present layout of the city and, indeed, on living conditions in entire urban districts. For the most part, the conglomerations correspond to the so-called centralities envisaged by the new urban master plan.[1] The purpose of this plan was among other things to regenerate the outer suburbs, but its consequences were very different: They took the form primarily of real-estate and financial transactions that benefited private promoters. This type of process seems to symbolize the current phase of development in Rome and the public policies that support it, a phase characterized by a quest for modernization, often in emulation of other "advanced" capital cities but without having undergone the maturing process of a "modernity" based on the riches and potential of the city aiming to have its own "high" profile.

This chapter is an analysis and appraisal of one of these "centralities," situated in the city's northeast quadrant near the ring road and comprising the Bufalotta district and the adjacent Porta di Roma shopping mall. It illustrates the characteristics of this new "market city," its effects on overall urban structure, including changes in types of housing and forms of dwelling. It focuses on the "centrality" in its entirety, rather than merely on the shopping center and its internal life.[2]

Centralities and Nonplaces: Approaching the Shopping Centers from within the Roman Context

Urban development related to the construction of shopping centers took place in Rome (and in Italy in general) much later than elsewhere—especially Britain and the United States, where the phenomenon spread many years ago and is now a very typical characteristic of the urban landscape, giving rise to subsequent generations of malls. In Italy, mainly up to the late 1980s, there was a certain resistance to grand projects of this kind because they were at variance both with the traditional models of shopping that were more inclined toward small- and medium-sized local shops and because of conservative policies of an administrative bureaucracy that certainly did not favor them. Thus, while these large business centers were becoming widespread in other European countries (France, Germany, and so on), their presence in Italy was very limited until the early 1990s, when a certain amount of liberalization and the initiative of some entrepreneurs brought about their development in Rome. Since then, they gradually found favor in the market and have seen a growing interest on the part of consumers in an urban development model that was strongly orientated toward and conditioned by consumption.

In this respect, Italy seems to have partially assimilated well-established and standardized foreign models, uncritically and tardily. Writings in Italy on this subject are relatively thin on the ground and focus mainly on the critique of the "shop window city" (Amendola 2006) and of the shopping center as a consumerist and standardized model. There are far more studies in other countries, especially Britain and the United States, that focus on the characteristics and the effects of the phenomenon.[3] Much high-level work has taken the shopping mall as a symbolic reference point of a model of urban development which signals a change in the history of cities. As is well known, Marc Augé (1992) regards the shopping center, along with airports, railway stations, and other spaces that are so widespread and so typical of our urban existence, as a "nonplace" *par excellence*. Lewis Mumford (1938, 1961) repeatedly returns to this issue and the model of urban development connected to it, based on the exponential growth of travel by private car. This, he says, has turned the city into a kingdom ruled by the car: a distorted interpretation of "progress," for the most part expressed in a predominant obsession with the car that goes beyond true human needs; a false interpretation of modernity, reduced to "modernization," the victim of the "religion of motoring." Lefebvre (1968), in light of the urban growth in Europe that was already in evidence in the 1960s, refers to shopping centers as a model of urban development and a strategy of the ruling classes, based on the logic of "planned consumption."

The novelty, speed, and intensity of the phenomenon in Rome has sparked an intense debate that for the most part is critical of urban development policies and focuses on the shopping center as such. The construction and existence of Porta di Roma has provoked a flood of criticism from eminent authors (Erbani 2008), architects, intellectuals, and commentators in local and national newspapers, on the Internet, and in television programs and documentaries. Only in a few cases has the matter been treated in depth, though. For example, an interesting collection of critical and problematic writings covers the evolution of Rome in its entirety, with particular attention to the switch of urban conglomerations toward the outer areas, the shift of the urban center of gravity to the area between the centralities and the outer suburbs, the radical change in the relationship between town and countryside and the creation of the linear city of the GRA, which is becoming an axis of urban gravitation (Ilardi 2005).

The creation of centralities and in particular of so many shopping centers around the GRA (including Porta di Roma) is viewed as symptomatic of an extremely speculative urban development and of very negative consequences from both the social and the environmental perspective. It is considered typical of a more comprehensive model of Rome's development dubbed Modello Roma (the Rome Model), widely promoted at the political and national level as a concept but much criticized in substance (Scandurra et al. 2007).

But all these comments (along with some interesting research: Scarso 2005; Di Lorenzo 2009; Regione Lazio 2007) have focused for the most part on the proliferation of shopping centers or on individual shopping malls, also seen as symbolizing a dubious and rapidly changing lifestyle. By contrast, little attention has been given to the new districts near the centers, to housing models, types of accommodation, and the sort of city that evolves from them. More attention is paid to the urban development model and modes of living in the market city in a very interesting essay by Belmessous (2009) about the Val d'Europe district that was constructed by the Disney Corporation near Disneyworld in Paris. The essay, much discussed in France, highlights the role of the state and public policies in this remarkable housing and financial project that was executed by a private company. Literature and cinema have also opened up very interesting perspectives on issues of this kind.[4] In particular J. G. Ballard in *Kingdom Come* paints a vivid, ruthless, and apocalyptic (typical of his writings) picture of life and housing in a situation of this type, providing an image that is perhaps a bit far-fetched but certainly points to our future horizons in a very problematic fashion.

The research presented in this chapter was conducted following a methodology that interweaves a more traditional town planning approach with one that is sociological and ethnographic.[5] Thus, the phenomenon is analyzed through available data from the neighborhoods, maps, and analysis of projects, plans, and local government policies and actions, through the creation of a dedicated geographic information system. In addition, recent studies of a sociological and anthropological nature are taken into consideration. Fieldwork was carried out in particular by means of "strolls through the district" with local residents, in-depth interviews with certain selected witnesses, participation in public meetings and online discussions, and observation of activities within the neighborhood.

The Bufalotta–Porta di Roma Affair:
The "Engine" of Centrality and of the Shopping Center

The affair of the new Bufalotta district and the Porta di Roma centrality has a symbolic value because it was the first operation of this type in Rome, and, furthermore, it signaled the development of similar subsequent projects. It opened the way to a certain type of urban development and a certain modus operandi in public administration, with the consent of Rome's property developers and building firms.[6] Its sixteen million visitors per year are now turning Porta di Roma, one of the most visited shopping centers in Italy,[7] into a very important phenomenon that also prompts reflection on changes in social behavior.

It was in the early 1990s that the project got off the ground. The urban master plan of 1962–1965, then in force, envisaged—with some perspicacity—the creation in the Bufalotta district of a Rome *autoporto,* or exchange and inspection area, for heavy goods vehicles arriving from the north on the A1 Milan-Rome motorway. Two million cubic meters of space, basically sheds, were planned for this area. The *autoporto* never materialized, and at the beginning of the 1990s, the Toti brothers, in a consortium with other construction companies (especially the Caltagirone family), acquired the area and requested a change of proposed use from industrial sector to residential area and services, with the same cubic capacity. A quick calculation makes it easy to realize the exponential growth in the value of the area and, given the projected value of the housing to be constructed, the consequent income that the proprietors and construction firms would receive (at least ten times what it would have been from the use originally intended).

The request was not only welcomed by Rome city government but was also supported by them in approaching the Lazio regional authority, which had to approve the amendment to the urban master plan. The center-left regional authority opposed the plan and the city council then approached the central government, obtaining a change in the national law so that the area could be dedicated to residential development and services, mainly offices. Once this change had been made, the city council used the tool of a "program agreement"—a form of public-private partnership that constituted an abuse of planning and programming mechanisms—to adopt the amendment to the urban master plan. This step heralded the start of a long period in which the program agreement became the main tool for governing urban development, making the planning and programming instruments in place completely ineffective. Subsequently, the plan for the Bufalotta district, drawn up by the private sector and agreed with the municipal government, was taken up by the city council and inserted into the new urban master plan then being drawn up, to provide details of the location and planning of Porta di Roma, the new centrality of Bufalotta.

The construction work began at the end of the 1990s, starting with the new branch of IKEA and the shopping center, which opened in July 2007. The residential buildings came next. Work on the housing estates was nearing completion in December 2011 (although the project will not be finished for some years), as was work on a large hotel. This way of proceeding was entirely in keeping with the economic and financial focus of the project. The completion of the shopping area was a priority, since there were buyers lined up and shopkeepers waiting to start trading. The whole shopping center is a huge economic and financial machine. The main infrastructure, especially the link with the ring road (which was built with public money), was also given priority so as to allow the shopping center to function. The capital accrued during this first stage was then invested in the gradual construction of the residential areas (in accordance with market demand), which increased returns and allowed investments to be capitalized. Public services were provided next (especially schools, which were completed very quickly), while the green spaces are not yet finished.

The interior of the shopping center also functions like a big machine. Its strength lies in the "magnets": IKEA, Auchan, Decathlon, Leroy Merlin, FNAC, Zara, Mediaworld, and other attractions such as the multiplex cinema and food courts. There are 220 shops in the center; many of them are franchises of Italian, European, or multinational chains, but there are also (though fewer) local Roman brand names, chosen because they were well placed in relation to the Roman shopping scene and therefore in a position to meet the cost of rent. The presence of global commercial organizations is a sign of both the local economic effects of globalization and the transition toward globalized and standardized tastes and social behavior. Furthermore, the layout of the shops corresponds to the functional demands of the machine. The magnets are located at the ends of the main routes through the center while less popular businesses are located in the shopping galleries along the routes. This overview shows how we are faced with a very weighty and complex economic, housing, and financial operation that has little to do with the regeneration of the outer suburbs, one of the fundamental objectives of the centralities envisaged. A more important aspect to be emphasized is that the public authorities are in charge of an initiative that is of most benefit to private operators.

The Policy of the Centralities and the Regeneration of the Outer Suburbs

According to Rome's new urban master plan, the centralities were to play an important (if not exclusive) role in the regeneration of the outer suburbs. The creation of Bufalotta–Porta di Roma seems manifestly to fail this objective, even though the planners paid particular attention to the neighboring district and the relationship between district and shopping center[8]—and Porta di Roma is one of the best planned, designed, and executed shopping centers in Rome (Valle 2005). The centralities envisaged by the urban master plan were progressively and ever more exclusively regarded as large shopping centers that at most, in some cases, involved the construction of residential districts in the areas next to the new mall. The shopping center was presented as a structure at the service of the neighborhood that would tend to raise its profile, causing property prices to rise; whereas the residential district was intended as the main catchment area for the shopping center. In reality, the catchment area that justified a project of such magnitude was (and could not have been other than) on a much more than local scale, revealing the entrepreneurs' lack of concern for the local context.

The actual creators of centralities of this kind hardly ever foresaw or brought in any productive activities even at a high level (for example, high-tech managerial or service industries) that might constitute a significant factor of production, job creation, or a driving force for development. One of the major grounds for criticism in Bufalotta (though it was the only centrality where this was envisaged) was that the original plan to include an office complex, which residents felt would raise the profile of the district, was never fulfilled. Very few of the staff employed in the shopping center, who often work demanding shifts on temporary contracts through agencies, come from the surrounding districts. The new districts with a reasonably high standard of building remain mostly residential and are indeed "dormitory neighborhoods," giving rise to further features of commuting that certainly do not lead to the regeneration of the outer suburbs. Instead, they attract vast crowds of visitors to the shopping centers and the resultant cars that fill up the huge existing car parks,[9] another feature that blights the area.

The unfulfilled objective of regenerating the suburbs and the lack of concern on the part of those in charge of the project for the neighboring districts is borne out by the physical organization and the structure itself of the project. The shopping center is a large, basically monolithic, structure that is entirely projected on to its interior and creates an insurmountable distance between itself and the world outside. The expanse of car parks that surround it, with their acres of asphalt and the metal of the parked cars, confirm and reinforce this distance and become an overwhelming barrier. What primarily concerns people is access for cars from far outside the district, rather than from the locality. Pedestrian access from the neighboring districts is forbidden or extremely difficult. The considerable distance and the lack of direct routes obliges local residents to drive and join the heavy traffic flows on the ring road and motorway in order to reach the shopping center that is literally next door.

It is notable that in these areas, which are meant to be desirable parts of the city, there are in fact citizens' protests and demonstrations, which are often organized by committees who are trying to make the authorities respect the commitments made by the administration and the construction firms, to stop further speculation, and to reach the quality standards that were boasted when they acquired their homes and which induced them to live in these new settlements.

Lastly, the lack of services and facilities in the district complete the picture of an utterly failed policy of regenerating the suburbs, and it was very easy to predict that this objective would not be met. We are dealing with completely inadequate urban public policies, as well as an easily standardized concept of a city that has lost the rich resources and the whole experience of living together in a community; a concept of a city that is dominated by other interests and, in view of the results of the entire process, seems to be guilty of having deceived people.

The Effects on the Organization of the City

It is important to analyze the effects on the city's organization that have resulted from the creation of the shopping center and the districts linked to it. The first effect has been a slump of commercial activities in the nearby neighborhoods. Many traders are tempted to move to the shopping center, but this is a high-cost operation and not always successful. One can indeed find a place in the mall, but with certain conditions attached. The contract—with respect to provision of services, ability to attract a very large number of customers, marketing, and promotion—stipulates that the shopkeeper pays an annual fee commensurate with his or her expected turnover. At the end of the year, the fee to be paid is fixed, even if the expected turnover has not been achieved. If the turnover has been achieved or exceeded, it becomes the reference point for next year's fee. Thus, the fee to be paid each year tends to increase and takes no account of possible slack periods. This means that traders not infrequently give up. The company that runs the shopping center regards a periodic "turnover" of shops as normal. Obviously, it is only the traders of some substance who sell well-known and recognizable brand names who can succeed under this pressure. Therefore, it is not easy to transfer a local store to the shopping center.

At the same time, however, the stores in the shopping center meet almost all the demands of middle- and upper-middle-class shoppers. The traders in the neighboring districts accordingly experience not so much a disappearance of local shops (which to some extent does happen) as their reorientation toward the lowest or very high segments of the market (from the viewpoint of costs and product quality). There has been an unprecedented proliferation of Chinese shops; bars selling slices of pizza, kebabs, and other types of fast food; or stores selling commodities of little worth. This brings about a radical change in the shopping streets, which lose their character of "a bustling thoroughfare" in the neighborhood and a meeting place where the shopkeeper often plays a social role that goes beyond the mere selling of products. What happens therefore is a major reduction in people visiting these streets, giving rise to a perception of uncertainty in a downward spiral that leads to an overall impoverishment of life in the district.

Another consequence is the magnetic attraction of the shopping center: Young people, in particular, are drawn away from the traditional shopping streets to spend their spare time in the mall. Whereas in the past people who lived in Rome, especially the young, made for the historic center of Rome (when they could, given the distance from their homes) or toward other intermediate destinations, they now make a beeline for Porta di Roma (and only in certain cases for the city center, in search of alternatives and skilled employment). The shopping center, furthermore, serves as a "filter" for the crowds that come from outside the city and inverts the direction of the traffic flows outward from more central districts (which is entirely new for Rome).

In short, the most obvious consequence of the shopping center is that it is completely changing the organization of the city and ways of living in it. Its powerful attraction, its strategic location next to the ring road, its easy accessibility (except for local residents!), and its projection toward the huge catchment area in the northern zone of Rome mean that there is a predominance of nonlocal visits and traffic. Porta di Roma is a structure that has scant regard for the locality and the neighboring areas: it is a structure that "thinks" and functions on an urban and territorial scale and imposes a different way of experiencing the city. The scale of housing is metropolitan, no longer local. The ring road is no longer just an infrastructure for speedy connections and a barrier that holds back the spread of the city into the countryside; it is an axis of gravitation (almost like a metropolitan boulevard) around which ordinary city life revolves (in addition to the twenty-eight big shopping centers that have arisen in the past few years), ever more oriented toward life in the car, a place of concentration of the city's activities that is now seen with a reversed perspective (Ilardi 2005). Its effects on infrastructural organization and mobility are substantial, exacerbated by the inadequacy of public transport and entailing an increase in local traffic.

Social behavior is also changing from other points of view. I will point out just two aspects. First, there has been an enormous increase in private car use that is becoming the normal (though not the only) form of transport, with a clear add-on effect on both congestion and unsustainable environmental pollution. Second, as noted in my field research and indications from managers of the shopping center, it has become normal for whole families to spend the weekend at the mall, arriving early in the morning, staying for lunch, and finishing with a visit to the cinema in the afternoon. The shopping center thus fulfils all of life's requirements in the space of a single day.

Living in Bufalotta

It is interesting to analyze and evaluate the experience of living in the district next to the shopping center,[10] an experience that reveals a clear evolution in a concept of living that is even more important in a cultural context like that of Rome. This context is partly linked to the Mediterranean culture, where housing is strongly connected with sociability, communal life, the direct appropriation, and shared dimension of common spaces. Bufalotta is one of the new residential districts of the market city; today it marks the "frontier" of middle-class housing. The housing is mostly private and of good quality, a form of expression and acknowledgement of its own social status. The entire area affected by the project and the Bufalotta–Porta di Roma complex is organized in housing units that differ from each other, but certain common features can be traced. Flats are generally very small (sizes range from 20, 40, or 60 m^2 to—sometimes—90 m^2, obviously for small families), but they have large balconies that compensate for the limited space indoors (thus many of the household appliances are put on the balcony). They are clearly aimed at single people, young couples, and nuclear families without small children (or at the most one small child). The availability of spacious balconies and especially the finishing touches and high quality of building, however, tend to compensate for the limited space and to replicate the models of more luxurious housing. This is the concept of residential accommodation that is promoted by the construction companies' marketing and publicity.

Similarly, the small blocks of flats are often grouped in complexes with their own swimming pool, an internal garden, a playground for children, and security systems to control access. Some of them are true residential complexes that can be described as luxurious. In others, everything (including the swimming pool and playground) is on a smaller scale and tends to replicate residential models for the less affluent classes. A further difference is that the larger and smaller blocks of flats can be regarded as "rabbit warrens" that are no different from other blocks in Rome's outer suburbs.[11] Residing in Bufalotta–Porta di Roma is no more than an imitation of good living.

The large shopping center around which the new district is constructed absorbs all the other functions of living. It trivializes the collective dimension of residing in a place and reduces it to a sum of separate functions. Although there are a few "squares" inside the neighborhood, some of them with colonnades and a few shops, people seldom make use of these public spaces and they are reduced to serving as car parks. The few shops there are those that cannot find a place in the shopping center: bars selling slices of pizza, some restaurants, services such as drycleaners and plumbers. They are not enough to liven up these places. Likewise, the shops envisaged in other areas remain empty, creating—already at this early stage—an atmosphere of desolation. And the schools, already constructed to a high architectural standard, are isolated complexes, far from the residential areas and barely integrated with them: The children have to be taken to school by car.

It is also interesting to note how some of the new residents in Bufalotta–Porta di Roma perceive the big shopping center, an inescapable presence in the cityscape and daily life: a "nightmare," an "octopus," a "black hole" that swallows up all life, especially during leisure time. That is what many residents think, and these are their words. In the absence of an alternative during one's spare time, and in order simply to buy some bread,[12] the shopping center becomes an unavoidable landmark with important effects on the perception of space, and public space in particular: People leave their own homes (where they spend the whole of their private life); they go to the garages; they get in their cars; they go to the underground car park in the shopping center; and they take the lift or the escalator up to the mall. Sometimes they spend the entire day there. The intermediate space, even in its physicality, disappears from the horizon of residents' lives and from their imagination; all that exists is one's own home and the shopping center, which is certainly not a "public space" in the traditional sense of the word (these areas are private property, placed under surveillance). This so-called public space in turn loses its whole character of a place of intersection of routes and stories in residents' lives, both because of the dispersal and alienation caused by the physical character of the spaces and because the shopping center with its nonlocal character witnesses a large number of visitors who do not live nearby. The physical public space (the square, the street) that still exists and is well looked after in these districts thus completely loses its meaning and for the time being has no visitors. The only areas to be visited are the playgrounds for children, who are always accompanied by parents or grandparents.[13] By the same token, mental and social public space, the collective dimension of living, disappears from the residents' horizon of life.

The ways of delineating spaces that are characteristic of most of the city of Rome and that mark a city's vitality do not exist in this district; sometimes a couple of market stalls are stationed outside the private perimeter of the shopping center, on the route to the bus stop. Community spirit is out of the question; people's behavior is determined by the organization of the space; the sense of ownership of the places is thwarted. Even the district's management committee, which still exists, meets via the Internet and not in real places. Thus, the district committee's pronouncements address the failure to create the areas intended for the office complex (which, according to the committee, would prevent Bufalotta–Porta di Roma being reduced to a solely residential district, that is to say a "dormitory quarter")[14] without perhaps being aware that the quality of housing would not change.

Modernization without "Modernity"

This chapter has attempted to illustrate and appraise one example of the housing developments that have become typical in Rome in recent years, especially the last decade, based on a multiplication of centralities, which are complexes of shopping centers and residential quarters. These private initiative projects, incorporated into the new urban master plan with the ostensible purpose of regenerating the outer suburbs, have completely failed to meet this objective and have turned out to be in essence financial and housing operations that have created whole segments of a market city. Operations of this kind, which imply a commonplace and standardized city aimed mainly at the middle classes, have not been opposed, but instead supported, by the public administration; the latter have played an important role and therefore have considerable responsibility in this type of urban development. As I have said, it is an operation that benefits only the private sector (yet proclaimed as being in the public interest) and creates a synergy between the city government and entrepreneurs. The boundary between public and private interest is thus made uncertain and ambiguous and has become a typical feature of urban development in Rome in recent years. Such completely inadequate urban public policies seem questionable, as does the easy standardized concept of a city that has lost its riches and the entirety of communal living and forms of coexistence: a concept of a city that is dominated by other interests reflecting a trivialization of housing, where the sense of ownership and the significance of places is thwarted and where the collective dimension of the city disappears from residents' lives.

This massive style of development of the market city in Rome confirms the limitations of the "Rome Model" and the creation of a modernization without modernity. That is to say, it lacks that quality that truly characterizes a modern capital city and could certainly characterize a city like Rome, endowed as it is with a magnificent historical and cultural heritage and extensive social resources. The policies, both private and public, that continue to typify the Rome model seem to be pursuing a modernization made up of buildings and infrastructure that is "abreast with the times," supposedly an instrument of fitting competitiveness at the international and global level, without aiming at an overall development of the city—on the contrary, bringing about an impoverishment of it. Indeed, the economies that derive from it, such as those relating to the market city, are in fact short-term: They aim obviously at the exploitation of existing resources (land use, trade, salaries, financial activities, etc.) without creating new resources and without playing a driving role for the entire city, in a course whose consequences have already been seen in the recent economic crisis.

Notes

1. Rome's Urban Master Plan; the main instrument of urban planning, adopted in 2003 and approved in 2008.

2. There exists a huge amount of research and a wide-ranging debate on shopping centers, slanted almost exclusively toward a radical (if not ideological) critique of the shopping center as such and the consumerist model that it embodies.

3. See Scarso (2005) for a vast and complete survey of the bibliography.

4. For example, Daniele Lucchetti's Italian-French film *La nostra vita* (*Our Life*, 2010), which won an award at the Cannes Festival, was a great success in Italy; it was set in an outer suburb of this type that was under construction.

5. The architect Sara Seravalle and the engineer Dario Colozza also participated in the research.

6. Recently (December 2011), the municipal authorities were authorizing, or had already authorized, the construction of sixteen more large "business parks."

7. More precisely, Porta di Roma was the shopping center "most visited in Italy" in 2008, with 16.4 million visitors.

8. For example, the numerous car parks are all situated underground, and there is a pedestrian entrance that reflects the search for an important and suitable link with the neighboring district.

9. Porta di Roma has 7,000 parking spaces, which provide a lot of parking when added to the service roads, but not enough for the weekend. When this happens, the overflow of cars leads to parking right on the orbital motorway.

10. I will not dwell on the modalities of experiencing the shopping center, but refer the reader to the texts on the subject and the ethnography that has been built up (Di Lorenzo 2009); nor do I intend to pass a full judgment on shopping centers, which despite everything have important elements of usefulness and economic advantages for families.

11. One balcony can overlook six to eight flats; one row of balconies, even with only one French window, can also overlook six flats.

12. Note that there are now certain public services such as post offices and banks in the shopping center.

13. These days, the big parks do not have many visitors (except for runners and joggers); their size, bleak character, and distance from residential areas make them rather uninviting.

14. The perceived decrease in the dimensions of living accommodation and the very high relative cost of accommodation has caused many residents to feel defrauded, or in more popular terms "ripped off." It should be noted that residents in the nearby unlawful settlements (*Cinquina*), even though they are in a more logistically inconvenient area lacking local services and indeed are seeking new accommodation, say that they would never move to Bufalotta–Porta di Roma.

References

Amendola, Giandomenico, ed. 2006, *La città vetrina: I luoghi del commercio e le nuove forme del consumo.* Naples: Liguori.

Augé, Marc. 1992. *Non-lieux.* Paris: Seuil.

Ballard, James G. 2006. *Kingdom Come.* London: Fourth Estate.

Belmessous, Hacène. 2009. *Le nouveau bonheur français: Ou le monde selon Disney.* Nantes, France: Librairie l'Atalante.

Di Lorenzo, Andrea. 2009. *La città e i nuovi centri. Etnografia di uno shopping center: Porta di Roma.* Specialist degree thesis in the discipline of Ethno-Anthropology, Facoltà di Lettere e Filosofia, Sapienza Università, Rome.

Erbani, Francesco. 2008. "Porta di Roma." In *Uneternal City. Urbanism Beyond Rome.* Catalog of the 11th International Architecture Exhibition, Biennale of Venice, Marseilles, and Padua. Venice: Marsilio.

Ilardi, Massimo, ed. 2005. *Grande Raccordo Anulare.* Monographic issue, *Gomorra* 5 (9).

Lefebvre, Henri. 1968. *Le droit à la ville.* Paris: Éditions Anthropos.

Mumford, Lewis. 1938. *The Culture of Cities.* New York: Harcourt, Brace & Co.

———. 1961. *The City in History.* New York: Harcourt, Brace & Co.

Regione Lazio. 2007. *La casa dello specchio: Indagine sul rapporto tra gli adolescenti e i centri commerciali*. Rome: La Maieutica-Ricerca e Formazione.

Scandurra, Enzo, Bruno Amoroso, Paolo Berdini, Alberto Castagnola, Antonio Castronovi, Giovanni Caudo, Carlo Cellamare, et al. 2007. *Modello Roma: L'ambigua modernità*. Rome: Odradek.

Scarso, Ilaria. 2005. "Una main street di asteroidi." *Gomorra* 5 (9): 84–89.

Valle, Pietro. 2005. "Porta di Roma: Il progetto urbanistico *Bufalotta*." *Gomorra* 5 (9): 80–83.

PART III
ROME AND ITS FRACTURED MODERNITIES

10 Roma, *Città Sportiva*

Simon Martin

Sᴘᴏʀᴛꜱ ᴀɴᴅ ꜱᴘᴏʀᴛɪɴɢ events have played a crucial role in shaping Rome, stimulating major transformations in urban planning and the evolution of the cityscape throughout its history. One of the largest urban footprints was left upon the city by the 1960 Olympic Games, which resulted in infrastructural changes and planning decisions that continue to resonate in the capital and among its inhabitants. As Rome prepared its bid to host the 2020 Olympic Games, the question of whether the planners had learned any lessons from the past was inevitably posed. The decision not to back the bid, which was taken by the leader of Italy's technical government Mario Monti and resulted in its withdrawal, suggested that at least the lesson of financial prudence had finally been understood. While good sense left Monti with almost no alternative, there was nonetheless huge potential for this major sporting event to, once again, radically affect urban development in the capital. Nonetheless, as analyses of Rome's central role in Italy's hosting of the 1990 World Cup finals and the more recent 2009 World Swimming Championships reveal, the positive potential has often come at significant cost. While leaving their marks upon the city, these international tournaments also revealed the type of internecine struggles for local and national political power and resources that have wracked Italy and Rome's postwar history. Providing opportunities for illicit practices and corruption, such events were still fundamental moments in the capital's development that have too often been overlooked and thereby warrant this overview.

Sport and Place

Karl Raitz's suggestion that the creation of a sense of place is largely based around the history and past events associated with that site (Raitz 1995) can clearly be directly applied to almost all sporting venues. It is as much their history as the current event—if not more so—that gives meaning and importance to fans and thereby roots stadiums into the fabric of the city. Applied to Rome, with its over two thousand years of sporting heritage, the concept becomes clearer.

Raitz's theory reflects much of John Bale's extensive work on sport and place in which he suggests that the relationship between fans and the sport venue is determined by the various meanings attributed to the stadiums as "religious" sites that provide a sense of "home," as "heritage" sites, and as "educators" (Bale 1993). Encouraging the development and dissemination of rules, hierarchies, rituals, and symbols that contribute to the integration of mind and spirit, they become secular sites of collective worship that can change according to results. Fans may view their regular home venue as a church or cathedral of sport, while a succession of away defeats sees enemy territories morbidly mutate into graveyards full of bad luck and memories. The concept of "home" and "away" sporting venues is clearly fundamental in creating a sense of place, pride, and affection. Forging sentiments of belonging that are rooted in the celebration of past glories and epic defeats, this further adds to developing the concept of sporting sites as heritage. Furthermore, such past achievements and great victories in sporting venues are means by which rules and values are imparted and role models created. In this way, if the Italian political theorist Antonio Gramsci's Marxist interpretation is applied, stadiums become key actors in the elite's establishment of a cultural hegemony that maintains the status quo in society. These factors that affect the relationship between fans and the sports venue are integral in the development of national-, regional-, local-, and city-based identities. As Bale suggests, these are what make sport "one of the few things that binds people to place simply through ascription" (Crawford 2004, 67).

Historical Context: Rome as Ludic City

To demonstrate the relationship between sport and place there is arguably no better city than Rome, where sport is so defined, evident, and enduring and where, consequently, it has had a profound impact upon the capital's character and growth. Where other metropolises have developed around trade, industry, economy, or religion, Rome is a city of sport and leisure: a ludic city. Ever present, integral features, Rome's stadiums and events have both encouraged and influenced its ever-changing nature, preceding that of its most obvious rival as the principal city-shaper, the Catholic Church.

Rome's relationship with sport dates back to the antics of antiquity: the ancient games, chariot racing, and gladiatorial contests. Yet even if "bread and circuses" did contribute to creating a degenerate society and the empire's downfall, it left a legacy of impressive structures around which the city would evolve and thoroughfares would pass. Like the ancient Greek hippodromes, Roman circuses were large, open-air, and among the most important entertainment sites of the time. Hosting horse, mule, and donkey races, with and without chariots and riders in the Republican period, they were almost exclusively reserved for competitive chariot racing during the time of the empire. Initially possessing religious and triumphal significance, the increasing dedication of races to the creation of spectacle and entertainment demanded circuses capable of accommodating significant numbers of spectators. With its long lateral terraces, the Circus Maximus seated in the region of 250,000 spectators prior to its destruction in the great fire of 64 A D.

In addition to the circuses, ancient Rome saw the construction of numerous stadiums. Reflecting their Greek origins, where stadiums were often situated at the foot of a hill from which spectators could view the entertainment below, Rome's early arenas took advantage of natural slopes, where possible, with terracing conforming to the Greek-style, U-shaped arena. Used primarily for athletic competitions, the first permanent stadium to be constructed was that of the Emperor Domitian, following his election in 81 A D. Based upon the design of the stadiums in Olympia and Athens, the elongated rectangle was capped by a curve at the northern end of the arena and a short straight at the south.

Like many Roman structures, following its abandonment the remains of the walls provided the foundations for the construction of civil and religious buildings that conformed exactly to the perimeter of the arena, thereby leaving the central area free. Renamed Campo Agonis, the area would later become known as Piazza Navona, which, from the 1600s to the 1800s, would be flooded every weekend in August to host the performance of mock maritime battles.

In the modern age, the Tiber River also made its contribution to the ludic city by hosting one of Rome's oldest and most distinguished societies. Two years after the city had been seized by the new Italian state, the Società Ginnastica dei Canottieri del Tevere introduced gymnastics and rowing to the city. Recognized by the Savoy Royal family, the club's merger with the Anzio-based Circolo del Remo created one of Italy's most aristocratic sports associations. At the same time as the Liberal Italian regime tried to establish a better relationship between the king and his new capital, the Reale Circolo Canottieri Tevere Remo's nationalist ideals encapsulated the ethos of the era.[1] With such huge lengths of coastline to defend, swimming had long been recognized as a military skill and, consequently, was promoted in united Italy as the perfect type of physical training to contribute to the creation of the citizen soldier. With the Tiber, one of the first organized swimming venues in Italy, the first clubs naturally came from the capital; the Società Rari Nantes and Società Romana di Nuoto (Rome Swimming Society) were based on the river just beyond the Porta del Popolo. Developing the sporting dimension of what had long been considered a health and fitness activity, affluent members of these clubs organized the first official competitive race in 1893. The Rome Championship was a 7.5 km swim along the Tiber.

From this point onward, sporting Rome and the now-capital city would develop symbiotically; the bid to host the 1908 Olympic Games was its first major entry onto the international field of play. Rome was the front-runner among the candidate cities of Berlin, Milan, and London, even after the visit of International Olympic Committee founder and chief Baron Pierre de Coubertain, whose positivity was matched by King Victor Emmanuel III and the city mayor Prospero Colonna. Others, however, held serious reservations. Most notable were Angelo Mosso, the Turin Gymnastic Society president and founder of modern Italian sport, and Giovanni Giolitti, the Italian prime minister from 1903 to 1905. Arguing that the city's lack of preparation and incapacity to host such a large event would result in international embarrassment, both opposed Rome's bid to host the Olympic Games. Preparations continued unabated, all the same, and included the adaptation of ancient Roman facilities such as the Baths of Caracalla for fencing and wrestling—offering both atmosphere and practicality—and the use of the Tiber for swimming events.

Rome's eventual withdrawal of its candidacy saw the tournament go to London, but plans to host the 1908 Olympic Games had been closely related to the city's modernization and the development of its new industrial zone in the southern Ostiense district. Furthermore, it also contributed to the national recovery from the fin-de-siècle crisis that had seen anarchists assassinate King Umberto I in 1900 and the explosion of a real-estate bubble that forced government intervention to avoid a total collapse of the Italian banking system. In terms of Olympic history, it was too early for the buzzword of legacy to enter the discourse, but regeneration and the opportunity to place Rome on the international sporting map had unquestionably been major motivational factors behind the capital's bid.

Fascist Rome

Local and international considerations also underpinned Fascism's investment in sport in 1930s Italy. As the economy suffered under domestic and global economic pressures, the construction of stadiums and sports facilities secured the regime significant international prestige, provided work, and stimulated local economies. While this alone could not fight recession and the Great Depression, fascist Italy rode the economic storm of the 1930s better than some countries did.

The self-declared heir of Roman glory, power, civil, and military strength, fascist Italy demanded equality with other states at the same time as it tried to establish superiority, especially in the Mediterranean region. Recognizing architecture's power to subtly persuade and its potential for political propaganda and mass communication, Rome's archaeological and historic wealth was supplemented by a building campaign worthy of the new fascist "empire." Claiming to be modernist and revolutionary at the same time as it attempted to reconstruct the glory of imperial Rome, the regime sought to legitimize its rule by linking these two apparently incompatible influences.

With no "blueprint" of what constituted fascist architecture or art, by the mid-1930s, *romanità* (Romanness) and modernism had been combined to form a distinct style that was neither backward- nor forward-looking, but represented the fascist present. As highly prominent buildings in fascist Italy, sports arenas in particular represented the philosophical contradictions of the regime's broad cultural influences. By enabling it to market a modern, futuristic, revolutionary society while extolling the virtues of its Roman past, stadiums evidenced an architectural style that remained inclusive but avoided the need to make any concrete, potentially problematic, definitions. "More than just training grounds and 'theatres' for the masses, stadia unquestionably served as propaganda vehicles in the regime's attempt to construct a national culture and community" (Martin 2004, 80).

In its "era of stadiums," the construction of major, multisport venues was also intended to demonstrate fascist Italy's capacity to host large, prestigious events. Developing international awareness of the regime, tournaments such as the 1928 World Diving Championship—held in Bologna's Littoriale complex—and the 1934 Football World Cup boosted both the economy and the regime's credibility as an organizer and productive force, essential qualities if Mussolini was to achieve his ultimate desire of hosting the 1940 Olympic Games.

The key in fascist Italy's Olympic ambition was Rome's Foro Mussolini, which blended a strong neoclassical interpretation of the ancient past with fascist mosaics, symbols, and slogans. Contributing to its process of self-legitimization by association with ancient Rome, sports stadiums were perfect venues to which the regime "entrusted the materialization of its myth to the architectural world" (Gentile 1990, 246).

Begun in 1928, the complex was inspired and driven by Renato Ricci, head of the fascist youth organization Opera Nazionale Balilla, who launched the development of an entirely new zone in Rome's northwestern periphery. A direct response to the 1919 urban master plan that trebled the capital in geographical size,[2] the foro's development on reclaimed marshland on the banks of the Tiber was concrete evidence of fascist *bonifica* (reclamation) in action. Including the restoration of swampland to constructive use, such programs connected with the regime's ruralization campaign saw the draining of the Pontine Marshes, south of Rome, and, more metaphorically, the physical regeneration of society.

A residential training institute for prospective physical education teachers, the Foro Mussolini was celebrated as a physical, scientific, artistic, historic, and political expression of Fascism's intention to regenerate Italy. Situated at the foot of the Monte Mario Hill and set in a natural bowl, it too directly referenced the stadiums and theaters of classical antiquity that were often found in the most aesthetically pleasing peripheral areas of cities and towns.

Overseen by Enrico Del Debbio, one of fascist Italy's most influential architects, the complex's patron, Renato Ricci, was also deeply involved in all design, architectural, and engineering decisions. One of the largest building sites in Mussolini's Rome, artists and architects informally offered their services to Ricci in the hope of being co-opted to the project. Dedicated to the physical education of Italian youth and inspired by sport- and regime-sponsored cults of youth and the body, the "complex realized a physical education city in Italy. Modernizing and expanding the antique 'Gymnasium,' it raised the national importance of physical education and symbolized the intent to regenerate the physical culture of the future generations" (Del Debbio 1933, 65).[3] Representing continuity, progress, and change, the Foro Mussolini was laden with displays of myths and values around which a common identity could be built.

Key in the future memorialization of the new fascist civilization, the zone was tied to Mussolini, whose name was cut into a tall, white marble obelisk that still marks the entry to the now renamed Foro Italico and Via Piazzale dell'Impero. This walkway, leading to the site's principal stadium, was decorated with classically inspired fascist mosaics of sporting and historical scenes, as well as huge blocks of marble upon which the key events in the modern history of Italy were etched. Equally spectacular was the Stadio dei Marmi, the smaller arena for the use of academy students. Crowned by statues of imposing sporting figures from the ancient and modern periods, the venue saw the merger of imperial tradition and fascist modernity to create a striking identity that was specific to the regime. "After Caesar's Rome, Papal Rome, here is Rome of Fascist Italy," declared the journalist Vittorio Orazi, in 1934 (Orazi 1934, 5).

Higher, Faster, Further, Richer: The 1960 Rome Olympics

Following the fall of Fascism in 1943, the Foro Mussolini understandably continued to command attention, but not always from those who glorified it. In fact, with the war still raging, debate had already begun regarding its future, with many demanding it be razed to the ground. Following the liberation of Rome in June 1944, the foro's position just outside of the city center across the river, its size, and the ease with which it could be secured caused it to be occupied by U.S. and British forces who remained for some years. While Mussolini's Rome was subjected to an "iconoclastic" orgy of destruction, this occupation by Allied troops saved the foro almost in its entirety.

Despite Mussolini's desire to host the 1940 Olympic Games, for diplomatic reasons, Italy gave way to Japan, which, in return, agreed to support Rome's theoretical bid to host the 1944 event. This failed to take place due to the global conflict, but the capital's moment finally came when, in 1955, the International Olympic Committee awarded it the games. The 1960 Rome Olympic Games were the concluding chapter in postwar Italy's rehabilitation and an opportunity for its elite to display its vision of the reconstructed country and city to the global audience. Presenting a modern, thriving democracy that had moved on from its fascist past, the Olympic Games provided a unique opportunity to establish rejuvenated Italy as an important and developed international actor, no longer reconstructing but in full and healthy economic growth.

Analysis of preparations for the tournament, however, reveals the nature and extent of the deeply conservative Christian Democrat Party's (DC) postwar hegemony over national political life. The dominant force in Rome's municipal government, the DC's monopoly of power was reflected in the controversial and deeply flawed decision to site the Olympic Games at opposite ends of the city. In the decade that began with preparations for the Catholic Church's Jubilee in 1950, construction for the Rome games was the final act in ten years of plundering of the city's real estate that became known as the twentieth-century "Sack of Rome" (Martin 2011a, 84).

Headed by DC Deputy Giulio Andreotti, the Rome 1960 Organizing Committee had two options for the Olympic park. The most obvious and expected was the redevelopment and expansion of the Foro Italico site. Alternatively, there was a proposal to construct a series of completely new facilities in the city's eastern suburbs, roughly between the Roman consular roads of Via Salaria and Via Casilina. Holding the Olympic Games there would have guaranteed a huge boost to sport and leisure in one of the capital's poorest areas, which was in need of drastic regeneration. Even though legacy was yet to become an International Olympic Committee prerequisite, the lack of interest in this potentially long-lasting benefit was indicative of the Italian Olympic Committee's approach to mass sport.

With development in the needy, eastern sector of the city excluded, the games were divided between the Foro Italico site and the Esposizione Universale Roma district. Almost diametrically opposite in the north and south of the capital, this choice demanded new infrastructure and a connecting road. As one of Italy's first environmentalists, Antonio Cederna, protested, the decision did not correspond with the demands of the city's master plan (Cederna 1965, 59). Moreover, its contempt for the elementary norms of reasonable urban planning marked it as a truly decisive turn for Rome.

Connecting these two distant sporting centers, the Via Olimpica was projected as a fast-flowing highway. In reality, it consisted of some new road sections stitched together with existing, redeveloped streets. So incapable was it of dealing with traffic during the event that its use was restricted to athletes and accredited journalists. More significant, however, was the road's impact on land prices in the northwestern sector of the city, much of which was owned by the Società Generale Immobiliare (General Estate Agency). Among its major shareholders were the Vatican, FIAT, and the cement producer Italcementi.

Enquiries by the left-wing newspapers *L'Espresso* and *L'Unità* exposed an alleged carve-up to the exclusive advantage of the land's religious proprietors (Benedetti 1960, 1; Cancogni 1960, 11; Perria 1960, 3). With values rising by 150 percent in ten years, the Vatican was proposed as *the* Olympic winner. As Terry Kirk argued in his architectural study of the city: "For the same reasons that Mayor Ernesto Nathan had turned down the idea of hosting the Olympics in

1908—encouraging real-estate speculation—Mayor Salvatore Rebecchini of the Christian Democrat party accepted" (Kirk 2005, 196–197).

Thus, the DC stranglehold over Rome's city administration was a microcosm of its unchallenged role in national government that led to stagnation, corruption, and minimal reform. The result was an eruption of violence, from the late 1960s onward, in the form of student and worker protests and a reaction from the extreme right.

Italia Novanta

Italian society's unrest continued long beyond the hot summer of 1968. In 1978, former Prime Minister Aldo Moro was executed by the communist Red Brigades. This was followed, two years later, by the murder of eighty-five citizens in a bomb blast at Bologna station which was eventually attributed to extreme right-wing forces. Sport provided welcome relief from the violence of the "years of lead," with the 1982 World Cup victory giving Italians good reason to celebrate. Moreover, the victory made a significant contribution to the country's successful bid to host the 1990 tournament, the final of which would be held in Rome.

Preparations for the event included the modernization of existing stadiums and the construction of new ones across the peninsula and an accompanying program of infrastructural development. From the original estimates, costs rose astronomically in order to "satisfy the hunger for bribes that regulated the relationship between big business and the political class" (Triani 1994, 81). Another snapshot of the type of corruption that had developed since the 1960s, it was a warning of the impending political earthquake to come following the exposure of the Tangentopoli scandal and the subsequent Clean Hands inquiry. "Italia 90" provided a huge opportunity to move money. Irregular, direct transfers of state funds to families and businesses, the creation of a massive tax avoidance system, the construction of "World Cup facilities" in cities that would not host a single match were accompanied by lax building controls and dangerous working practices that left 24 workers dead and 648 injured (Martin 2011b, 206).

As the showpiece arena that would host the final, Rome's Stadio Olimpico received a face-lift and a roof, for the first time in its history. A new station was opened at nearby Vigna Clara, but it functioned on only eight days during the tournament after which it was closed and never reopened. Expected to alleviate public transport pressure in this area of the city once the event had been concluded, it was supposed to have been connected to the Nomentana station, but the track was never laid.

2009 World Swimming Championships

A number of swimming pools were built across the capital theoretically for the 2009 World Swimming Championships, but with a certain legacy in mind. The failure, however, of some contractors to meet construction deadlines for facilities projected as training camps for the various national teams once again raised serious questions about transparency and the extent to which lessons from the past had been learned.

As accusations of corruption began to dog the construction process, the irreverent investigative television journalists of Mediaset's *Le Iene* asked some very difficult and very public questions following a series of articles in the daily newspaper *La Repubblica* in 2009. Four hundred million euros were allocated for the creation of five major venues, the bulk of which was dedicated to a new Palazzo dello Sport, nicknamed La Vela (the sail). An unmistakable addition to the skyline in Rome's eastern periphery, visible from as far away as the Janiculum Hill, four years after the event the building remained unfinished. To be completed in two stages—the first for the swimming championship and the second in time for the following year's volleyball tournament in April 2009—the structure was intended to be a key part of Italy's expected 2020 Olympic bid. However, only four months before the world's elite swimmers were due to perform, *Le Iene*'s journalists revealed that works had barely begun and the tournament was moved to the fascist-built Foro Italico. In July 2011, responding to the suspension of works, the Rome City Councilor Marco Corsini stated: "The figure of €408 million in the current economic circumstances is significant and it is difficult to predict a quick solution, but certainly if public finance difficulties continue the Olympic bid will be decisive" (Boccacci 2011).

Given the huge expenditure of public money, equally worrying was the construction of dozens of private pools with no connection to the event beyond their apparent necessity as training venues. One case described by Corrado Zunino, in April 2009, was that of three new pools built on land owned by the city council but used by members of the exclusive rowing club Canottieri Aniene in Rome's affluent Parioli quarter. Costing almost fourteen million euros, funds were raised through the public body Credito Sportivo and would be repaid over twenty years. Club president Giovanni Malagò, who also happened to be president of the Swimming World Championships Organizing Committee, promised that the pools would be open to schools and citizens of the local area in which, incidentally, there were already twenty within a radius of 1 km of the Foro Italico (Zunino 2009, 7).

To serve the apparent needs of the World Championships, a further eight pools were also projected in this most affluent part of the city. At its complex near the Foro Italico, the Club Tevere Remo also joined the fray, pursuing authorization to build a pool despite the municipal government's initially negative assessment. Two other societies also began works on their own projects thanks to the efforts of their managing director Luigi Barelli, whose brother was president of the National Swimming Federation and vice president of the 2009 event's organizing committee. In the Villa Flaminia dei Fratelli delle Scuole Cristiane (Villa Flaminia of the Brothers of Christian Schools), a 12 m pool was deemed necessary for athletes to warm up prior to entering the already existing 25 m version. Following the closing ceremony, it was destined to become part of a private health club. At the nearby Flaminio Sporting Club, the diggers were already excavating for a second pool, in an area that the city authorities had previously declared untouchable, when permission was granted for a huge pool for children (Zunino 2009, 7).

Further out of the city on the banks of the Tiber at Settebagni, the Salaria Sport Village's imposing additions to its existing facilities resulted in the first inquiry. At the expense of thirty eight million euros, the members-only club would be blessed with a covered, Olympic-sized, ten-lane pool, plus two more 25 m versions, one covered and one open-air. Launched in January 2009, the investigation considered any irregularities in the approval of these projects by the Extraordinary Commission for Rome 2009, after officials of the Rome municipality and the Region of Lazio had earlier "definitively" rejected the plans. It was the sort of affair into which the president of the parliamentary Green Party, Angelo Bonelli, demanded an inquiry in April 2009: "We need to verify if all of the buildings authorized by the Commission for the Swimming World Championships were directly tied to the event and if public money or the benefits of sporting credit intended for the championships were used to build facilities that had nothing to do with this important sporting competition" (*La Repubblica* 2009, 5).

Roma Sportiva Futuristica

As the Comune di Roma and the Italian Olympic Committee assembled the city's bid to host the 2020 Olympic Games, the capital's development around sport and the questions raised by the World Swimming Championships were particularly relevant. In addition to the plan to use four sites, the proposed infrastructural changes such as metro improvements, the return of the Tiber embankments as a central axis of road traffic in the city, and the pedestrianization of the center raised valid questions as to the extent that past lessons had been learned in terms of the relationship between sport and urban development. The removal of Rome from the bidding process, however, left this unanswered.

As pressure on space in Rome increases it seems inevitable that sporting facilities will begin to encroach upon the Lazio countryside, which will maintain sport's omnipresent role in the city's development. Nonetheless, it is highly likely that this will affect the capital's sporting identity, especially with the proposed plans of AS Roma and SS Lazio to leave the Stadio Olimpico for their own stadiums outside of the city center. Should such moves materialize, responses to them will offer an interesting comparison with the often fierce objection from many English fans to their club's relocation. As Bale (1993) suggests, many fans' love of place (topophilia) or specific venue is augmented by the atmosphere within the ground, the emotions associated with attending a match, and the memory of shared past experiences. While almost all English professional clubs have their own stadium that ties them closely to their location and thus creates importance and meaning for fans, there already appears to be significant difference for Roma and Lazio supporters who not only share their "home" but also rent it from the Italian Olympic Committee.

Somewhat belatedly, Italian sports venues and the sporting "experience" are beginning to change. This comes primarily in response to outdated, poor facilities and stadiums that have contributed to a malaise in attendance figures and the significantly reduced revenue that football clubs are able to raise when leasing rather than owning their own grounds. While the importance that Bale attaches to space and place is unquestionably valid, the moving of stadia to the periphery must be expected to change the relationship between sports venues, fans, and the city and, consequently, the meanings attached to them by supporters, spectators, and citizens.

With the recent construction of huge out-of-town shopping centers, such as Roma Est and Euroma2, there is a clear future direction: expansion (see chapter 9). Equally, the Italian obsession with cars, partly created by the necessity for personal over public means of transport, makes the move to out-of-town venues quite logical. Furthermore, the reduction of personal associations with the shared, Italian Olympic Committee–owned Stadio Olimpico makes such moves potentially less traumatic for Roman fans, especially those of Lazio whose supporter base has always been far stronger in the region's countryside. With the plans made even more intriguing following Roma's purchase, in 2011, by an Italo-American consortium, the comparison of Italian sports stadiums with those in America, as described by Gary Crawford, is striking:

> By the 1950s many North American baseball parks were over forty years old and increasingly outdated and "ageing fast," and the suburbanization increased affluence and mobilization (largely due to the rising popularity of the motor car), of America's middle class saw many baseball teams relocate to suburban or out-of-town venues. The American middle class had left behind the overcrowded city centres, and many were reluctant to travel back into these for their leisure and entertainment. In growth which mirrored out-of-town shopping malls, North American sports stadiums began to appear on development sites on major road networks away from city centres and located within convenient distance of other entertainment and leisure facilities (Crawford 2004, 72).

Since the end of the Second World War and the cultural and economic penetration of Italy by the United States, principally through European Reconstruction Aid (Marshall Plan) money, there appears to have been an inexorable wave of American influence over Italian society and its cultural development in particular (Forgacs 1990, Forgacs and Gundle 2007, Scrivano 2005). Whereas Italian cinema suffered considerably following the repeal of Fascism's 1938 Monopoly Law and the subsequent influx of Hollywood B movies that had been stockpiled over the years, Italian sport has resisted U.S. influence arguably more than any other cultural form. However, with new out-of-town stadiums being proposed across the country, it is questionable how long some of the intrinsically Italian aspects of the stadium and football will remain.

Juventus's new ground in Turin, inaugurated in September 2011, is now generally considered to be the model to which Italian clubs must aspire. Containing a shopping center and a museum, it was envisaged that the stadium would be hired for corporate events and used seven days a week. Built on land acquired from the city, Juventus's own venue has certainly allowed the club to begin making the sort of profits that will enable it to be competitive on a European level once again. Yet the multisport, multiuse, out-of-town stadium is not a new concept in Italy, with Bologna's 1928 Stadio Littoriale being a case in point. Despite having been lauded for its innovation, beyond football, the concept failed and the stadium was rarely full.

With both Roman clubs now proposing fifty-thousand-plus-seat venues in the Lazio countryside, which will include shopping malls and housing complexes, one wonders if their fans are ready for such grand plans. Even if America's influence upon Italian life might make such moves logical, the practice may well be different. Either way, there can be no doubt that Lazio's and Roma's abandoning of the urban center will once again have a major psychological and physical impact upon the future of this sport city.

Notes

1. Approximate translations for these organizations' names are: Tiber Gymnastics and Rowing Club (Società Ginnastica dei Canottieri del Tevere), Rowing Society (Circolo del Remo), Royal Tiber Rowing Club (Reale Circolo Canottieri Tevere Remo).

2. The population of Rome reached 1 million inhabitants in 1931 and 1.4 million by 1941. By the end of Fascism, the population had doubled with respect to that of 1922 (Insolera 1962).

3. All translations are my own unless otherwise indicated.

References

Bale, John. 1993. *Sport, Space and the City*. London: Routledge.
Benedetti, Arrigo. 1960. "Un record italiano. Affari e Olimpiadi." *L'Espresso*, 21 August.
Boccacci, Paolo. 2011. "La città dello sport, l'incompiuta dove svetta la Vela di Calatrava." *La Repubblica*, 17 July. http://roma.repubblica.it/cronaca/2011/07/17/news

/la_citt_dello_sport_l_incompiuta_dove_svetta_la_vela_di_calatrava-19240963/. Accessed 28 September 2013.

Cancogni, Manlio. 1960. "Dietro il sorriso di Rebecchini quattrocento miliardi." *L'Espresso,* 11 December.

Cederna, Antonio. 1965. *Mirabilia Urbis: Cronache romane 1957–1965.* Turin: Einaudi.

Crawford, Garry. 2004. *Consuming Sport: Fans, Sport and Culture.* London: Routledge.

Del Debbio, Enrico. 1933. "Il Foro Mussolini in Roma.," *Architettura* February: 65–75.

Forgacs, David. 1990. *Italian Culture in the Industrial Era, 1880–1980: Cultural Industries, Politics, and the Public.* Manchester: Manchester University Press.

Forgacs, David, and Stephen Gundle. 2007. *Mass Culture and Italian Society from Fascism to the Cold War.* Bloomington: Indiana University Press.

Gentile, Emilio. 1990. "Fascism as a Political Religion." *Journal of Contemporary History* 25 (2/3): 229–251.

Insolera, Italo. 1962. *Roma Moderna. Un secolo di storia urbanistica.* Turin: Einaudi.

Kirk, Terry. 2005. *The Architecture of Modern Italy, Volume II: Visions of Utopia 1900–Present.* New York: Princeton Architectural Press.

La Repubblica. 2009. "Aprite un'inchiesta sulle nuove piscine." *La Repubblica,* 24 April. http://ricerca.repubblica.it/repubblica/archivio/repubblica/2009/04/24/aprite-un-inchiesta-sulle-nuove-piscine.html. Accessed 28 September 2013.

Martin, Simon. 2004. *Football and Fascism: The National Game under Mussolini.* Oxford: Berg.

———. 2011a. "Bikila's Aria: Rome 1960." In *Sport and the Transformation of Modern Europe: States, Media and Markets 1950–2010,* edited by Alan Tomlinson, Christopher Young, and Richard Holt, 83–99. London: Routledge.

———. 2011b. *Sport Italia: The Italian Love Affair With Sport.* London: IB Tauris.

Orazi, Vittorio. 1934. "La città eterna." *La Citta Nuova,* 5 January.

Perria, A. 1960. "Lo stato del Vaticano ha vinto le Olimpiadi." *L'Unità,* 2 August.

Raitz, Karl. 1995. *The Theater of Sport.* Baltimore, Md.: Johns Hopkins Press.

Scrivano, Paolo. 2005. "Signs of Americanization in Italian Domestic Life: Italy's Postwar Conversion to Consumerism." *Journal of Contemporary History* 40: 317–340.

Triani, Giorgio. 1994. *Bar sport Italia: Quando la politica va nel pallone.* Milan: Elèuthera.

Zunino, Corrado. 2009. "Circoli, la carica delle piscine Mondiali." *La Repubblica,* 18 April. http://ricerca.repubblica.it/repubblica/archivio/repubblica/2009/04/18/circoli-la-carica-delle-piscine-mondiali.html). Accessed 28 September 2013.

11 Football, *Romanità*, and the Search for Stasis

Mark Dyal

In Search of Glory

Rome is a city whose past is rich in images of warfare, conquest, and glory. From Virgil's proclamation that the Romans were a people predetermined to rule the world, to Mussolini's desire to reestablish Roman control of the Mediterranean, the idea that Rome and glory are interrelated has a long history. In contemporary Rome, it is an idea that has been adopted by the fans of the city's football teams. As Associazione Sportiva Roma (AS Roma) and Società Sportiva Lazio (SS Lazio) search for wins in Italian and European football, both teams' fans use a set of symbols culled from classical and fascist Rome designed to connect victory on the field, and often in the streets, with the idealized supremacy of Roman culture. However, these symbols are often at odds with the demographic realities of contemporary Rome. While the city is moving toward the multiculturalism found in other world capitals, many of its football fans embrace *romanità*, a deep affection for Rome and things Roman, in an effort to identify with a primordial Rome that is impervious to contemporary political and social trends. This chapter explains how football keeps alive a sense of Roman-ness that originated with the fascist regime, while also explaining the affinities and contrasts between the fans of AS Roma and SS Lazio.

Framework and Methodology: Symbols of Identity between the Local and the Global

This chapter examines the complex relationship between Rome's cultural and political past and contemporary football fandom. As such, it draws not only from those like Allen Guttman (1981), who study sports spectators, and from anthropologists of sport like Richard Giulianotti (1999) and Gary Armstrong

(1998), who study football fans and cultures, but also from authors like Simon Martin (2004), Michael Herzfeld (2009), and Paul Baxa (2010) who study the more specific social and political fields in which Roman football and fandom occur.

While not necessarily designed to address the built environment of Rome, a topic that Martin, Herzfeld, and Baxa—like Painter (2005)—cover extensively, this study nonetheless converses with those authors on the topic of *romanità* and its ability to influence contemporary Romans. As a concept, *romanità* is rather self-congratulatory, which might be considered an oddity given how prominently it was used by Fascism (see Gentile 1996; Falasca-Zamponi 1997; Griffin 2007; Baxa 2010). *Romanità* does have a long history, having been used by both liberal and fascist Italy as a universalizing narrative designed to give Italians a national worldview. At the same time, *romanità* is the exclusive purview of the Romans, a discourse of cultural and historical particularity and uniqueness.

This understanding of *romanità* comes from the competitive environment of professional football. In Europe, but especially Italy, football teams are deeply ingrained aspects of well-developed local identities. Rome is no different in this than Udine, Florence, or Palermo, for instance. Unlike those cities, however, Rome has two high-level professional teams and, hence, a divided populace. And while every Italian city can boast a long history of unique economic, social, and political developments, none can rival the depth or importance of Rome's contributions to Italian and world history. Thus, the field of symbols and images that Rome provides to its citizens and football fans is arguably the broadest and deepest in Italy. These symbols, such as the Lupa Capitolina (Capitoline She-Wolf—henceforth Lupa) and the Roman Imperial Eagle, not only represent the teams that use them, but also influence the ideologies utilized by their fans to identify with the city itself. This is important to remember when assessing the role played by football and fandom in the city.

During 18 months (2006–2008) of ethnographic study among AS Roma's Ultras, I learned how football operates as a nexus between the global nature of capital and human labor flows, and the lived experience of a highly local (and localist) cultural system. With European football teams fielding many foreign players and being sponsored by multinational corporations, local fans are forced to come to terms with the business aspects of the game that often overshadow the local meaningfulness of the teams they follow. In Rome, this has never been more apparent as in 2011, when a consortium led by American Thomas Di Benedetto bought AS Roma with an eye toward turning the team into a "global brand." Furthermore, the fans themselves negotiate the inter- and intranational migration of peoples. This chapter, therefore, wrestles with the discontent, but also spectacle, produced by globalization, while also suggesting that the local Roman context is constantly reimagined through the lens of football fandom.

Football: The Game of Passion

In his study of sports spectators, Allan Guttman (1981) explains that for the ancient Romans, sport had a purpose that went beyond social control and distraction. Roman spectators were extremely partisan; enough so that partisanship seems to have been the point, or at least the draw, of watching sports. Pliny the Younger, Guttman tells us, had difficulty understanding the passions of the masses for sports. If the masses had had a genuine appreciation for the skills one needs to properly control a speeding chariot, perhaps he would have been more sympathetic to their passions. Instead, Pliny said, "it is the racing colors they really support and care about, and if the colors were to be exchanged in mid-course . . . they would transfer their favor and enthusiasm. Such is the popularity and importance of a worthless shirt" (Guttman 1981, 11).

So deep were the passions for chariot teams that violence between sets of fans was common (Guttman 1981, 12). Furthermore, identification as a fan of a certain team bound one to a common body that had political clout. Certain colors, as teams were divided by color, were historically affiliated to certain parties. "Whatever differences in behavior and even social class there may have been," Guttman explains, "partisans of both colors moved in much the same world" (1981, 12).

This is one ancient tradition that remains in contemporary Rome, as the will to rivalry and partisanship is just as strong among contemporary Romans as it was with their ancient forebearers. There is no question that football is the Italian national game. While other nations, like the Netherlands and Brazil, associate the game with beauty, the Italians seem to have always associated football with warfare. Simon Martin reports on the failure of Serie A (Italy's top professional division) to unite the peninsula as Mussolini had intended because of the extreme partisanship of local fans (Martin 2004, 27). Similarly John Foot summarizes the origins of Italian football by explaining the game's exacerbation of civic rivalries (Foot 2006, 1–41). However, while football ignites and maintains civic rivalries associated with *campanilismo* (extreme localism) and politics all over the peninsula, it is in Rome that "the beauty of rivalry," as Federico, a 24-year-old AS Roma fan told me, "flows forth like the Tiber," making the city home to the most contentious and raucous fans in Italy.

Why this is the case is debated in popular and academic circles. In bars, cafés, and piazzas, it is common to hear that "Rome is a place of extremes" or that football "is a game of passion" that mixes freely with the fiery temperament of the people. In the words of Marcello, a 31-year-old barman and AS Roma supporter, the Romans possess a "ferocious spirit that seeks rivalry at every opportunity." Elsewhere, Maurizio Stefanini (2009) and Giovanni Francesio (2008) agree that in Rome football lies at the heart of a battleground mentality. My own research uncovered a deep connection among hardcore Roman football fans between an understanding of football in militaristic terms and a particular model of Rome gathered from the long Roman tradition of military aggression, glory, and greatness (Dyal 2010).

In Virgil's *Aeneid,* we are given reason to believe in the providence of Roman greatness. Later, the church made use of what it saw as the universal mission of Roman greatness, and the Risorgimento adopted what has been called the "myth of Roman continuity" (Gentile 1996, 103) in order to justify the establishment of an Italian state. Similarly, Fascism utilized Rome as the central reference point for statecraft, virtue, "discipline, and the secret of greatness" (Gentile 1996, 76). In contemporary Rome, although a recent right-wing political movement Popolo di Roma (People of Rome) has taken up the belief in the greatness of Rome and the triumph of those who share that belief, it is an idea more commonly expressed by fans of the city's football teams than by politicians.

Romanità: A Contemporary Myth

AS Roma and SS Lazio share Rome's Olympic Stadium. The stadium, redesigned for the 1960 Olympics and upgraded for the 1990 World Cup, was born as part of the Foro Mussolini (now Foro Italico—Italic Forum), a fascist sports complex located under Monte Mario, northwest of Rome's center. Introduced by Mussolini's obelisk, the stone and marble forum is a complex of four stadiums and four buildings linked by a mosaic boulevard, tiled with images of the fascist revolution and the 1922 March on Rome. The Stadio dei Marmi (Stadium of the Marbles), one of the four stadiums, is ringed by sixty statues of various sporting disciplines (Baxa 2010, 73–75). To reach the Olympic Stadium, football fans must traverse this mythical fascist landscape (Martin 2011, 152–153). That professional football takes place in this environment makes perfect sense given the fascist regime's role in creating Serie A and in professionalizing Italian sport (Martin 2004, 9–27).

However, far from being merely fascist, it is a space that is full of *romanità.* As the marble athletes and the neoclassical but modernist architecture of the complex attests, this is a structure designed to inculcate against bourgeois passivity with the virtues of classical athleticism. It is designed to aggrandize and ennoble the mythical Roman spirit in modern men and women (Baxa 2010, 117). For Roman football fans, some of the most rabid in Europe, the environs help motivate a commitment to participating in, rather than merely watching, their team's games. For the Ultras, the most committed and impassioned fans, the forum is proof of the superiority of Roman cultural forms. This sensation is part of *romanità.*

Romanità is defined by Piergiorgio Zunino as a premodern and mythical (as opposed to historical) form of collective mentality best expressed in nostalgia for ancient Rome (Fogu 2003, 23). Claudio Fogu found this definition useful as he attempted to explain how an idea of Rome operated in the fascist understanding of history. Fascist history, according to Fogu, was structurally dependent upon a break with the past. He argued that Fascism did not seek a continuation of classical Roman identity within a fascist context. Instead, it sought to use Rome, through *romanità,* to lessen the influence of a modern, linear view of history among Italians. In other words, Fascism used a concept of history that aimed at diminishing the conceptual import of the metanarratives creative of modern political subjects (Fogu 2003, 20–23).

Tracy Koon (1985), meanwhile, was less concerned about the functioning of history and historiography during the fascist era. Instead, he linked *romanità* first with liberal risorgimento thinkers and their desire to find a unifying discourse for all peoples of the peninsula. Second, he pursued *romanità* through to the fascist period to show how then, as well, the greatness of Rome's imperial power was glorified as a unifying discourse. Thus, contrary to Fogu (2003), he presented *romanità* as a narrative that created links between the classical and modern periods. By focusing more upon Mussolini's speeches and the symbolic finery of fascism, Koon understood *romanità* as a powerful tool in Mussolini's drive to create, via Fascism, a Third Rome. Indeed, part of the power of *romanità* was that as a discourse it demonstrated the supposed classical origins of Fascism (Koon 1985, 19).

For Julius Evola, *romanità* is a suprahistorical agent. He acknowledged that the radical Left perpetuated an idea that *romanità* was "antihistorical" in that it motivated attachment to ideology at the expense of commitment to class conflict and was thus an example of irrational reaction to historical dialectical processes (Evola 2002, 181). Even as he used the antihistorical concept to attack the liberalization of the world, however, he described Rome and *romanità* in Nietzsche's terms. There are immutable principles, he said, that have been useful in creating ascending cultural forms. These principles can only be found by looking toward the past, toward tradition. In his words, "tradition is neither servile conformity to what has been, nor a sluggish perpetuation of the past into the present. [It] is something simultaneously meta-historical and dynamic: it is an overall ordering force, in the service of principles that have the chrism of a superior legitimacy" (Evola 2002, 115).

Romanità has value, then, for Evola, because it does not seek to reestablish the institutions of classical Rome, but the principles of which such institutions were expressions. Some of the principles to which Evola attributed so much power were inherent in the Roman cultural and psychological characteristics to be striven for in the present. These were self-control; enlightened boldness; concise speech and determined and coherent conduct; a cold and dominating attitude; virile spirit and courage; spiritual strength; thoughtfulness and awareness; love for self-given law and form; loyalty and faithfulness; studied and moderated seriousness; respect and veneration for the gods; deliberate actions; realism as love for the essential, not the material; the ideal of clarity; inner equilibrium and suspicion of confused mysticism; love of boundaries; and unity in pursuit of higher goals (Evola 2002, 259).

Romanità and the Roman Football Clubs: AS Roma versus SS Lazio

SS Lazio was founded in 1900 in the Prati neighborhood of Rome. Prati, along with other aristocratic neighborhoods like Parioli and Flaminio, was central to the club's foundation, not only socially but also politically. The club in fact competes in a variety of sports. Thus, it chose the blue and white colors of Greece as its own, seeking a link to the Olympic tradition of excellence in multiple sporting disciplines. According to Massimiliano, owner of a pizzeria in Monteverde and local expert on his team, the founding members of SS Lazio, among them Luigi Bigiarelli, sought a "universal" color scheme and symbolic reference point in choosing the Greek colors and eagle mascot. The cosmopolitan founders of SS Lazio did not consider Rome "universal enough."

By 1927, however, SS Lazio's eagle was seen less as Greek and universal than Roman and imperial. The fascist campaign of *romanità* was busy rewriting Italy, Italians, and Rome in neoclassical style. And, despite SS Lazio being the favored football club of Mussolini, he proposed that the sporting societies of Rome be conjoined and reborn as a club competing "in the name of Rome" (Foot 2006, 112). Perhaps because of the Duce's backing, SS Lazio was able to resist the proposed merger, while three other Roman clubs were not.

In any event, in 1927, AS Roma was born and centered in the working-class neighborhood of Testaccio. Because the club was formed at the behest of the fascist regime, its boardroom was populated with leading fascists of the day, including Italo Foschi. When, in 1942, it became the first team south of Bologna to win the Italian championship, the assumption of many was that the state had played a role in this rare success (Foot 2006, 114). AS Roma chose ancient yellow and maroon-red, the colors of Rome, as its own. Similarly, its mascot is the Lupa, Rome's symbol since antiquity.

It is these founding narratives that form the terms of debate among rival fans in Rome. While both teams have had relatively modest success in an Italian football dominated by teams from the north, with AS Roma having won three championships to SS Lazio's two, the fans are left to argue over symbolism and, often, politics. For despite being founded by a mandate from the fascist regime, AS Roma was historically seen as the "people's" team while SS Lazio was seen as the team of the regime itself.

Fans, Symbols, and *Romanità*

In July 2011, SS Lazio President Claudio Lotito shocked many in Rome by questioning AS Roma's right to use the Lupa as the club's symbol. In his words, "AS

Roma's original symbol was not the *Lupa* but merely a mangy wolf . . . and besides, the *Lupa* is the symbol of Rome, not AS Roma. Therefore [SS Lazio has] as much right to use the *Lupa* as [AS Roma]."[1] It was evident from the flood of calls made to Rome's sports radio stations that SS Lazio fans were worried about Lotito demeaning their own symbol, or worse, actually considering using the Lupa on SS Lazio's jerseys.

This was an interesting move by Lotito, considering that he had recently (2009) purchased an American bald eagle to act as official team mascot. Yet, even though the bird is named Olympia, very few SS Lazio fans associate the eagle with Zeus or Greece. Instead, as so many pointed out in the wake of Lotito's comment, the eagle accompanied the Roman Legions into battle. The Lupa, it was said, was never a battle emblem. Throughout my research in Rome, fans repeatedly returned to their understanding of these two symbols as a key topic of discussion.

Augusto, a 32-year-old waiter and SS Lazio fan, dismisses the Lupa. "The eagle," he explained, "was with those who fought for Rome—and those who fought for Rome built Rome. That wolf is just a symbol of the whorish behavior of Roman women." Augusto's explanation of the symbols reflects the deep commitment of many football fans in Rome to understanding the history of the city. And while his narrative is less than accurate, it is difficult to say whether working-class Romans would discuss this history with such an impassioned point of view without the lens of football.

Manuele, a founding member of *Fedayn* (an AS Roma Ultra group), explained *romanità* to me in simple terms: "*Romanità* is the thing that makes Romans different from and superior to any others. It links us with the past and future of the city, and our city is more steeped in glory and conquest, in veneration and honor, than any city in the world. Others love their cities, as they should, but when looking for glory, they have no choice but to envy us." Those populating the Ultra groups are especially prone to understanding Rome as a city of glory and conquest, as well as of honor and veneration—ideals that drove Mussolini's project to transform, aggrandize, and render more fascist the center of Rome (Painter 2005, 1–5). However, there is an important distinction between the *romanità* of the Ultras and that of Fascism. Fascism utilized *romanità* not only to lend itself legitimacy by linking its rule with imperial Rome, but also to undermine the power of *campanilismo* in the provinces. *Romanità* was to be the unifying narrative of the Italian fascist state. Thus, its universal aspects were highlighted (Falasca-Zamponi 1997, 90).

In Rome, *romanità* motivates an inversion of the universal mission, being reserved, rather, as the rarified domain of Romans. It is not a universal phenomenon or mission, but what separates Romans from the Milanese, for example. Nor is it a will to unity as part of Italian nationalism. Instead, *romanità* is useful as a discourse that limits the scope of altruistic inclusiveness. It is apparent that the Roman celebration of self is done at the expense of feelings of inclusion with others. Although many scholars and journalists lament the Italian tendency to identify with narrow scopes (hence the concept *campanilismo*), Romans understand this part of fandom to be entirely positive.

Politics, Football, and *Romanità*

The most important consequences of *romanità* and football fandom occur away from the football field, in the politics shaping contemporary Rome. Roman football fans use *romanità* in a way that subverts the fascist desire to Romanize all Italians. For the Roman football fans, *romanità* is what makes them different in a sports culture that relishes difference and, given that football is very much a part of Italian and international politics, this perspective has significant political repercussions.

Luca is a 33-year-old member of both Boys Roma (another of AS Roma's Ultra groups) and Forza Nuova (New Force—a neofascist movement). He studied political science and enjoys discussing the links between politics and sport. While discussing the Ultras' stance against globalization, he explained that multinational corporations are a menace to local cultures because they tend to demand a marketplace that acts within the strictures of American multiculturalism. The sting of a "moral prohibition" against local pride in football was already being felt, with recent governmental crackdowns on freedom of expression during games. "Why would anyone have a problem with our love of Rome?" he asked, before responding, "Only if they feared being excluded. There are many people who believe that the world belongs to them and that anywhere people build a wall against them is a sign of ignorance." "And not pride or protection," I interjected. "We are not allowed pride," he answered. "Our pride is what [Americans] call racism."

In this way, *romanità* may be understood as a bulwark against the world and it points to an exclusionary tendency in contemporary Rome, where many racially and culturally diverse immigrants are viewed with scorn. According to Caritas, Rome is home to some four hundred thousand non-Italian immigrants, comprising 14.8 percent of the city's population. These come primarily from Eastern Europe (40 percent), other European Union states (20 percent), Asia (20 percent), and Africa (10 percent). Immigrants make up 9.4 percent of the city's workforce (Nozza 2010, 16–27). While this type of immigration has seen a steady increase, Italian migration to Rome has slowed since the late 1990s (Nozza 2010, 27).

In Italian popular political discourse, unlike in America, it is still possible to debate the consequences of immigration in terms of its impact on culture. Maurizio, a 27-year-old SS Lazio fan, mirrored Luca's comments about Romans wishing to disconnect from contemporary Rome. "Our Rome," he said, "is that of the true Romans. What makes Rome special is not Chinatown, but the altar where Caesar was cremated (in the Roman Forum). Our Rome is something of value that must never be taken for granted." In this way, *romanità* may be understood as a positive force. If it acts as a bulwark against the outside world, it is doing so to protect valued traditions. If it stems the influence of foreign peoples, it does so to prohibit cultural degeneration.

Fabrizio, a lifelong SS Lazio fan, lives in Monteverde. He sells small machinery to farmers just outside Rome. His job therefore takes him in the opposite direction to the many commuters who come into Rome's center for work. "I wouldn't have it any other way. I can't stand to be around the tourists and immigrants who take our city to be a big playground or some kind of joke," he told me. He and his friends became politicized during the late 1990s renaissance of SS Lazio, which won the Italian championship and UEFA Cup between 1999 and 2000.[2] To their chagrin, though, they noticed that the team that represented them and their city was bereft of Romans. "In the past," he said, "both Lazio and Roma had local players on their teams. It was normal that [the fans] might even know some of them. Now, though, just like in the city—even in our neighborhood—we know fewer and fewer people. We see fewer faces that have shared our history and our passion for the city."

Fabrizio was a rarity in that he acknowledged the heterogeneous nature of ancient Rome. In fact, no other Roman with whom I conversed about Rome and *romanità* would admit to such a thing. "Rome," he said, "has always been an immigrant destination, even for the ancients. So it is hard to know what is ours and what is just a facade created by foreigners. The historic center [of Rome] is largely of the latter variety for us. We [residents of Monteverde] want to walk our streets and hear our language." I asked him about the monetary influence of tourism in Rome, and the way the city caters to tourism. "When drunken Poles swim in the *Trevi* [fountain], Roma stab and rape, or American students destroy Trastevere, we can do nothing and thus the Romans are enslaved by them."

Fabrizio's parents were part of a generation that saw Rome flourish as a tourist destination and that likewise flourished itself. However, his parents, like some Ultras' parents I encountered, became disillusioned with the changes tourism had brought. Especially given Monteverde's proximity to Trastevere, his parents often lamented that small restaurants and Roman butchers had closed their shops to make way for "Indians selling postcards and gaudy t-shirts." Their desperation fed Fabrizio's early passion for football, which he, like many others, saw as a way to connect with something Roman that was not tainted by the changes affecting the city. I asked if he thought Roman culture was not strong enough to withstand a few immigrants and a lot of tourists. "Fair enough," he said, "I should have more faith in my culture. It is just that we have seen so much of it change. Romans used to be proud but happy, even my parents were like that until recently. Now, we are proud and angry. We are defensive because we see that in a few more generations, the city might be more immigrant than Roman and more commercial than cultural. We've already lost political autonomy [because of the European Union] and the right to keep our city ours."

The parents' desperation points as well to a process of "cultural dispossession," wherein the economic and political system is aligned with foreign interests that ultimately eliminate the options for local people to live in a locally meaningful way (Creed 2011, 1–27). This sense of dispossession is strong among Romans, as Herzfeld (2009) has also discovered. Whereas the celebration of selfhood among Europeans is often unacknowledged before it is irrevocably under attack (Southgate 2010, 124–131), there are other possibilities—most notably the experiences of postcolonial peoples who actually achieved peoplehood as a result of a struggle for cultural survival (Said 1993, 97–111). Romans resemble the latter, in some ways, having long been keenly aware not only of their patrimony but also how their inheritance entitles them to feelings of distinction (Herzfeld 2009, 3). There is a birthright to Rome that Romans often feel is undermined by the city also being a world capital (Herzfeld 2009, 3–4). Instead of turning their backs on the intellectual and material heritage that comes to define being Roman, many Romans I met embrace it to the point of rejecting what Rome may mean to anyone else.

I recently walked in the neighborhood south of the Vatican called Borgo. The area, like other Roman neighborhoods, is a self-contained universe. Almost every corner is covered in Ultra graffiti and the area's Ultras walk the streets with a sense of pride. Most of them know everyone, from the merchants to the men and boys standing in front of each café or mechanics shop. The neighborhood is also home to a recent addition, a kebab stand. Typically associated with Turks, kebab stands are opening throughout Rome. The owners of this particular stand are not Turks but Indians. The first time I encountered the stand with Ultras, there was derision and a dismissive silence. The only comment made was that "a few years ago there were no kebab stands in Rome. Now they are everywhere."

A few weeks later, I received a call from Danillo, one of the dismissive Ultras. Danillo, a 29-year-old waiter in a restaurant near Campo dei Fiori, lives with his mother, father, and aunt. His girlfriend lives on the next block. They met when she was a student in need of a Latin tutor. Now they work together in her family's small restaurant. Like so many others of that generation, Danillo's parents are extremely proud Romans, even going so far as to show me the family's modest collection of antique espresso cups adorned with images of turn-of-the-century Rome.

Danillo told me that he had eaten kebabs from the stand after a recent game (as no restaurants were open at that hour on a Sunday night). He had enjoyed the kebab and said the people were friendly. He was quick to add, though, that this did not signal a change in his negative attitude toward the proliferation of kebab stands in Rome. "Rome," he said, "is opening up to foreigners because the government and the EU are forcing it to do so. [The Roman people] are left to lament the changes in their neighborhoods and an influx of people who neither speak our language nor take an interest in our culture. How do these people have the right to come here and do very little to be accepted and those who have been here for generations, who can trace their Roman heritage seven generations [as he could, his mother proudly added], have no right to defend the form of life that we have created in that time?" He went on to say that Rome was his city, not theirs. He would never dream of going to another country to set up a shop. Such a move would be "the most vulgar [form] of materialism." I asked him what he feared in the presence of the Indians. "The eventual destruction of Roman culture," he said.

Conversely, Mario, an AS Roma fan in his mid-forties who has been attending games since he was seven, told me "[not to] worry about traditions collapsing in Rome. The rest of the world lives without tradition because their history, culture, existence itself, is not real. But here in Rome, the past is so important that you cannot even live in it. We have a perpetual present (*il presente permanente*) that stretches back 2,700 years." Mario's statement reminded me of Michael Polanyi's struggle to justify the forms of knowledge generated by zealotry, through which violence and terror are given fuel. Borrowing from Hannah Arendt, he explains that revolutionary education is designed to abolish the line between truth and fiction, thereby making every knowable thing a "statement of purpose" (Polanyi 1974, 242). Leaving aside his epistemology (and political aversion to extremism), his understanding of knowledge serving a purpose but also being pliable is reflected in Mario's statement. And there is no mistaking that this devotion to Rome is a form of extremism. Rome's visibly multilayered history makes the city's historical importance a constant reminder of what is "at stake" for the Romans. In effect, their feelings of ownership are manifested in every evening stroll they take.

This chapter demonstrates the complexities of the deep affection for Rome and things Roman among the city's football fans. Far from being "just a sport," football is an integral part of the Roman social and political landscape. While football fans have become politicians and politicians are often football fans, the politicization of football fans into a particular (and particularist) cultural understanding is a process that brings together influences and symbols from a broad social field. As has been explained, the two large professional football teams in Rome both have important historical connections with the fascist regime. Today, both teams share the highly fascist Foro Italico complex. And both teams can count extreme right-wing activists among their most passionate fans. Yet, among these fans, Fascism is overshadowed by what was one of its most useful tools: *romanità.*

In this context, *romanità* acts as a will to connect with something eternally Roman—"ours"—in Rome. In a Rome that is home to almost half a million immigrants, Italian Romans are using football and its deep connections with the discourses of imperial greatness and valor—both of which are part of Fascism's self-understanding and *romanità*—as a salve against the immigrant city. This is replete with its own political struggles and ironies, as football itself is a highly visual battleground between traditional and commercial conceptions of cultural property and heritage. That football has become a successful global business is certainly not lost on Roman football fans. Instead, some of them, the Ultras, work actively to attempt to minimize the impact of global capital and labor on the game (Dyal 2014, 360–400).

Here we see a process similar to theatrical politics. Theatrical and cultish politics, Kertzer explained, function in modern societies just as they did in what were assumed to be "traditional" societies. These political forms are based on ritual practices and liturgies that attach great meaning to action. They are also based on mythical or ideational discourses, like *romanità,* which "give meaning to the world around us" and provide the fabric of order in the face of chaos. Far from lulling their audiences to sleep, these discourses and narratives transform ideas into a lived reality (Kertzer 1988, 13).

Notes

1. "Lotito: Lazio prima squadra della Capitale simbolo Roma era un lupo spelacchiato," *Il Messaggero,* 4 July 2011, http://www.ilmessaggero.it/articolo.php?id=154935&sez=HOME _SPORT&ctc=220 (accessed 2 October 2013).

2. The Union of European Football Associations (UEFA) is the governing body of European football. Its two professional competitions are the UEFA Champion's League and the UEFA Cup, now known as the Europa League.

References

Armstrong, Gary. 1998. *Football Hooligans: Knowing the Score.* Oxford: Berg.

Baxa, Paul. 2010. *Roads and Ruins: The Symbolic Landscape of Fascist Rome.* Toronto: University of Toronto Press.

Creed, Gerald. 2011. *Masquerade and Postsocialism.* Bloomington: Indiana University Press.

Dyal, Mark. 2010. "War as a Form of Life: The Agonistic Culture of Italian Ultras." *International Journal of Sport and Society* 1 (2): 11–22.

———. 2014. *Ultras Contra Modernity.* London: Arktos Media.

Evola, Julius. 2002. *Men among the Ruins: Post-War Reflections of a Radical Traditionalist.* Translated by Guido Stucco. Rochester, Vt.: Inner Traditions.

Falasca-Zamponi, Simonetta. 1997. *Fascist Spectacle: The Aesthetics of Power in Mussolini's Italy.* Berkeley: University of California Press.

Fogu, Claudio. 2003. *The Historic Imaginary: Politics of History in Fascist Italy.* Toronto: University of Toronto Press.

Foot, John. 2006. *Calcio: A History of Italian Football.* London: Fourth Estate Press.

Francesio, Giovanni. 2008. *Tifare contro: Una storia degli ultras italiani.* Milan: Sperling and Kupfer.

Gentile, Emilio. 1996. *The Sacralization of Politics in Fascist Italy.* Translated by Keith Botsford. Cambridge, Mass.: Harvard University Press.

Giulianotti, Richard. 1998. *Football: A Sociology of the Global Game.* Oxford: Polity Press.

Griffin, Roger. 2007. *Modernism and Fascism: The Sense of a Beginning under Mussolini and Hitler.* New York: Palgrave Macmillan.

Guttman, Allen. 1981. "Sports Spectators from Antiquity to the Renaissance." *Journal of Sport History* 8 (2): 5–23.

Herzfeld, Michael. 2009. *Evicted from Eternity: The Restructuring of Modern Rome.* Chicago: University of Chicago Press.

Kertzer, David. 1988. *Ritual, Politics, and Power.* New Haven: Yale University Press.

Koon, Tracy. 1985. *Believe, Obey, Fight: Political Socialization of Youth in Fascist Italy, 1922–1945.* Chapel Hill: University of North Carolina Press.

Martin, Simon. 2004. *Football under Fascism: The National Game under Mussolini.* Oxford: Berg.

———. 2011. *Sport Italia: The Italian Love Affair with Sport.* New York: I. B. Tauris.

Nozza, Vittorio, Giancarlo Perego, and Enrico Feroci. 2010. *Dossier Statistico Immigrazione 1991–2010: 20 anni per una cultura dell'altro.* Rome: Caritas.

Painter, Borden W, Jr. 2005. *Mussolini's Rome: Rebuilding the Eternal City.* New York: Palgrave MacMillan.

Polanyi, Michael. 1974. *Personal Knowledge: Towards a Post-Critical Philosophy.* Chicago: University of Chicago Press.

Said, Edward. 1993. *Culture and Imperialism.* New York: Alfred Knopf.

Southgate, Troy. 2010. *Tradition and Revolution: Collected Writings of Troy Southgate.* London: Arktos Media.

Stefanini, Maurizio. 2009. *Ultras: Identità, politica, e violenza nel tifo sportivo da Pompei a Raciti e Sandri.* Milan: Boroli Editore.

12   Rome's Contemporary Past

Valerie Higgins

Is ROME'S ANCIENT past a blessing or a curse? This may seem a strange question to ask seeing that classical heritage is an essential part of the identity of the city and revenue from cultural tourism underpins its economy. On the other hand, its patrimony can also be seen as a block to development and an insurmountable obstacle to Rome taking its place as a dynamic twenty-first-century global city. During the twentieth century, there was a conservative approach to cultural heritage which sought to protect historic cities by isolating them from economic development. Recently there has been a greater acceptance that heritage can be a functioning part of a modern economy and an increased awareness that turning cities into fossilized open air museums generates intractable social, economic, and conservation problems. Rome has remained somewhat resistant, though not immune, to these new trends. This chapter will explore the relationship between cultural heritage protection and urban development in Rome since 1960 with particular reference to the impact on three groups: the local population of Rome, the wider Italian nation that looks to Rome as its capital, and the international community attracted by heritage tourism. Discussions concerning development in Rome are often dominated by the practical difficulties generated by its dense cultural patrimony, but equally important are the ideological issues concerning what the city symbolizes, what past it seeks to protect, and to whom this past belongs.

Developments in Heritage Protection in the Later Twentieth Century

In 1960, a conference held in Gubbio, in central Italy, established what would become normal practice for heritage protection in Italy's historic cities. The Gubbio Charter, as it came to be called, viewed the historic center as, in effect, a single monument that was to be preserved intact and isolated from all modern development. Indeed, it was this document that first coined the phrase *centro storico* (historic center), a term that is now in such common use that it is hard to believe it has existed for only half a century. Although the Gubbio conference took place during the postwar economic boom in Italy, it was far from forward-looking in its objectives. Its aims were distinctly retro, even by the standards of the time. It looked to recreate the kind of romantic approach of nineteenth-century savants, such as John Ruskin and Viollet-le-Duc, that conceived of archaeological sites as picturesque ruins, situated in verdant spaces, quarantined from the chaos, noise, and dirt of daily life during the Industrial Revolution. The goal of the Gubbio Charter was analogous; it aimed to provide a *cordon sanitaire* between the sacred space of the past and the contemporary commercial and industrial development that was sweeping Italy (Dainotto 2003, 69).

The impact of this approach can be clearly seen in postwar Rome where the historic center entered a period of stagnation. This was in sharp contradistinction to the outskirts of the city where there was rampant, often uncontrolled, new development. The contrast between the two areas could not have been starker, but whatever the political and demographic realities of its spatial boundaries, Rome was symbolically conceived as the historic center with its ancient monuments (Salvagni 2005, 13). Its designation as the Eternal City rendered any idea of modernizing it a contradiction in terms;[1] it had already reached a state of perfection and, as it had been there for eternity, clearly nothing needed to be done to safeguard its future. Thus the monuments of the city center were not threatened by new development, but neither were they cared for. In practical terms, two cities existed: the historic city center which was the locus of social and cultural life and the magnet for foreign tourists (particularly the well-heeled variety), and a polycentric periphery that housed increasing numbers of local people pushed out of the center by rising prices. These areas suffered from social deprivation, high levels of unemployment, poor facilities, and weak transportation links (Anselmi 2005, 131).[2] This extended period of urban neglect came to a clamorous end in 1978 when the archaeological monuments began, quite literally, to fall apart. Chunks of masonry fell off the Column of Marcus Aurelius and the state of many other monuments gave cause for concern; the situation was further exacerbated by a small earthquake the following year. As well as structural damage, relief sculptures on many ancient monuments had all but disappeared, a clear indication that the primary cause of the damage was chemical degradation resulting from traffic pollution (La Regina 1985, 7). The archaeological superintendent of the time, Adriano La Regina, drew up an ambitious plan to turn a large area of central Rome into a traffic-free archaeological park that, on the eastern side, would segue into the archaeological park of the Via Appia (Cagnardi 1985, 45). This idea found favor with the minister for cultural patrimony, Oddo Biasini, who passed a law to finance the project, setting aside 180 billion lire for it (Packer 1989, 40).

Although presented as a practical and aesthetic solution to conservation issues, the plan was not without its political agenda: the making of such a park would have involved ripping up three wide boulevards built by Mussolini for fascist parades. The construction of a new metro line was an essential part of the project, as there would be no vehicular traffic, and indeed hardly any roads, in the center of Rome. Few details were presented on exactly how the stations would deal with either buried archaeological remains or surface buildings except for specifying that the imposing fascist public records office would have to be demolished to create space for a metro station; a sacrifice the authors seemed more than willing to make (Podestà 1985, 105).

The concept of an archaeological park was taken up with enthusiasm by the Communist-led city council of Rome and not only because it would have meant getting rid of hated fascist structures. The mayor, Luigi Petroselli, was a product of the periphery and was acutely aware of the need to provide a program to develop Rome after decades of inactivity: "The historic center of Rome must live, and its life must push the whole city towards new values of civic association." (Quoted in Bosworth 2011, 272.)

The archaeological park offered a platform for action that would give Romans a sense of pride in their city and the people in the marginalized periphery would be drawn back into the center by means of free events to be staged at the monuments. The plan immediately attracted a great deal of media attention. Predictably, it provoked a backlash from the right that was at times very bitter, but further served to make it good copy. Within Rome, the plan revived local enthusiasm for archaeology and, according to some newspaper articles, resulted in 8,000 people visiting the Roman Forum in one day (Insolera and Perego 1983, xv, xxiii, 244). However, notwithstanding the fact that the argument was played out in the national press and concerned the national capital, it was essentially a local dispute that failed to ignite the rest of the country and had little resonance beyond the city boundaries.

The plan ultimately came to nothing. The merry-go-round of Italian politics ensured that Biasini was removed from office before any progress could be made on the ambitious pedestrianization scheme and subsequent ministers squashed the project. Aside from political opposition to removing the fascist boulevards, the lack of a credible plan to deal with traffic made certain that the vast archaeological park was never seriously considered, though certain aspects of it were implemented and were very important from the point of view of preserving the historic center. For example, a road across the Roman Forum was removed and traffic was diverted away from the Colosseum and Arch of Constantine (Insolera and Perego 1983, 254). However, even those without nostalgia for Mussolini baulked at the notion of turning the clock back by canceling reminders of an uncomfortable past. As one American archaeologist put it, the fascist boulevards are "themselves part of Rome's history and sections should perhaps be left intact to commemorate the character of the city in the first three decades of the 20th century" (Packer 1989, 141).

If the 1980s were dominated by the aborted archaeological park, during the 1990s, it was the preparations for the Jubilee of 2000 that took center stage. The plans were somewhat complicated by the fact that this was, primarily, a religious celebration and the timing and scale of events depended on the Vatican.[3] Francesco Rutelli, who was the mayor of Rome in the run-up to the Jubilee, had high hopes for what could be achieved:

> Rome hopes to offer visitors from all over the world an avant-garde metropolis with the ability to combine the patrimony of its glorious past with an improved quality of life, a modern and compatible infrastructure, efficient services and cultural stimuli. (Quoted in Kirk 2005, 253.)

Sadly the reality fell far short of this ideal. Secular authorities focused their activities on museums and areas around the main Christian basilicas: the inability to tackle transportation infrastructure in any meaningful way was noted as a weakness (Scoppola 1998, 46, 54). Even more problematical were the controversies caused by the building of a multistory car park near Saint Peter's Basilica and the construction of a complex of new musical auditoria in the northern suburbs (Parco della Musica) which were originally intended to be opened in 2000.

The car park for the anticipated influx of pilgrims to Saint Peter's was excavated into the adjacent Gianicolo Hill. The designated area was in the grounds of a pontifical institute and therefore came under the jurisdiction of the Vatican, making it exempt from Italian heritage laws. Rumors began to circulate that a Roman villa and even possibly early Christian tombs had been destroyed in the course of its construction. These rumors appeared to be confirmed when Roman artifacts were found on the spoil heaps. The Italian archaeological superintendency became involved when it was discovered that the ramps for the car park were on Italian, not Vatican, land. Some cursory excavation was carried out, but the damage had already been done and the car park was well behind schedule by this stage. There was little political will to push for the kind of expensive and time-consuming excavation that would have been required, even if the legal issues of land ownership could have been resolved. The prospect of tens of millions of pilgrims arriving with no parking facilities available was simply unconscionable.

Another reason why the archaeological superintendency was probably reluctant to take on the Vatican was that it already had its hands full with issues concerning the Parco della Musica. This was a prestigious project of three concert halls by the world famous architect Renzo Piano whose design was intended to be a contemporary evocation of Roman architecture. Unfortunately for him, Roman architecture became rather too involved when it was discovered that one of the halls was projected to be directly on top of the remains of a Roman villa. Not only did work have to stop for excavation to take place, but the design had to be adjusted to avoid disturbing the site. It was literally back to the drawing board for Renzo Piano who had to relocate not only one of the halls, but the access roads as well, at considerable cost. As a result, the Parco della Musica missed its symbolically important opening date. It eventually opened two years later and very much over budget. For many people, it served as confirmation that Rome's economic development is continually held hostage to archaeology.

One sector that was notably more successful, and that has had a lasting impact on Rome's development, was the provision of tourist accommodation. Preparations for the Jubilee saw a fundamental restructuring of the hotel industry to provide many more beds. New international chains of hotels such as the Marriott arrived in Rome for the first time and a system of licensed bed and breakfast accommodation was promoted. These sectors have continued to grow steadily since 2000 and have been crucial to advancing Rome as a global center for heritage tourism. Hotels also constitute a major source of employment in Rome today, with mixed results for local people, as will be elaborated (Berdini 2010, 319).

Plans for the Twenty-First Century

The urban master plan (Piano Regolatore Generale) adopted in 2003 was a step forward in that it recognized the need to link more effectively the ancient historic center with modern peripheral developments and to create a synergy between the two elements in order to fully exploit the value of Rome's past for its contemporary population (Salvagni 2005, 13).[4] From the point of view of monuments and artistic heritage, the city and the metropolitan areas possess a unique world patrimony covering thirty centuries of history, set within an environment that could potentially be one of the most important driving forces of the whole economy of Rome, especially if it were connected to creating services for tourism and leisure activities (Salvagni 2005, 19, my translation).

Central to the economic and social regeneration envisaged in the 2003 plan is the development of an integrated mass transportation system which will link the periphery with the center and reduce the number of vehicles, especially private cars, on the city center roads. The key element of this is a coordinated network of overland and underground trains including, finally, the construction of a third metro line. Line C will be 39 km long and will traverse the historic center. It was originally projected to have forty-two stations and to serve half a million residents (Martone 2010, 4). In order to avoid destroying archaeological remains, the train galleries have been placed at a depth of more than 30 m, well below the level of even the earliest human settlement. However, at the point where stations are placed, access tunnels will have to be created through wells, 25 m in diameter,

Local residents protest the lack of accountability in the construction of Rome's new metro line. *Photo by Valerie Higgins.*

which will cut through all archaeological layers (Bottini 2010, x). The difficulties in placing these so they do not destroy important archaeological structures were emphasized at the planning stage by the archaeological superintendency, who stressed the importance of carrying out all archaeological investigations before costing and awarding contracts. Failure to do this, they warned, would result in changes having to be made in the course of construction, which would lead to losses of time and money (Martone 2010, 3).

Results have shown that their fears were well founded. Three of the four stops projected in the area that was the heart of the ancient city (Campus Martius) have been canceled, raising concerns over how useful the line will be in reducing surface traffic (Bottini 2010, xi; Suttora 2010). The station in Piazza Venezia, the symbolic heart of the city, was originally intended to be in the center of the square, making it easily accessible from all sides, but this is now under review. The discovery of significant Roman remains, possibly the Atheneum of Emperor Hadrian, a building hitherto known only from texts, will necessitate some adjustments. However, the fact that the station is going ahead at all and that there is cooperation between the archaeologists and the developers in finding a solution to the problem is a sign of a less rigid approach to development (Cecchi 2010, viii). Progress is slow, as the archaeological superintendency warned it would be in 1996 and again in 2002 (Martone 2010, 3). The metro, which was originally scheduled to open in 2011 and cost two billion euros, is now unlikely to open before 2018 and will cost nearer five billion euros (Suttora 2010). The constant delays, expense, disruption of traffic, and lack of transparency in the awarding of public contracts have frustrated local residents.

Impact of Heritage Protection

At a distance of more than fifty years since the first Gubbio Charter, this seems a good moment to take stock and assess the long-term impact of heritage protection on the city of Rome. The most notable impact has been the loss of local population from the historic center, a phenomenon repeated in other tourist-historic cities (Ashworth and Tunbridge 2000, 127). The abandonment of the city center by residents began in the postwar period and has persisted to the present day as prices continue to rise. Most areas of the city have lost 60–70 percent of their local residents since 1980. In 1951, 370,000 permanent residents lived in the historic center, today the figure is estimated to be less than 100,000 and there is no sign that the trend is reversing. Their place has been taken by tourists who now outnumber permanent residents by two to one in some areas (Berdini 2010, 322–323). For those forced to migrate to the periphery, the failure to provide the promised new integrated transportation structure, and the cancelation of stations in the city center where they are most needed, makes life at best uncomfortable and at worst unsustainable.

The palace of the Emperor Nero remains closed indefinitely due to stability concerns. *Photo by Valerie Higgins.*

Scaffolding supports unstable Roman monuments. *Photo by Valerie Higgins.*

Residential, industrial, and commercial property continues to be converted into various types of tourist accommodations. According to some statistics, Rome now hosts thirty million visitors per annum (Berdini 2010, 318). While public authorities (and doubtless tourists themselves) like to think that tourism benefits local people, the evidence is far less clear cut. Research into tourist-historic cities shows that aside from the loss of homes and breakup of communities and social support systems that this entails,[5] local businesses which might provide genuine career opportunities for young people get forced out in favor of tourist-oriented activities with a fast turnover that can pay higher rates. Often, local products are a casualty of this, as multinational chains move in and price them out of the market (Timothy 2011, 166). Tourist-historic cities lose their distinctiveness and part of their local identity as they acquire the veneer of a global city of culture. Economically, the jobs created in tourist areas are overwhelmingly in the poorly paid service sector and offer little in the way of a career structure. The low wages make it unlikely that those employed will be able to live in the areas they work in. Some have likened this type of exploitation to a twenty-first-century version of imperialism (Smith 2009, 61).

There are also real questions concerning the sustainability of the monuments that this tourism depends on. The palace of the Emperor Nero (Domus Aurea) in the center of Rome is closed indefinitely because of fears that it is now structurally unsafe.

Several sections of the towering walls that surrounded the Roman city have collapsed in recent years. Concerns have been expressed for the stability of the Colosseum and restoration work becomes ever more urgent, just as finding the money for it becomes ever more difficult. For an idea of what the future might bring if there is not a steep change in attitudes to ongoing conservation, we need look no further than a few hundred kilometers south to Pompeii. Here the overnight collapse of buildings due to a chronic lack of maintenance resulted in the resignation of a government minister and an emergency rescue fund of one hundred million euros from the European Union to prevent the situation becoming catastrophic (Richeldi 2011). However, the funds that would be needed to carry out such interventions in Rome would be of an order of magnitude many times greater. Pompeii was a small town with mostly domestic buildings and provincial-sized public buildings. Rome was the capital of the empire and its monuments were built to impress. Environmental degradation is just as threatening to tourism as building dilapidation is. Tourist-historic cities rely on their narrow streets, enchanting piazzas, and atmosphere of timeless charm to attract visitors. Such settings have a limited carrying capacity and are particularly vulnerable to overexploitation (Montanari and Staniscia 2010, 309).

The great winner from the last fifty years of heritage protection appears to be the international tourist, largely at the expense of the local resident. Rome's visitors are now no longer primarily the glitterati of the *dolce vita* era, but they are the consumers of mass tourism, served by low-cost airlines whose flights have increased at an exponential rate in the last decade. The change in the tourist type ensures that the sharp rise in numbers is not directly reflected in increased revenue. Mass tourists do not have a high spending capacity and their spending patterns favor commercialized products rather than characteristic local goods (Montanari and Staniscia 2010, 309). Today's visitor can enjoy a historic center that has been protected from modern development. The traffic may be chaotic, but many of the monuments are close enough to walk between, so the lack of transport infrastructure is less problematic. Specially chartered tourist buses can also ensure that the delays and overcrowding regularly endured by local residents on public transport are avoided. It has been estimated that the daily quota of tourist buses circulating in the center of Rome is the equivalent of 12 km long (Berdini 2010, 327).

Rome's popularity in the global cultural marketplace was further demonstrated by the Colosseum being nominated one of the Seven New Wonders of the World. Between 2001 and 2007, in a widely publicized global campaign, one hundred million people voted for seven contemporary monuments to rival the ancient list. The Colosseum was elected (the only European monument) ahead of the Giza Pyramids and the Parthenon, which failed to make the cut.[6] Once the haunt of the rich, Rome now belongs to everyone. It has become one of a handful of cities that people feel they have to experience at least once in their lives.

Whose Past?

Early photographs taken in the mid-nineteenth century show a Rome which had a very different relationship with its population. In these pictures, local people are hanging out their washing on a temple in the Roman Forum and buying their bread from a baker who has set his oven into the wall of the Forum of Nerva, presumably taking advantage of the fact that these thick Roman walls also functioned as firebreaks. Texts from this period and earlier speak of local people living in the arches of the Colosseum, in the attic stories of triumphal arches, and in old aqueducts (Higgins 2012, 209–214). Before Rome became the capital of a united Italy, the relationship between the city and its inhabitants was intimate and unquestioned. When Rome became the nation's capital, its heritage had to symbolize the grandeur of Italy and, therefore, clearly there was no place for washing lines, bakeries, or squatters.

The marginalization of local people that began with the Risorgimento was rapidly accelerated under the fascist plan to modernize Rome. Large areas of housing were pulled down in order to isolate the monuments, and the residents were forcibly evicted to the periphery. From the postwar period up to the present day, inexorably rising prices have continued the work of Mussolini's jackboots; local people have become economic migrants in their own city as wages have failed to keep up with increased living costs. The past that is presented today in

Tourism at the Colosseum. *Photo by Valerie Higgins.*

Rome is one that is packaged for the global mass tourist. The buildings are unique but the packaging—the souvenirs, the guides, the merchandising—is anything but. As Rome has become elevated on the global stage, so it has progressively surrendered its local identity.

There is a third group, or stakeholder in modern parlance, identified in the introduction to this chapter whose concerns have not yet been addressed. Rome also functions as the capital city for Italians and its cultural heritage is of particular importance in this context. Unlike London, Paris, Brussels, or pretty much any other European capital, Rome is not, and never has been, the financial powerhouse of the nation (for further discussion, see Thomassen and Vereni, chapter 1). That accolade goes to Milan. Rome was chosen as the capital at the time of the Risorgimento because of its cultural heritage. It was hoped that its ancient past could represent a rallying point for the new country, a modern-day foundation myth that everyone from Piedmont to Sicily could buy into. This was never completely successful, even in the nineteenth century, and it has become notably less so with the passage of time. Impressive as the ancient monuments are, they also evoke a slight unease. As a political and social system, the Roman Empire is entirely at odds with twenty-first-century values. Ancient Rome conjures up images of constant war, loss of liberty for conquered peoples, unspeakable cruelty (vividly portrayed in modern cinema), and mass slavery. Whereas Athens can proudly showcase its heritage as embodying the very foundation of Western democracy (glossing over the fact that this too was based on slavery and that the majority were not enfranchised), Rome's legacy is perceived primarily as being the inspiration for some of history's worst despots and dictators from the Middle Ages down to Mussolini. The very heritage which in the nineteenth century symbolized a greatness that would unite the disparate regional groups now seems more of a liability in terms of its political symbolism.

As a national capital, Rome has always lacked the authority that other European capitals have within their own country and it has struggled to compete against strong regionalism and a widespread disdain among Italians from outside Rome. In the 1960s, the Italian weekly *L'Espresso* described Rome as "a corrupt capital of an infected nation"; in 1974, the Catholic Church criticized "the ills of Rome." More recently, center-right political parties, most notably the *Lega Nord*, have questioned the whole concept of Rome as a national capital (Salvagni 2005, 15). For many ordinary Italians, "Rome" has become shorthand for a caste of politicians and bureaucrats who parasitically live off the taxes of hardworking ordinary people—much as the corrupt emperors of ancient Rome did.

Whose Future?

Historic cities like Rome are part of the tourist industry but unlike other branches of industry, they have very little limited scope for capacity building. The ancient monuments can only withstand so many pairs of feet and so much traffic pollution before they are either irreparably damaged or conservation costs outstrip income. This has been recognized by local politicians of all persuasions. The center-left mayor Walter Veltroni boasted in 2005 that he had created economic prosperity in Rome by developing other sectors of the economy so that the city no longer had to rely on "the spent motor of the historic center" (Bosworth 2011, 287–288). Mayor Gianni Alemanno, leader of the center-right city government from 2008, also recognized that the historic center had reached its limits. He advanced plans to develop a second tourist pole on the outskirts based on theme parks (including one on ancient Rome with a full-size replica of the Colosseum), sports facilities, and conference centers. In this way, he aimed to raise the number of annual tourists to fifty million (Dipartimento Turismo di Roma Capitale 2012). It is debatable whether this could in the end help to conserve the historic center: it seems rather presumptuous to assume that these extra millions of tourists will want to come to Rome without ever visiting the Colosseum or the Pantheon, and clearly there would be no way of preventing them should they so desire. As this book was going to press (September 2013), Rome had just elected a new mayor, Ignazio Marino. He has revived the plan to pedestrianize the center of Rome around the ancient monuments and to remove the fascist boulevard that runs from the Colosseum to Piazza Venezia. It is, as yet, unclear how this will be financed. The complexity of the situation was made clear when, in the same week that he gave an interview to the Italian version of the *Huffington Post* outlining his ambitious plans for Rome's heritage, all of the work on the new metro line ceased due to lack of funds.

The conservative approach to cultural heritage in Rome that has been dominant since the end of the Second World War has undoubtedly been responsible for the uniquely preserved ancient city that we now enjoy, and it certainly was never the intention to create a city center that was more like a museum than a living city. However, changing social and economic factors have combined to create just such a scenario and that should make us question whether this will continue to be the best approach. The development of tourism on the scale we are now seeing could not have been predicted even a generation ago. The strain this puts on ancient buildings, combined with the sheer volume of heritage that has to be cared for, makes the cost of ongoing conservation prohibitively high. After the fall of buildings at Pompeii, some archaeologists were bold enough to state an uncomfortable truth—that decay is the natural state and that in trying to prevent it we are attempting the impossible. Instead of trying to keep everything as it is, we should acknowledge that all we can do is arrest decay, and even that is very expensive (Flohr 2010). We may yet be forced to admit that we do not have the resources for ongoing conservation of all the remains currently exposed and that covering over some monuments, such as the Domus Aurea, might be the best option, allowing them to be preserved for future generations who might have better solutions. This could also release funds to care adequately for other monuments where interventions might be more successful.

Often in discussions of the future of tourist-historic cities, the symbolic role of the heritage for the community, and the economic potential of heritage tourism, are considered as separate items to be traded off against each other, but in Rome there is a good argument for seeing them as interdependent. Rome's heritage cannot support an increase in mass tourism and if Rome is to continue to enjoy the economic and status benefits of being one of the world's most loved cities, it needs to direct heritage tourism onto a more sustainable path. This could include the development of niche tourism based on the distinctive local Roman culture, which is fast disappearing, or it could be the expansion of tourist routes beyond the narrow confines of the center, to the very many equally interesting places throughout the city. This would spread out the impact and would encourage longer stays. The average tourist stays only two nights in Rome (Berdini 2010, 327) and as long as this is the case, it is clear that all activity will be funneled into a limited number of well-known sites within a small area. But new approaches rely on something that is a dwindling resource in Rome—a local population. Reclaiming the center of Rome for permanent residents is not only right for symbolic reasons, it is also the key to a more sustainable exploitation of its cultural heritage.

Acknowledgments

Much of the work for this chapter was completed during a period of sabbatical leave at the McDonald Institute for Archaeological Research, University of Cambridge. I am grateful to the McDonald Institute and in particular its director, Prof. Graeme Barker, for his generosity in hosting me. The weekly heritage seminars held at the McDonald were of immense value in developing the arguments put forth here. I am also grateful to The American University of Rome for their support of my sabbatical leave.

Notes

1. Mussolini stridently proclaimed that he was "modernizing" Rome when he demolished large parts of the city center. Thus, the idea of conserving and protecting Rome could also be seen as part of an antifascist agenda (cf. Dainotto 2003, 70).

2. This trend has been noted in many historic walled cities (cf. Creighton 2007).

3. The year 2000 was designated a Holy Year in which pilgrims who visited Rome and performed certain rites would be given a plenary indulgence for their sins.

4. The increased emphasis on seeing the historical city in a broader territorial context, and the importance of historical cities as symbols of identity, are both central tenets of an update of the Gubbio Charter published in 1990 (cf. Lazzarotti 2011).

5. Michael Herzfeld (2009) has charted the impact of these social changes on the community of Monti, an area close to the Colosseum, in *Evicted from Eternity: The Restructuring of Modern Rome.*

6. See http://world.n7w.com/new-7-wonders/the-official-new7wonders-of-the-world/ (accessed 15 September 2012).

References

Anselmi, Alessandro. 2005. "Roma galassia urbana di centro città." In *Roma Capitale nel XXI secolo: La città metropolitana policentrica,* edited by Piero Salvagni, 127–132. Rome: Palombi Editori.

Ashworth, G. J., and J. E. Tunbridge. 2000. *The Tourist-Historic City: Retrospect and Prospect of Managing the Heritage City.* Oxford: Pergamon.

Berdini, Paolo. 2010. "Rome: The Inevitable Decline of a Center with No Rules." *Rivista di Scienze del Turismo* 2 (2010): 317–330.

Bosworth, Richard J.B. 2011. *Whispering City: Modern Rome and Its Histories.* New Haven, Conn.: Yale University Press.

Bottini, Angelo. 2010. "Archeologia e metropolitana a Roma: Qualche considerazione." In *Archeologia e infrastrutture: Il tracciato fondamentale della Linea C della Metropolitana di Roma: Prime indagini archeologiche,* edited by Roberto Egidi, Fedora Filippi, and Sonia Martone, ix–xiv. Florence, Italy: Bollettino d'Arte Speciale.

Cagnardi, Augusto. 1985. "Il quadro urbanistico." In *Studio per la sistemazione dell'area archeologica centrale,* Soprintendenza Archeologica di Roma, edited by Leonardo Benevolo, 45–56. Rome: De Luca Editore.

Cecchi, Roberto. 2010. "Presentazione." In *Archeologia e infrastrutture: Il tracciato fondamentale della Linea C della Metropolitana di Roma: Prime indagini archeologiche,* edited by Roberto Egidi, Fedora Filippi, and Sonia Martone, vii–viii. Florence, Italy: Bollettino d'Arte Speciale.

Creighton, Oliver. 2007. "Contested Townscapes: The Walled City as World Heritage." *World Archaeology* 39 (3): 339–354.

Dainotto, Roberto M. 2003. "The Gubbio Papers: Historic Centers in the Age of the Economic Miracle." *Journal of Modern Italian Studies* 8 (1): 67–83.

Dipartimento Turismo di Roma Capitale. 2012. *Second Polo Turistico.* http://www .secondopoloturistico.roma.it/. Accessed 15 September 2012.

Flohr, Miko. 2010. *MikoFlohr Research.* http://www.mikoflohr.nl/working_papers /dealing_with_decay/. Accessed 15 September 2012.

Herzfeld, Michael. 2009. *Evicted from Eternity: The Restructuring of Modern Rome.* Chicago: University of Chicago Press.

Higgins, Valerie. 2012. "Rome—The Unauthorised Version." *Acta ad Archaeologium et Artium Historiam Pertinentia* 25: 207–236.

Insolera, Italo, and Francesco Perego. 1983. *Archaeologia e città: Storia moderna dei fori di Roma.* Bari-Rome: Editori Laterza.

Kirk, Terry. 2005. *The Architecture of Modern Italy. Volume 2: Visions of Utopia, 1900–Present.* New York: Princeton Architectural Press.

La Regina, Adriano. 1985. Introduction to *Studio per la sistemazione dell'area archeologica centrale,* Soprintendenza Archeologica di Roma, edited by Leonardo Benevolo, 7. Rome: De Luca Editore.

Lazzarotti, Roberta. 2011. "Historical Centers: Changing Definitions." *Italian Journal of Planning Practice* 1 (1): 73–89.

Montanari, Armando, and Barbara Staniscia. 2010. "Rome a Difficult Path between Tourist Pressure and Sustainable Development." *Rivista di scienze del turismo* 2: 301–316.

Martone, Sonia. 2010. "La linea C della metropolitana di Roma. Procedure e nuove Prospettive." In *Archeologia e infrastrutture: Il tracciato fondamentale della Linea C della Metropolitana di Roma: Prime indagini archeologiche,* edited by Roberto Egidi, Fedora Filippi, and Sonia Martone, 1–38. Florence, Italy: Bollettino d'Arte Speciale.

New Open World Corporation. *New 7 Wonders.* http://world.n7w.com/new-7-wonders/the-official-new7wonders-of-the-world/. Accessed 15 September 2012.

Packer, James. 1989. "Review article. Politics, Urbanism and Archaeology in 'Roma Capitale': A Troubled Past and a Controversial Future." *American Journal of Archaeology* 93: 137–141.

Podestà, Claudio. 1985. "La proposta dei sistemi di trasporto." In *Studio per la sistemazione dell'area archeologica centrale,* Soprintendenza Archeologica di Roma, edited by Leonardo Benevolo, 99–107. Rome: De Luca Editore.

Richeldi, Anita. 2011. "Le dimissioni di Sandro Bondi e il silenzio del premier." *Politica e società 2.0.* http://politicaesocieta.blogosfere.it/2011/03/le-dimissioni-di-sandro-bondi-e-il-silenzio-del-premier.html. Accessed 15 September 2012.

Salvagni, Piero. 2005. *Roma Capitale nel XXI secolo: La città metropolitana policentrica.* Rome: Palombi Editori.

Scoppola, Francesco. 1998. *Piano di intervento in preparazione del Giubileo dell'anno 2000. Roma e Area Metropolitana. Ministero per i Beni Culturali e Ambientali.* Rome: Palombi Editori.

Smith, Melanie K. 2009. *Issues in Cultural Tourism Studies.* 2nd ed. London: Routledge.

Suttora, Mauro. 2010. "Roma: Metro senza stazioni." Blog entry for 22 September. http://maurosuttora.blogspot.com. Accessed 15 September 2012.

Timothy, Dallen J. 2011. *Cultural Heritage and Tourism: An Introduction.* Bristol, U.K.: Channel View Publications.

PART IV
THE INFORMAL CITY

13 The Self-Made City

Carlo Cellamare
(translated by Jennifer Radice)

NEARLY 30 PERCENT of the city of Rome has been built illegally and the phenomenon is in constant development. Numerous forms of squatting, mostly of housing, are to be found throughout the city; similarly, there are widespread areas, some more marginal than others, under self-management and self-organization. Still more widespread are the misappropriations (and reappropriations) of the built environment by the city's inhabitants. In many respects Rome, acknowledged (or aiming to present itself) at the national and international level as a great "modern" Western capital with a strong and stratified historical and cultural heritage, can be regarded as a "self-made city" whose urban development is driven less by centralized urban planning and more by spontaneous private initiative and improvisation. In this sense, Rome is unique among European capital cities.

This chapter considers the "informal city," focusing especially on unauthorized construction: its general characteristics, its historical evolution, its more recent manifestations. This construction is characterized as one of the basic structural modalities of the city's development: a sort of "parallel housing market" that responds to a demand based on "necessity," as well as—sustained by speculative intentions—to one based on "affordability" for the poorer but also middle classes.

Unauthorized building in Rome is primarily a response to the lack of adequate housing and town planning policies. A modality of urban government has evolved in recent years, and there now exists a veritable policy of unauthorized urban development, as is demonstrated by the building amnesties enshrined in recent national and regional housing laws. Rather than eradicating the problem and finding alternatives, the public administration has adopted forms of negotiation and consultation (if not downright delegation of authority) with builders

and proprietors of the areas and construction firms that allow and indeed encourage irresponsible land use.[1] Political weakness and the absence of an administrative culture in the face of powerful forces in Rome's planning and economy
are coupled with widespread social attitudes; these in turn are rooted in Rome's
laissez-faire urban ethos and in the "sin and be pardoned" mindset.[2] The research
methodology interweaves a traditional urban planning approach with one that
is sociological and ethnographic. The informal city is analyzed through available
data from local authorities, mapping, the spatial distribution of self-built areas,
planning, urban development programming, and the policies and actions of the
government. I also take into consideration recent sociological studies, in particular by supplementing maps produced by the geographic information system with
extensive interviews. My fieldwork included "strolls through the neighborhood"
with local residents, in-depth interviews with selected witnesses or small groups
of residents, participation in public meetings, and observation of activities within the district.[3] This type of methodology allows one to look at phenomena both
"from outside and above" and "from inside and below," thus permitting them to
be analyzed in more detail and depth.

The Debate on Unauthorized Construction and the Informal City

As well as arousing political and social concern, unauthorized construction in
Rome was the subject of intensive scholarship between the late 1970s and the
1980s (Berlinguer and Della Seta 1976; USPR 1981; Clementi and Perego 1983; Della Seta and Della Seta 1988). It was also in the front line of sociological research at
the national and international level (Ferrarotti 1970, 1974, 1981; Martinelli 1986).
The issue thus became the focus of political attention by local administrations
(Unione Borgate 1986). The victory of the center-left in Rome in those years was
closely connected to the effort that subsequent administrations invested in the
renewal of the working-class peripheries (*borgate*). From then on, however, the
problem of unauthorized building was no longer studied and recent works focusing on the problem of Rome's suburbs (Ilardi and Scandurra 2009; Ferrarotti and
Macioti 2009) pay little attention to it. Only a few publications have tried to give
a systematic and overall picture of the phenomenon today (Cellamare 2010; Cellamare and Perin 2010), in some cases drawing attention to it at a national level
(Berdini 2010). This lack of attention is worrying. It may be true that unauthorized building is no longer perceived as a social emergency, yet it remains a very
important phenomenon with a major bearing on serious problems in the city and
shortcomings in urban development (land use, lack of services, inadequate and
unsustainable public transport, low urban standards, and so on).

The question of unauthorized construction, or rather of the informal city,
has by contrast received greater attention in international debate and research
(Davis 2006; Roy and AlSayyad 2004; Porter 2011; Barberi 2010; Duhau and Giglia 2008; Fernandes and Varley 1998) with particular focus on large cities of

Latin America, the Middle East, India, Southeast Asia, Africa, and elsewhere. In these places, the phenomenon has assumed massive proportions and is regarded as a very serious urban and social issue because of the proliferation of shanty-towns. The situation in Rome is very different. Here we are talking about a large modern Western European capital that is affluent and endowed with a strong heritage of historical and cultural strata and a major system of infrastructure. Conditions in the Southern Hemisphere stem from serious problems of housing and poverty. In Rome, the problem has its origins in unauthorized building, but it has become intrinsic, indeed functional, to the evolution of the city. This can call into question the very idea that Rome can be considered a "modern and advanced" Western capital,[4] yet the incidence of unauthorized building can be considered a variant, if only a "low-profile" one, of advanced "predatory capitalism." It also suggests that Rome's "modernity" cannot easily be subsumed under any existing model or category (see also Thomassen and Vereni, chapter 1). Some more recent studies have considered the situation in European or Western countries (UN-Habitat 2010), but the phenomenon is more in evidence in eastern and southern European countries such as Albania, Macedonia, Greece, and Montenegro. In the recent past, the problem was invariably seen as an emergency, linked to urban migration of large numbers of people following the changes in the economies of those countries. By contrast, the phenomenon in Rome had very different features: Although it originated out of "necessity," especially for housing, today it has assumed the character of a standard modality of town planning; it affects the middle class, it has become speculative and no longer affects only residential building.

Characteristics of the Informal City in Rome

In Rome, informal housing assumes a range of characteristics, reflecting a process which is variegated, massive, and spread over a wide area. In many ways, it assumes the characteristics of deep-rooted social behavior, a way of responding to the inadequacy of public administration, a basic way of building a city.

First, we have "classic" unauthorized building, that is to say unauthorized building originating from a need for housing and motivated by "necessity"; this led, and leads, to the construction of residential buildings for one or at the most two families (which could have one, two, or three stories). We are dealing here with unauthorized self-building, where the builder also lives there with his whole (maybe extended) family. He does not own the land, but the operation is carried out with the agreement of the landowner, indeed often requested and granted, or at least offered by the landowner who sees to the unauthorized dividing-up and illegal sale of the sites even though they are unsuitable for building. This type of "classic" unauthorized building has come to be used not only for housing but also for shops, workshops, and farms; is often for speculative purposes; and is carried out directly by the individuals who own the land. This "unauthorized city," extending to some 30 percent of the built-up area of Rome, is now used by or intended for the middle class and reaches urban quality standards that are minimal but regarded as acceptable for housing purposes. The people who live there are now well-organized and capable of dealing with the authorities who in turn accept them and acknowledge them often as legitimate counterparts. It is on situations of this type that I shall concentrate in this chapter.

Second, we have a form of unauthorized building that bears a marked resemblance to the classic model because it is intended for housing and constructed by self-builders, but has come into being without ownership of the land and without the permission of the landowners. Here we are dealing with squatting, and the locations are thus for the most part public areas or land that is disused or abandoned. Areas, therefore, that are seldom checked and in which the owners have little interest.

Unauthorized building in privately owned areas tends to be of short duration and to generate greater problems and conflicts. This is an aspect of informality that has its origins and roots in the prevalence of "shanty dwellers" (such as the historical shanties built next to the Felice aqueduct). In this type of informal city conditions are diverse. Some are extensive areas, now historically established and also well-known and recognizable, that generate entire housing conglomerations (like the Idroscalo di Ostia—see Trabalzi, chapter 14). Then there are the less consolidated and structured sites that can generate small nuclei, still partly hidden and not well known, as in Magliana. Finally, there are sites closer to being shantytowns that are very precarious (people live in shacks), short-term in nature, with a very low standard of living, and unacceptable housing conditions. These sites, fewer in number, for the most part occupy a small area but are dotted around the city, along the Tiber, on wasteland, building sites, and under flyovers (Scandurra et al. 2009). Such conditions are frequently linked to the presence of immigrants. In recent years, the administrations of both political groupings have dealt with the phenomenon by means of policies based on clearances and removal of the residents from the city to areas fitted out on an ad hoc basis and generally fenced in, thus turning settlements into veritable ghettos. In short, we have "occupations" for housing purposes and squatting in existing buildings, usually publicly owned ones, that have fallen into disuse or been abandoned (Caudo and Sebastianelli 2008). The occupations are generally supported by committees and associations (such as the Committee for the Struggle for Housing or *Action*) that lead people to become organized and interact, sometimes harshly and violently, with the authorities.

The Evolution of Unauthorized Building

Classic unauthorized building came into existence in Rome as a response to the housing problem. It is hard to identify the precise moment when it started, not least because it has its roots in circumstances going far back (Martinelli 1986; Insolera 1993, 2001). It was already occurring when Rome became the capital of Italy in 1870. But it was in the 1930s, during the fascist period, that the birth of the *periferia*, or outer suburbs, and the run-down areas in particular was noted. It was an era of demolition in the historic center, of moving people into settlements of very poor quality in rural areas a very long way from the center and the established part of the city. The colonization of the countryside and the expansion of the city evolved from these developments (see also Mudu, chapter 4).

The process became more aggressive and dramatic during the postwar period and finally exploded in the 1960s and 1970s. After 1945, the devastation caused by war and the weakness of the production system forced huge numbers of people to move to the cities in search of a job and adequate public services. This state of affairs caused Rome, certainly not an industrial city, to experience a number of issues simultaneously: a marked population increase, generally of those with a low income; insecurity and low levels of employment and productive activity; widespread employment of new immigrants in the building trade; and very rapid growth of settlements and a significant increase in demand for housing. The public administrations that succeeded each other in governing the city were not capable of responding adequately to these developments or to the housing problem. Although Rome was the Italian city that built the largest volume of "public housing," this had turned out to be insufficient. Hence, the progressive and widespread development of unauthorized building that moved from the construction of makeshift shacks, often extremely unhygienic and unhealthy, to the building of small blocks of flats for one, two, or three families according to their needs and the prospects for their children. All this took place entirely as self-construction, outside the rules laid down by the urban master plans, often involving neighbors and other families in a system of exchanges of services and mutual assistance. For many new residents, this phase was experienced as an epic period.

At the same time, unauthorized building was closely linked to speculation and to the deeds of the landowners who divided up and sold their own land, tricking the new residents while knowing that these operations were illegal and covering themselves legally in every possible way. The operations of these landowners were unquestionably systematic and intentional and these individuals therefore have a great deal to answer for. Vast areas of the countryside around Rome, some of it valuable land and furthermore where building was not allowed, were broken up into plots, partially urbanized, and then sold.[5] Such a glaring case of speculation, together with the low (sometimes very low) housing density, involved an enormous use of land and irremediable damage to large parts of the countryside with serious consequences for the environment.

All this put the residents in a complex situation. On the one hand they were lawbreakers, engaging in illegal behavior that was often damaging for the city;

on the other hand they were victims of deceit and widespread acts of injustice. Their attempts to regularize the situation, paying what was due and in addition acknowledging the damage to the community that they were willing to pay compensation for, often ended badly or took many years to sort out. They felt that they were living in an insecure condition, an insecurity that was not formally acknowledged and entailed a long wait for all those things that are part of city life: services, infrastructure, facilities, urbanization, public spaces, parks. They lived in an incomplete city, forever waiting and uncertain of their future.

The matter of unauthorized building may have been closely linked, at any rate in its initial stages, to a struggle for housing, but many aspects of it evolved with the passage of time: its relationship with the housing model, the typology of buildings and the construction process, the changing social requirements and objectives of the developers, and the areas that were affected. In the end, a system was created around unauthorized building that was at the same time a housing regime and an economic regime.

The problem was also affected by speculative building, as well as by three successive building amnesties (in 1985, 1994, and 2003) that triggered a mechanism of implicit and silent acceptance of an unauthorized process of building development, in the expectation of more amnesties and related legislation. More recently, the housing laws at national and regional levels have tended to reinforce this trend, favoring deregulation and supporting small-scale and scattered building development and furthermore putting a premium on cubic capacity, seeing this incentive to building activity as a response to the global economic crisis. Indeed these low-profile policies can be seen as a local consequence of the global economic situation.

So unauthorized building moved on from being based on "necessity" to being based on "affordability" that aims at affordable good-quality dwellings that often have a garden (or even a swimming pool). These aspired to a higher standard of living, meeting the future requirements of children and foreseeing an increase in nuclear families (mostly houses of various sizes and other one-family units, often built by small construction firms, but also small blocks of flats, typical of Rome's building style, or other two-family or multifamily buildings). The next stage was a type of economic and speculative construction where the builder was not necessarily the occupier and user of the building and where the end use was not only residential (unauthorized building has also spread to industrial, commercial, and artisans' areas). The final stage was the organized and "industrialized" forms of speculative building (creating entire residential complexes), where the enterprise was supported by specialized technicians and lawyers.

What also changed from the 1980s was the typology of the residents: one could observe the simultaneous presence of "original" residents, the "pioneers" of these areas, and of strangers to the neighborhood who were renting their homes, and even immigrants to whom people sublet their former cattle sheds and hen-houses, these being in a very worrying state of decay and social exclusion. There was also naturally a change in the relationship of these various residents and workers with their own territory and their willingness to invest in its regenera-tion. The growing presence of immigrants (coming mainly from Eastern Europe) brought about a further local effect of globalization but one that invariably kept a low profile.

Policies toward Unauthorized Building in Rome: Involving Residents in Management

Unlike what happened in most central and southern Italian cities, there have been attempts in Rome in recent years to confront the problem by trying out feasible and innovative courses of action through town planning and urban re-generation policies. Rome is thus an interesting case, if a problematic one. The attitude of Rome's administrations over the years has certainly been equivocal. On the one hand, unlawful building is illegal and should be prosecuted; on the other hand, local government was not in a position to respond to the growing demand for housing and unlawful building; therefore, it acted as a safety valve. The weakness of control mechanisms, inadequacy of public housing policies, lack of planning, absence of genuine political will, and an inadequate culture of ad-ministration and government made the problem ever more intractable, the more so as it grew and turned into speculation.

It was only at the end of the 1970s, and in particular with the advent of the center-left administrations, that policies were adopted for the regeneration of un-authorized housing in the suburbs. This was done in particular through a process of negotiation and consultation with the interested parties in order to bring the problem under public control. From this emerged the experiment of plans for the rehabilitation of the unauthorized areas, designated as the "O Zones" in a variant of the 1962 Urban Master Plan (Rossi 2000). This was a very demanding and long, drawn-out operation that in the end did not deliver the hoped-for results. After much foot-dragging by the government, it was not until the 1990s, with the new center-left municipal governments, that new courses of action were developed both at the planning level and from the management perspective.

The city authorities introduced an innovative procedure permitted by region-al legislation that was the only one of its kind in Italy: such urbanization works could also be carried out by a consortium of landowners in the area, known as a consortium of self-regeneration. The members paid in their own agreed share that included not only a minimum subscription for the functioning and manage-ment of the consortium but also the expenses that the proprietors would have had to pay to the city government to rectify the situation and for the works of ur-banization envisaged. Leaving aside the specific mechanisms that were features of the functioning of the consortia and the execution of the works, the substance of the matter was that the landowners, through these consortia, were able to self-manage the execution of the works including the planning stages, prioritization, the tendering and choice of firms, the execution, quality control, and so on.

In this process, certain organizations were tasked to coordinate and support the consortia, such as the Unione Borgate (Union of Borgate) or the Consorzio Periferie Romane (Consortium for Rome's Peripheries). These organizations often became the direct interlocutors with the city council, intermediaries between the self-regenerating consortia and the administration. All the decisions of the consortia relating to the running of the properties, planning, design, and such were taken in meetings with the landowners. The funds collected were paid into a bank account controlled by the city council (which authorized the expenditure) and managed directly by the chairman of the consortium. The city administration played a role of support, supervision and coordination, and financial guarantee, but above all of quality control and approval of projects, effected by means of rules, guidelines, and public notices explaining the plans and projects.

The experience of the consortia was regarded by several parties, starting with city government, as a participatory experience. The city council gains considerably from the lightening of its burden of creating and managing works: The administration is routine and very small-scale and focuses mainly on projects of particular importance. Moreover, the consortia in practice deal with minor disagreements, thus preventing them from reaching the municipal administration. But above all, the landowners by and large delegate the running of projects to the consortia, preferring to take care of their own special interests, like a sort of large residents' association in a condominium. There were undoubtedly some aspects of a participative character, but the experiment seemed to be characterized mainly by a sort of "shared management," limited in terms of the ideal of constructing a "public space" (Allegretti and Cellamare 2007).

The *Toponimi*

The experience of the Consortia for Regeneration was regarded as so important and effective that the city government extended it to the new unauthorized areas, the so-called *toponomi*, not merely for managing the regeneration but also for its planning. The incidence of unauthorized building was not in fact brought to an end after the defining of the O Zones' boundaries, nor even after the last amnesty.

The *toponimi* in Valle Borghesiana are emblematic (Cellamare and Perin 2010). This is a very extended area (150 ha), situated between the Via Casilina and the Via Prenestina, in Rome's eastern outskirts (18 km along the Via Casilina, about 7 km outside the Grande Raccordo Anulare ring road). It is situated to the north of the Borgata Finocchio, another zone with unauthorized building that is now established. The few services and shops in Borgata Finocchio (including public spaces and green areas with recreational facilities) are used by residents of the much wider area since Valle Borghesiana itself has no such services. Valle Borghesiana has a population of just over ten thousand, which, added to Borgata Finocchio and the neighboring *toponimi*, amounts to over forty thousand people: an entire town that is completely unauthorized and deprived of essential services.

The city council envisaged the possibility of setting up consortia for the *toponimi* (though, in many cases, existing consortia would be enlarged) that would target not only the execution of the works, but also the planning and drawing up of detailed plans that here—unlike in O Zones—were lacking and therefore could be dealt with by private as well as public initiatives. Clearly they had in mind a sort of "urban planning contract" or a "collaboration with the unauthorized landowners." The city government, through a number of public notices, set out the criteria for drawing up plans and subsequently evaluated them and approved them. The planning process is proving extremely time-consuming and is still ongoing.

The True Dynamic of a Consortium

The experiment with consortia for self-regeneration seems interesting and, in some ways, effective, but if the concrete dynamics are studied in depth, the facts prove to be more complex, diversified, and at the same time problematic and ambiguous.

The consortia came into being originally in response to pressure from people who were motivated and committed to regeneration, often gathering around an original nucleus of people with a concrete interest in carrying out such regeneration in their own residential area. In this sense, the consortia appeared to be (and in part were) an opportunity to finally make changes that had always been difficult to achieve, owing largely to the shortcomings of the administration. At the same time, the consortia were founded on a relationship of trust, on delegation to people at the core of the organization and in particular to the chairman, and on participation relating to small concrete issues and not to big policies.

With the passage of time, the consortia, especially through their small management teams, evolved, combining diverse characteristics. In some cases, they stayed tied to a sort of community dimension mixed with friendly relationships that were linked to the joint character and mutual assistance of the pioneering enterprise of colonizing wild territory. In others, they gradually grew into small centers of management, local interest networks, and local micropowers, where there was an uncertain and blurred boundary between the leader who was seriously committed to the local community and the "village despot" whose interest tended toward the local and municipal levels.

As I have already pointed out, a new development has brought about the creation of a number of organizations, generally resembling consortia, that have joined together or supported various consortia for self-regeneration. These organizations have given greater powers to the consortia and have provided important technical and logistical support for the individual units that are unquestionably weaker. They have become the preferential interlocutors of Rome's administration and have come to constitute an intermediate level of micropower in the huge panorama of the outer suburbs. The city council benefits from the reduction of interlocutors and conflicts, but the participatory dimension aimed at the creation of the common good seems clearly to have faded away. In truth, the participatory processes relating to consortia of self-regeneration differ greatly from one to another, and the processes offer a huge variety according to the specific individuals involved and the particular conditions on the ground.

It should be noted that within these areas, many committees have sprung up, characterized by varied relationships with the consortia; thus distinctions emerge between the people who look after the landowners' interests and those who concern themselves with the regeneration of the urban area around their homes, often fighting important battles.

Forms of Housing

The most common form of living accommodation is the private house: This becomes a microcosm that is a home not only for oneself and one's own family but often for the families of one's children (although most of these tend today to leave home and seek a place somewhere else that is more like "living in a city"). But especially within one's own plot, there is room for a garden or a swimming pool as well as a kitchen garden and other installations that complete a style of living based on self-sufficiency and a microcosm that induces a sense of the family nucleus, even if it is extended. The person who can afford it will seek to enlarge and smarten up their own space; the person who cannot will settle for simply having their own house. People show no great interest in what happens beyond the boundary of their own plot, or they expect others to see to those spaces. That is why anything to do with roads, pavements, initial town planning, public spaces, minimal services, and parks is in effect absent, or completely neglected if it exists.

The maximization of land exploitation by division into plots and unauthorized construction nullifies the chance of creating public spaces of any type. Living is pared down to the minimum. The public dimension is likewise minimal, since it manifests itself only occasionally. This is even more the case in recent instances of speculative unauthorized building, while it was less in evidence in the initial phases when illegal building stemmed from necessity. In the latter case, the collaboration between informal builders brought about the creation of a community spirit, implanted a sociability based on solidarity and stabilized personal and social relationships that stood the test of time and became stronger. From this derived a perceptible public dimension, although it did not always manifest itself in a corresponding physical space. In Borghesiana, the only places to meet are certain people's houses or some very rare bars. In some ways, even the public dimension became privatized. This dimension was limited but important; however, it later faded away with the younger generations who had not experienced that epic phase and with the increase of unlawful building that was mainly speculative.

In some more restricted circumstances, either because people originated from the same places, or because of the enterprise and leadership of more sensitive people or for other reasons, there was a more collaborative spirit that led to the creation of infrastructures, spaces, and communal facilities, even if totally self-built and self-managed. For example, in Cerquette Grandi, people created, among other things, a sports and recreation center (with a football training pitch, other playing fields, changing rooms, picnic sites, etc.), a park in the nearby ravine with footpaths and poster art, and a photovoltaic field that supplies energy to the *borgata*.

In most cases, and in the most extended areas of illegal building in Rome, there nevertheless prevails a style of living that is strongly focused on the private dimension, entailing a reduction of the depth and complexity of social living. This style of living was probably never dreamed of by the first residents, but it became entrenched and became the only form of living imaginable there to the young people and the more recently arrived residents (while those with experience outside these areas have tended to move away). The younger generation lack spaces, facilities, and things to do in their spare time and are thus obliged to go away and spend their time in the nearest shopping malls that offer amusement, distractions, and somewhere to hang out. These are all very basic and homogenizing activities, but at least they are opportunities for leisure that are geographically and financially accessible. At the weekend, especially on Saturdays, the whole family spends an entire day in the nearest shopping mall.

Unlawful building is to all intents and purposes an acknowledged and accepted modality (as well as a spontaneous process) in the construction of Rome: it is functional in its development and forms a part of the very nature of the city and its mode of governance. One could say that it is a widespread form of social behavior and a culture that is typical of Rome, as is testified above all by the spread and importance of these developments but also by the legal system and measures taken by the administration.[6] The administration is aware of all this, accepts the process, has a policy for it, regards it as an integral part of building a city, and aims at intensive cooperation with the private sector. From such a perspective, we may find it difficult to regard Rome as a modern Western capital, but at the same time, we ought to question more closely what we mean by a Western *capitalist* city. Rome represents, even if in a "degraded" form, the expression of a "predatory" capitalism that stops at nothing and demands deregulation, indiscriminate exploitation of resources and intensive speculative building, "sacrifice" of the public interest, and haggling over the public good. All this relates not so much to a lack of policies for the city, but rather to a very clear idea of urban development and of the forces and processes that govern its transformation and the role that the public administration could play in this connection. And the idea that was proposed as a form of co-involvement of citizens in governing the city now reveals its principal character of "shared administration," giving rise to a form of externalizing urban planning: that is to say an offloading of burdens and responsibilities to outsiders, a lightening of the citizen's load, but at the same time a delegation and a subservience to the workings of the property market and a relinquishment of the development of an organic program and of an effective political and urban policy.

Notes

1. This has occurred in a context of deregulation declared at the national level, not without opposition.
2. Ennio Flaiano used to say about Rome: "A great city *manqué*! The only city in the world whose inhabitants lack civic pride. There is no sense of collective ownership, ownership is universal or rather entrusted to Providence. Everyone washes their hands of it" (1994, 49).
3. The districts researched were Cerquette Grandi (in the northwestern outskirts of the city), Saline and Stagni of Ostia, the Idroscalo of Ostia, Saxa Rubra in the north, but in particular Borgata Finocchio and Valle Borghesiana, a huge area in the far eastern outskirts of Rome. The project also involved a multidisciplinary research group: Self-Made Urbanity (http://smu -research.net/). Particular thanks to the architect Antonella Perin for her cooperation with the research, the activities she arranged, the information she supplied, and her strong support in the field. Special thanks also to Dario Colozza for technical and geographic information system support.
4. In a certain phase of history, on the strength of condemnations that emerged later and from the voice of the pope himself, Rome was unveiled as a "third world city."
5. The average size of each plot was between 800 and 2,000 m².
6. For example, at least fifty thousand requests were registered for the latest building amnesty, most of them—it must be noted—in the historic center, one of the most affluent parts of the city. This demonstrates that we are not dealing here with behavior driven by necessity.

References

Allegretti, Giovanni, and Carlo Cellamare, eds. 2007. *Les dispositifs participatifs locaux en Ile-de-France et en Europe: Vers une démocratie technique? Le cas de Rome.* Paris: Centre National de la Recherche Scientifique.

Barberi, Paolo, ed. 2010. *È successo qualcosa alla città.* Rome: Donzelli.

Berdini, Paolo. 2010. *Breve storia dell'abuso edilizio in Italia: Dal ventennio fascista al prossimo futuro.* Rome: Donzelli.

Berlinguer, Giovanni, and Pietro Della Seta. 1976. *Borgate di Roma*. Rome: Editori Riuniti.

Caudo, Giovanni, and Sofia Sebastianelli. 2008. "Dalla casa all'abitare." In *L'Italia cerca casa: Progetti per abitare la città*, edited by Francesco Garofalo, 40–47. Milan: Electa.

Cellamare, Carlo. 2010. "Politiche e processi dell'abitare nella città abusiva/informale romana." *Archivio di Studi Urbani e Regionali* 97–98: 145–167.

Cellamare, Carlo, and Antonella Perin. 2010. "Consorciando os habitantes: As experiências das 'zonas O' e dos 'topónimos' em Roma." *Revista Crítica de Ciências Sociais* 91: 237–254.

Clementi, Alberto F., and Francesco Perego. 1983. *La metropoli "spontanea."* Bari, Italy: Dedalo.

Davis, Mike. 2006. *Planet of Slums*. London: Verso.

Della Seta, Pietro, and Roberto Della Seta. 1988. *I suoli di Roma*. Rome: Editori Riuniti.

Duhau, Emilio, and Angela Giglia. 2008. *Las reglas del desorden: Habitar la metropolis*. Romero de Terreros, Mexico: Siglo XXI Editores.

Fernandes, Edesio, and Ann Varley, eds. 1998. *Illegal Cities: Law and Urban Change in Developing Countries*. London: Zed Books.

Ferrarotti, Franco. 1970. *Roma da capitale a periferia*. Bari-Rome: Editori Laterza.

———. 1974. *Vite di baraccati*. Naples: Liguori.

———. 1981. *Vite di periferia*. Milan: Mondadori.

Ferrarotti, Franco, and Maria I. Macioti. 2009. *Periferie: Da problema a risorsa*. Rome: Sandro Teti Editore.

Flaiano, Ennio. 1994. *Diario notturno*. Milan: Adelphi.

Ilardi, Massimo, and Enzo Scandurra, eds. 2009. *Ricominciamo dalle periferie: Perché la sinistra ha perso Roma*. Rome: Manifestolibri.

Insolera, Italo. 1993. *Roma moderna: Un secolo di storia urbanistica 1870–1970*. Turin: Einaudi.

———. 2001. *Roma moderna. Da Napoleone I al XXI secolo*. Turin: Einaudi.

Martinelli, Francesco. 1986. *Roma nuova: Borgate spontanee e insediamenti pubblici. Dalla marginalità alla domanda dei servizi*. Milan: Franco Angeli.

Porter, Libby. 2011. "Informality, the Commons and the Paradoxes for Planning: Concepts and Debates for Informality and Planning." *Planning Theory and Practice* 12 (1): 115–153.

Rossi, Piero O. 2000. *Roma: Guida all'architettura moderna 1909–2000*. Bari-Rome: Editori Laterza.

Roy, Anania, and Nezar AlSayyad, eds. 2004. *Urban Informality: Transnational Perspectives from the Middle East, South Asia and Latin America*. Lanham, Md.: Lexington Books.

Scandurra, Enzo, Giovanni Attili, Sara Braschi, Carlo Cellamare, Alessia Cerqua, Alessia Ferretti, Alice Sotgia, and Anna M. Uttaro. 2009. *Lungo il tevere: Episodi di mutazione urbana*. Milan: Franco Angeli.

UN-Habitat. 2010. *Informal Urban Development in Europe: Experiences from Albania and Greece*. Nairobi, Kenya: UN-Habitat.

Unione Borgate. 1986. *Dieci anni di lotte dell'Unione Borgate. 1976–1985*. Rome: Tipografia DACAR.

———. 2010. *Periferie di mezzo: Condizione sociale, economica e territoriale nei quartieri ex abusivi di Roma*. Rome: Associazione Italiana Casa and Unione Borgate.
USPR (Ufficio Speciale del Piano Regolatore, Comune di Roma). 1981. *Il recupero degli insediamenti abusivi*. Rome: Comune di Roma.

14 Marginal Centers

Learning from Rome's Periphery

Ferruccio Trabalzi

FINIS TERRAE, MEANING "end of the earth" in Latin, is our starting point for the story of Idroscalo: an informal, illegal, self-built multicultural neighborhood located where the mouth of the Tiber River meets the Mediterranean Sea. An agglomeration of about three hundred homes in varying conditions of conservation and of uncertain aesthetics, Idroscalo has grown amid the benign neglect of all political coalitions that have governed Rome since the early 1960s. Idroscalo and its two thousand residents are an important example of a persistent urban practice that, since the end of World War II, has determined the form and shape of most of Rome's periphery: unauthorized building. The history of this site reveals a further characteristic of Rome's urban development: the negligent approach of city government toward the peripheries, which it often treats as if they were not part of the city but rather as accidents of the contemporary urban landscape. It is thus not surprising that when Rome's authorities address the issue of the urban poor's right to decent accommodation, they often do so in a violent manner.

The fate of Idroscalo is currently in limbo because city officials and powerful private investors have unilaterally decided that the site is to become part of Rome's "second tourist pole," with marinas, hotels, and other private amenities. In the middle of this urban renewal fever stand the residents, the majority of whom have invested all their savings in their homes. The city government is promising their relocation into completely different housing situations: from living together in small, single-family homes they will be scattered around Rome in small apartments in concrete tower blocks, where the daily face-to-face interactions they are accustomed to will be replaced by anonymous encounters in elevators and parking lots.

The history of Idroscalo allows us to study Rome beyond conventional clichés such as "eternal city," city of the "arts" and of the "dolce vita." Indeed these clichés are still part of Rome's global identity but they do not exist in isolation from other processes which Idroscalo is evidence and a manifestation of. To capture the complexities and contradictions of Rome requires a dialectic effort that brings together the city's rich historical center with its anonymous peripheries, the art of Bernini and Borromini with the self-made architecture of hundreds of unknown masons, of the right to the city granted to some and denied to many. In this way, we also touch on a fundamental issue concerning Rome's urban form and quality of life: the relationship between archaeology and architecture, that is, how an "imagined" understanding of the past has consequences for the "real" present and future identity of the city. Rome's imagined past as *caput mundi* of the caesars was used as justification for the creation of fascist suburban working-class ghettos. Just as in the 1970s, the ideology of preserving the Roman past again fueled a new generation of peripheries, today an imagined "natural" past at the mouth of the Tiber is in part shaping the future of the residents of Idroscalo.

Looking at Rome from Idroscalo is not an exercise in postmodern neorealism; we do not intend to romanticize the margin. Rather, it is an attempt at reading the peripheries as integral parts of urban agglomerations and not as mere accidents in an otherwise coherent and rational development. In doing so, we further a critical perspective on modern urban planning that, since the end of World War II, has theorized that the best way to deal with urban growth is to concentrate people in large complexes located in whatever empty areas of the city are still available (La Cecla 2008). This perspective allows us to consider Idroscalo as a place where social and environmental degradation coexist with hopes and opportunities for a qualitatively different urban future. This view is not based on wishful thinking but on the observation that in many parts of the world—less so in Rome unfortunately—approaches to urban peripheries such as Idroscalo "have generally shifted from negative policies such as forced eviction, benign neglect and involuntary resettlement, to more positive policies such as self-help and *in situ* upgrading, enabling and rights-based policies" (United Nations Human Settlements Programme 2003, xxvi). To such an end, UN-Habitat observes that

> informal settlements, where most of the urban poor in developing countries live, are increasingly seen by public decision-makers as places of opportunity, as "slums of hope" rather than "slums of despair." While forced evictions and resettlement still occur in some cities, hardly any governments still openly advocate such repressive policies today.
>
> There is abundant evidence of innovative solutions developed by the poor to improve their own living environments, leading to the gradual consolidation of informal settlements. Where appropriate, upgrading policies have been put in place, slums have become increasingly socially cohesive, offering opportunities for security of tenure, local economic development and improvement of incomes among the urban poor. However, these success stories have been rather few, in comparison to the magnitude of the slum challenge, and have yet to be systematically documented (Ibid., 23).

Within the sociospatial landscape of modern Rome, the history of Idroscalo is both unique and conventional. It is unique because it is the last surviving self-built small *borghetto* (illegally constructed neighborhood), and it is conventional because its history follows that of other illegal, informal settlements in this city that have grown to become large neighborhoods. It therefore offers a unique opportunity to study twenty-first-century urban processes whose roots go deep into the making of Rome.

The chapter develops as follows: the first part includes a brief history of Idroscalo since the early 1960s. The purpose of this section is to emphasize and clarify a process of city-making that befuddles foreign observers, that is, how it is possible for private citizens to build on public land without formal permits. To answer this legitimate question, it is necessary to briefly discuss urban development in Rome since Unification in 1870, intertwined with that of Idroscalo. The second section begs the question of how squatters are able to live in their makeshift communities for years without being evicted or formally recognized by the city. Searching for an answer highlights the relationship between the city authorities and working-class citizens living in informal, illegal neighborhoods. The contemporary proposal to relocate Idroscalo residents to subsidized apartments that have yet to be built and the violent police operations underway to "convince" them to abandon their homes fits into this section. The chapter ends with the question of why, if all is bad, people want to stay at Idroscalo. Answering this question leads the discussion to individual motivations and the very system of social relations that simultaneously unites and divides the residents. Such an ethnography highlights the difficulties of self-organization and coordination and, at the same time, some of the reasons why residents continue to resist moving out. The methodology used is both quantitative and qualitative. Surveys, interviews, videos, photographs, and informal meetings with residents and institutional actors, as well as secondary data for comparing Idroscalo to other illegal neighborhoods, have been used in the research, which started in 2007 and is still ongoing.

Idroscalo: A Roman History

The peninsula of Idroscalo covers an area of approximately 10 ha (500 m by 200 m). On the northwest side, it borders with Fiumara Grande (as the Tiber mouth is known there), and on the southeast with the Tyrrhenian Sea and the new port of Rome. Topography varies from a minimum of -0.70/-0.90 m in relation to average sea level near the river, to -2.0 m at the center of the settlement, and -1.4 m along the shoreline. The mouth of the Tiber at this point is about 200 m wide with an average depth of 5 m and the medium slope of the sea bed is approximately 1:100. During winter, atmospheric pressure and northwesterly winds create trains of waves that raise the sea level further. Although flooding occurs frequently on the Tyrrhenian side and appears more dangerous there, the risk of inundation is actually greater on the Tiber side. This is because the sea water entering the mouth of the Tiber prevents the increased river flow during the winter from discharging into the sea, thereby often pushing water onto the land. On the left side of Fiumara Grande, there is the little peninsula of Idroscalo. The name derives from a seaplane base located there since the 1930s. Before the postwar colonization, Fiumara Grande was, and in part still is, a popular fishing spot and a place for collecting firewood brought to shore by the river and the sea. The peninsula is public property, which makes Idroscalo residents de facto illegal.

The takeover of the area began in 1961 when fishermen from Roman neighborhoods as varied as Garbatella and Primavalle built makeshift huts to use at weekends and in the summer. Well aware that the authorities tolerated their squatting, it did not take long before the colonists converted their huts into more solid constructions. According to long-time residents, the second phase of Idroscalo's history began in the mid-1970s when a second series of occupations transformed the site from weekend refuge to year-round community. Residents explain that this new phase was caused by a housing crisis and foreign immigration; like other informal communities in Rome, squatting at Idroscalo was now fueled by necessity. To understand how a group of unorganized citizens could occupy public property without permission, it is necessary to briefly discuss how the periphery of Rome developed after Unification.

Patchy Urbanization

The Roman periphery occupies what was known as the Campagna Romana, or Agro Romano (Roman Countryside), before Rome became Italy's capital in 1871. This was an enormous territory that was partly abandoned, partly cultivated, and partly used as grazing ground, surrounding the city which until then was confined within the Aurelian Walls of antiquity (Caracciolo and Quilici 1985). This territory urbanized in parallel with the simultaneous development of Rome inside the walls (Mancini 1982, Sanfilippo 1933), through a process which scholars divide into four main periods: from 1870 to 1914, the interwar period of 1918–1945, the postwar years until the 1970s, and the contemporary period (Della Seta and Della Seta 1988; see also Mudu, chapter 4, and Cellamare, chapter 13).

The first period corresponds to the creation of the capital, whose inhabitants grew from 250,000 to 700,000 in less than thirty years. Its new buildings (government offices, theaters, museums, railway stations, and residences for the emerging bureaucratic class) took the place of villas, gardens, and vineyards that constituted the so-called uninhabited areas: rural portions of the city located within the Aurelian Walls (Krautheimer 1980). The city of the working class, mainly immigrants from the center and south of Italy who relocated in search of jobs in the burgeoning construction and tertiary business, rose outside the Aurelian Walls along the main access roads, near newly created railway stations and other minor infrastructures such a post offices, police stations, and health offices that were dotting the eastern part of the Agro (Bortolotti 1988). Several suburbs also emerged on former ecclesiastical properties rented to bourgeois entrepreneurs or on properties owned by the aristocracy who sold or rented it to land speculators. The most important characteristic of such a tumultuous development is that it happened without an urban master plan (the first such plan is dated 1873) but followed the private interests of landowners, insurance companies, banks, and developers. These groups, taking advantage of the increasing demand for new housing, took over the responsibility for deciding which areas were to be developed by means of ad hoc agreements with the government or simply without permission.

The second period of urbanization corresponds to the interwar period, particularly the twenty-two years of fascist government (1922–1944), when rural to urban migration continued relentlessly, piling the issue of unemployed in search of new accommodation on top of an already difficult housing situation. This is when private speculators and cooperatives, aided by permissive state legislation, began or completed the construction of Garbatella and Montesacro, "garden cities" located at a significant distance from the city center and which were then expanded by the regime to house masses of workers.[1] The suburbanization of Rome also responded to ideological requirements of the fascist regime. The exaltation and reconstruction of the myth of "Roman-ness" led to dramatic urban renewal projects that radically changed the fabric of vast areas in the city center, the life of thousands of its residents, and the direction of urban development, which shifted its axis from the east to the west, toward the sea. The realization of a neo-Augustan Rome with the blessing of the Vatican required the relocation of thousands of working-class families from the center to twelve peripheral *borgate:* suburban low-income enclaves built according to state-of-the-art rationalist principles (Trabalzi 1989). This official suburbanization was mirrored, during the same years, by an informal, self-made urbanism developed by rural immigrants along major roads leading to the city, around and inside aqueducts and along railways. Lacking basic infrastructures such as electricity and sewers, and with improvised connections to the water system, the Roman press named these workers' agglomerations "Abyssinian Villages" to emphasize both their precarious state and improbable aesthetic, as well as the subordinate status of their residents.

Through the years, some of these nuclei were transformed into more solid and coherent agglomerations. Mud, carton, tin, and wood were substituted with more solid materials such as brick, so that the original "Abyssian Villages" became veritable *borghetti,* slumlike agglomerations often equipped with roads, water, and sewage systems. Some of the *borghetti* became precursors to the wild urbanism of "necessity" which accompanied the economic boom of the postwar period. Prior to the 1950s, self-made urbanism was represented by two ideal type situations, both located at the margin of the legal city: slums built on squatted public land and single-family homes or apartment buildings on private land which was divided into lots and sold on the market. Slum residents were progressively relocated to mass-produced apartment buildings in the *borgate,* while the second type of dwellers' homes were regularized in 1935 (Cazzola 2005).

The third wave of urban development started immediately after World War II and has continued into the present. This renewed expansion includes legal and self-made, uncontrolled urbanism which increases urban density and reduces public space. The new development was left in private hands, which shifted the burden of primary urbanization—infrastructures such as roads, sewers, electricity, public transportation—to the state. From grottoes to ruins, and from shacks to cellars, the 1958 census counted about 13,000 illegal housing situations (Olivieri 1983). Contrary to the past, however, this form of spontaneous self-made urbanism was not provisional and transitional in character; it was a real alternative housing production. Along the Via Casilina, Via Prenestina, Via Boccea, and around Ostia, pre-existing, illegal, and later legalized urban nuclei provided the basis for further illegal agglomerations that eventually covered about 4,000 ha of prime agricultural land just outside the city walls. From 1949 to 1962, about 162,000 ha fell prey to land speculation, contributing to widening the city limits by about 80 percent. Such irrational urbanism, which continues unabashedly today, has not occurred covertly or overnight (Olivieri 1983). In fact, it is the result of conscious political choices that have sacrificed the legal and rational development of the city in favor of party and personal gain. Idroscalo is but one egregious example of the modern urbanization of Italy's capital.

Living at the Edge: Fighting for Visibility

Following this background to the origins of places like Idroscalo, the next question concerns what type of relations exist between low-income residents of illegal, self-made communities and public institutions. I argue that such relations are of dependency and subordination on the part of the residents and of benign neglect on the part of city officials. The first is motivated by the fact that the residents depend on the goodwill of the city government for the provision of water, sewers, electricity, mail, and public transportation. Knowing the residents' needs, and aware that no court would legitimate squatting on public land, the authorities can keep them on a tight leash for decades, providing services in bits and pieces as long as they do not create too much trouble. Benign neglect allows the authorities to achieve several objectives: to delay or forgo the construction of low-income housing; to reserve the right to use public land according to political advantages of the moment; to keep at its disposal a reservoir of votes that can be utilized (bought and exchanged) at election time. This, in short, is the story of Idroscalo: always on the verge of becoming legitimate and always on the verge of being destroyed. The ambiguous behavior of the city government raises false hopes among the residents which in turn creates diffuse mistrust preventing the development of virtuous civic behavior. To complicate things further, benign neglect does not stop residents from creating a sense of community and investing their life savings in ameliorating their living conditions. The informality of the settlement becomes their lived world and their home the only tangible property upon which to construct a present for themselves and a future for their children. It is thus understandable that residents resist plans for their relocation, at times violently.

Since the mid-1970s, Idroscalo residents have negotiated with city authorities to obtain visibility and legitimacy, but to no avail. As noted by residents in interviews and documents sent to the city government, the site is practically devoid of primary and secondary infrastructures and existing services are temporary and incomplete. Internal roads are made of packed earth and, apart from a few canalizations made by the residents at the end of the 1980s to drain gardens and channel rain water into the river, there is no proper sewage system. Roads are constantly flooded, therefore, making walking and driving particularly difficult.

The distribution of drinking water is another exercise in creativity. Most homes receive water from three drinking fountains. The water is collected into large tanks and then flows through exposed metal pipes to smaller containers placed on rooftops; from there it is distributed into homes and gardens with the help of small electrical pumps. Residents have built all these connections, using water that is public and therefore free, with the full knowledge (and blessing) of the Azienda Comunale Elettricità e Acque (ACEA). Not all homes receive water in this way, though; some are hooked up to the communal aqueduct, and residents therefore pay for it. This paradoxical situation came about because in the mid-1990s, ACEA offered residents the possibility of signing a contract to connect their houses to the grid. This initiative, however, was short-lived and not well advertised so that only a few informed and well-organized residents were able to take advantage of the brief window of opportunity.

Cooking is done at Idroscalo by using gas cylinders. Most homes have electricity from the city grid but, as with water, the history of their access to electric power is a convoluted one. According to residents, before 1977, it was possible to get electricity simply by making a request to the power company. Since then, two laws concerning illegal settlements (Law No. 10/1977 and Regional Law No. 28/1980) have prevented further access. At Idroscalo, therefore, homes built before 1977 have a regular contract with the power company, whereas the majority, built after 1977, connect illegally to the grid. This practice is also known to ACEA and to the city government.

There is no garbage collection inside the settlement because the municipal authorities consider its internal roads to be "private"; refuse is collected only in a few spots along the main road connecting Idroscalo to the neighborhood of Ostia. As many residents note, the "dumping" that happens at Idroscalo is only in part due to the practices of locals. Most of the garbage that lies abandoned around the settlement (from old sofas to refrigerators) is brought there by outsiders. The sensation of living in an abandoned place reinforces psychological mechanisms such as cynicism, resignation, and mistrust that constitute the basis of the social psychology of the community. Mistrust is mostly directed at city hall, as the most common comments during our interviews underlined: "we feel abandoned"; "we have asked many times and received nothing"; "as far as they're concerned, we do not exist"; "everything you see here we made ourselves"; "when they come here they only do so to show off"; "nobody protects us."

The feeling of being isolated and abandoned is further reinforced by events concerning the construction and, more recently, the expansion, of the marina. For about forty years, the community of Idroscalo was the only built zone in an otherwise rural area. In early 2000, a consortium of local entrepreneurs, backed by local administrators, built a marina for three hundred boats on previously unspoiled land, radically and permanently altering the area's ecosystem. To keep Idroscalo residents quiet and win their tacit approval of the project, the city government promised that the new port would employ locals. In reality, though, no Idroscalo residents have been given work there. Indeed, if anything, the perimeter wall and the gates of the marina have further isolated the community from the city. In 2008, the authorities granted the same consortium permission to expand the marina, de facto severing Idroscalo from what little access to the sea they had left. Moreover, municipal architects have now put forward plans to bulldoze the community and build a "nature" park in its stead. The fact that there is a living community on the site appears irrelevant to these planners whose projects do not even indicate the presence of a settlement. In a purely imperial fashion, the city of Rome considers Idroscalo empty and devoid of life. Its residents, like their twentieth-century predecessors in other parts of Rome, are now plunged into urban planning processes much larger than themselves and, as in the past, the city government continues to show its violent side when dealing with poor citizens.

Uprooting and Relocation

It is worth briefly returning to the fascist program of urban renewal mentioned earlier in this chapter. The forced relocation of thousands of residents from the *centro storico* to isolated suburbs with no job opportunities was a traumatic experience not least because it uprooted them from their social environment, jobs, and friends, forcing them to reinvent their lives from scratch amid strangers. The event left a strong mark on the collective memory of thousands of elderly Romans and their children.[2] From the 1970s onward, when the left-wing city government decided to demolish the remaining illegal and informal settlements inside the city, scores of residents in Valle Aurelia, Mandrione, Prenestino, and Casilino experienced similar traumas as they were relocated from their homes to low-income dormitory neighborhoods such as Spinaceto, Laurentino 38, or Corviale, together with other families with whom they shared nothing but their sad predicament. Even when the relocation was within reasonable distance, the violence and the pain of the event remained and was often not psychologically processed at the individual and collective level for years. Indeed, as Antonello d'Elia has shown in his movie *Il silenzio di Corviale* ("The Silence of Corviale"), it can stay for generations (D'Elia 2008).

The practice of forced removal follows an established script, irrespective of whether it is carried out by left- or right-wing city governments. It starts with sending municipal officers, who are generally not from the area, to survey the settlement and collect information on homes and residents. Residents, worried about the official presence of the city in their neighborhood (police usually visit informal communities only to conduct arrests or harass residents), ask officers the reason for their presence. The latter keep their answers vague, or in the case of Idroscalo, they bluntly reply that they are there because the community will soon be evacuated. In either case, rumors spread like wildfire and groups of concerned citizens drive to city hall asking for clarification. If they are received, they are told not to worry because the process will take time and, in any case, the authorities will give them a rent-controlled apartment. This does not occur, though, and one morning, usually before dawn, police in riot gear and bulldozers occupy the settlement. From then on, depending on local circumstances, it is just a matter of time (hours, days, weeks, or months) before it is razed to the ground. In the case of Idroscalo, such a nightmare materialized on the morning of 8 March 2011 when about two hundred riot police and four huge bulldozers appeared in the main piazza, reminding the residents of their subordinate and illegal status as citizens. In a few hours, over a hundred homes along the sea shore were demolished and the residents were distributed in different short-stay "residences" in the city at a cost of about 2,000 euros per month. Since then, and notwithstanding a temporary halt to the demolition following rising protests from the residents, the fate of Idroscalo and its remaining inhabitants has been sealed; this last bastion of urban contradictions is to be removed and its residents scattered to new, distant peripheries.

The official discourse used by the authorities to justify the forced removal of residents from informal settlements usually focuses on concerns about public health, public security, and human decency. In the case of Idroscalo, there is also a moral imperative: to protect the lives of the residents from possible flooding. Underlying these discourses, though, is the much more pressing motive of political opportunity. Here the utility of the policy of benign neglect becomes clear.

By allowing squatting on public land, the city government de facto abdicates its civic and political responsibility to provide decent housing to poor citizens. At the same time, it transforms what should be citizens' constitutional right to housing into a favor to the most needy. In order to secure a roof above their heads, poor citizens forgo their rights and recreate the conditions of their subalternity, at the same time enabling institutions and elected officials to use public land as it suits their personal and party interests. The case of Idroscalo is illuminating. Until private interests changed the status quo, presenting local politicians with new opportunities for their political advancement, the health and security of the residents did not seem a high priority for the administration. The question "why now?" asked by residents to local officials in many dramatic and emotional meetings, is nothing but appropriate.

The Advantage of Being Marginal

All the problems with the municipality and with the site notwithstanding, the social system of Idroscalo is what makes this place different from the anonymous, formal, and detached ways of living typical of many other neighborhoods in Rome. At Idroscalo, people are inserted in complex networks thick with informal relations and connections that are important especially in times of need. They provide physical as well as psychological support in a site which otherwise offers few opportunities for social aggregation. Indeed, apart from a little chapel managed by a very active and generous priest who provides counseling and other services necessary to residents' spiritual and practical well-being, Idroscalo is a cultural and social desert: no shops, no community center, no library, no piazza, no gardens or city offices, let alone any pharmacies or doctors. From this perspective, the recent attention of the authorities toward the health and security of the residents assumes a farcical and tragic dimension.

Social life at Idroscalo is by no means idyllic. Long-standing feuds between individuals, violent personal histories, physical violence, unemployment, poverty, and borderline personalities are all present, mixing with very different realities: church goers, people with formal employment, retired workers with decent pensions, artists, young couples raising children, and immigrants who struggle between integration and exclusion. The social network is thus coherent and fragmented, solid and weak, open and closed, proactive and passive. In part this is due to the way people communicate, or not, with each other: within the neighborhood, incomplete and distorted information often circulates and does not help to create a coherent and sustained sense of identity. Many residents explain the psychological state of their community in terms of personality traits. As one of them (Anna) says: "One cannot change people's minds, you either accept them as they are or you don't." As radical an affirmation as this may sound, it is nonetheless based on personal, lived experiences. After forty years of projects, discus-

sions, meetings, rallies, appointments with city officials and politicians, Idroscalo residents have seen it all. People within the community they have trusted have
betrayed them. One infamous story concerns a long-time resident, Signor Giulio,
who, according to many, organized a fake robbery to keep the money collected by
the residents to have their neighborhood's streets graded and tarred. Signor Armando remembers when Signor Franco kept for himself the money collected for
the *festa* of the patron saint (Santa Maria Assunta, 15 August). The opposite exists
as well: Signora Domenica who helped Chiara while her husband was in jail or
Enza who cooks for two elderly widows, Vittoria and Teresa. Stories such as these
abound even if the selective memory of the informant and the place or moment
in which it is recounted mean that there are always multiple and contrasting versions of each one. In other words, the ways in which Idroscalo residents relate
with each other is neither "typical" nor "exceptional," rather it is "normal" if
normal means frequenting or avoiding people based on one's personal experiences. Nevertheless, the community would certainly benefit from stronger ties
but, as Cipriani et al. (1988) have pointed out in their sociological analysis of Valle
Aurelia near the Vatican (bulldozed in the late 1970s), slum people "discover"
their common identity only when their community is about to die, when external
factors threaten to destroy their settlement. Indeed, on the morning in which
riot police entered Idroscalo to facilitate the removal of the residents, everybody
came out, women and children in front, shouting and yelling their rage against
city government with one voice. And again they won, at least until next time.

Why I Stay Here

It is not difficult to imagine why the Idroscalo peninsula must have appeared
a sort of exotic paradise to its first residents. The light, the wind, the colors of
the sky, the crashing of the waters, the sound of the sea waves, and the breath-
ing river flowing nearby, the sight of birds and flying fish, wild flowers, and fine
grained sandy beaches remind one that Rome is also "nature." All the residents
agree on one point at least; that they live in a beautiful place. Indeed, when they
describe it, they unconsciously change their postures, gestures, and voices. Broken by years of living precariously amid violence, abuses, and injustices, almost
by magic, their skeptical and cynical expressions soften and their language turns
poetic when they talk about the nature around them. From them, one learns that
the river "breaths" and that one can "feel" it passing by their homes, that south-
westerly winds "burn" your plants but bring in the smell of the sea. Old and
young know about seagulls and cormorants that dive to catch fish; of sea bass
and dolphins that at times pass by; of white herons, howls, swallows; of a mother
swan that crosses the street with her chicks to her nest in the lagoon; and of stray
dogs and cats. Above all, sunrises and sunsets capture their imagination: (Fabio)
"have you ever seen such beauty in Rome?" (Domenica) "I could never live in a

place where I cannot see the sun set," (Enza) "I come here to relax," (Franca) "this place disgusts and enchants me." When setting aside for a brief moment their objective living conditions, residents speak about a man-made world that can still produce strong emotions. It is when the researcher asks why they keep resisting in a "hopeless" place where they are not welcome, in homes put together piece by piece with no formal plan or aesthetic, that these residents show a capacity for sensorial detail, an absence of temporality, an ability to collapse space and time typical of the writings of Roh, Borges, or Garcia Marquez. It is this capacity to be simultaneously realists and utopians, anarchic and integrated, ethical and amoral that make the residents of Idroscalo "special" and their community one of the last pieces of Rome that, at least from a formal and structural point of view, is not anonymous. A new vision for Rome could well start from here.

Notes

1. The oldest nucleus of Garbatella, neighborhood Concordia, was initiated before Fascism, on 18 February 1920. The construction of Montesacro began in 1924 with the name of Città Giardino Aniene (the "garden city of Aniene").

2. To understand the effects of relocalization on collective psychology in the U.S. context, see Fullilove (2004).

References

Bortolotti, Lando. 1988. *Roma fuori le mura*. Bari-Rome: Editori Laterza.

Caracciolo, Alberto, and Folco Quilici. 1985. *Roma, una capitale singolare*. Bologna, Italy: Il Mulino.

Cazzola, Alessandra. 2005. *I paesaggi nelle campagne di Roma*. Firenze, Italy: Firenze University Press.

Cipriani, Roberto, ed. 1988. La *comunità fittizia nella borgata romana di Valle Aurelia*. Rome: Euroma La Goliardica.

D'Elia, Antonello. 2008. *Il silenzio del Corviale*. Film, directed by Marco Danieli, produced by Chiara Grassi. Rome: Comune di Roma.

Della Seta, Piero, and Roberto Della Seta. 1988. *I suoli di Roma: Uso e abuso del territorio nei cento anni della capitale*. Rome: Editori Riuniti.

Fullilove, Mindy Thompson. 2004. *Root Shock: How Tearing Up City Neighborhoods Hurt America and What We Can Do About It*. New York: Ballantine Books.

Krautheimer, Richard. 1980. *Rome: Profile of a City, 312–1308*. Princeton, N.J.: Princeton University Press.

La Cecla, Franco. 2008. *Contro l'architettura*. Milan: Bollati Boringhieri.

Mancini, Oscar. 1982. "Il territorio agricolo dell'area metropolitana di Roma." In *Metropoli e agricoltura*, edited by Piero Bolchini and Daniela Lorandi, 255–278. Milan: Franco Angeli, 1982.

Olivieri, Mauro. 1983. "1925–1981: La *città* abusiva." In *La metropoli "spontanea." Il caso di Roma*, edited by Alberto Clementi and Francesco Perego, 280–394. Rome: Dedalo, 1983.

Sanfilippo, Mario. 1933. *Le tre città di Roma: Lo sviluppo urbano dalle origini ad oggi.* Bari-Rome: Editori Laterza.

Trabalzi, Ferruccio. 1989. "Primavalle: Urban Reservation in Rome." *Journal of Architectural Education* 42 (3): 38–46.

United Nations Human Settlements Programme (UN-Habitat). 2003. *The Challenge of Slums—Global Report on Human Settlements.* London: UN-Habitat.

15 Residence Roma

Senegalese Immigrants in a Vertical Village

Cristina Lombardi-Diop

THIS CHAPTER EXAMINES the dwelling practices that Senegalese immigrants devised—in one specific location in the city of Rome—as an attempt to respond to the failure of the capital's integration policies. The site under consideration is Residence Roma, a residential building in the neighborhood of Forte Bravetta, located in the northern outskirts of Rome's XVI municipality, where over two thousand immigrants lived between 2001 and 2006. Among them were at least eight hundred citizens of Senegal (most of whom were Wolof immigrants linked to the Sufi brotherhood of Mouridiyya), who established themselves in rented studio apartments. All of the Senegalese residents were evacuated at the end of 2007, the site was demolished, and new and expensive villas are being built in its place. Yet this story speaks to the city today. As a telling example of Rome's transformation from national to global capital, it testifies to the existence of historical events that are not lost, but only removed from the present. They can be brought back to light by simply digging into them. The work of digging is exactly what this essay does, as this work fits the history of the city of Rome perfectly. When Mussolini during the 1930s decided to remember the imperial past, all he had to do was to "dig out" monumental places such as the Roman Forum. Yet, such an operation required the removal of other pasts, such as the medieval one. In Rome, some pasts are more easily forgotten than others, and some are simply too disturbing to deserve monuments to their memory. Against the grain of such forgetfulness, the work of this essay envisions Rome as a city that "has [. . .] learned the art of growing old by playing on all its pasts" (de Certeau 1994, 91).

The events that occurred in Residence Roma exemplify how contemporary Rome has been, and continues to be, highly affected by the major spatial transformations brought about by global migrations. The focus of the chapter is on the dwelling practices among Senegalese immigrants, for this transnational commu-

nity evidences salient features connected to larger spatial practices that characterize the reterritorialization of urban spaces in globalization. In particular, the
chapter discusses the creation, near Rome's *centro storico,* of "vertical villages"
that are an alternative to the ghettoization of many immigrants and specific to
the Senegalese communities in diaspora. Moreover, the chapter explores the
gendered dimension of housing discrimination practices by looking at the way
in which Senegalese women creatively transformed the private, mono-familial
apartments of Residence Roma into hybrid spaces, a practice that responded
more closely to their cultural and gendered dimension and ultimately critiqued
the very concept of integration from within.

The premise of my approach rests upon Michel de Certeau's important theory of everyday consumption (of space, food, goods, and texts) as a form of alternative production. According to de Certeau, daily practices of consumption of
dominant economic systems do not necessarily imply passivity on the part of the
consumers. On the contrary, daily operations (such as walking, dwelling, cooking food, watching TV, and reading) very often constitute forms of consumption
that appropriate and utilize the products of a dominant economic system in ways
that are foreign to that system but functional to other specific ends (de Certeau
1994, xii–xiii). The vertical villages are thus a form of alternative production of
space in the face of urban dispersal, segregation, and housing discrimination.

The existence of vertical villages counterbalances the ambiguous de facto/de
jure logic of discrimination that privileges Italian nationals over non-European
Union foreigners in housing and rental policies. Housing constitutes one of the
major problems immigrants experience in Italy and shortage of housing is a lingering issue in the history of the country (see also Mudu, chapter 4). Although,
in 2005, 14.4 percent of houses sold on the real-estate market in Italy were bought
by foreign residents, 36.5 percent of them lived in precarious housing conditions.
In 2006, shortage of housing figured as the number one problem for migrants in
Italy, listed before the issue of finding a job and the nostalgia of home (Caritas/
Migrantes 2006, 159).The difficulty immigrants experience in finding a home in
Italy is an emblematic sign not only of the breaking of the social "pact of hospitality" on the part of state institutions, but also of the breaking of the "absolute hospitality" given to nameless migrants in a just society.[1] Two theoretical paradigms
contribute to my discussion: the concepts of linguistic and cultural hybridity,
and transnationalism. More specifically, I draw part of my argument from the
model provided by the type of urban Wolof that has developed during the last decades among transnational Senegalese traders as a new linguistic hybrid (Swigart
1992) that mixes Wolof, French, and any of the other languages dominant in the
host country of the Senegalese diaspora. The code switching between different
languages is a normative practice (Swigart 1992) that does not disrupt the linguistic and social integrity of the speaker. In the paradigm I assume as the one that

is most useful for reading the Senegalese dwelling practices devised at Residence Roma, distinct cultural forms, set against each other dialogically, intermix but do not merge.

Rather than hybridity understood as a condition of radical disjunction and unstable in-between-ness, my idea of hybridity shares common elements with a definition of transnational space as a process of deterritorialization of people and goods but also as a reterritorialization in another place. Emphasis on the specific context of reterritorialization shows that globalization does not necessarily entail the disappearance of place; rather, it is very much a process that involves locality and new ways of settlement (Jackson et al. 2004). Transnational migration studies analyze migrations as part of the broader phenomenon of globalization: "The recent use of the adjective 'transnational' in the social sciences and cultural studies draws together the various meanings of the word so that the restructuring of capital globally is seen as linked to the diminished significance of national boundaries in the production and distribution of objects, ideas, and people" (Schiller et al. 1995, 49). Contrary to previous views of past immigrations, in which immigrant settlements were often understood as an incorporation and transformation of immigrants and their communities, followed by a decline of the immigrant's ethnicity and cultural distinctiveness, transnational migration studies allow for a new understanding of the immigrant's continuous and uninterrupted involvement in cross-border activities and exchange between the country of origin and the host country. These contacts, which often involve family networks, extend to the larger sphere of economic, political, and social relations (Gowricharn 2009).

Multiple factors affect contemporary transnational migrations, including the new technologies of transportation and communication facilitating sustained and multiple contacts with the countries of origin. Transnational affiliations also represent "a response to the fact that in a global economy contemporary migrants have found full incorporation in the countries within which they resettle either not possible or not desirable" (Schiller et al. 1995, 52). The creation of sustained and constant links with the homeland implies the transformation of the cultural forms of the country of origin and a reelaboration of the idea of integration within the destination country. In a similar vein, the Algerian sociologist Abdemalek Sayad has repeatedly warned against the temptations of looking at migrations from the ethnocentric and partial perspective of the host country. A migrant is, in his view, always caught in the dialectical relationship between departure and arrival: Emigration and immigration are complementary aspects of the same phenomenon and cannot be separated. His analysis, based on the Algerian experience in France, sheds light on the complex layering of motivations and multiple influences implicated in the process of adaptation to the destination country. Sayad's critique of the practice of "integration" stems from his realization that, behind this politically coded word, lay the power relations that often orient cultural transformation in the direction of the migrant's social cooptation within the host country's social system (Sayad 1999).

Senegalese Transnationalism

The Senegalese community in Italy is made of approximately eighty thousand people, a highly mobile, young Wolof-speaking population that predominantly comes from the center-western regions of the country and the *banlieues* (peripheries) of Dakar (Caritas/Migrantes 2011; Riccio 2007, 2008; Tall 2008).[2] Senegalese migrants are involved in social and economic activities that cross national borders in a circulatory migration characterized by a "specific blend of dwelling and moving" (Riccio 2004, 930). Many of them keep links with the Mourid Sufi brotherhood of Senegal, an autochthonous religious group founded in the nineteenth century by the Senegalese marabout Cheikh Amadou Bamba Mbacké. Although highly dislocated in urban centers worldwide, the Mourids' geography is centered around the sacred city of Touba, founded by the Cheikh Amadou Bamba and considered the spatial and spiritual point of reference of their "sacred geography" (Carter 1997, 61). The Mourids' ritualization and sacralization of the Italian space (Riccio 2004) maintains as its center the sacred city of Tuba, which is constantly imagined as a point of reference distinct from the real geography of settlement.

The religious networks play a very important organizational role for migrant Mourids (Riccio 2004). Their urban diaspora was spurred by a gradual abandonment of the commercial production of groundnuts in Senegal, introduced by the French in the nineteenth century and which came to dominate the Senegalese economy during the colonial period. By incorporating themselves into the colonial agricultural system, the Mourids managed to preserve Wolof rural values, but renegotiated and reinvested in the institutional structure of French colonialism (Diouf 2000). Until the 1980s, the groundnut economy was still the major source of income for the Mourids (Salzbrunn 2002). The lack of crop diversification coupled with crop failures and prolonged drought in much of the Sahel region contributed to internal urban migrations, throughout the rest of Africa, as well as to the countries of Europe, Asia, and the Americas (Carter 1997; Diouf 2000). In the 1990s, the implementation of structural adjustment programs in West Africa prompted the removal of taxes on imported goods. Mourid traders began to import electronic and computer products directly from Southeast Asian countries. Today, remissions from Mourid migrants allow major social projects in Touba and elsewhere. In the eastern part of Senegal, for instance, the electrification of entire villages has been funded with remissions from Senegalese immigrants living in Naples (Salzbrunn 2002).

Ligeey (work) is both a social and spiritual value of the Mourid brotherhood. For many immigrants without a work permit in Italy, *ligeey* means commerce and trade. In the 1990s, their products were fake Lacoste shirts, jeans, and fake leather purses, cheaply produced in China and in Naples and sold to Italian clients. In the 2000s, there are bootlegged CDs and videos (Lombardi-Diop 2005). Trade activities facilitate the organization of mobility from and to the country of origin, in a constant flux of people, goods, and information. Travel and technology (TV, telephone, and Internet) contribute to fast and constant contacts with home (Mboup 2000). The diasporic movement from Africa to Europe is no longer simply from place of origin to host country, but it is a movement into and out of different types of spaces.

Rome and the New Immigration

Residence Roma is a space at the threshold of the historic center of Rome. Its inhabitants, when asked, say that they live "*in centro.*" In fact, it is a few miles away from centrally located sites such as Gianicolo, Saint Peter's, and Trastevere, where many of the Mourid traders set up makeshift shops to sell their goods. But Residence Roma also exists at the threshold of the late modernity of Rome. Its history is a layered one linked to the transformation of Rome from a city of internal migrations to a city that now hosts over 440,000 foreign residents (almost 10 percent of its total population) from such diverse countries as, Romania, Albania, Poland, the Philippines, Sri Lanka, China, Bangladesh, Egypt, and Peru (Caritas/Migrantes 2011, 474).[3] When Rome became the capital of the newly founded Italian state, the city was still to be created in terms of modern housing and infrastructures. Its basic industry soon became the construction industry, which created a "building proletariat" (Casacchia, Calvosa, and Sonnino 2006), subject to much exploitation. While it was used to build the official city, the internal proletariat was housed in shacks and little houses built along the main consular roads. Gradually, Rome's lower classes were expelled from the city center and moved to the *borgate* in the outskirts, where the new labor immigrants from regions close to Lazio also settled (Casacchia, Calvosa, and Sonnino 2006). The process of remixing and decentering Rome's working-class and low-income populations, which first targeted internal immigrants, is now affecting non-European Union foreigners. From the early 1990s onward, they established themselves in historic working-class areas, where internal immigrants moved from the 1920s onward, such as Pigneto-Torpignattara, Centocelle, Alessandrino, Primavalle, and Magliana (Mudu 2006; see also Mudu, chapter 4). The southern axis of settlement along the Casilina road was marked by the occupation of the Pantanella complex, an ex-factory brutally evacuated by the police in 1990. Its inhabitants were arrested and the building set on fire. Similar to what will happen to Residence Roma, the Pantanella complex was entirely restructured and put on the real-estate market for high profit. These two cases show that contemporary urban immigrant settlements are subject to patterns of displacement that seem constitutive of Rome's formation process as a global capital; like previously decentered native communities, today's immigrants are often the target of evacuation and demolition practices that decentralize and disperse immigrant communities away from the city's historic and central districts. These practices determine clear boundaries of settlement that define categories of exclusion from privileged areas of Rome's walled center.

Vertical Urban Villages

Senegalese transnational migrants in France, Italy, and the United States tend to privilege physical proximity by settling in large numbers in single units or buildings. These dwelling places in the urban context have been defined as *vertical villages* (N'Diaye and N'Diaye 2006). These are

> an outward expressive form of a complex network of long-standing practices, structured relationships, and values growing out of the experience of interdependence in long-distance trade, craft apprenticeship, and teamwork in farming that bridged rural and urban—a mechanism of survival and community building rooted in and relating to these overlapping and intertwined occupational traditions (N'Diaye and N'Diaye 2006, 97–98).

The vertical villages can be conceived as counterpart of the compound or family residence in Africa where extended family members live (Carter 1997), sharing close-knit ties with neighbors and friends. In the early 1980s, in the Borgo Dora area of Turin, Ibrahim Wade, a former peasant turned trader in Italy, established the first house inhabited exclusively by Senegalese. By the early 1990s, more than 120 people lived there by sharing six rooms (Carter 1997). In Rome, decayed old buildings near the Termini station, which are no longer attractive for the local population, usually provide temporary shelter for those newly arrived in Italy or lacking a stable job and a permit to stay. As they gradually insert themselves in the labor market, most immigrants improve their housing conditions by seeking more stable types of housing, usually rented private houses occupied by one person or the whole family (Natale 2006). Many Senegalese immigrants settled in the same residential complex, thus forming an extremely large community. In the late early 2000s, Residence Roma soon became one of the largest sites of settlement for Senegalese in Italy. It was composed of five buildings, each of which was seven stories high, and divided into studio apartments (*monolocali*) averaging 30–40 m² in size.[4] The entrance to each building opened onto a large courtyard, the only communal space of the complex, where residents gathered—usually divided by ethnic community—for socializing and trading goods.

On each floor, at least forty units were distributed along a labyrinth of corridors and halls. The buildings were named in alphabetical order, with each unit labeled in progressive numerical order. In 2005, over two thousand people, including one hundred Italian families lived there in the rented *monolocali*. The focus of my research was uniquely on Palazzina A, where, according to my rough estimate, a yearly average of five hundred Senegalese lived in the 2001–2006 period by renting the apartments at a price of 500–700 euros per month.[5] The residence was managed by Costruzioni Edili Immobiliari, a private company, but owned by another private enterprise, Enpam. Behind Enpam is the Mezzaroma family, a well-known family of Roman real-estate investors who, since the beginning of the 1990s, have made a fortune and now, ironically, own *"mezza Roma"* ("half Rome").[6] In 1983, when the city of Rome experienced a particularly acute crisis in housing shortage, the residence, which had been recently inaugurated, opened its doors to at least nine hundred low-income Italian families. As many as six hundred Italian families lived there until the end of the 1990s. Then, gradually, the Italians were transferred elsewhere. The media focused their attention on Residence Roma when the surrounding neighbors started complaining about illegal activities taking place inside the residence. For many, these began with the arrivals of immigrants around the year 2000, when the city council stipulated an agreement with the Libyan Embassy and Enpam began renting out some of the apartments left by the Italians. After the Libyans, other communities arrived, including Albanians, Maghrebians, Senegalese, Peruvians, and Rom Napulengre, and were housed there by the municipal government. At the time of the research, the largest community was the Senegalese, which occupied the entire Palazzina A.

In November 2005, Walter Veltroni, then mayor of Rome, signed the final deliberation authorizing the evacuation of Residence Roma. The eviction order, although implemented without any major act of violence, came at the end of street demonstrations and lengthy negotiations between the city council, the XVI district where the residence is located, its Senegalese and Italian inhabitants, the private owners of the buildings, Enpam, and the owners of the extended land surrounding the property, Fineuropa. Thanks to an agreement signed between Enpam and the city government, after its demolition, the land is to be transformed into a green area furbished with a playschool, a library, public offices, and other public infrastructures conceived as part of a general plan for its *"riqualificazione"* (requalification or regeneration). What this requalification also envisions is the construction of small living units, *villette*, to be sold on the real-estate market for high profit.

What happened to the inhabitants of Residence Roma after the evacuation? Many of the tenants have found new apartments to rent outside the city, in small provincial towns such as Pomezia, Torvaianica, and Ladispoli, along the southern shores of Lazio (see also Cervelli, chapter 3). Some have already relocated in other historically important peripheral neighborhoods such as Pigneto-Torpignattara and Centocelle. A study conducted by Scenari Immobiliari, a real-estate firm, affirms that the number of immigrant house owners grew by 5.4 percent in 2005. Immigrant buyers then represented almost 15 percent of the total real-estate market in Italy (Caritas/Migrantes 2006). They have been buying in degraded peripheral neighborhoods or in rural areas around Rome, some of which have been abandoned by Italians in the course of the last twenty years. These areas, such as Settecamini, Castel di Leva, Castel di Decima, Ponte Galeria, Castel di Guido, Casalotti, Ottavia, and Cesano (Mudu 2006), are now being revitalized by new immigrant presence through another transformative process in the history of Rome's urban space. And this is an ongoing process.

From Ghetto to Village: The Transformation of Space

Like other "ghettos" in Italy, Residence Roma's dilapidated conditions soon became a self-fulfilling prophecy: piles upon piles of accumulated rubbish; the infesting presence of rats; the unsafe conditions of the place where elevators did not work, emergency exists were locked, rain and water from broken pipes leaked through the ceilings, and common areas were blocked by trash. These conditions were caused, over the years, by programmatic neglect on the part of the private owners of the residence, with the complicity of unreliable and intermittent public services such as the one provided by Agenzia Municipale Ambiente (the municipal agency for trash collection) but were allowed to foster in order to serve multiple purposes. From an economic perspective, they justified the need for demolition of an immigrant residential center located in an area so close to the historic center and thus targeted by rampant property speculation. The area is now becoming a tourist hub with the development of hotels, restaurants, and transport networks that cater to them. Once conceived only as a temporary dwelling for Italian families, with their removal, the residence area can now be turned into a much more profitable business. On a sociocultural level, its degraded conditions became a symbol of the radical incompatibility of the immigrant presence of Africans in central Rome.

In spite of the *degrado urbanistico* (urban blight), the Senegalese had organized themselves in ways that seemed organic to their ends and cultural references. They had set up networks of support based on internal communal rules, as well as resources useful for the sacralization and ritualization of their urban space. These ranged from small house-based restaurants, a small grocery shop with food imports from Senegal, a tailor's shop where ceremonial dresses were made, a photographer's studio in order to catch moments of important events such as baptisms and weddings, and a praying room for the Mourid *dahiras*.

These spaces for prayer and gatherings, typical of the religious brotherhood of Muridiyya, have an important function for the Senegalese in diaspora. The *dahiras* help to maintain links between the migrants and their religious leaders. They also constitute vital centers of exchange and socialization. The social organization of space within Residence Roma was functional to the Mourid transnational diaspora but was not limited to it. It also created hybrid forms of space fulfilling different economic and social functions.

A study of participation of different immigrant communities in the socio-economic life of the province of Rome, taking as indicators their demographic behavior, their insertion in the labor market, and their relationships with the native population, shows that, during the 1990s, the level of integration of Senegalese communities in the city, compared to other communities, was rather low (Casacchia, Calvosa, and Strozza 2006). As part of a transnational labor diaspora, the Senegalese in Rome show a low propensity to family reunification, a low rate of mixed marriages, and an extremely low rate of naturalizations.

My field observations nonetheless revealed that women and children were proportionally overrepresented within Residence Roma. They were busy with organizing ceremonies such as weddings, baptisms, and the consumption of religious ritual meals. Their presence contributed greatly to transform its degraded isolation in economically and culturally productive ways. B., one of the Senegalese tenants who first moved to Residence Roma, lived with his wife in a neat and perfectly furnished room on the fifth floor. He arrived at Residence Roma in 2001, after having shared apartments in small towns such as Ladispoli and Palmarola. He heard about it through a friend. B. first lived on the first floor, in a smaller room, and eventually moved up to the second and third floors, where rooms were bigger and pipes did not leak, but the apartments were also more expensive. As he moved up the ladder of Residence Roma's society and found better rooms to rent, he called in first his brothers and then his cousins, who occupied the rooms he had previously inhabited. At the time of the interview, B. was perfectly comfortable with what he had achieved. His current room was large, well lit, and extremely well kept. His wife joined him and opened a restaurant in their apartment. This catered almost exclusively to a clientele internal to Residence Roma.

In order to be able to cook for many people, B.'s wife transformed the *mono-locale*'s balcony into a kitchen. There she prepared Senegalese dishes and sold them at lunch and dinner for 5 euros a plate. The food was rigorously Senegalese, made with all the right ingredients, the dried fish, the *bisap* leaves, the tamarind seeds, and the *Maggi poullet*. These she purchased at the market of Piazza Vittorio, behind Termini Station, or had them brought directly from Senegal. Yogurt bought at the nearby GS supermarket substituted the *lait callè*, which is not sold in Italy. This combination of different ingredients and food preparation marks constant shifts between Senegalese affiliations and Rome's ethnic mapping. In apartment 200, M., a young Senegalese woman who lived one floor below, traded merchandise among Italy, France, and Senegal. She also braided hair at home or on the Italian beaches in summertime. A., in another room on the fifth floor, also cooked for residents; like F. and L., she transformed the balcony into a kitchen.

As they explained, at home, in Senegal, kitchens are often open air areas, separate from the enclosed quarters. On the balcony, the fumes and the smell of food are easily dispersed.

Inside Residence Roma, the gendered separation between the public and the private spheres also marked a separation between different gendered spatial practices such as operations of production and consumption. The daily practices of Senegalese male vendors, publicly visible on the streets of Rome, are very different from those of Senegalese women, who operated inside the invisible spaces of Residence Roma, where they cooked or braided hair. F. emphasized how she did not like to cook because she preferred to be out in the public. She would rather do what she did in Senegal, that is, work with her mother who owned a small cleaning service. Cooking is a hard business, F. explained, because it is very tiring and, besides, you cannot leave home, you are always indoors, from day to night. When it does occur that they sell in the streets, the visibility women acquire often meets the scorn of Senegalese men or, as Coumba suggests, the pity of Italian women who, out of a sense of Christian charity, constantly address her as "*la poverina*" (the "poor thing") (Perrone 1995, 111–112). For women, selling more often happens indoors, where they buy and sell goods and products for their own consumption. This is in many ways similar to what happens in Senegal, where many women have opened their own home boutiques. In the privacy of their apartment, they showcase and sell what they have bought during their transnational trading travels, that is, cosmetics, accessories, as well as clothes and jewelry.

The gendered separation of daily spatial practices within and without Residence Roma adds an interesting dimension to our understanding of female subjectivity in transnationality. The rearrangement by women of the balcony as a cooking space constitutes one of the most creative acts of appropriation of the space of Residence Roma. The kitchen-balcony served multiple purposes, both economic and social. On the one hand, it transformed the alienating one-dimensional *monolocale* into a space reminiscent of home. On the other, it also allowed the setting up of a rather profitable indoor business for women who did not want to or could not sell in the streets. The kitchen-balcony signals the high degree of hybridity, flexibility, and creativity of the Residence Roma experience. Yet, as we have seen, Senegalese transmigrant women must constantly renegotiate their subjectivity, caught in the tension between the advantages of a flexible appropriation of their present migrant reality and the persistent models of their role in both Western and African societies, which would like them to be invisibly confined to the domestic walls.

The Residence Roma experience indicates that the formation of a hybrid identity as a state of radical heterogeneity seems unthinkable, and certainly counterproductive, to transmigrant politics and daily social practices. The analysis of new sites of placements, distinct from the original ones, shows how diasporic communities engage with their surroundings and create new forms of belonging. My discussion of the space of Residence Roma shows how the real and imagined cultural systems of both origin and host countries are constituted through a dialectical relationship that involves belonging and displacement, grounding and movement, and real and imagined geographies. In the case of Residence Roma, the material geography of urban Rome combined with the symbolic and imagined geography of urban Senegal. The *monolocale,* transformed into a restaurant and a gathering place, highlights the dialectical relationship of individual/ communal and private/public dimensions within Residence Roma. As an act of intentional hybridity, the creation of the kitchen-balcony allowed a degree of preservation of cultural difference that was crucial for many of the Senegalese residents of Palazzina A, especially women. Moreover, it also proved useful for contestatory actions. Once migrant solidarity networks were preserved, political action became possible. It was indeed through constant engagement with other residents in such places as the praying rooms and the women's restaurants that the residents of Palazzina A managed to come together to form an association, called Jappo. Jappo Solidarietà Senegal was an association born in the spring of 2005 to mobilize all residents during the negotiations set up to avoid Residence Roma's evacuation. In Wolof, *jappo* means "holding hands" and the image of the association shows white and black hands holding each other. Membership in Jappo was open to and strongly encouraged for Italians, as a way to show solidarity with the Senegalese community of Residence Roma. Demonstrations in the streets of Rome and repeated encounters with the city council brought a compromise resolution. After the evacuation, all the residents with a legal permit of stay were granted temporary lodging in municipal housing.

Jappo provides a unique example of the concerted effort of Senegalese diasporic nonreligious association with local, municipal political forces in the Italian urban context. Its crucial role in the resolution of the political negotiations with the city authorities shows that both localized and transnational affiliations contributed to the degree of hybridization of political action "from below" by different actors (such as local oppositional forces, the Senegalese Mourid traders, and the Senegalese intellectuals). Yet, all immigrants without a legal permit to stay, who were and still are the weakest subjects of globalized and transmigrant politics "from above," were the ones who succumbed to the sheer pressure of the political power of local real-estate speculations and to the larger, globalized dimension of restrictive immigration policies. Under their pressure, those who have been denied the rights of legal visibility, citizenship, and hospitality succumb to these forces without possibility of resistance.

Acknowledgments

A previous version of this chapter first appeared as "Residence Roma: Senegal, Italy, and Transnational Hybrid Spaces" in *Interventions* 2009, vol. 11 (3): 400–419. I would like to thank Routledge of the Taylor and Francis Group for permission to reprint material from this essay.

Notes

1. On the articulation of the difference between these two concepts see Derrida (2000).
2. The figure does not include immigrants without a legal permit of stay, who remain outside statistics and whose mobility is severely restricted by their illegal status. An approximate estimate of Senegalese illegal immigrants is given by the number of applications for work permits received by the Ministry of the Interior on the occasion of the December 2007 deadline for admission to Italy under the quota decree: 14,836 Senegalese without a work permit applied, that is, approximately 33 percent of the actual total legal number. Yet only one thousand work permits were allocated for Senegal. The number of applications received for other African communities included: 97,085 for Morocco, 16,010 for Tunisia, 12,057 for Ghana, 5,889 for Nigeria, 1,904 for Algeria, 159 for Somalia. See Polchi (2007).
3. The Caritas/Migrantes figure refers to data for 31 December 2010.
4. Another large settlement was Residence Prealpino of Bovezzo, near Brescia, evacuated in January 2008.
5. My estimate was made on the basis of an average of four people per rented apartment (Palazzina A included 220 apartments) and not on the number of actual rental contracts. The director manager of Residence Roma did not make data available concerning the actual rental contracts. These would have not been of much use anyway since, according to my calculations, at least three-fourths of the inhabitants of Palazzina A were not on the director's records because of their status as illegal immigrants.
6. Pierpaolo Mudu (2006) explains how the city council has been selling apartments in the historic center of Rome in order to buy others in the outskirts, thus pursuing a policy of economic investment rather than one of preservation of the city's real-estate patrimony. Rome's real-estate business had seen the involvement of the Mezzaroma family on different occasions, such as the restructuring of the ex-deposit Sefer on Via Appia Nuova. Residence Roma is a further example of this powerful family's involvement in the city's exploitative business of decentralized investments and gentrification.

References

Caritas/Migrantes. 2006. *Dossier Statistico Immigrazione 2006*. Rome: Centro Studi e Ricerche IDOS.
———. 2011. *Dossier Statistico Immigrazione 2011*. Rome: Centro Studi e Ricerche IDOS.
Carter, Donald Martin. 1997. *States of Grace: Senegalese in Italy and the New European Immigration*. Minneapolis: University of Minnesota Press.
Casacchia, Oliviero, Fiammetta Mignella Calvosa, and Eugenio Sonnino. 2006. "Social and Demographic Trends in Rome: Population, Migration, and Social Structure." In *Rome and New York City: Comparative Urban Problems at the End of the 20th*

Century, edited by Victor Goldsmith and Eugenio Sonnino, 301–332. Rome: Casa Editrice Università La Sapienza.

Casacchia, Oliviero, Fiammetta Mignella Calvosa, and Salvatore Strozza. 2006. "Foreign Population and Integration: Theoretical Models and Empirical Results." In *Rome and New York City: Comparative Urban Problems at the End of the 20th Century,* edited by Victor Goldsmith and Eugenio Sonnino, 333–355. Rome: Casa Editrice Università La Sapienza.

de Certeau, Michel. 1994. *The Practice of Everyday Life,* translated by Steven Rendall. Berkeley: University of California Press.

Derrida, Jacques. 2000. *Of Hospitality: Anne Dufourmantelle Invites Jacques Derrida to Respond,* translated by R. Bowlby. Stanford, Calif.: Stanford University Press.

Diouf, Mamadou. 2000. "The Senegalese Murid Trade Diaspora and the Making of a Vernacular Cosmopolitanism." *Public Culture* 12 (3): 679–702.

Gowricharn, Ruben. 2009. "Changing Forms of Transnationalism." *Ethnic and Racial Studies* 32 (9): 1619–1638.

Jackson, Peter, Philip Crang, and Claire Dwyer, eds. 2004. *Transnational Spaces.* London: Routledge.

Lombardi-Diop, Cristina. 2005. "Selling and Storytelling: African Autobiographies in Italy." In *Italian Colonialism: Legacy and Memory,* edited by Jacqueline Andall and Derek Duncan, 217–238. Oxford: Peter Lang.

Mboup, Mourtala. 2000. *Les Sénégalais d'Italie: Emigrés, agents du changement social.* Paris: L'Harmattan.

Mudu, Pierpaolo. 2006. "L'immigrazione straniera a Roma: Tra divisioni del lavoro e produzione degli spazi sociali." In *Roma e gli immigrati: La formazione di una popolazione multiculturale,* edited by Eugenio Sonnino, 115–164. Milan: Franco Angeli.

Natale, Luisa. 2006. "Non-EC Immigrants in Rome: The Housing Inclusion." In *Rome and New York City: Comparative Urban Problems at the End of the 20th Century,* edited by Victor Goldsmith and Eugenio Sonnino, 395–408. Rome: Casa Editrice Università La Sapienza.

N'Diaye, Diana Baird, and Gorgui N'Diaye. 2006. "Creating the Vertical Village: Senegalese Traditions of Immigration and Transnational Cultural Life." In *The New African Diaspora in North America: Trends, Community Building, and Adaptation,* edited by Kwadwo Konadu-Agyemang, Baffour K. Takyi, and John A. Arthur, 96–106. Lanham, Md.: Lexington Books.

Perrone, Luigi. 1995. *Porte chiuse: Cultura e tradizioni africane attraverso le storie di vita degli immigrati.* Naples: Liguori Editore.

Polchi, Vladimiro. 2007. "Immigrati, 350 mila domande ma è bufera sul sistema online." *Metropolis, La Repubblica,* 15 and 16 December.

Riccio, Bruno. 2004. "Transnational Mouridism and the Afro-Critique of Italy." *Journal of Ethnic and Migration Studies* 30 (5): 929–944.

———. 2007. *'Toubab' e 'vu cumprà.' Transnazionalità e rappresentazioni nelle migrazioni senegalesi in Italia.* Padova: Cooperativa Libraria Editrice Università di Padova.

———. 2008. "West African Transnationalisms Compared: Ghanaians and Senegalese in Italy." *Journal of Ethnic and Migration Studies* 34 (2): 217–234.

Salzbrunn, Monika. 2002. "Hybridization of Religious and Political Practices amongst West African Migrants in Europe." In *The Transnational Family: New European*

Frontiers and Global Networks, edited by Deborah Fahy Bryceson and Ulla Vuorela, 217–229. Oxford: Berg.

Sayad, Abdelmalek. 1999. *Le double absence: Des illusions de l'émigré aux souffrances de l'immigré.* Paris: Seuil.

Schiller, Nina Glick, Linda Basch, and Cristina Szanton Blanc. 1995. "From Immigrant to Transmigrant: Theorizing Transnational Migration." *Anthropological Quarterly* 68 (1): 48–63.

Swigart, Leigh. 1992. "Two Codes or One? The Insiders' View and the Description of Code Switching in Dakar." *Journal of Multilingual and Multicultural Development* 13 (1–2): 83–102.

Tall, Serigne Mansour. 2008. "Les émigrés sénégalais en Italie: Transferts financiers et potentiel de développement de l'habitat au Sénégal." In *Le Sénégal des migrations: Mobilités, identités et sociétés,* edited by Momar Coumba Diop, 153–177. Dakar, Senegal: Crepos, Karthala, Onu-Habitat.

16 Where Is Culture in Rome?

Self-Managed Social Centers and the Right to Urban Space

Pierpaolo Mudu

> Would not specific urban needs be those of qualified places, places of simultaneity and encounters, places where exchange would not go through exchange value, commerce and profit?
>
> —Lefebvre (1996, 148)

In Rome, the construction of political spaces has changed significantly due to transformations in the social composition of the population and the development of the city. During the last twenty-five years, many abandoned buildings have been converted to self-managed social centers by leftist activists and other diverse groups. A social center is a space which originates through squatting an abandoned place, within which people experiment with forms of noninstitutional action and association through self-management (*autogestione*). Self-management means opting for a form of decision making which keeps out racism, sexism, social hierarchies, and all forms of oppression.

This definition provides only a partial picture of the complex political and organizational patterns of social centers, though. The characteristics of social centers are far from easy to define, but their history does reveal a number of features that are worth exploring. Most Italian ones are located in big cities such as Milan, Naples, Rome, and Turin, although some are also present in small towns in the north and center (Mudu 2004). Positioned outside the framework of mainstream institutions, social centers are significant and sophisticated grassroots initiatives, particularly when most of the people participating in their activities are "simply" there "to be with others" and to be part of a process of cultural production from below. Gathering together in a squatted place generates challenges and debates on various topics such as decision-making processes, local opposi-

Explicit "welcome" slogans of a social center. *Website of the social center Zona a Rischio.*

tion to speculation, glocal resistance to capitalism and consumerism, queer spaces and the emergence of new urban forms and identities, and alternative modes of economic production and exchange. Social centers have complex histories and participate as nodes in larger networks that connect the local to the global. The centers represent vital engines for both cultural and political life in Italy's urban centers; any attempt to grasp urban change must take their presence into serious account. The aims of this chapter are: (1) to introduce the reader to the development and complexity of social centers; (2) to analyze the particular experience of such centers in Rome; (3) to discuss some of the political trends that frame this experience; and (4) to engage with relevant theoretical approaches that support our analysis of this phenomenon.

The Origins of Social Centers

The Christian Democrat Party, which held power uninterruptedly from 1948 until the early 1990s, steered the country's transition to the post-Fordist economy against great odds, not least of which was the emergence in the mid-1960s of a strong antagonistic movement which advocated an alternative approach to modernity by stoutly opposing capitalism, consumerism, and a hierarchical organization of society (Balestrini and Moroni 1997). In the mid-1970s, evidence was mounting that the political hegemony of the Christian Democrats was about to be broken. In 1974, the more reactionary sections of society were defeated in an antidivorce referendum; the Italian Communist Party was gaining votes; and, for the first time, there seemed to be some possibility of a left-wing government coming to power. All the same, in 1976, the Italian Communist Party chose to form an alliance with the Christian Democrats, the so-called "historic compromise," which resulted in three years of national coalition governments. The first generation of social centers arose within this context in the latter half of the 1970s, when part of the antagonistic movement dropped practices of institutionalized conflict and adopted more radical forms of struggle, including armed protest (Virno and Hardt 1996). A long series of pro-housing initiatives led thousands of people in Rome, Milan, and Bologna to become squatters in unused apartments (Lotringer and Marazzi 2007). The collective needs of young proletarians and women, the marginalization of entire neighborhoods in metropolitan areas, and the diffusion of heavy drugs were some of the issues tackled by the Italian antagonistic movement. One of its major groups was Autonomia, a patchy federation of spontaneously formed collectives which mobilized thousands of people from 1976 onward and had its major hubs in Rome, Padua, Milan, and Bologna. Workplaces, factories, universities, and schools were the scene of protests against the Italian establishment as well as the Communist party and the major leftist trade union (CGIL, or Confederazione Generale Italiana del Lavoro).

The more distant origin of social centers can be traced back to working-class organizations that emerged at the end of the nineteenth century, such as Mutual Aid Societies and *case del popolo* ("houses of the people) (Cecchi et al. 1978), which were linked to the socialist movement and the creation of communes by the anarchist movement. The compound noun *social center* was already in use in Italy in the 1950s, though at that time it denoted organizations run by municipalities to provide social assistance (Ibba 1995). The first generation of Italian social centers dates back to the mid-1970s. They were founded in Milan, an industrial city which at the time was experiencing a brutal transition to post-Fordism through the dismantling of many of its factories (Cecchi et al. 1978, Balestrini and Moroni 1997). In Milan, as well as in Turin later on, the growth of social centers was prompted by the need for alternative political meeting places in a period when the economic role of factories was declining. The peculiarity of the Roman movement was instead its strong presence in "traditional" public spaces, neighborhoods, *piazzas,* and schools.

At the end of the 1970s, the antagonistic movement including Autonomia and other organizations came under heavy attack from reactionary forces and the coalition of Christian Democrat and Italian Communist parties (Melucci 1996). Hundreds of people were put in jail or prosecuted without cause, and at the beginning of the 1980s, the movement underwent a crisis. Few of the social centers set up in the 1970s were still in existence after 1979, and those few opted for a lower profile of political action, rarely attracting the attention of the population or the media. Three major developments took place in the 1980s, though, which contributed to the rebirth of social centers. The first was a network of radio stations, bookshops, and political collectives which had been set up in the 1970s and continued their activities in the 1980s. In Rome, Radio Onda Rossa (still on air, FM 87.9), Radio Proletaria (now Radio Città Aperta, FM 88.9), Radio Città Futura (now linked to the Democratic Party, FM 97.7), and the Via dei Volsci political group of Autonomia kept a climate of confrontation alive (e.g., antinuke struggles).[1] The second was the mobilization of high school students in 1985 in an attempt to build new forms of political opposition. The punk movement was the third important force behind a fresh squatting campaign which gave birth to second-generation social centers in the 1980s.

What Is a Self-Managed Social Center?

Each social center has its own history and political tendency, which makes it very difficult to generalize about this heterogeneous phenomenon spread throughout Italy and in many metropolitan areas (Dines 1999). However, it is possible to argue that they mutated from mere physical places of social aggregation into a symbol, a label to classify a social group (Adinolfi et al. 1994; Ibba 1995; Montagna 2006), developing a number of common traits whose analysis may also clarify the differences between them.

Most social centers were created through squatting or, in a few cases, by occupying sites assigned to them by the local municipal government at no cost. A social center originating from a squat is termed Centro Sociale Occupato Auto-gestito, CSOA (Self-Managed Squatted Social Center), while a social center that has some kind of legal recognition uses the acronym CSA (Self-Managed Social Center). Recently, new denominations have emerged such as Laboratorio Occu-pato Autogestito (Self-Managed Squatted Laboratory), Spazio Occupato Liberato (Squatted Liberated Space), or Spazio Pubblico Autogestito (Self-Managed Public Space). Squatting is an essential event in the life of a social center, not only be-cause this action entails breaking the law, but also because it is a way of appropri-ating what has been withheld and denied by urban policies (Solaro 1992; Adinolfi et al. 1994; Maggio 1998). Most social centers have taken as their symbol a "flash of lightning piercing a circle" (Tiddi 1997).

Self-management is at the core of any social center activity (Mudu 2012). Self-managed social, political, and cultural activities are carried out based on a complex decision-making process and usually decisions are reached at open meetings, held on a weekly basis.

Activities are funded with money collected during events, such as concerts or movie projections, and by selling food and drinks. The members of social cen-ters are mostly unpaid volunteer workers. As activities are self-managed, the gen-eral rule is that there cannot be any regular paid jobs (Lombardi and Mazzonis 1998), although, in the last fifteen years, various social centers have decided to pay people who can keep their activities going within a logic of social enterprise (Membretti 2007). It must be recognized that social centers make an efficient use of the funds they collect, especially considering the difficulty of restoring large buildings or organizing big events unless one has significant funds and the work is done for profit.

Social centers tend to network based on their political affiliations, mainly Communist or anarchist (Mudu 2012). The groups linked to the Communist ex-perience either adopt collective, anticapitalist, or antifascist approaches linked to autonomist, situationist, poststructuralist and neo-Marxist theories (e.g., Debord, Foucault, and Negri) or, in a few cases, Leninist strategies. Conversely, anarchist groups prioritize the creation of small decentralized communities over the strategies traditionally advocated by theorists such as Bakunin or Kropotkin or the creation of "Temporary Autonomous Zones" (Bey 1993).

Who Participates in Social Center Activities?

In some social centers, people have their homes within the complex and keep it open seven days a week, while in other cases, they are run by one or more collec-tives that keep the space open three or four days a week. Investigations carried out in the 1990s provide a clear picture of the fact that although visitors differ in terms of age, gender, and education, they reflect the structure of the labor market, especially as far as the younger generations are concerned (Consorzio Aaster et al. 1996, Senzamedia 1996). For many years, most of the members of social cen-

Ladyfest in two social centers: Strike and Forte Prenestino. *Websites of the individual social centers.*

ters were either young students or proletarians. A study carried out in 1994 in Rome showed that 72 percent of people visiting social centers were between 18 and 26 years old (Senzamedia 1996). Today, though, the fact that several social centers have existed for a long time has made them very diverse in terms of generations participating in activities. At least until a few years ago, in Rome, there was a marked gender imbalance among supporters, with males accounting for 67 percent of the total versus a 33 percent share of females (Senzamedia 1996). But recently, feminist and queer events, for example, the ones organized by the Ladyfest network, are regularly scheduled, making social centers much more mixed places than before.

Squatters and people attending meetings; organizing activities; or just going to listen to music, discussions, and events form various small and large networks. Networks must be conceptualized on at least four different levels: (1) the individuals participating in a single social center, (2) clusters of social centers, (3) the movement in its entirety, and (4) connection with other social movements and political actors. Each social center builds its distinctive identity because people have multiple affiliations and are willing to move in order to meet others who share their views (Consorzio Aaster et al. 1996). At the same time, each individual who temporarily joins the network and who perhaps does not identify with just one social center, sharing only some elements of the activity and political orientation of each center, helps shape a collective practice with magmatic borders (Consorzio Aaster et al. 1996; Mudu 2005). A long chain of activities and narratives in which neoliberal policies are critically addressed and different perspectives are offered constitutes an important component of identity building for each social center. These issues include topics such as globalization, racism, war, Chiapas, Palestine, minority rights, genetically modified foods, prisoners' rights, copyright laws, the legalization of marijuana, and artistic noncommercial performances. Initiatives in which different social centers join together are mostly connected to organizing and participating in demonstrations, and their focus has constantly changed over the years.

Furthermore, during the last twenty years, social centers have started receiving and working with rising numbers of foreign immigrants, particularly in Rome. In Italy, they have vehemently opposed the construction of Centers for Temporary Detention (Centri di Detenzione Temporanea), now Centers for Identification and Expulsion (Centri di Identificazione ed Espulsione), where undocumented migrants are held before being expelled. At present, struggles against the high speed railway project between Turin and Lyon (the so-called NO TAV movement) represent a significant intersection-link for the wider network of social centers. Similarly, struggles against privatization of common goods, such as water, represent another strong link to other social movements.

Self-Management and Self-Production

Self-production is a basic component of the life and experience of all social centers and is particularly related to artistic activities such as music, theatrical productions, and graphic arts. The list of such activities is long indeed: for example, concerts; film projections; art exhibitions; ballroom dancing for senior citizens; production and distribution of books, records, and CDs; solidarity actions in favor of Roma; courses in music, photography, dancing, yoga, juggling, open source software, and so on.[2] Other facilities offered by the social centers include libraries, pubs, restaurants, discos, music rehearsing halls, theaters, gyms, and legal advisory centers for migrants and the homeless. For many years, they demonstrated great originality in playing with symbols, codes, and logos. In the 1990s, some began to publicize their activities with leaflets, posters, and graffiti, and a few years later some of their graphics were found to have been adopted by the mainstream advertising industry. Social centers explored and used the potential

Leaflets to promote concerts and initiatives in Rome: ex Snia and Torre Maura. *Websites of the individual social centers.*

for networking and web-mediated transmission of knowledge and political action (e.g., net strikes) well ahead of institutional political actors. Hack labs and open source software have been supported since the early 1990s.

The Development of Social Centers in Rome

After the 1970s, we usually distinguish three phases in the development of social centers: a first wave of squatting between 1985 and 1989, a second phase of growth which followed student protests against the proposed reform of the Italian university system that took place in 1990, a third phase after the anti-G8 demonstrations in Genoa in 2001.

Hai Visto Quinto (Have You Seen Quinto) was the first self-managed social center to be created in Rome, in March 1986, located in an abandoned school building in the Prati Fiscali neighborhood after a previous squatting attempt in 1985 had proved unsuccessful. Approximately fifteen social centers operated between 1985 and 1989; two of those—Forte Prenestino (within an abandoned fortress that covers 13 ha) in the Centocelle neighborhood and Ricomincio dal Faro (I Start Again from the Lighthouse) within an abandoned movie theater in Trullo—are still active today. At the beginning, all the social centers were, more or less, linked to Autonomia and a significant proportion of their members were punks; the only exceptions were Alice nella città (Alice in the City), which liaised with the small new Left party named Proletarian Democracy (Democrazia Proletaria), and the Leninist Blitz. All of them had been set up in suburban areas outside the city center, in reaction to the transformation of the historic center into a district catering primarily to mainstream politics, business, tourism, and leisure (Mudu 2002). Over the preceding twenty-five years, cultural and social initiatives had been increasingly concentrated in central areas. Entire neighborhoods where thousands of people were living suffered from the absence of cinemas, theaters, libraries, and even bookshops. As other chapters in this volume discuss further, the development of the Roman suburban area, the *periferia*, was led by real-estate speculation, offering nothing except bad housing and bad public services (e.g., insufficient transport connections). Social centers instead provided spaces of amalgamation where heterogeneous radical subjects, different generations, and networks could come together. Between 1985 and 1989, social centers mainly engaged in building their own network and producing new languages and symbols. Politically speaking, they concentrated on small-scale initiatives to combat the spread of heroin abuse locally and participated in international solidarity projects in support of Palestinians and Nicaraguan Sandinistas.

The second wave of squatting initiatives occurred after the 1990 mobilization of university students. To mention a few, Askatasuna, Brancaleone, Corto Circuito, Maggiolina, Magliana, Villaggio Globale were all set up between 1990 and 1991. Magliana was turned into a social center using premises occupied back in 1973. Intifada, Pirateria, ex Snia Viscosa, Strada, and Torre followed between 1993 and 1995.[3] Additional centers, for example, Acrobax, Rialto, SCOLA (later Strike), and Bencivenga 15 were created between 1996 and 2001. Forty-nine social centers were in operation between 1990 and 2001 in Rome. In 1994, a large survey was carried out within them (Senzamedia 1996). Regular supporters and occasional visitors interviewed described a social center as a "politically committed group" (45.6 percent) or a "hub for political action" (20.8 percent). People visiting or participating in their activities traveled on average 5 km from home to the center (Senzamedia 1996). An increasing number of sympathizers and visitors was the main feature of the 1990–2001 phase, when social centers often hit the headlines and were able to attract greater flows of visitors thanks to more effective communication methods (Transform! 2004). Their increased visibility also meant a greater involvement with the local political scene.

In 1993, various social centers supported the election of the center-left candidate for mayor of the city, defeating the right-wing candidate. In 1993–1994, the municipal administration started discussing the possibility of legalizing squats with some of them. After a long and harsh debate among centers and between them and the city government, some squats were legalized and officially assigned for use to social centers in 1995 (Comune di Roma 1995); Brancaleone, Corto Circuito, and Torre were among those that benefited from this resolution. Legalization means that the owner of the building recognizes a formal association's right to run activities in the squatted premises and a (usually very low) rent is agreed for a few years. Whether to accept or reject relations, negotiations, and/or agreements with local authorities has always been an issue that has created fractures within the movement. From the late 1980s, the Roman social centers met regularly—regardless of political inclination—in order to work out schedules of events that would prevent competition between them (Mudu 2005). This effort at general coordination came to an end in 1995, though, following friction caused by disagreement over the legalization of squats by the municipal government.

The Current Situation of Roman Social Centers

In the last twenty years, speculation has become primarily about advancing political gain, on the one hand, and private profit, on the other, making it very difficult to support the common good as in the past. The current development of social centers and their capacity for resistance are interesting because they are again promoting and experimenting with new forms of social relations and cultural production. Approximately thirty-four social centers are now active in Rome, located mainly in the eastern and southern parts of town, although six are in central areas (Angelo Mai, Garage, Rialto, San Papier, Villagio Globale, Volturno occupato) and half of them are now legal.[4] Very close to the center, in the San Lorenzo neighborhood, are 32 and ESC (or Eccedi, sottrai, crea). In the northeastern areas there are Astra19 and Centro Donna LISA. Along Via Nomentana, we find Bencivenga 15, Brancaleone, la Torre, and Casale Podere Rosa. Along Via Tiburtina are Strike, Zona a Rischio, and Intifada. In the eastern part of the city along Via Prenestina and Via Casilina are ex Snia Viscosa, Casale Garibaldi, ex Casale Falchetti, Forte Prenestino, CIP (or Centro Iniziativa Popolare), Torre Maura, and El CHEntro Sociale. Spartaco and Corto Circuito are located along Via Tuscolana. Moving from the center of the city toward Ostia we find la Strada, Acrobax, Laurentino occupato, Auro e Marco, Ateneo Occupato, and Zk. On the west side of the Tiber River, in the southern part, there are Macchia Rossa and Ricomincio dal Faro.[5] Ex 51 is located in the west side of the city, in the Aurelio neighborhood. To complete the picture, it is important to note that in Rome there is a considerable circuit of bookshops, cafés, and other types of squatting; for example, there are two squatted student houses Point Break and Puzzle that network with the social centers.

The current map of social centers is akin to that of institutional left-wing parties in terms of territorial distribution (the city's east side has traditionally supported leftist parties), but completely different as far as spatial network mobilization and attitudes are concerned (Mudu and Pessina 2007). Some social centers, such as Lab 00128 (CSOA Auro e Marco 1995), El CHEntro, and Laurentino Occupato, are located in the city's most dilapidated areas,[6] although some social centers operate in the center and squats in the San Lorenzo district have so far managed to resist the pressures from neoliberal policies now prevailing in the city. The most recent example of a social center located in a central neighborhood is the Angelo Mai that resisted gentrification processes in Monti between 2004 and the end of 2006 before negotiating a move to a new space close to the Caracalla baths (Cellamare 2008). The situation on the opposite side of the Tiber River has proved somewhat tougher: Alice nella città, Break out, and Interzona ceased their activities many years ago, and Askatasuna was attacked and destroyed by the police in 1992.

Social centers vary considerably in terms of the scale of their activities. For example, ex Casale Falchetti can be considered just a meeting point for the neighborhood, while Forte Prenestino is part of an international circuit. One of the network's major features is its ability to mobilize thousands of people quickly—thanks in part to remarkable information technology skills—to help prepare big events, such as concerts or illegal raves, or demonstrate against neoliberal political moves. From this perspective, they differ greatly from center-left institutional parties, which often take weeks or months to prepare political initiatives in public spaces. Since the beginning of the 1990s and before any other movement or party began to do so, social centers have played a major role in organizing street parades and other types of happenings.

Perspectives and Challenges

Links among social centers have usually proved rather volatile despite the fact that "official" networks were generally formed based on similar political affiliations. Initially, there were two major subdivisions: groups close to Autonomia and Radio Onda Rossa, and pro-anarchist groups. In the second phase, the mapping of political affiliation became somewhat more complex, since social centers liaising with the institutional left and others close to Leninist groups, in particular the Proletarian Anti-capitalist Movement, arose alongside the former two. At the time of the Genoa countermobilization against the G8 summit, the Italian CSA movement linked to the antiglobalization movement was divided into five main networks (Membretti and Mudu 2013). Given these different political backgrounds, it comes as no surprise that social centers have had difficulty liaising with institutional left-wing parties and have seldom had any contact with more conservative or neofascist parties, which tend to dub them criminals. In addition, in Rome, neofascists organized three pseudo social centers, of which Casa Pound, close to Piazza Vittorio, is the most famous.[7] Most recently, the referendum against water privatization and the debate on the commons has created a small opening for dialogue between social centers and the most progressive portion of the left-wing parties.

The continuity and survival of a social center is heavily dependent not only on the attitudes of the police, in terms of repression, and a continual generational turnover, but also on the extent to which the members are able to reconcile personal needs with their involvement in the center's activities. Issues such as the organization of volunteer work, the assignment of tasks to different people and ongoing membership turnover are the object of incessant debate in each social center alongside the need to secure free spaces and ensure that people who organize activities also have time off (Romano 1998). When internal conflicts are too strong or strategic visions too divergent, they are usually solved through separation (in 1990, the Brancaleone collective came out of Sisto V), while conflicts between social centers can lead to ostracism (in 2007, Villaggio Globale was blamed for having hosted homophobic reggae singers).

The principle that members of social centers should be unpaid volunteer workers held true at least until the mid-1990s. From then on, some centers started paying salaries to their regular volunteers and, in very few cases, accepting funds from private corporations or local governments. There is ongoing debate about just what kind of actions will prove most effective in the political arena and should therefore be prioritized. Issues under discussion include the extent to which social centers can strike financial compromises without renouncing their political identity and means of acquiring visibility at the cost of a biased communication feedback. The current phase is characterized by a transition toward new political organizational patterns and involves a concomitant redefinition of social center activities, for example, through building networks with independent food producers and urban community gardens (see Trabalzi, chapter 17). Since 2002, Acrobax has organized a rugby team that is now in the league's C division. More importantly, in the last ten years, squatting for housing has seen renewed struggles, supported by organizations such as Action or Coordinamento Cittadino di Lotta per la Casa (Citizens' Committee for Housing). The link with protests in universities and against precarious work have also been reestablished. For example, since 2004, ESC has provided alternative university classes and seminars (Libera Università Metropolitana—Free Metropolitan University) or free wireless connection. The latest significant focus concerns how best to counter the consequences of the financial crisis.

Theoretical Implications

In social science research, what has been described in this chapter is linked to many keywords—social movements and resistance, participation and democracy, rights and justice, public space and the commons—to name a few. Two main approaches, new social movement and resource mobilization theories, are usually employed within social movement studies, and thus their applicability to Italian social centers should be discussed. Other theoretical models have also been proposed (e.g., Fitzgerald and Rodgers 2000), but it is worth considering the most prevalent. According to the new social movement approach, a social movement is a collective actor who intervenes in the process of structural social change, usually formed to tackle temporary or single-issue themes, such as feminism and antiracism (Castells 1983). The resource mobilization scholars instead view social movements as composed by goal-oriented actors making collective claims and employing various forms, or repertoires, of actions (Tilly 2006). The long-term experience, activities, and connections of social centers make it difficult to examine them in conjunction with new social movements made up of temporary or single-issue organizations or to consider them as resource mobilization centers. In fact, social centers develop much more complex actions: on the one hand, their activities are consistent with traditional class struggles, geared toward reappropriating social space and time; on the other hand, their collective demands intend to deny the legitimacy of power and the current uses of social and intellectual resources. Both mainstream approaches emphasize movement participation and claim to be incorporated in the dominant trends, something that is at odds with most of the social centers. We can to a certain extent accept the idea that social centers are a container for new social movements and they make use of resources with a distinctive repertoire of struggles, but if we want to expand our knowledge, we have to shift our analysis to power relations. Geographers tend not to use the term *social movement* in their analysis; instead, *resistance*, which is a much broader term, is increasingly being used (Miller 2000). According to Foucault (1982, 780): "[to] understand what power relations are about, perhaps we should investigate the forms of resistance and attempts made to dissociate these relations." Antiauthority struggles are transversal, not limited to one country; people criticize instances of power that are the closest to them, in particular, uncontrolled power over bodies, health, life, and death. In short, they are "immediate" struggles (Foucault 1982). The resistance and immediate struggles set up by social centers are threefold: First, squatting of empty buildings is arranged as visible public action. Second, this public action challenges urban speculation, housing scarcity, private property rights, and the neoliberal production of space on behalf of speculation and private interests—this also provides an exhibition of new power relations in order to transform a piece of the city. Third, new public space is proposed within a framework of commons, or better, it aims to turn the noun *common* into a verb, into an action. In fact, there are no commons without incessant activities of commoning, of (re)producing in common (De Angelis 2010).

This resistance has to address urban entrepreneurialism, organized, for example, through competition to hold sport events and privatization of services that has increasingly governed the city on a global scale (Harvey 1989). In a post-political framework, contestation is replaced by techno-managerial planning, the disappearance of spaces of dissent, and the development of depoliticized public space (Swyngedow 2009). This means that, as theorized by Lefebvre, the right to the city "legitimates the refusal to allow oneself to be removed from urban reality by a discriminatory and segregative organization" (Lefebvre 1996, 195). The right to the city is becoming the "constitution or reconstitution of a spatial-temporal unit, of a gathering together instead of a fragmentation" (ibid.). This right is asserted through the restoration of public spaces, or better a construction of a new common space, within a climate of conflict touching several fields, for example, culture. But, what is culture? We cannot assume culture has a single meaning (Zukin 1995). Summarizing Williams's (1983) analysis, Mitchell pointed out that the term *culture* had come to be used in three different ways in scientific and common discourse: (1) a general process of intellectual, spiritual, and aesthetic development; (2) a particular way of life, whether of a people, a period, a group, or humanity in general; (3) the works and practices of intellectual and especially artistic activity (Mitchell 1995). Social center activities are located within all three definitions proposed by Williams. Moreover, it is very hard to separate *culture* from *economics* and *politics* (Mitchell 1995). Cultural goods are openly integrated as commodities in the market-based circulation of capital, and the power to frame things symbolically turns into a form of material power (Zukin 1995). Culture is socially constructed and always contested, and it is thus best understood as a process, a set of relationships that gain efficacy as they are reified. What if the term *culture* becomes a means for representing power relations? (Mitchell 2000). Again, we turn to power relations and through culture, we can turn our attention to considering *participation*. Is there culture without participation? Although the answer is trivial it opens new discussions; in fact, if people do not participate in the production of their culture, colonialism emerges. But, what is participation? "Participation is a popular buzzword in contemporary urban studies" (Silver et al. 2010, 453). For some, it implies a support of democratic deliberation for the public good, while for others, it represents grassroots resistance to elites' top-down control and neoliberalization (Silver et al. 2010). Participation has to be contextualized within increased trends of inequality and modifications in governance structures that amplify the roles of the private sector as provider of social and cultural services. In combination, these trends have altered the relationships between citizens, as well as between citizens and governance structures. These new relationships, in turn, have significant implications for the ability of all citizens to gain access to the city's resources. Thus, when discussing the experience of social centers, we are challenged to reconsider general questions that are too often neglected, such as those of power relations and the right to the city. To be more precise, we have to critically engage with the ways in which power relations act to restrict and confine the possibility of being autonomous and not in competition with others.

> In all these years of history of Social Centers in Rome the paths have been many and the directions taken have inevitably been varied. . . . There are many which have now become fashionable clubs even with multinational corporate sponsors:-([*sic*] others that have lost self-management and self-production along the road and cooperate with and are funded by the municipality, others have become places of/for political parties, others that have become internationally famous, others that have stuck to the neighborhood, those that keep their original spirit, etc. Time will tell which of these paths is/will be the best way to proceed. In short, as usual, use your head and get an idea of your own.[8] (Translation by author.)

Social centers arose under the pressure of a social crisis sparked off by the transition to a postmodern age during the 1970s. In the 1980s, the social centers highlighted a practicable approach to the use of space thoroughly different from that advocated by the hegemonic majority. A social center is a self-managed nonprofit organization which operates in a squatted place mostly on the periphery of a city. They conduct and support a mix of social, political, and cultural activities devised as alternatives to and in stark contrast with neoliberal practices. Over three hundred social centers have been active throughout Italy over the past twenty-five years. Similar organizations have also developed, although on a decidedly smaller scale, in other countries such as Germany, Switzerland, Spain, Holland, and more recently in the United Kingdom (Common Place 2008). Rome is the city with the greatest number of social centers in Italy. More than sixty centers were operating in the capital between 1986 and 2012; we must thus recognize that the city is rich in social movements. In a social environment characterized by discriminatory hegemonic neoliberal policies and an increasing shortage of public spaces, social centers have represented an important experience characterized by a particular approach to a number of major issues: First, the restoration of disused public sites and uninhabited private properties and their reappropriation as new public spaces, and the concomitant effort to contrast speculation and mastermind collective actions designed to eradicate social marginalization and exclusion in Italian cities. Bearing in mind that most social centers are located in peripheral areas, this issue is closely associated with the unequal spatial distribution of resources. Second, social centers promote the growth of the "public sphere" by securing public spaces to be used as forums for discussion and experimenting with cooperative work modes not governed by legislation on wage labor (Vecchi 1994). Third, the social centers try out organizational modes alternative to the bureaucratic organization of many aspects of political and social life and highlight areas which may provide scope for direct democracy and nonhierarchical structuring.

Social centers have managed to shed light on a new urban geography based on a close-knit network of social activities which, though conducted at various levels, are invariably connoted by the suspension of the hegemonic neoliberal laws of profit and repression. In this way, they have managed to build a critical space in which dominant neoliberal policies can only be enforced by recourse to conflict and violence. The originality of this space is the fact that, by involving struggles which are simultaneously economic, cultural, and political, it draws public attention and challenges what is considered possible within the existing dominant social trends. Social centers represent unique spaces of recognition and respect for diversities that are worth knowing because they constitute radical factors of change in the city's dynamics.

Acknowledgments

Many topics covered in this chapter were discussed with the people in the Squatting Europe Kollective network, and I thank them for their questions and comments.

Notes

1. Approximate translations for these organizations are: Red Wave Radio (Radio Onda Rossa), Proletarian Radio (Radio Proletaria), and City of the Future Radio (Radio Città Futura).

2. For more details, see the websites of individual social centers.

3. Most of these names are untranslatable, except for: Corto Circuito (Short Circuit), Villaggio Globale (Global Village), Pirateria (Piracy), ex Snia Viscosa (Former Chemical Products Factory), Strada (Road), and Torre (Tower).

4. In the center of Rome, the Teatro Valle, one of the most prestigious theaters in the city, has been occupied by dozens of artists and workers of the entertainment sector since June 2011, following the occupation of Cinema Palazzo in San Lorenzo in April 2011. This successful occupation generated a national simulation effect, and it was followed by the occupations of Teatro Coppola in Catania, Teatro Garibaldi in Palermo, Teatro Marinoni, and S.a.l.e. Docks in Venice; ex Asilo Filangieri in Naples; Teatro Rossi Aperto di Pisa, Macao in Milan; Teatro Pinelli in Messina; and Cinema America in Rome.

5. The names for which translations can be attempted are: San Papier (Undocumented), Volturno occupato (Volturno Squat), Centro Donna LISA (LISA Women's Center), Zona a Rischio (No-Go Area), Casale Garibaldi (Garibaldi Farmhouse), ex Casale Falchetti (Former Falchetti Farmhouse), Ateneo Occupato (Squatted Atheneum), and Macchia Rossa (Red Stain).

6. See http://www.tmcrew.org/laurentinokkupato/story.htm (accessed 19 September 2013).

7. Squatting by neofascists takes the form of two different projects: ONC (Non-Standard Occupations) and OSA (Occupation for Housing Purposes). Neofascist occupations are characterized by a strong connection with right-wing and neofascist parties and politicians (that represent the main source of their funds), a hierarchical organization, and by the idea of creating closed spaces, symbolically invoked by the idea of *casa*, home, a private sphere to be de-

fended. Finally, their diffusion is operated by a franchising strategy replicating the Casa Pound label in different cities and the fundamental point is that Casa Pound runs for the national, regional, and municipal elections with its symbol, something never done by the social centers.

8. Original text is available at: http://www.tmcrew.org/csa/csa.htm (accessed 19 September 2013).

References

Adinolfi, Francesco, Marco Bascetta, Massimo Giannetti, Marco Grispigni, Primo Moroni, Livio Quagliata, and Benedetto Vecchi. 1994. *Comunità virtuali: I centri sociali in Italia*. Rome: Manifestolibri.

Balestrini, Nanni, and Primo Moroni. 1997. *L'orda d'oro*. Milan: Feltrinelli.

Bey, Hakim. 1993. *T.A.Z.: The Temporary Autonomous Zone, Ontological Anarchy, Poetic Terrorism*. New York: Autonomedia.

Castells, Manuel. 1983. *The City and the Grassroots*. Berkeley: University of California Press.

Cecchi, Raffaello, Giò Pozzo, Alberto Seassaro, Giuliano Simonelli, and Claudia Sorlini. 1978. *Centri sociali autogestiti e circoli giovanili*. Milan: Feltrinelli.

Cellamare, Carlo. 2008. *Fare città: Pratiche urbane e storie di luoghi*. Milan: Elèuthera.

Common Place. 2008. What's this place? University of Leeds. http://socialcentrestories .wordpress.com/. Accessed 19 September 2013.

Comune di Roma. 1995. *Delibera 26 1995 Regolamento per la regolarizzazione e l'assegnazione ad uso sociale di spazi e strutture di proprietà comunale* [Rules for the legalization and assignment for social use of spaces and structures owned by the municipality]. Rome: Comune di Roma.

Consorzio Aaster, Centro sociale Cox 18, Centro sociale Leoncavallo, and Moroni, Primo. 1996. *Centri sociali: Geografie del desiderio*. Milan: ShaKe Edizioni Underground.

CSOA Auro e Marco. 1995. "Metropoli: Conflitto continuo." In *Culture del conflitto*, edited by Massimo Canevacci, Roberto De Angelis, and Francesca Mazzi, 48–54. Genoa, Italy: Costa and Nolan.

De Angelis, Massimo. 2010. "The Production of Commons and the 'Explosion' of the Middle Class." *Antipode* 42 (4): 954–977.

Dines, Nick. 1999. "Centri sociali: Occupazioni autogestite a Napoli negli anni novanta." *Quaderni di Sociologia* 43: 90–111.

Fitzgerald, Kathleen J., and Diane M. Rodgers. 2000. "Radical Social Movement Organizations: A Theoretical Model." *The Sociological Quarterly* 41 (4): 573–592.

Foucault, Michel. 1982. "The Subject and Power." *Critical Inquiry* 8 (4): 777–795.

Harvey, David. 1989. *The Condition of Postmodernity*. Oxford, U.K.: Blackwell.

Ibba, Alberto. 1995. *Leoncavallo. 1975–1995: Venti anni di storia autogestita*. Genoa, Italy: Costa and Nolan.

Lefebvre, Henry. 1996. *Writings on Cities*. Oxford, U.K.: Blackwell.

Lombardi, Erika, and Martino Mazzonis, eds. 1998. *Lavori autorganizzati: Inchiesta sull'economia alternativa a Roma*. Rome: Privately printed, free distribution.

Lotringer, Sylvere, and Christian Marazzi. 2007. *Autonomia*. New York: Semiotext(e).

Maggio, Marvi. 1998. "Urban Movements in Italy: The Struggle for Sociality and Communication." In *Possible Urban Worlds*, edited by INURA, 232–237. Basel, Switzerland: Birkhauser-Verlag.

Melucci, Alberto. 1996. *Challenging Codes*. Cambridge, Mass.: Cambridge University Press.

Membretti, Andrea. 2007. "Centro Sociale Leoncavallo: Building Citizenship as an Innovative Service." *European Urban and Regional Studies* 14: 252–263.

Membretti, Andrea, and Pierpaolo Mudu. 2013. "Where Global Meets Local: Italian Social Centres and the Alterglobalization Movement." In *Understanding European Movements*, edited by Cristina Flesher Fominaya and Laurence Cox, 76–93. New York: Routledge.

Miller, Byron. 2000. *Geography and Social Movements*. Minneapolis: University of Minnesota Press.

Mitchell, Don. 1995. "There's No Such Thing as Culture: Towards a Reconceptualization of the Idea of Culture in Geography." *Transactions of the Institute of British Geographers* 20: 102–116.

———. 2000. *Cultural Geography*. Oxford: Blackwell.

Montagna, Nicola. 2006. "The De-commodification of Urban Space and the Occupied Social Centres in Italy." *City* 3 (10): 295–304.

Mudu, Pierpaolo. 2002. "Repressive Tolerance: The Gay Movement and the Vatican in Rome." *Geojournal* 58 (2–3): 189–196.

———. 2004. "Resisting and Challenging Neo-liberalism: The Development of Italian Social Centers." *Antipode* 36 (5): 917–941.

———. 2005. "Changing Backdrops in Rome: An Exploration of the Geography of Social Centers." In *Rights to the City*, edited by Doris Wastl-Walter, Lynn Staeheli, and Lorraine Dowler, 265–275. IGU—Home of Geography Publication Series 3. Rome: Società Geografica Italiana.

———. 2009. "Where is Hardt and Negri's Multitude? Real Networks in Open Spaces." *ACME* 8 (2): 211–244.

———. 2012. "At the Intersection of Anarchists and Autonomists: Autogestioni and Squatted Social Centers." *ACME* 11 (3): 413–438.

Mudu, Pierpaolo, and Daria Pessina. 2007. "Rome: Administrative Spatial Divisions and Citizens' Mobilization Patterns." In *Urban Problems and Shared Solutions*, edited by V. Goldsmith and Eugenio Sonnino, 101–142. New York: University of Rome, 2007.

Romano, Alessandra. 1998. "Liberated Spaces—Possibilities for Liberating Everyday Life." In *Possible Urban Worlds*, edited by INURA, 238–341. Basel, Switzerland: Birkhauser-Verlag.

Senzamedia. 1996. "Aggregazione, autogestione, punti di riferimento e libertà di espressione una ricerca sui frequentatori dei Centri Sociali romani." http://www.tmcrew.org/csa/ricerca/index.htm. Accessed 19 September 2013.

Silver, Hilary, Alan Scott, and Yuri Kazepov. 2010. "Participation in Urban Contention and Deliberation." *International Journal of Urban and Regional Research* 34 (3): 453–477.

Solaro, Alba. 1992. "Il cerchio e la saetta: Centri sociali occupati in Italia." In *Posse italiane: Centri sociali, underground musicale e cultura giovanile degli anni '90 in*

Italia, edited by Carlo Branzaglia, Pierfrancesco Pacoda, and Alba Solaro, 11–68. Florence, Italy: Tosca.

Swyngedouw, Erik. 2009. "The Antinomies of the Post-Political City. In Search of a Democratic Politics of Environmental Production." *International Journal of Urban and Regional Research* 33 (3): 601–620.

Tiddi, Andrea. 1997. *Il cerchio e la saetta*. Genoa, Italy: Costa and Nolan.

Tilly, Charles. 2006. *Regimes and Repertoires*. Chicago: University of Chicago Press.

Transform! 2004. *La riva sinistra del Tevere: Mappe e conflitti nel territorio metropolitano di Roma*. Rome: Carta.

Vecchi, Benedetto. 1994. "Frammenti di una diversa sfera pubblica." In *Comunità virtuali: I centri sociali in Italia*, edited by Francesco Adinolfi, Marco Bascetta, Massimo Giannetti, Marco Grispigni, Primo Moroni, Livio Quagliata, and Benedetto Vecchi, 5–14. Rome: Manifestolibri.

Virno, Paolo, and Michael Hardt, eds. 1996. *Radical Thought in Italy*. Minneapolis: University of Minnesota Press.

Williams, Raymond. 1983. *Keywords*. London: Fontana Press.

Zukin, Sharon. 1995. *The Cultures of the City*. Oxford: Blackwell.

17 Greening Rome

Rediscovering Urban Agriculture

Ferruccio Trabalzi

As in many other cities in the world, urban gardening and farming are gaining space and relevance in Rome. Community gardens, vegetable gardens, playgrounds with a garden attached, cultivated tracts along the Tiber River and places in between buildings, under freeways in the periphery and in urban parks are slowly revitalizing abandoned or underutilized areas of the city and bringing them back into the public arena. The city is not new to urban farming. Vineyards and vegetable gardens existed within the old city walls until the nineteenth century; war gardens in the 1930s and 1940s were planted in the periphery as well as amid Roman monuments in the center; while post–World War II immigrants from the countryside of central Italy squatted empty plots on private and public land in the eastern periphery and along the Tiber and Aniene riverbanks to plant vegetables and fruit trees without official permission. Urban farming is thus both a new and an old feature of this city; the recent revamping of the practice, however, departs from local tradition in at least three distinctive ways.

The first is the nonprofessional nature of the actors involved. Instead of being experienced farmers, as was the case in the past, the new urban agriculturalists (individual citizens and civic associations) are city people with little or no experience in farming. The second characteristic is that farming and gardening are taking root in what Gilles Clement (2004) calls "third landscapes," that is, on marginal, polluted, or abandoned areas near roads, railways, or rivers, and more generally on fragments of empty land. The third difference is that contrary to past practice, today's urban farmers do not cultivate for profit, for sustenance, or out of a desire to become entrepreneurs. Indeed, the long-term objective of the movement is mostly symbolic of a different approach to the city and to city living, one that is civically responsible, environmentally sustainable, and associative.

Although it is progressive and even desirable, the movement for urban farming and gardening in Rome clashes against three main barriers that limit its development: media silence, lack of practical support from the institutions, and lack of coordination among the actors involved. The relative silence in the media and the indifference to the subject on the part of city institutions force the movement to assume a sort of "underground" identity which is able to survive mainly through interpersonal connections and, especially, via blogging and other forms of virtual communication. Lack of coordination among its participants instead limits the movement's efficiency and political strength. Institutional, communicative, and cultural bottlenecks notwithstanding, it has been estimated that about seventy urban gardens existed in Rome in 2011, distributed from the center to the extreme periphery, and covered over 90 ha.[1] By comparing the urban farming and gardening movement in Rome with similar initiatives internationally (United States, Northern Europe, and in poor countries from Africa to Asia and South America), it is possible to note further specificities. First, urban farming in Rome is not driven by social and economic necessity (FAO 2011; Gottlieb and Joshi 2010). Even in times of economic crisis when Roman families are forced to restructure their expenses, the prices for fruit and vegetables in the market remain relatively affordable even to those in the lower income brackets. This is not because fruit and vegetable prices are supported by state policies and thus kept artificially low but, rather, because the industrialization of Italian agriculture since the end of World War II, although radical and deep, has not erased the network of family farms. These still persist and are able to supply local markets in urban areas with fresh produce at relatively cheap prices.

Second, in part for the preceding reason, urban farming in Rome is not driven by the need to access local, fresh food. The Italian diet, and Roman cuisine in particular, are highly flexible and dependent on what is available in the market seasonally, thus placing a high premium on local produce. Third, urban farming in Rome is not about promoting entrepreneurship (Kaufman and Bailkey 2000). A lack of startup capital, barriers to accessing the market, and bureaucratic obstacles discourage cultivating small plots of land in the city for profit or as an employment opportunity.

More than anything else, the majority of urban farming and gardening initiatives in Rome represent a critique of and a reaction to contemporary urban planning and policies for sustainable urbanization (Mougeot 2000, 2005, 2006; Moustier and Danso 2006). The immediate objective of the movement is instead to foster community-making and identity (Bailkey et al. 2007). This is not a weakness but indeed a merit in a city where half the surface area is urbanized and over 90 million m^2 of new constructions are forecast as part of the municipal government's plan for social housing (Erbani 2012).

This chapter traces the origins of urban gardening in Rome and maps its contemporary social and cultural landscape. The image that emerges is one in which residents of all ages and social conditions in different parts of the city use farming and gardening (on different scales and with different degrees of success) to manifest the desire to take control over fundamental issues of everyday life for a better city with a qualitatively higher sense of community and urban living.

The methodology used for this research includes literature reviews and interviews with relevant actors. The work does not aim to exhaustively cover all urban farming and gardening experiences in Rome; however, the cases chosen are indicative of the typologies and heterogeneity of the movement in general. As one of the first studies in English of this feature of contemporary Rome, its goal is to map the situation and provide a foundation for further and more in-depth research.

What Is Urban Agriculture?

Urban agriculture is the practice of producing, distributing, and selling food; raising livestock; and growing plants and trees within the urban and peri-urban boundary (Smit et al. 1996). As such, the practice can be geographically limited within a village or a town or, as in the case of Rome, spread throughout the over 128,531 ha of its administrative boundaries, of which 82,000 ha are considered "green" (i.e., safeguarded and protected by law) (Comune di Roma 2004). The most striking feature of urban agriculture is its interaction with the wider urban ecosystem. Such linkages include the use of urban residents as laborers, the utilization of typically urban resources (like organic waste as compost and urban wastewater for irrigation), the direct link with urban consumers, participation in the urban food system, and the direct competition for land with other urban functions.

Urban agriculture is not a new phenomenon. In the mid-1960s, Ester Boserup (1965) addressed the issue of population growth in (Asian) primitive societies as the impulse to further rationalize agricultural practices, while in her *Economy of Cities*, Jane Jacobs (1969) made the argument of a coevolution, indeed coexistence, of cities and agriculture. More recently, Edward Soja (2000) took on the same argument, analyzing the evolution of proto-urban places such as Çatalhöyük in Southern Anatolia as an urban agro-artisan node in a geographically vast trading network.

The urban-rural divide as we know it today did not emerge before the modern understanding of plant nutrition developed by Justus von Liebig, among others, in the nineteenth century (Brock 2002). A real impulse which stimulated the separation of agriculture from the urban environment was the invention of ammonia synthesis by German chemists Carl Bosch and Fritz Haber (the Haber-Bosch process) which allowed the German manufacturer BASF to mass-produce synthetic nitrogen, the fertilizer that sparked the green revolution, that is, the industrialization of agriculture (Smil 2001). Such technological innovations allowed the development of a rural world functional to the economy of urban centers yet distant from them both culturally and socially.

If the development of agricultural activities for commercial purposes outside the urban limits in the technologically advanced, industrialized Western world is a modern occurrence, informal farming within cities and peri-urban areas is still practiced in most of Africa, South America, and Asia (Cole et al. 2008; Dubbeling et al. 2009; Liu et al. 2005; Gonzales-Novo and Murphy 2000). The vegetable gardens in many backyards tended by migrant families in the United States are evidence that the majority of people outside western Europe and the United States see urban farming as nothing new (Bevilacqua 2008). Indeed as a Chinese grandmother asked when visiting the university town in Iowa where the author was living in 2008: "Why do all these people [mostly white Americans] use their gardens only for growing inedible plants?"

Urban Agriculture in the Western Metropolis

The international literature on the topic is growing fast (Smit et al. 1996; Pothukuchi and Kaufman 1999; Jacobi and Dresher 2000; Beatley 2000; FAO 2000, 2011; Halweil 2002; Feenstra 2002) but a major inventory of European, U.S., or Australian experiences has yet to be made. Systematic information on urban agriculture systems, actors, and trends in Europe and elsewhere is therefore lacking and the existing evidence is mostly anecdotal. This is not to say that there are no groups, formal and institutionalized, working on developing and supporting urban agriculture. The Civic Trust in London, the *Bundeskleingartengesetz* (the federal law for allotment gardens) in Germany, the European Support Group on Urban Agriculture, the European Coordination of Gardeners Associations, the International Coalition for Local Environmental Action, and the European League of Local Authorities are just a few examples of local- and state-supported institutions interested in promoting community gardening in particular and urban agriculture in general in major European countries. In France, for example, urban gardening is facilitated by the state. The so-called *jardins partagés* (shared gardens) have become a consolidated reality since 1997 thanks to the Charte Main Verte (Green Charter) that allows the utilization of municipal land by associations of citizens for six years. Accordingly, the city provides water and potting compost while the residents manage the garden, including opening hours and the organization of a social event once a year (Jardinons Ensemble 2013). The example of France is currently being exported to other countries as distant as New Zealand and the United States, where, increasingly, local administrations try to foster and regulate urban farming.[2] Modern urban agriculture is a global movement whose origins in the industrialized West go back to the 1800s, in part connected with factory workers for whom home gardening was seen as a supplement to their salary and in part as an aesthetic solution to blight.[3] The City Beautiful Movement, for example, promoted urban gardening because uncultivated backyards and vacant lots were seen as eyesores (Bassett 1981). During the two world wars, urban farming took the form of war gardens that continued and expanded on the tradition started in the 1800s.[4] War gardens prepared the basis for what would become, from the 1970s onward, a veritable international concern for realistic and desirable land use options in urban areas and sustainable urban productive systems. Since the 1990s, such a concern has found renewed energy within many cities in Europe, the United States, and Australia, developing urban programs aimed at distributing plots or "allotments" to foster community-managed gardens on vacant or unused parcels of land (Armstrong 2000; Baker 2004; Bartolomei et al. 2003; Englander 2001; Lawson 2005).[5] There is a crucial difference among them, however: Whereas in rich and polluted western Europe (from Germany to Sweden), the main interest in urban agriculture is on environmental management and recreational activities and only secondarily on income-generating activities, in poor and polluted eastern Europe the focus is on urban agriculture's potential for enhanced food security, employment creation, and small enterprise development. Similarly, in the United States, the rhetoric on urban farming has been constructed as a concern over a new urban productive system and a potential way out for the urban poor in central districts. To this end, it is interesting to note that until 2005, the American Planning Association (the association of professional planners) did not have a food section among its interests. Since a landmark American Planning Association conference in San Antonio, Texas (2005), where a food working group was funded for young planners, a growing number of planning schools—including architecture—deal with the issue of food from the points of view of policy and design, recognizing this growing interest in urban agriculture, which has now spilled into the mainstream (Pothukuchi and Kaufman 2000; Quon 1999).

The Forgotten Landscape of Rome: The *Disabitato*

A frescoed bird's eye view of Rome by Simone Lagi (1631) in the Map Room of the Vatican Museums shows the mausoleum of Saint Helen along Via Nomentana at the boundary between city and countryside. The fresco highlights the nonbuilt area internal to the city walls known as the *disabitato,* that is, the once urbanized part of Rome that reverted into countryside at the end of the Roman Empire. The presence of farmland inside the urban area well into the nineteenth century is a peculiarity Rome shares with no other large city in Europe, the majority of which grew progressively from a central nucleus toward the countryside.

In *Rome: Profile of a City, 308–1308,* Krautheimer (1980) reminds us how from the Rome of Constantine to the early fourteenth century what had once been a bustling city of over a million inhabitants had reverted to an urbanized countryside. Important temples at the center of the city were stripped of their precious marbles and fell into ruin and were forgotten. The Roman Forum became known as Campo Vaccino, or Field of Cows, the Capitolium became Monte Caprino, or Goats Hill, while the once orderly space of the Imperial Fora was progressively occupied by houses with gardens or simply "covered with trees, fields and vineyards" (Krautheimer 1980, 311), while hills like the "Quirinal and the Pincio were entirely rural until in the sixteenth and seventeenth centuries they became a suburb of elegant villas" (ibid., 313). More recently, Jim Tice has been instrumental in bringing to the surface the historical relationship between Rome and urban agriculture by looking at one of the most important cartographic documents for studying the *forma urbis* and the historical landscape of the city: the Nolli map of 1748.[6] If the relationship between Rome and agriculture inside the perimeter of the Aurelian Walls defines land use historically, the rural characteristics of Rome's *disabitato* changed only, and forever, with the transformation of the city from the sleepy capital of Catholicism to the modern capital of a kingdom with industrial and imperial ambitions and its ensuing rapid urbanization. Following the first urban master plan of 1873, large tracts of urban countryside were surveyed, plotted, subdivided, developed, and eventually transformed into modern neighborhoods, institutional buildings, army barracks, railroad stations, bus depots, industrial and commercial areas, and roads (Insolera 1962; Agnew 1995). Today, leftovers of those centrally located vineyards and gardens exist within secluded monasteries and churches, for example, on Colle Oppio, San Giovanni, the Celio, and the Palatine, and are tended by monks and nuns who use them partly as subsistence gardens and as places for meditation and prayer (Frolet and Trabalzi, in press).

Urban Agriculture in Rome Today

It is interesting to note how agriculture reappears in the city. We have mentioned the transformation of Rome's urban landscape in the late nineteenth century as a product of urbanization and industrialization. In this section, we examine the opposite process: how agriculture persists, is fostered through habit, or is "rediscovered" in Rome.

In the first category, persistence, we include tracts of land cultivated by professional farmers for profit or used as pastures.[7] These rather large urban agricultural estates are thick with archaeological remains and are of immense naturalistic importance. They were part of the so-called Agro Romano (Roman countryside) described in innumerable texts and painted countless times by Italian and northern European travelers as part of their grand tours in search of the forgotten roots of Western civilization (Hodges 2000). Since the end of World War II in 1945, these areas have been targeted by wild and uncontrolled urban speculation and many have been buried under millions of cubic feet of reinforced concrete. The remaining areas all around the ring road are still under attack by private and ad hoc public sponsored urbanization following private development (Erbani 2012).

The main reason these areas are still cultivated (i.e., not built upon) is because they are included in nature reserves. In these areas, Roma Natura (Rome Nature) promotes eco-compatible activities such as agritourism, direct sale of agricultural products, and education programs.[8] In the city's nine nature reserves, there are currently twenty-seven multifunctional farms operating according to the guidelines of the institution and producing foods that range from vegetables to buffalo mozzarella. Of particular interest because they are located very close to residential neighborhoods are the 6,000 ha of nature reserve of Decima Malafede and the smaller Pineto and Caffarella urban parks. Decima Malafede hosts thirteen of the twenty-seven commercial urban farms. Agricoltura Nuova (New Agriculture) is one of the oldest enterprises in the nature reserve. It is a rural cooperative created by a group of unemployed young people and farmers who squatted the land in 1977. The two main objectives of the cooperative were the creation of labor in agriculture and opposition to construction in an area of great environmental and social value through squatting. In 1996, the cooperative, which manages 257 ha, won a twenty-year-long legal battle with the city and regional authorities, and its presence was finally officially recognized. The cooperative operates without going through wholesalers. The entire production is either sold on-site or through the Community Sponsored Agriculture Network, distributed in specific points of the city for pick up. The cooperative has integrated and built on its original fruit and vegetable production and has now diversified to include beef, cheese, honey, bread, and sweets. Since 1990, Agricoltura Nuova has converted to organic production, and in 1996, its livestock became organic. During the week, it is possible to have lunch for a symbolic price together with the workers in the cooperative's cafeteria. Of great importance is the cooperative's social service, which includes seminars as well as workshops with local schools. In any given day of the school year, it is possible to meet classes of students learning the fundamentals of environmental protection and of organic farming.

Smaller agro-pastoral activities like those of pre-Unification Rome persist in urban parks such as Pineto or Caffarella (Dierna and Orlandi 2007). Caffarella is particularly interesting; located between Via Latina and the Via Appia in east Rome, the park includes the Caffarella valley, which has been owned by the family of the same name since the 1500s. The Caffarella barons transformed the valley into a rural estate in which they built the Vaccareccia,[9] a fortified farm where it is still possible to buy locally made sheep's cheese. In west Rome, three miles from the Vatican, near the Villa Pamphilj Park, is the Valle dei Casali (Farmhouse Valley): 469 ha of countryside which has been preserved thanks to the efforts of a civic committee that has been able to stop the continuous, often illegal, urbanization of the area, in collaboration with the city authorities. The area now hosts

Il Trattore (The Tractor), a social cooperative constituted in 1980 with the objective of reinserting disadvantaged children in the social and economic fabric of the city through rural activities, particularly through the production of organic vegetables. Il Trattore manages 4.5 ha and has recently opened a shop selling its own vegetables and fruits as well as organic produce from other farms in the region. As part of its didactic activities, Il Trattore organizes visits to the stables, to the vegetable gardens, as well as seminars and lectures about techniques used on the farms. New activities such as honey production and cultivation of flowers are well underway. The cooperative sells its products to an organic bistro, La Casa del Parco (The House of the Park), located inside the park and which also organizes summer camps in situ for children. La Casa del Parco and Il Trattore are connected with other didactic farms located in the peri-urban areas of the city in such a way as to form a real urban farms system.[10] The final example of persistence and resistance of urban farming in Rome is the Acquafredda estate: 249 ha of cultivated farmland in the western part of Rome, half a mile from the busy ring road, transformed by the city authorities into an urban park/natural reserve in 1997. The following story shows how urban farming in Rome, both on the small and larger scale, is a preeminently political activity because it goes against powerful landowners and builders. Of the 249 ha estate, 11.7 ha are owned by the Vatican, specifically by the Capitolo San Pietro, which is the administrator of the landed patrimony of the Holy See. On this land live ten farming families who rent the land, continuing a practice rooted in the papacy's historic feudal role in the city. The Vatican had not used the 11.7 ha for over a century, but lately it has changed its mind. Given the relatively central location, the Capitolo San Pietro would like to develop its property with new apartments that eventually would be sold on the market. Consequently, the tenants have received eviction letters. Apart from ethical considerations, the main problem for the Vatican is that the 11.7 ha estate is preserved and building on it is de facto prohibited by the law.[11] When the interests of powerful Roman landowners pit against public interests, negotiations ensue. While the farmers and their political sponsors were demonstrating in Saint Peter's Square in early 2011, shouting "Benedict, why do you want to evict us?," the political representatives of the city and of the Vatican were making a deal. The city agreed on an exchange of land whereby the Vatican would give the municipality its 11.7 ha (to be left as agricultural land farmed by the same families), and the city would give the Vatican another 11.7 ha of unbuilt public land in another part of Rome where the Holy See, through its developers, has the right to build 210 m^2 of apartments.[12] The exchange has been criticized as the latest in a long series of gifts made by the city's lay administration to the Vatican. The *querelle* seems appeased for the moment. The farmers can keep their small homes, work the land, and sell their produce along the street; the Vatican has again successfully pressured the civic administration while Rome, the city, will see another slice of its precious countryside cemented over to the benefit of the usual unnamed real-estate speculators.

Urban Farming as Habit

A second category of urban agriculture in Rome includes private vegetable gardens scattered throughout the city as parts of single-family homes. This category is particularly interesting because it reflects not only the rural origins of many Roman residents but the very process of the formation of modern Rome discussed in other chapters of this book (especially chapters 13 and 14). These gardens are in fact part of the "illegal" and "informal" Rome built on small plots of land in the periphery which help to create a sense of community or small-town feeling in an otherwise anonymous and drab urban landscape. Within this category fall the myriad vegetable gardens located in between buildings and in leftover spaces, both on public and private land, occupied and tended by private citizens. Indeed, such examples are not far from the contemporary notion of "agrarian urbanism" trumpeted as the new way of thinking about cities for the future (Lindsay 2010). A prototypical example of such vegetable gardens is located in the neighborhood of Primavalle, where an entire ravine abandoned for decades and full of debris has been occupied by a couple of Bosnian refugees, Drazen and Dzenana, who have transformed it into a highly complex vegetable rain garden and one of the best maintained green areas in the whole neighborhood of over 160,000 residents.

The Rediscovery of Urban Farming and Gardening

A third category is communal gardens, which are the closest thing Rome shares with other world cities. The motivations behind the phenomenon are in part global, as an answer to environmental, economic, and health concerns (as Michelle Obama's efforts at promoting urban gardening clearly show), and in part local, that is, addressing specific Roman concerns: economic, historical (see the previous discussion about the Nolli map), and sociocultural (community making). It is this last aspect, namely the retrenchment and disappearance of spaces for socialization, that is sparking the contemporary phenomenon of urban gardening in Rome. As emphasized by architect Luca d'Eusebio, a founding member of Zappata Romana (Digging Rome), shared gardens "conquered" by groups of citizens "provide the opportunity to generate a number of social activities through which new social relations are forged, especially in marginal areas among disadvantaged groups that often lack such opportunities, such as seniors, people with disabilities, women, children, and the unemployed."[13] Indeed, shared gardening allows these groups the possibility for further social and economic integration via the learning of sustainable environmental practices. Shared gardens in Rome usually follow an established procedure which includes a formal request by a civic group to the city government for permission to occupy an area, and, if approved, an agreement between the group and the authorities is established. At this point, the city should provide water and soil. As in the case of Paris, in Rome too, the only requirement is that gardens be open to the public at least two days per year. In reality, as pointed out by Bianca Daniello, president of La Vanga Quadra (The Square Spade)—a civic association interested in creating urban gardens in Rome—the municipal authorities are often very inactive in this respect. Indeed, at times, the city goes against such activities due to the absence of a clear policy for urban gardens and the perpetuation of spatial policies favoring the covering of green areas with concrete rather than protecting the remaining green areas (Scarpa 2012). This position is shared by many people in the movement. As an example, Antonio Viglietto of the Circolo Garbatella (Garbatella Association) speaks for many when he says, "it is necessary to defend public green from the institutions." In the absence of a clear policy on this issue, it is easy for citizens to find themselves operating in situations of illegality, namely creating public gardens without having received permission. As pointed out by Lorenzo Parlati, president of the environmental group Legambiente Lazio (League for the Environment, Lazio branch), "the absence of a shared program and policy can lead to paradoxical situations because those who defend and protect the environment often have to operate illegally." Within this context of institutional vacuum and civic activism, the following section of the research presents a few examples of urban gardens in Rome.

In Via dei Galli in San Lorenzo, a centrally located neighborhood behind the main railroad hub of Termini, there is a garden managed by three local associations: Associazione Sportiva Popolare (Sporting Club of the People), Associazione Volsci 32, and Cooperativa Oltre (Cooperative Beyond). As explained by Antonella, the spokesperson for Associazione Sportiva Popolare, the garden, more of a playground for children in fact, is on public land and was created in 2006 after a long battle to prevent the area—by then reduced to a typical *terrain vague* used as a dump and colonized by thorny bushes—from becoming a parking lot.[14] The civic battle by the three associations, whose legal expenses were covered by the city, was eventually adjudicated in favor of the public. With other residents, especially families with small children who did not have places to play if not on the street in the middle of traffic, and with workers provided by the city, the three associations cleaned the space, created pathways, a playground, and seating. Later, the residents built toilets and a small cafeteria and planted trees, vines, and a vegetable garden around the area's perimeter. Today, the garden is bustling with activity and is trying to connect the experience with other experiments throughout the city via a mostly virtual association called Filoverde (Green Thread).[15] In the neighborhood of Garbatella, environmental associations and several families have occupied and cleaned a space near the offices of the Rome Province and are awaiting a decision by the city on whether they can permanently develop a communal garden. Nearby, in the Ostiense neighborhood near the Basilica of Saint

Paul's Outside the Walls, is the Utopia garden, which is the outcome of a collaborative project between the International Social Service and the Monte dei Cocci (Hill of Clay Pots) association of herbalists from the neighborhood of Testaccio. The group's mission is to manage and cultivate the green area around a farmhouse known as Casale Garibaldi (which supposedly housed the famous general when he arrived in Rome in the late 1870s), together with the neighborhood residents.[16] Along the Via Ardeatina, twenty former workers of the now-closed Eutelia computer factory have created EutOrto (Eut Kitchen Garden), a shared orchard and vegetable garden on the property of the Giuseppe Garibaldi high school, which specializes in agricultural studies.[17] EutOrto includes one thousand olive plants, vineyards, and a milk farm that produces over a thousand liters of milk per day. EutOrto is particularly important from a social point of view because it shows how urban farming, apart from generating income, can be fundamental to the identity and social role of workers who lose their jobs. As explained by Mario, EutOrto has been fundamental in making "them" (i.e., the group of unemployed workers) feel productive again. In particular, Mario describes how complex it is to explain this feeling to someone who has never felt "the sense of frustration, of being robbed of one's rights, of isolation caused by malfeasance on the part of management." Passing from the mouse to the shovel has not been easy for this group of workers. Nonetheless, reinventing their identity through urban farming has been the answer to seeking a job which, in a low-tech city such as Rome, could well take a whole lifetime of effort.

Since 2008, in Prato Fiorito, a social cooperative whose activities aim to integrate disadvantaged youths and seniors has managed a 1 ha urban vineyard called Parco dell'Acqua e Vino (Park of Water and Wine). The cooperative produces wine and, in addition to various local social integration programs, also supports a number of social projects in developing countries. In particular, the sale of wine helps the cooperative to provide drinking water to the Saharawi population of Western Sahara.

In the Aniene River park is Coltivatorre (The "Cultivatower"), a project initiated in 1997 by a cooperative for social promotion aimed at disadvantaged youths, whose activities include organic farming and gardening. In the far eastern periphery along Via Tiburtina, in Piazza Bozzi, a civic group has occupied and cleared an abandoned plot of land to create a soccer field and to foster other initiatives, including farming. In Via Capoprati near the Tiber River, on an abandoned property of the Ministry of Finance, volunteers of the environmental association Legambiente work with private citizens to manage a vegetable garden which also hosts other social endeavors throughout the year.

Quarto degli Ebrei in Via Domenico Montagnana in northwestern Rome, between the Rome-Viterbo railway and the ring road, is an area in which a number of civic associations manage over two hundred vegetable gardens. In the same part of town is Monumento Naturale Parco della Cellulosa, a 100 ha park where local residents have created another communal vegetable garden in collaboration with environmental groups such as Legambiente and Roma Natura. The only urban garden managed by the city administration itself is in Via della Consolata, in the Pisana neighborhood.

The different categories of urban farming in Rome summarily presented here show a creative civic society, which is highly heterogeneous, made up of different associations, cooperatives, families, private citizens, and professional farmers. The city authorities, although familiar with the need to protect green areas in Rome, are a reluctant partner to say the least. Urban farming is thus left to the individual efforts and will of private citizens and associations for whom it represents a political platform functional to expressing a multitude of needs and demands as well as to connecting with similar events and associations internationally.

During World War II, over 40 percent of U.S. vegetables were produced in the backyards of patriotic citizens. In Rome, urban war gardens, although useful, were more of a folkloric phenomenon organized for fascist propaganda than a real alternative to commercial farming. Today the enemies are not foreign armies but high prices, squalid and anomic peripheries, environmental degradation, and carbon footprint, that is, the impact of human activities on the biosphere. Urban agriculture in Rome is the latest and most interesting manifestation of the refusal of concerned citizens to give up the idea of living in a cleaner, healthier, and more humane city. Slowly yet progressively, vegetables, flowers, and trees have started to grow where garbage previously dominated. Open-air dumps are at times reclaimed, fenced off, and brought to new life by the energy and passion of dedicated citizens' associations and private individuals amid the indifference of public institutions. But the movement fueling agriculture in Rome is not yet formalized. Immigrant families denied refugee status, seniors living on meager pensions, urbanized farmers longing for a plot where they can cultivate fruit and vegetables, and residents of illegally built neighborhoods far from the center and isolated from social services and infrastructures, take over and maintain vegetable gardens out of passion, for leisure, and for subsistence without necessarily being in contact with each other. Could this be a possible future for the Eternal City, creating a city that is tended and loved, that is gentler, more delicate, healthier, and more sustainable? Major structural changes for a more just and equitable city need to happen before urban agriculture and gardens can become a viable alternative to conventional urban planning and socioeconomic development in Rome. Nevertheless, what is emerging with a lot of effort is one way for this city to climb out the dark hole that institutional neglect of the public good, collective disregard for the environment, disenchantment, lack of opportunities and of political vision have excavated in the last fifty years of its history.

Notes

1. Zappata Romana. http://www.zappataromana.net/ (accessed 12 May 2013).
2. See http://www.seattle.gov/util/Services/Yard/Natural_Lawn_&_Garden_Care/Grow ingFoodintheCity/ (accessed 10 May 2013). For more general and specific information on how to grow food in the city and to connect with city food growers in Australia, the United States, and New Zealand, see http://cityfoodgrowers.com.au/whats_new.php (accessed 12 November 2012).
3. For information on the history of urban farming in Europe and the United States, see http://www.cityfarmer.info/category/history/ (accessed 12 November 2012).
4. "In Dallas, Texas, in 1918 there were 20,000 gardens that produced over 17,500 cans of vegetables in just a few weeks. The Town of Marian, Indiana, had just 29,000 people and 14,081 gardens—that means that almost every other person in Marian had a garden. National-wide there were 3 million garden plots in 1917, according to the National War Garden Commission. In 1918, that number increased to 5,285,000 plots. Due to rising education level of gardeners, these 1918 plots were cultivated more intensely. Over 528.5 million pounds of produce has [sic] harvested that year (Pack 1919). It was here that the idea of the 'city farmer' was born." http://sidewalksprouts.wordpress.com/history/vg/ (accessed 8 May 2013).
5. See, for example, the experiences with community gardens in Los Angeles (http://lagar dencouncil.org/o), Boston (http://www.bostonnatural.org/communitygardens.htm), Seattle (http://www.seattle.gov/neighborhoods/ppatch/), and Houston (http://www.houstontx.gov /health/Community/garden.html). (All accessed 2 May 2013.)
6. See http://nolli.uoregon.edu/disabitato.html. Giovanni Battista Nolli created an elaborate plan map of Rome in 1748. The map showed Rome as a mosaic of public and private spaces whose boundaries were defined by streets and parks and, more interestingly, by privately owned interior public spaces. Many modern urban planners such as Rowe (1978), Caniggia and Maffei (1979) and Habraken (2000) have embraced this approach as a powerful instrument for urban design and study.
7. Typical examples are the gardens outside the Church of San Gregorio on the Celio, where the monks have given a large plot to Mario and his wife for the cultivation of vegetables. In the Castrense amphitheater by the Basilica of the Holy Cross of Jerusalem in San Giovanni, there is another well-kept vegetable garden managed by Cistercian monks. In Via delle Sette Sale on Colle Oppio, there is a vegetable garden cultivated by nuns of the order of Saint Claire. For a discussion on religious Rome in the early 1900s with some information on convents' agricultural economy see Iozzelli (1985).
8. Roma Natura is the city institution that is responsible for managing the over 16,000 ha of protected nature within the administrative boundaries of the city. The system includes nine nature reserves, two regional parks, three natural monuments, and a marine reserve off the coast of Ostia. See www.romanatura.it (accessed 3 November 2012).
9. This is an untranslatable name which refers to the farm's history of cow-rearing.
10. Didactic farms are part of the social and environmental function of farming. In this way, farms diversify their activities, creating new opportunities for connecting the city and the countryside. In particular, they offer the possibility of directly experiencing the activities, the food cycle, animal and vegetable life, the jobs and skills, and the social role of farmers in educating the public toward responsible consumption, respect for the environment, the recovery of local traditions, and cultural values. For didactic farms in Rome, see http://www .fattoriedidatticheroma.it/ (accessed 2 November 2012).
11. The only typology of buildings the city allows on the estate are public utility buildings: hospitals, schools, theaters, etc.

12. See the following: http://www.liberazione.it/succedeoggi-file/Cos—abbiamo-difeso-la
-Torre--i-contadini-e-il-Vaticano---LIBERAZIONE-IT.htm;   http://www.massimovalicchia
.net/gli-ultimi-contadini;   http://www.ecoblog.it/post/11926/contadini-del-parco-dell-acqua
fredda-sfrattati-dal-vaticano-nessuna-pieta; http://www.cafebabel.it/article/37259/papa-bene
detto-ambientalista-greenwasher.html. (All accessed 3 March 2013.)

13. See www.zappataromana.net (accessed 12 May 2013).

14. For the meaning of *terrain vague*, see http://www.atributosurbanos.es/en/terms/terrain
-vague/ (accessed 28 October 2012). The term, introduced by Catalan philosopher and architect
Ignasi Sola-Morales, goes together very well with the notion of "third landscapes" developed
by French landscape architect Gilles Clement (2004). Reading these authors together provides
a very interesting and provocative approach to urban gardening and farming.

15. See, for example, Paesaggio Critico (Critical Landscape) at www.paesaggiocritico.com
(accessed 22 July 2012).

16. See http://ricerca.repubblica.it/repubblica/archivio/repubblica/2012/05/06/da-garbatella-all
-aniene-boom-degli-orti.html (accessed 28 October 2012).

17. See www.eutorto.eu (accessed 13 May 2013).

References

Agnew, John A. 1995. *Rome*. Hoboken, N.J.: Wiley Academic Press.

Armstrong, Donna. 2000. "Survey of Community Gardens in Upstate New York: Implications for Health Promotion and Community Development." *Health & Place* 6 (4): 319–327.

Bailkey, Martin, Joanna Wilbers, and René van Veenhuizen. 2007. "Building Communities through Urban Agriculture." *Urban Agriculture Magazine* 18: 1–6.

Baker, Lauren E. 2004. "Tending Cultural Landscapes and Food Citizenship in Toronto's Community Gardens." *Geographical Review* 94 (3): 305–325.

Bartolomei, Linda, Linda Corkery, Judd Bruce, and Susan Thompsson. 2003. *A Bountiful Harvest: Community Gardens and Neighbourhood Renewal in Waterloo*. Sydney: The University of South Wales/New South Wales Department of Housing.

Bassett, Thomas J. 1981. "Reaping on the Margins: A Century of Community Gardening in America." *Landscape* 25 (2): 1–8.

Beatly, Tim. 2000. *Green Urbanism: Learning from European Cities*. Washington, DC: Island Press.

Bevilacqua, Piero. 2008. *Miseria dello sviluppo*. Bari-Rome: Editori Laterza.

Boserup, Esther. 1965. *The Condition of Economic Growth: The Economics of Agrarian Change under Population Pressure*. London: Allen and Unwin.

Brock, William H. 2002. *Justus von Liebig: The Chemical Gatekeeper*. Cambridge, Mass.: Cambridge University Press.

Caniggia, Gianfranco, and Gian Luigi Maffei. 1979. *Architectural Composition and Building Typology: Interpreting Basic Building*, translated by J. Faser. Florence, Italy: Alinea Editrice.

Clement, Gilles. 2004. *Manifeste du tiers paysage*. Paris: Sujet.

Cole, Donald C., Diana Lee-Smith, and George W. Nasyniama, eds. 2008. *Healthy City Harvests: Generating Evidence for Policy on Urban Agriculture*. Lima: International Potato Center/Urban Harvest and Makerere University Press.

Comune di Roma. 2004. "Studio sul verde pubblico nel comune di Roma." http://www .agenzia.roma.it/documenti/monitoraggi/415.pdf. Accessed 15 May 2013.

Dierna, Salvatore, and Fabrizio Orlandi. 2007. *Ecoefficienza per la città diffusa: Linee guida per il recupero energetico e ambientale degli insediamenti informali nella periferia romana.* Florence, Italy: Alinea.

Dubbeling, Marielle, Laura Bracalenti, and Laura Lagorio. 2009. "Design of Public Spaces for Urban Agriculture, Rosario, Argentina." *Open House International.* http:// www.openhouse-int.com/abdisplay.php?xvolno=34_2_4/. Accessed 12 June 2013.

Englander, Diane 2001. *New York's Community Gardens: A Resource at Risk.* San Francisco: The Trust for Public Land. http://actrees.org/files/Research/NYC _CommunityGardens.pdf. Accessed 12 June 2013.

Erbani, Francesco. 2012. "Su Roma una nuova pioggia di case: La campagna nelle mire dei palazzinari." http://inchieste.repubblica.it/it/repubblica/rep-it. Accessed 12 May 2013.

FAO (Food and Agriculture Organization of the United Nations). 2000. *Urban and Periurban Agriculture on the Policy Agenda.* Virtual Conference and Information Market. Rome: FAO Food for the Cities Multidisciplinary Initiative.

——. 2011. *Food, Agriculture and Cities: Challenges of Food Security, Agriculture and Ecosystem Management in an Urbanized World.* Rome: FAO Food for the Cities Multidisciplinary Initiative.

Feenstra, Gail. 2002. "Creating Space for Sustainable Food Systems: Lessons from the Field." *Agriculture and Human Values* 19 (2): 99–106.

Frolet, Elisabeth, and Ferruccio Trabalzi. In press. *I chiostri dimenticati di Roma.* Rome: G. B. Palumbo and Company Editore.

Gottlieb, Robert, and Anupama Joshi. 2010. *Food Justice.* Cambridge, Mass.: MIT Press.

Gonzales-Novo, Mario, and Catherine Murphy. 2000. "Urban Agriculture in the City of Havana: A Popular Response to a Crisis." In *Growing Cities, Growing Food: Urban Agriculture on the Policy Agenda. A Reader on Urban Agriculture,* edited by N. Bakker, M. Dubbeling, S. Guendel, U. Sabel Koschella, H. de Zeeuw, 329–347. Feldafing, Germany: Deutsche Stiftung für Internationale Entwicklung, Zentralstelle für Ernährung und Landwirtschaft.

Habraken, John N. 2000. *The Structure of the Ordinary.* Cambridge, Mass.: MIT Press.

Halweil, Brian. 2002. *Home Grown: The Case for Local Food in a Global Market.* Worldwatch Paper 163. Washington, DC: Worldwatch Institute.

Hodges, Richard. 2000. *Visions of Rome: Thomas Ashby, Archaeologist.* Rome: British School at Rome.

Insolera, Italo. 1962. *Roma moderna.* Turin: Einaudi.

Iozzelli, Fortunato. 1985. *Roma religiosa all'inizio del novecento.* Vol. 22. di Biblioteca di storia sociale. Rome: Edizioni di Storia e Letteratura.

Jacobi, Petra, and Axel Drescher. 2000. *Urban Agriculture: Justification and Planning Guidelines.* Eschborn, Germany: Deutsche Gesellschaft für Technische Zusammenarbeit.

Jacobs, Jane. 1969. *The Economy of Cities.* New York: Random House.

Jardinons Ensemble. 2013. http://jardinons-ensemble.org. Accessed 19 August 2013.

Kaufman, Jerry, and Martin Bailkey. 2000. "Farming Inside Cities: Entrepreneurial Urban Agriculture in the United States." *Lincoln Institute of Land Policy.* http://www

.urbantilt h.org/wp-content/uploads/2008/10/farminginsidecities.pdf. Accessed 27 May 2013.

Krautheimer, Richard. 1980. *Rome: Profile of a City, 312–1308*. Princeton, N.J.: Princeton University Press.

Lawson, Laura J. 2005. *City Bountiful: A Century of Community Gardening in America*. Berkeley: University of California Press.

Lindsay, Greg. 2010. "New Urbanism for the Apocalypse." *Fast Company*, May 24. http://www.fastcompany.com/1651619/the-new-urbanism-meets-the-end-of-the-world. Accessed 12 June 2012.

Liu, Shenghe, Janming Cai, and Zhenshan Yang. 2005. "Migrants' Access to Land in Peri-urban Beijing." *Urban Agriculture Magazine* 11: 6–8.

Mougeot, Lucia J. A. 2000. "Urban Agriculture: Definition, Presence, Potentials and Risks." In *Growing Cities, Growing Food: Urban Agriculture on the Policy Agenda, A Reader on Urban Agriculture*, edited by N. Bakker, M. Dubbeling, S. Guendel, U. Sabel Koschella, H. de Zeeuw, 99–117. Feldafing, Germany: Deutsche Stiftung für Internationale Entwicklung, Zentralstelle für Ernährung und Landwirtschaft.

——. 2005. *Agropolis: The Social, Political and Environmental Dimensions of Urban Agriculture*. London: Earthscan.

——. 2006. *Growing Better Cities: Urban Agriculture for Sustainable Development*. Ottawa, Canada: International Development Research Centre.

Moustier, Paul, and George Danso. 2006. "Local Economic Development and Marketing of Urban Produced Food." In *Cities Farming for the Future: Urban Agriculture for Green and Productive Cities*, edited by René van Veenhuizen, 174–195. Manila, Philippines: International Institute of Rural Reconstruction/ Resource Centres on Urban Agriculture and Food Security Foundation/International Development Research Centre.

Pack, Charles Lathrop. 1919. *The War Garden Victorious*. Philadelphia, P.A.: J. B. Lippincott Co.

Pothukuchi, Kameshwari, and Jerome L. Kaufman. 1999. "The Food System: A Stranger to the Planning Field." *Journal of the American Planning Association* 66 (2): 113.

Quon, Soonya. 1999. *Planning for Urban Agriculture: A Review of Tools and Strategies for Urban Planners*. Cities Feeding People Report Series 28. Ottawa, Canada: International Development Research Centre.

Rowe, Colin. 1978. *Collage City*. Cambridge, Mass.: MIT Press.

Scarpa, Giuseppe. 2012. "Roma tra antiche rovine e orti urbani." *Wired IT*, July 23.

Smil, Vaclav. 2001. *Enriching the Earth: Fritz Haber, Carl Bosch and the Transformation of World Food Production*. Cambridge, Mass.: MIT Press.

Smit, Jac, Annu Ratta, and Joe Nasr. 1996. *Urban Agriculture: Food, Jobs and Sustainable Cities*. New York: United Nations Procurement Division.

Soja, Edward. 2000. *Postmetropolis: Critical Studies of Cities and Regions*. Oxford, U.K.: Blackwell.

Contributors

ALESSANDRA BROCCOLINI is an anthropologist and researcher at the University of Rome, La Sapienza.

CARLO CELLAMARE is professor of Urban Planning in the Faculty of Engineering of the University of Rome, La Sapienza.

PIERLUIGI CERVELLI is professor of Communication and Social Research at the University of Rome, La Sapienza.

ISABELLA CLOUGH MARINARO is assistant professor of Italian Studies at John Cabot University, Rome.

ULDERICO DANIELE teaches in the Department of Education at the University of Rome, Roma Tre.

MARK DYAL is an anthropologist and independent scholar.

MICHAEL HERZFELD is professor of Anthropology at Harvard University.

VALERIE HIGGINS is associate professor of Archaeology at the American University of Rome.

CRISTINA LOMBARDI-DIOP is lecturer of Modern Languages and Literatures and Women's Studies and Gender Studies at Loyola University Chicago.

SIMON MARTIN is a research fellow at the British School at Rome.

PIERPAOLO MUDU is affiliate professor in the Faculties of Urban Studies and Interdisciplinary Arts and Sciences at the University of Washington, Tacoma.

MARCO SOLIMENE teaches in the Department of Anthropology at the University of Iceland.

BJØRN THOMASSEN is associate professor in the Department of Society and Globalization at Roskilde University, Denmark.

FERRUCCIO TRABALZI teaches International Relations at the American University of Rome.

PIERO VERENI is researcher at the University of Rome "Tor Vergata" and professor of Urban and Global Rome at the Trinity College Rome Campus.

Index

Note: Page numbers in *italic* indicate photographs and illustrations.

283

BOOKS IN THE NEW ANTHROPOLOGIES OF EUROPE SERIES

Sharing Sacred Spaces in the Mediterranean: Christians, Muslims, and Jews at Shrines and Sanctuaries
Edited by Dionigi Albera and Maria Couroucli

The Euro and Its Rivals: Currency and the Construction of a Transnational City
Gustav Peebles

Labor Disorders in Neoliberal Italy: Mobbing, Well-being, and the Workplace
Noelle J. Molé

Jewish Life in Twenty-First-Century Turkey: The Other Side of Tolerance
Marcy Brink-Danan

Political Crime and the Memory of Loss
John Borneman

Secularism Soviet Style: Teaching Atheism and Religion in a Volga Republic
Sonja Luehrmann

Hypersexuality and Headscarves: Race, Sex, and Citizenship in the New Germany
Damani J. Partridge

Loyal Unto Death: Trust and Terror in Revolutionary Macedonia
Keith Brown

Politics in Color and Concrete: Socialist Materialities and the Middle Class in Hungary
Krisztina Féherváry

Jewish Poland Revisited: Heritage Tourism in Unquiet Places
Erica T. Lehrer

Global Rome: Changing Faces of the Eternal City
Edited by Isabella Clough Marinaro and Bjørn Thomassen

CPSIA information can be obtained at www.ICGtesting.com
Printed in the USA
LVOW07s2352271114

415848LV00001B/135/P